Pagan Inscriptions, Christian Viewers

CULTURES OF READING IN THE ANCIENT MEDITERRANEAN

Series Editors
William A. Johnson and Chris Keith

This book series presents a home for original scholarship on the reading cultures of the wider ancient Mediterranean world. Broadly chronological—from the Iron Age to Late Antiquity—and geographical—from Western Europe to Mesopotamia—the series welcomes new work at the intersection of Classics, papyrology, epigraphy, Jewish Studies, early Christian studies, early Islamic studies, and ancient media culture.

Jeremiah Coogan, *Eusebius the Evangelist: Rewriting the Fourfold Gospel in Late Antiquity*

Anna M. Sitz, *Pagan Inscriptions, Christian Viewers: The Afterlives of Temples and Their Texts in the Late Antique Eastern Mediterranean*

Pagan Inscriptions, Christian Viewers

The Afterlives of Temples and Their Texts in the Late Antique Eastern Mediterranean

ANNA M. SITZ

OXFORD
UNIVERSITY PRESS

Oxford University Press is a department of the University of Oxford. It furthers the University's objective of excellence in research, scholarship, and education by publishing worldwide. Oxford is a registered trade mark of Oxford University Press in the UK and certain other countries.

Published in the United States of America by Oxford University Press
198 Madison Avenue, New York, NY 10016, United States of America.

© Oxford University Press 2023

All rights reserved. No part of this publication may be reproduced, stored in a retrieval system, or transmitted, in any form or by any means, without the prior permission in writing of Oxford University Press, or as expressly permitted by law, by license, or under terms agreed with the appropriate reproduction rights organization. Inquiries concerning reproduction outside the scope of the above should be sent to the Rights Department, Oxford University Press, at the address above.

You must not circulate this work in any other form
and you must impose this same condition on any acquirer.

Library of Congress Cataloging-in-Publication Data
Names: Sitz, Anna M., 1988– author.
Title: Pagan inscriptions, Christian viewers : the afterlives of temples and their texts in the late antique Eastern Mediterranean / Anna M. Sitz.
Other titles: Writing on the wall Description: New York : Oxford University Press, 2023. | Series: Cultures of reading in the Ancient Mediterranean | Revision of the author's thesis (doctoral)—University of Pennsylvania, 2017, under the title: The writing on the wall : inscriptions and memory in the temples of late antique Greece and Asia Minor. | Includes bibliographical references and index.
Identifiers: LCCN 2022051689 (print) | LCCN 2022051690 (ebook) | ISBN 9780197666432 (hardback) | ISBN 9780197666456 (epub)
Subjects: LCSH: Architectural inscriptions—Middle East. | Christianity and culture—Middle East. | Language and culture—Middle East. | Christianity and other religions—Middle East. | Social perception—Middle East.
Classification: LCC NA4050.I5 S58 2023 (print) | LCC NA4050.I5 (ebook) | DDC 729/.19093—dc23/eng/20221125
LC record available at https://lccn.loc.gov/2022051689
LC ebook record available at https://lccn.loc.gov/2022051690

DOI: 10.1093/oso/9780197666432.001.0001

To my family

So Paul, standing in the midst of the Areopagus, said: "Men of Athens, I perceive that in every way you are very religious. For as I passed along and observed the objects of your worship, I found also an altar with this inscription: "To the unknown god." What therefore you worship as unknown, this I proclaim to you.

Acts 17:22–23, English Standard Version

Contents

List of Figures — xi
Preface — xvii
Acknowledgments — xxi
Abbreviated Epigraphic Corpora — xxiii

1. Introduction: Afterlives of Inscriptions — 1
   Epigraphic Reincarnation at Megara — 1
   Manufactured Violence — 7
   Inscribed Sanctuaries — 15
   Literacy in Late Antiquity — 17
   Chapter Outline — 20
   The Fine Print — 23

2. The Use of Real or Imagined Inscriptions in Late Antique Literature — 28
   The "Arch of Alexander" and the Ends of the Earth — 28
   Writing the Past from Inscriptions — 30
      Agathias and the Remarkable Afterlife of Chairemon — 34
      Kosmas Indikopleustes: Hellenistic History in Late Antique Ethiopia — 38
      Prokopios' Inscribed Ships — 43
   Prophesying from Stone: Invented Oracles — 45
      Epigraphic Omens at Chalcedon, Alexandria, and Carthage — 45
      The *Tübingen Theosophy*: Converting Temples — 48
   Plagiarizing for the Saints: The *Life of Abercius* — 52
   Conclusion: The Literary Afterlives of Ancient Inscriptions — 65

3. Preservation: Tolerating Temples and Their Texts — 69
   Touring Temples — 69
   Inscribed Text and Figural Imagery at Unconverted Temples — 74
      Ephesos: Embodying Emperors on the Embolos — 74
      Museumification at Priene's Temple of Athena? — 77
      Performative Bureaucracy at the Temple of Augustus and Roma at Mylasa — 84
      A Fallen God at Magnesia on the Maeander — 88
      Congregated Graffiti at Delphi — 90
   Secular or Sacred? Imperial Documents on Temples of Uncertain Use — 95
      The *Res Gestae divi Augusti* in Late Antique Ankara — 96
      A Tale of Two Temples at Aizanoi: Zeus at Church — 113
      Tolerance at Palmyra — 120

viii CONTENTS

    Priests, Talking Columns, and Unreadable Texts at
    Christianized Temples   121
        Diokaisareia-Olba: A Careful Conversion   121
        "Archaeophilia" at Sardis's Artemision   122
        Lagina: Early Christian Economics   128
        Everyday Hieroglyphs at Medinet Habu   134
        Reading Nonsense at Didyma   139
    Conclusion: Kings of the Past on Display   143

4. Spoliation: Integrating and Scrambling tions-Inscrip   147
    (T)reading the Past: Epigraphic Spolia Underfoot   147
    Constructing Churches with Inscribed Text   155
        The Korykian Cave: Building with Inscriptions   155
        Scrambling Apollo Klarios at Sagalassos   165
        Gods and Angels in the Temple-Church at Aphrodisias   172
        Uncertain Reuse at Baalbek   183
        Klaros: Exporting Spolia   185
    Epigraphic Spolia Elsewhere   188
        Not Only Christians: The Synagogue at Sardis   188
        The Temple of Zeus at Labraunda: Spolia *in medias res*   191
    Conclusion: Mixed Re-Views of Old Texts in New Buildings   195

5. Erasure: [[Damnatio Memoriae]] or Conscious Uncoupling?   202
    Unnaming the Gods   202
    Violence against Statues   208
        Heads or Tails?   208
        Out of Sight, Out of Mind   213
        Ambiguous Afterlives   215
    Violence against Inscriptions   217
        Damnatio Memoriae   218
        Beyond Damnatio Memoriae   220
    Selective Erasures   223
        Identity Crisis at Aphrodisias   223
        Labraunda: A Rasura Out of Place   232
        A Tale of Two Temples at Aizanoi: Artemis in Absentia   236
        Roll of the Dice at Antioch ad Cragum   241
    Indiscriminate Erasure and Destruction   244
        Reverse Graffiti at the Korykian Cave Clifftop Temple   244
        Breaking the Past at Pisidian Antioch?   247
    Conclusion: Epigraphic Unnamings and a Fresh Start   254

6. Conclusion: Unepigraphic Readings   265
    Reading at the Temple of Augustus at Ankara Once More   265
    An Archaeology of Reading   266
    Spolia: Breaking the Monolith   270

Word and Image: Inscriptions and Statues 271
Land, Men, and Gods 273
Epigraphy: A New Direction 274

Bibliography 277
Index 311

List of Figures

Map 1	Eastern Mediterranean in the time of Diocletian and Constantine, with the province names in western Asia Minor. Ancient World Mapping Center © 2023 (awmc.unc.edu). Used by permission, with modifications.	xxvii
Map 2	Western Asia Minor, with sites discussed in the text. Ancient World Mapping Center © 2023 (awmc.unc.edu). Used by permission, with modifications.	xxviii
1.1	Megara. Late antique inscription (*IG* VII 53) honoring the Persian War dead with a reinscribed epigram of Simonides of Keos. Wilhelm 1899, 238.	2
2.1	Tralles. Honorific base for Chairemon (*SEG* 61.880). Photo courtesy of Murat Aydaş.	36
2.2	Manuscript of *Christian Topography* by Kosmas Indikopleustes. Illustration of the inscriptions of Abdulis. Ninth century. Vatican Library, Vat. Gr. 699, Folio 15v. © 2023 Biblioteca Apostolica Vaticana, all rights reserved.	40
2.3	Hier(o)polis. Inscription of Abercius (*SEG* 30.1479). Late second/early third century. Vatican Museum no. 31643. © Governorate of the Vatican City State-Directorate of the Vatican Museums, all rights reserved.	54
2.4	Hier(o)polis. Inscription of Alexandros, son of Antonios (*IGR* IV 694). 216 CE. Istanbul Archaeology Museum. Ramsay 1897, 721.	57
3.1	Ephesos. Façade of the "Temple of Hadrian" with *I.Ephesos* 429. Quatember 2017 Pl. 22. Used by permission.	75
3.2	Priene. Dedication of Alexander the Great (*I.Priene B—M* 149) and following documents on the front of the northeast anta of the Temple of Athena Polias. British Museum no. 1870,0320.88. © The Trustees of the British Museum.	78
3.3	Priene. Plan of the sanctuary of Athena Polias. Hennemeyer 2013, Fig. 4. Used by permission.	80
3.4	Priene. Marble female head identified as Ada, found in the Temple of Athena Polias. British Museum no. 1870,0320.138. © The Trustees of the British Museum.	81
3.5	Mylasa. Temple of Augustus and Roma. Inset detail of the inscribed architrave (*I.Mylasa* 31). Pococke 1745, Pl. 55, with modifications.	85

xii   LIST OF FIGURES

3.6   Mylasa. Plan of the Temple of Augustus and Roma. Approximate locations of *I.Mylasa* 613 on the podium indicated. Author and Yasmin Nachtigall, after Rumscheid 2004, Fig. 17. 87

3.7   Magnesia on the Maeander. Temple of Zeus Sosipolis, section reconstruction. Humann 1904, Fig. 165. 89

3.8   Magnesia on the Maeander. Temple of Zeus Sosipolis, plan. Humann 1904, Pl. 18. 91

3.9   Delphi. Altar of the Chians. Amandry 1981, Fig. 60. Courtesy of the École française d'Athènes. © Hellenic Ministry of Culture and Sports / Archaeological Resources Fund. 94

3.10 Ankara. Plan of the archaeological remains of the city. Author and Yasmin Nachtigall, modified from Kadıoğlu, Görkay, and Mitchell 2011. 97

3.11 Ankara. Temple of Augustus, current state plan. Author, after Krencker and Schede 1936, Pl. 2. 98

3.12 Ankara. Temple of Augustus, view of the annex from the exterior (permit no. 64298988-155.02E.218252). Author, courtesy of the Turkish Ministry of Culture and Tourism. 99

3.13 Ankara. Temple of Augustus, section of the exterior southeastern façade. Cross graffiti and Byzantine inscriptions (*I.Ancyra* 497–499) below the Greek *Res Gestae* are marked. Author and Yasmin Nachtigall, modified from Krencker and Schede 1936, Pl. 6. 108

3.14 Ankara. Temple of Augustus, detail of cast of the exterior southeastern façade. Greek *Res Gestae* with Byzantine grave text *I.Ancyra* 498 below. Mommsen 1883, Pl. 9. 108

3.15 Aizanoi. Apse in the proanos of the Temple of Zeus. Rudolf Naumann 1979, Fig. 44. Used with permission. 114

3.16 Aizanoi. Temple of Zeus. Author, courtesy of the Aizanoi Excavations. 115

3.17 Aizanoi. Exterior wall of the Temple of Zeus with graffiti, below the Eurykles dossier (*OGIS* 504–507). Courtesy of the Deutsches Archäologisches Institut Istanbul (D-DAI-IST-R31242). 116

3.18 Sardis. View toward Temple of Artemis and Chapel M. Author, courtesy of the Archaeological Exploration of Sardis. 123

3.19 Sardis. Plan of the Temple of Artemis area in late antiquity. © Archaeological Exploration of Sardis/President and Fellows of Harvard College. 124

3.20 Sardis. Christian graffiti on the southeastern door jamb of the Temple of Artemis. Courtesy of the Howard Crosby Butler Archive, Department of Art and Archaeology, Princeton University. 124

3.21 Sardis. Nannas Bakivalis monument. Courtesy of the Howard Crosby Butler Archive, Department of Art and Archaeology, Princeton University. 126

LIST OF FIGURES   xiii

3.22 Lagina. Plan of the sanctuary of Hekate with the basilica in grey.
      Gider 2012, Fig. 1. Used with permission. 129

3.23 Lagina. General view of propylon, the Temple of Hekate, and the area
      of the basilica. Author, courtesy of the Stratonikeia Excavations. 130

3.24 Lagina. Graffiti on the stylobate of the Temple of Hekate. Author, courtesy
      of the Stratonikeia Excavations. 131

3.25 Medinet Habu. View of church in the temple, before 1903. Antonio Beato,
      Yale University Art Gallery. 137

3.26 Didyma. Church in the adyton of the Temple of Apollo.
      Wiegand 1924, Pl. 2. 141

3.27 Didyma. Masons' marks on wall (south wall, eastern part). *I.Didyma*,
      Fig. 51. Used with permission. 142

3.28 Miletos. *Erzengelinschrift* ("archangel inscription") on a wall of the theater.
      Photo: E. Steiner. Courtesy of the Deutsches Archäologisches Institut
      Istanbul (D-DAI-IST-Perg.86/311-1). 143

4.1   Korykian Cave (Kilikia). Section showing the sinkholes and the opening
      of the cave system, as well as the chapel and the temple-church. Author
      and Yasmin Nachtigall, after Bayliss 2004, Fig. 109. 157

4.2   Korykian Cave (Kilikia). Clifftop temple-church plan. Author and Yasmin
      Nachtigall, after Bayliss 2004, Fig. 110. 159

4.3   Korykian Cave (Kilikia). Clifftop temple-church plan, detail. Inscribed faces
      (A, B, and C) of the anta marked. Author and Yasmin Nachtigall,
      modified from Bayliss 2004, Fig. 110. 160

4.4   Korykian Cave (Kilikia). Clifftop temple-church, anta, inscribed faces
      A, B, and C. Author, courtesy of Hamdi Şahin. 161

4.5   Korykian Cave (Kilikia). Drawing of the three uppermost courses of the
      inscribed faces of the Clifftop temple anta (A, B, and C, *I.Westkilikien Rep.*
      Korykion Antron 1). Heberdey and Wilhelm 1896, 73, Fig. 10. 162

4.6   Sagalassos. Façade reconstruction of the Temple of Apollo Klarios with
      I.Sagalassos 20. Lanckoroński 1892, Pl. 25. 167

4.7   Sagalassos. Plan of the temple-church with Lanckoroński's proposed
      placement of the architrave (dotted lines). Author and Yasmin Nachtigall,
      modified from Lanckoroński 1892, Fig. 123. 169

4.8   Aphrodisias. Site plan. Courtesy of NYU Excavations at Aphrodisias
      (Harry Mark). 173

4.9   Aphrodisias. Composite plan showing the Temple of Aphrodite and the
      temple-church. Courtesy of NYU Excavations at Aphrodisias (Harry Mark). 176

4.10 Aphrodisias. *Tabulae ansatae* (marked) with inscriptions on the north
      colonnade of the temple-church (*I.Aphrodisias* 2007 1.4–1.8). Author,
      courtesy of NYU Excavations at Aphrodisias. 177

xiv LIST OF FIGURES

4.11 Aphrodisias. Door lintel of the northern entrance into nave with
I.Aphrodisias 2007 1.102. Courtesy of NYU Excavations at Aphrodisias. 179

4.12 Sardis. Plan of the synagogue, fourth phase. © Archaeological Exploration
of Sardis/President and Fellows of Harvard College. 189

4.13 Sardis. Epichoric inscription in an unknown Anatolian language found
in the synagogue. Sardis IN63.141. © Archaeological Exploration of Sardis/
President and Fellows of Harvard College. 190

4.14 Labraunda. Interior of Andron A with *I.Labraunda* 137 marked.
Courtesy of the Labraunda Excavations. 193

4.15 Labraunda. Upper surface of the stone with *I.Labraunda* 137, showing
original and later cutting marks. Courtesy of the Labraunda Excavations. 194

4.16 Phoenix. Doorway into the nave of the Kızlan Deresi church with
a dedication to Apollo (detail); the dedication to Eleithya is below it.
Author, courtesy of the Phoenix Archaeological Project. 198

5.1 Aphrodisias. Bust of Alexander the Great with cut mark on the neck.
Author, courtesy of NYU Excavations at Aphrodisias. 210

5.2 Perge. Statue of a Grace (Antalya Museum Inv. 2018/133) with damage
to the pubic area and breast. Author, courtesy of the Antalya Museum. 213

5.3 Burdur Museum. Inscribed spolia (*I.Mus. Burdur* 184) in a baptistery
from Uylupınar (permit no. 51544244-155.02-E.158017; 64298988-155.02-
E.156523). Author, courtesy of the Turkish Ministry of
Culture and Tourism. 222

5.4 Aphrodisias. Northeast gate with erased and replaced inscription
(*I.Aphrodisias* 2007 12.101ii). Courtesy NYU Excavations at Aphrodisias. 224

5.5 Aphrodisias. Theater with *skene* architrave and *frons pulpiti* marked.
Author, courtesy of NYU Excavations at Aphrodisias. 226

5.6 Aphrodisias. Chiseled relief of Aphrodite from the Sebasteion, with cross
added at lower left. Author, courtesy of NYU Excavations at Aphrodisias. 228

5.7 Aphrodisias. Door lintel from the Temple of Aphrodite
(*I.Aphrodisias* 2007 1.2), reused at the main entrance into the nave of the
temple-church. Author, courtesy of NYU Excavations at Aphrodisias. 229

5.8 Labraunda. Site plan with the South Propylaea and find area of the architrave
blocks marked in dashed lines. Courtesy of the Labraunda Excavations. 234

5.9 Labraunda. Architrave of the South Propylaea (*I.Labraunda* 18), unerased
and erased blocks. Photos: Arthur Nilsson, Labraunda Excavation 1949,
courtesy of the Labraunda Archives, Uppsala University Library
(LabArP:1949:399 and LabArP:1949:328). 235

5.10 Aizanoi. *Säulenstraße*, erased and unerased sections of the Artemis architrave
(*SEG* 45.1708). Photos: D. Johannes, courtesy of the Deutsches Archäologisches
Institut Istanbul (D-DAI-IST-Ai-93-454 and D-DAI-IST-Ai-93-342). 238

5.11 Aizanoi. *Säulenstraße*, partially erased dedication to Zeus and Nero (*SEG* 45.1711). Photo: D. Johannes, courtesy of the Deutsches Archäologisches Institut Istanbul (D-DAI-IST-Ai-94-1). 239

5.12 Antioch ad Cragum. Northeast Temple block with dice oracle inscription (*I. Westkilikien Rep.* Antiocheia epi Krago 19). Bean and Mitford 1965, no. 43. 242

5.13 Korykian Cave (Kilikia). Clifftop temple-church, *I. Westkilikien Rep.* Korykion Antron 1, partially erased. Author, courtesy of Hamdi Şahin. 246

5.14 Pisidian Antioch. Fragments of the *Res Gestae divi Augusti*. Ramsay and von Premerstein 1927, Pl. 11. 251

6.1 Ankara. Temple of Augustus within the Hacı Bayram complex in 1881 or 1882. Photo: John Henry Haynes (HayAr.239 AKP160). Courtesy of Special Collections, Fine Arts Library, Harvard University. 275

Preface

Why are the famous Parthenon marbles currently sitting in the British Museum? Because of Lord Elgin, of course. But Elgin could only take down the pedimental statues and reliefs from the Parthenon because they were still in place up to his time: because a series of decisions had been made centuries earlier. In late antiquity—sometimes called the early Christian period—the decision was made *not* to remove or edit much of the figural imagery of this pagan temple at the heart of Athens, even when it became a church in approximately the seventh century, nor to dismantle the temple completely. The Parthenon is often lauded as a remarkable instance of the tolerance of early Christians toward ancient statuary, although some figural reliefs were chiseled away (at an uncertain time). In sanctuaries and cities throughout the late Roman empire, the relationship of Christians to older carved figural images can perhaps best be described as "it's complicated." Some statues were destroyed or edited even as others were preserved in place or sought out as desirable elements—and these decisions were informed by the discourses on statuary taking place in the literature and homilies of the day.

Marble statues were not the only elements of the ancient world to remain prominent in our period. For decades, scholars of late antiquity have attempted to document and understand the enduring value of the classical past in this new era of "Christianization." They have pinpointed the ways that ancient Greek and Roman myths, oratory, histories, and poetry inflected Christian texts and thought-worlds. St. Jerome (c. 342–420) may have claimed to give up Cicero for Christ (*Ep. 22*), but his writings remained permeated with classical rhetoric—and he could not resist praising the pious Christian Paula for her ancestry leading back to the Gracchi, to the Scipiones, and even to Agamemnon himself (*Ep. 108*). The most famous Greek poet of all, Homer, was still read, emulated, adapted, annotated, and illustrated in our period; St. Basil of Caesarea (330–379) encouraged his students to seek virtue in the verses or sayings attributed to Homer, Hesiod, and Solon (*Ad adulescentes*). Herodotos' tale of Kroisos and the oracle at Delphi appears in the proem of the fifth-century *Miracles of St. Thekla* as a foil for the more reliable (and less tricky) wisdom of the Christian saint. Prokopios' literary style in the sixth century is founded on the tradition of classicizing histories stretching back to the same Herodotos and to Thucydides. He claimed that the late antique population of Rome took great care of their classical patrimony—even keeping the ancient ship of Aeneas on view. Meanwhile, at Gerasa in Jordan, a Christian priest bearing the name Aeneas put up an inscription that quoted from the *Iliad*, but at the same time denigrated the pagan rituals that had formerly taken place at the site of his church. Late antique pagan intellectuals—who came to be called Hellenes ("Greeks" or "pagans") by their Christian contemporaries—likewise built upon and grappled with the ideas of ancient poets and philosophers.

Not only in the discursive sphere, but in the physical one as well, late antique individuals made the decision to keep monuments of the classical past front and center in cities and landscapes. Older buildings with their classical façades continued to stand and be maintained throughout the empire. Greek and Roman architectural marbles from disassembled or destroyed buildings were repurposed in new structures as spolia. Objects both elite, such as the mid-fourth-century silver Projecta casket bearing an image of Aphrodite, and banal, such as wine flasks emblazoned with Dionysos, drew on classical iconography. Some ancient deities, such as river gods and winged Victory, were relegated to the realm of "personifications" and continued to appear in explicitly Christian art for centuries.

Aesthetically, materially, and conceptually, then, the late antique world was deeply indebted to its classical forebear, even as fundamental paradigms shifted. The continued vitality of Hellenism, as well as Roman and local or indigenous cultures, has been well documented in numerous works of scholarship. There are now few researchers who would countenance the portrayal of the early Christian period as a fundamental and complete break from the classical past, regardless of where one finds oneself in the debate on *decline and fall*.

When I started my research for this project, I thought that just about every iota of evidence for late antique attitudes toward the classical past had been examined. Short of newly excavated finds or newly deciphered papyri, we are limited in the data set we can use to interrogate "Christianization" or the reception of classical culture in our period. Certainly, there is still a need to re-examine old evidence with fresh eyes, with new and diverse theoretical perspectives or in innovative combinations. But I was surprised to realize that a significant body of evidence for the late antique reception of the classical past has been largely overlooked: the fates of ancient inscriptions.

Whereas the reading of Greek and Roman *literature* in late antiquity has been widely acknowledged and analyzed, the reading of Greek and Roman *inscriptions* has not—never mind that, in the telling of Acts 17:22–23, St. Paul himself initiated the use of an ancient inscription ("to the unknown god") in the Christian world-building project. So too has the study of reusing ancient *architectural* marbles proven to be a rich space in which to tease out attitudes toward the past, but this has not been the case for *inscribed* marbles. I am not presenting in this book truly new evidence, in the sense of unpublished or re-edited inscriptions, but I am collecting and bringing this data set to bear on questions of reception and attitudes toward the Greek, Roman, and local pasts for the first time in a comprehensive way. I do this by examining the discourses surrounding inscriptions—carved in a variety of eastern Mediterranean languages, legible and illegible—in the late antique literary sources, and by examining the fates of the physical inscribed stones themselves at various archaeological sites. Inscriptions were not very likely to receive the kind of scholia that clues us in to the reception received by Homer, for example, nor to receive the lengthy theorization in treatises and hagiographies that ancient statuary did. But if our evidence is more taciturn than that for the reception of ancient literature and art, it only means that we have to listen to it more closely.

Acknowledgments

This book would not have been possible without a great deal of institutional and personal support. First and foremost, I want to thank Bob Ousterhout, who, as my PhD advisor, deftly guided this project from its conception; his support (and an endless supply of good puns) has not waned in the intervening years. Brian Rose, Elizabeth Bolman, Ivan Drpić, and Dale Kinney offered valuable feedback during the project's formative stages. Franz Alto Bauer helped to bring my ideas into a more coherent form. He, Christian Witschel, Stephan Westphalen, Klaus Hallof, Ruth Bielfeldt, Stefan Ritter, and Christof Schuler (among many others) aided me in making the transition from American to German academia; this book reflects, I hope, the synergy of the two academic systems. Angelos Chaniotis and Charlotte Roueché were kind enough to discuss my material and offer important corrections and expansions. Stephen Mitchell has been exceptionally generous with his time and energy in sharing his expertise on a number of topics, especially Ankara and early Christian Phrygia.

Several directors of archaeological excavations or surveys kindly gave their permission for me to use images, plans, or materials from their sites: Nick Cahill; Gökhan Coşkun; Olivier Henry; Sabine Ladstätter; İbrahim Hakan Mert; Jeroen Poblome; Hamdi Şahin; R. R. R. Smith; Bilal Söğüt; and Asil Yaman. Other image permissions were granted by: the Ancient World Mapping Center; the Antalya Museum; Murat Aydaş; Richard Bayliss; the British Museum; the Burdur Museum; the Deutsches Archäologisches Institut (DAI); the École française d'Athènes (EFA); Zeliha Gider Büyüközer; Harvard University's Special Collections, Fine Arts Library; Arnd Hennemeyer; Princeton University's Howard Crosby Butler Archive; Uppsala University Library's Labraunda Archives; Ursula Quatember; the Yale University Art Gallery; the Turkish Ministry of Culture and Tourism; Verlag Mann; the Vatican Library; and the Vatican Museum. Assistance in obtaining images, permits, or drawings was provided by: Dila Akgün; the American School of Classical Studies at Athens (ASCSA); Timuçin Alp Aslan; Harvard's Center for Hellenic Studies (CHS); Kalliopi Christophi of the EFA; Elif Denel of the American Research Institute in Turkey (ARIT); Berna Güler of the DAI Istanbul; Yasmin Nachtigall; Kerri Sullivan of the Archaeological Exploration of Sardis; and Athanasios Themos of the Epigraphic Museum in Athens.

Fellowships and grants both before and after I completed the PhD supported my research and travel: a CHS/DAI Joint Postdoctoral Fellowship; a Phi Beta Kappa Sibley Fellowship; a Louis J. Kolb Society of Fellows Junior Fellowship; a Penn Museum Colburn Fellowship; and a Council of American Overseas Research Centers (CAORC) Mediterranean Regional Fellowship. The resources of ASCSA, ARIT (Ankara), the CHS, the Kommission für Alte Geschichte und Epigraphik (Munich), the Institut für Klassische Archäologie of Ludwig-Maximilians-Universität (Munich), the DAI (Berlin), and the American Research Center in Egypt (Cairo) were of great importance in my research. This publication was largely written while I was employed at the Universität Heidelberg in the Collaborative Research Centre (CRC) 933 Material Text Cultures: Materiality and Presence of Writing in Non-Typographic Societies (subproject A01, "Inscriptions in Urban Space in the Greco-Roman Period and Middle Ages"). The CRC 933 is funded by the German Research Foundation (DFG). The support of the CRC and its many members made my time in Heidelberg both productive and pleasant.

Various individuals commented on drafts, offered insight on specific case studies, or pointed me toward relevant material: Benjamin Allgaier, Jesper Blid, John Camp, Angela Commito; Gülşah Gunata, Edward Harris, Pontus Hellström, Ine Jacobs, Troels Myrup Kristensen, Stephanie Larson, Polly Low, Muriel Murer, Philipp Niewöhner, Chris Ratté, Scott Redford, Felipe Rojas, Peter Talloen, Marco Tentori, Rhys Townsend, Nikos Tsivikis, Loreleï Vanderheyden, and Maria Xenaki. This book would not exist if not for Alden Smith's first-year Latin course, which introduced me to the world of Classics. Over the years, too many people to name have accompanied me on research travels, offered hospitality, or shared their specialized knowledge on site; a few of them are: Ayşe Belgin Henry, Olivier Henry, Sarah Nash Hollaender, Julian Hollaender, Sam Holzman, Friederike Kranig, Regina Loehr, Kate Morgan, Agnieszka Szymanska, Kurtis Tanaka, Tasos Tanoulas, and Banban Wang. The anonymous reviewers made many important contributions and corrections; any errors or oversights that remain are my own.

Finally, I wish to thank my family, who have always been supportive of and interested in my research, even when it took me very far from home. I also thank Maxim Korolkov, whose presence made the final months of manuscript preparation a pleasure. This book is for them.

Abbreviated Epigraphic Corpora

Abbreviations follow the *SEG*

AE	1888–. *L'Année épigraphique*, Paris.
CIG	1828–1877. *Corpus Inscriptionum Graecarum*, Berlin.
CIJud	Frey, J. B. 1936–1952. *Corpus inscriptionum Judaicarum*, Vatican.
CIL	1863–. *Corpus Inscriptionum Latinarum*, Berlin.
F.Delphes III	1909–1985. *Fouilles de Delphes III. Épigraphie*, Paris.
I.Ancyra	Mitchell, S., D. French. 2012–2019. *The Greek and Latin Inscriptions of Ankara (Ancyra)*, Munich.
I.Aphrodisias 2007	Reynolds, J., C. Roueché, and G. Bodard, eds. 2007. *Inscriptions of Aphrodisias (2007)*, http://insaph.kcl.ac.uk/iaph2007/index.html.
I.Byzantion	Łajtar, A. 2000. *Die Inschriften von Byzantion*, Bonn.
ICG	Breytenbach, C., K. Hallof, U. Huttner, P. Hommel, S. Mitchell, J. M. Ogereau, M. Prodanova, E. Sironen, M. Veksina, and C. Zimmermann, eds. 2016. *Inscriptiones Christianae Graecae: A Digital Collection of Greek Early Christian Inscriptions from Asia Minor and Greece*, http://repository.edition-topoi.org/collection/ICG.
I.Chr. Macédoine	Feissel, D. 1983. *Recueil des nscriptions chrétiennes de Macédoine du IIIe au VIe siècle*, Paris.
I.Cret.	Guarducci, M. 1935–1950. *Inscriptiones Creticae*, Rome.
I.Didyma	Rehm, A., R. Harder. 1958. *Didyma II. Die Inschriften*, Berlin.
I.Ephesos	1979–1984. *Die Inschriften von Ephesos*, Bonn.
I.Ethiopie	Bernand, E., A. J. Drewes, and R. Schneider. 2000. *Recueil des Inscriptions de l'Éthiopie des périodes pré-axoumite et axoumite.* Vol. 3, *Les inscriptions grecques*. Paris.
I.Gerasa	Welles, C. B. 1938. "The Inscriptions" in *Gerasa. City of the Decapolis*, ed. C.H. Kraeling, New Haven, CT, 355–494.
IG	1873–. *Inscriptiones Graecae*, Berlin.
IGLS	1929–. *Inscriptions grecques et latines de la Syrie*, Beirut.
IGR	1906–1927. *Inscriptiones Graecae ad Res Romanas Pertinentes*, Paris.
I.Iasos	Blümel, W. 1985. *Die Inschriften von Iasos*, Bonn.

I.Ikaria	Matthaiou, A. P. and G. K. Papadopoulos. 2003. Ἐπιγραφὲς Ἰκαρίας, Athens.
I.Knidos	Blümel, W. 1992-2019. *Die Inschriften von Knidos*, Bonn.
I.Kibyra	Corsten, T. 2002. *Die Inschriften von Kibyra*, Bonn.
I.Kourion	Mitford, T. B. 1971. *The Inscriptions of Kourion*, Philadelphia.
I.Labraunda	Crampa, J. 1969-1972. *Labraunda. Swedish Excavations and Researches 3: Greek Inscriptions*, I-II. Lund.
I.Laodikeia Lykos	Corsten, T. 1997. *Die Inschriften von Laodikeia am Lykos*, Bonn.
I.Lindos	Blinkenberg, C. 1941. *Lindos. Fouilles et recherches.* Vol. 2, *Fouilles de l'acropole. Inscriptions*, Berlin.
I.Magnesia	Kern, O. 1900. *Die Inschriften von Magnesia am Maeander*, Berlin.
I.Milet	1997-2017. *Milet VI. Inschriften von Milet*, Berlin.
I.Mus. Burdur	Horsley, G. H. R. 2007. *The Greek and Latin Inscriptions in the Burdur Archaeological Museum*, London.
I.Mus. Iznik	Şahin, S. 1979-1987. *Katalog der antiken Inschriften des Museums von Iznik (Nikaia)*, Bonn.
I.Mylasa	Blümel, W. 1987-1988. *Die Inschriften von Mylasa*, Bonn.
I.Pergamon	Fraenkel, M. 1890-1895. *Altertümer von Pergamon VIII. Die Inschriften von Pergamon*, 1-2, Berlin.
I.Perge	Şahin, S. 1999-2004. *Die Inschriften von Perge*, Bonn.
I.Phil.Dem.	Griffith, F. L. 1937. *Catalogue of the Demotic Graffiti of the Dodecaschoenus*, Cairo.
I.Priene B—M	Blümel, W., E. Merkelbach. 2014. *Die Inschriften von Priene*, Bonn.
I.Rhodische Peraia	Blümel, W. 1991. *Die Inschriften der rhodischen Peraia*, Bonn.
I.Sagalassos	Eich, A., P. Eich, and W. Eck. 2018. *Die Inschriften von Sagalassos*, Bonn.
I.Sardis I	Buckler, W. H., D. M. Robinson. 1932. *Sardis VII. Greek and Latin Inscriptions*, Part 1, Leiden.
I.Sardis II	Petzl, G. 2019. *Sardis. Greek and Latin Inscriptions.* Part 2, *Finds from 1958 to 2017*, Cambridge, MA.
I.Stratonikeia	Şahin, M. Ç. 1981-2010. *Die Inschriften von Stratonikeia*, Bonn.
I.Westkilikien Rep.	Hagel, S., K. Tomaschitz. 1998. *Repertorium der westkilikischen Inschriften nach den Scheden der Kleinasiatischen Kommission der Österreichischen Akademie der Wissenschaften*, Vienna.
MAMA	1928-2013. *Monumenta Asiae Minoris Antiqua*, London.

OGIS	Dittenberger, W. 1903–1905. *Orientis Graeci Inscriptiones Selectae*, Leipzig.
RIB	1965–2006. *The Roman Inscriptions of Britain*, Oxford.
SEG	1928–. *Supplementum Epigraphicum Graecae*, Leiden.
TAM	1901–. *Tituli Asiae Minoris*, Vienna.
Tit. Calymnii	Segre, M. 1952. *Tituli Calymnii*, Athens.

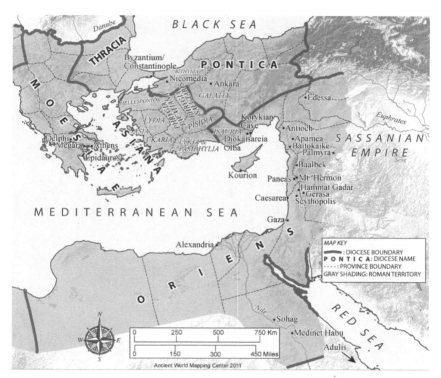

Map 1 Eastern Mediterranean in the time of Diocletian and Constantine, with the province names in western Asia Minor. Ancient World Mapping Center © 2023 (awmc.unc.edu). Used by permission, with modifications.

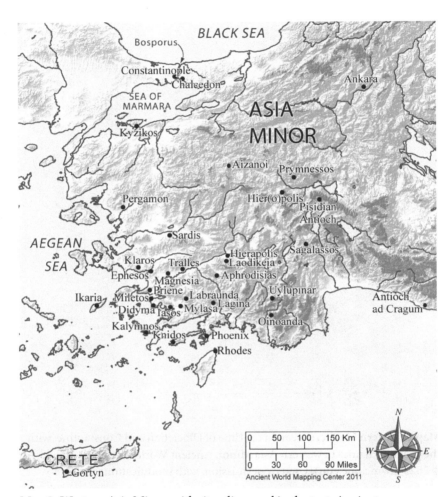

Map 2 Western Asia Minor, with sites discussed in the text. Ancient World Mapping Center © 2023 (awmc.unc.edu). Used by permission, with modifications.

1
Introduction
Afterlives of Inscriptions

Epigraphic Reincarnation at Megara

In 480 BCE, Xerxes' invasion of Greece brought death to the citizen-soldiers of Megara, a *polis* neighboring Athens. In late antiquity, nearly a full millennium after the Persian Wars, the memory of the Megarian fallen had not burnt out. An inscription, dated to the fourth or fifth century CE based on letter forms, opens with the heading:

> The epigram of the heroes who died in the Persian war and who are buried here, which the head priest Helladios had inscribed when it had been damaged by time, for the honor of the fallen and of the city. Simonides composed it.[1]

A nine-line epigram follows on the stone, naming the battles in which the Megarians fell (Figure 1.1). The text concludes by stating that the city continued to sacrifice a bull on behalf of the dead up until the present. Despite the extraordinary potential of this verse inscription to shed light on late antique engagement with the inscribed past, the scholarly discourse surrounding it has centered on the putatively Classical epigram and how much of it, if any, can really be attributed to Simonides of Keos, the prolific lyric poet of the sixth/fifth century BCE.[2] To my knowledge, only a drawing and a

---

[1] *IG* VII 53, *ll.* 1–4; revised and regularized edition from Tentori Montalto 2017: 162: τὸ ἐπίγραμμα τῶν ἐν τῶι Περσικῶι πολέμωι ἀποθανόντων καὶ κειμένων | ἐνταῦθα ἡρώων, ἀπολόμενον δὲ τῶι χρόνωι, Ἑλλάδιος ὁ ἀρχιερεὺς ἐπιγρ|αφῆναι ἐποίησεν εἰς τιμὴν τῶν κειμένων καὶ τῆς πόλεως. Σιμωνίδης | ἐποίει. Throughout, I use bars to indicate line breaks on the stone, except when otherwise noted. The inscription is not lost, *contra* Bravi 2006: 66 and Proietti 2019: 34, but is in the collection of the Archaeological Museum of Megara (Inv. no. 146) after being removed from the wall of the twelfth/thirteenth century Hagios Athanasios church at Palaiochori. For the latest discussion of this stone and its late antique context, see Robu 2020.

[2] Throughout this book, I use "Classical" with a capital "C" to refer to the discrete period of Greek history from roughly 500 BCE to 323 BCE. When I use "classical" with a small "c," I am referring

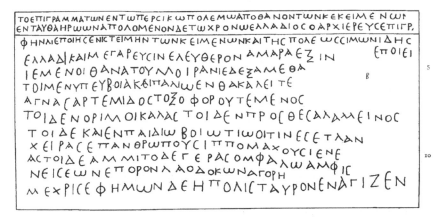

Figure 1.1 Megara. Late antique inscription (*IG* VII 53) honoring the Persian War dead with a reinscribed epigram of Simonides of Keos. Wilhelm 1899, 238.

general photo of this inscription, which is carved on a narrow, parapet-like block originally joined with other blocks to the left and right, have so far been published, but an examination of a squeeze and the stone itself confirms a late date on palaeographic grounds.[3] Indeed, both the letter forms *and* the layout are explicitly non-Classical: the lines were not laid out prior to carving (they are uneven and the final word of the heading, ἐποίει, "made," is crammed below the name Simonides); the letter forms include lunate sigmas, lunate epsilons, and w-form omegas; the letter sizes vary significantly.

This inscription from Megara raises many questions: Did the city really sacrifice bulls for the war dead in the fourth or fifth century CE? Had Christianity made so few inroads into this region of Greece that Helladios, a presumably pagan priest, could set up such a monument? Was Helladios really able to comprehend and copy an epitaph inscribed in the early Classical era? Some lines of the epigram are most likely later elaborations on Simonides' theme, so Helladios may have been working from a Hellenistic or Roman inscription rather than a Classical one; even so, the stone in question

---

instead to classical antiquity in general, a category created by scholars to encompass the Greek and Roman worlds from roughly the period of the Homeric poems to the dominance of Christianity.

[3] The stone measures 1.75m (length) × 0.925 (height) × 0.225 (depth). It is sometimes incorrectly described as a stele. Drawing: Wilhelm 1899: 238; photo Robu 2020: Pl. 2; squeeze courtesy of Marco Tentori Montalto.

was old enough to be "damaged by time."[4] The republication of this epigram indicates the continued relevance of older inscribed texts in the late Roman world—and, critically, the ability to read and engage with them. This copying is not simply evidence of "antiquarian" interests on the part of Helladios; it is rather an act of reception and the production of a specifically late antique monument at the moment when the sacred canopy over Megara was being pulled in a new direction.[5] As Angelos Chaniotis has argued, the bull sacrifice mentioned at the end of the inscription probably does not represent a continuous tradition stretching back to the Classical era, but rather a revival of cultic activity in response to fourth-century imperial legislation prohibiting animal sacrifices: "Not so many people bothered to write epigrams commemorating the fact that they had offered sacrifices before the fourth century AD."[6] The long-dead Megarian soldiers were deployed anew against a novel threat: Christianization. The copied text of the epigram stayed the same (perhaps with a few errors introduced in the republishing process), but its significance was fundamentally altered.

Another late antique inscription found at Megara has a similar pedigree: it records the setting up of the *mnema* (monument or memorial) for a Megarian named Orsippos (or Orrippos) on the advice of Delphi.[7] According to the second-century CE traveler Pausanias, the tomb of Orsippos stood in the city's agora, occupying this place of honor because of its occupant's remarkable feats: he was the first to win the Olympic footrace while naked (in 720 BCE, if Eusebius of Caesarea's *Chronicon* is to be believed), followed by a successful career as *strategos* of Megara, in which he expanded the city's territory.[8] The same information is included in our inscribed copy. This inscription is written in the Doric dialect (e.g., μνᾶμα instead of μνῆμα), but based on the palaeography, it dates as late as the fifth century CE, long after the Doric dialect had fallen out of use.[9] It is written on a reused architectural

---

[4] For the date of the epigram: Petrovic 2007: 194–208; Tentori Montalto 2017: 162–164; Robu 2020: 50–52. Note that one verse from the epigram (of whatever date) is missing on the stone: perhaps it was left out by accident during the process of copying, or was too worn to be read.

[5] I follow McKechnie 2019 in using Peter L. Berger's concept of the "sacred canopy" as a convenient shorthand for describing religious change.

[6] Chaniotis 2005: 166.

[7] *IG* VII 52. Photos: Robu 2020, Pl. 3 and 4.

[8] Pausanias 1.44.1; Eusebius *Chronicon* 1.195.

[9] Date and earlier bibliography: Schörner 2014: 152; photo: Montecalvo 2007: 980. Proietti 2019: 41–45 argues that the copying of both the Simonides epigram and the Orsippos text reaffirmed Megarian civic-military identity in the wake of Alaric's Visigothic invasion of Greece in 395/6 CE (cf. Zosimos 5.6.4; Tzavella 2012: 353–357), while Robu 2020: 57 suggests that a revitalization of hero cult in late antiquity was responsible for both these inscriptions and a fragmentary third one, all of which may have been attributed to Simonides in this era. The two inscriptions under consideration

block with a frame only at the right and lower edges. Yet again, a hero from the distant past has been epigraphically reincarnated, this time affirming the importance of two gradually declining Panhellenic institutions: the Delphic oracle and the Olympic games. The reasons for this decline were as much internal, the reflection of changing tastes, as the result of Christianizing imperial legislation, but pagans may have preferred to blame Christians, some of whom were probably all too happy to take credit.[10] These two republished inscriptions, the Simonides epigram and the commemoration of Orsippos, indicate that Megara used ancient epigraphic material to perpetuate the memory of their city's heroes and push back against newly ascendant Christian idea(l)s of history. These late inscribed copies make claims on the continuing vitality of Hellenic identity in a Christianizing Roman world that espoused complicated, even contradictory, views of the pre-Christian Greco-Roman past.

As we will see in this book, Helladios and his fellow Megarians were not alone in their engagement with older inscriptions—but not everyone read and interacted with inscribed texts in the same ways. Many people in late antiquity commissioned newly cut inscriptions that were *not* copies of older texts, even if they continued long-standing epigraphic habits. Given the marked drop-off in epigraphic production in most regions in our period, however, the majority of inscriptions on display in cities were actually centuries older.[11] Our strict periodization of material—the neat categorization of inscriptions under labels such as "Hellenistic" or "Roman" or "late antique"—cannot stand. All these inscribed stones were in fact part of late antique material culture, even if some inscriptions would have struck late Roman viewers as old-fashioned, difficult to read, or even mysterious. And each of these texts held in its stony materiality and textual content the seeds of its potential fate: preservation, reuse, or obliteration.

Our exploration of the late antique reception of ancient inscriptions focuses on eastern Mediterranean contexts stretching from Greece to Asia Minor to the Levant to Egypt between the fourth and seventh centuries CE. And exploration it is: no previous study has centered on the late Roman afterlife of ancient inscriptions or habits of viewing older inscribed stones in

---

here, however, are palaeographically distinct and in my view should not be attributed to a single program of memorialization.

[10] Remijsen 2015; Heineman 2018.
[11] Nawotka 2020.

this period, so we must chart our own path.[12] Jennifer Westerfeld has recently documented late Roman attitudes about Egyptian hieroglyphs (including inscribed ones) in the textual sources; a volume edited by Jonathan Ben-Dov and Felipe Rojas explored (late) classical reception of ancient Near Eastern rock-cut monuments, some inscribed; both Rojas and Christina Maranci have detailed the reuse of Iron Age Urartian inscriptions in medieval Armenian churches and their potential interpretation as predecessors of the unique Armenian writing system; and Jason Moralee has articulated how pagan dedications were appropriated to create a triumphalist Christian narrative at churches in Gerasa (Jerash, Jordan).[13] Other authors have treated individual instances of ancient inscriptions in late antique contexts, and they are cited throughout this book. But the topic as a whole has garnered little attention. It is rather Persia, the eastern neighbor and competitor to the Roman empire, that has provoked consideration of the continued power of inscriptions across centuries: Matthew Canepa has documented how Sassanian kings (224–642 CE) staged their power in relation to their distant Achaemenid predecessors (550–330 BCE) by inscribing monumental rock-cut texts onto landscapes, as earlier kings had done. Although they could not read the Achaemenid texts (typically in Old Persian, Elamite, and Babylonian Akkadian), the Sassanian rulers carved lists of deeds remarkably similar to the older texts at sites of historical import, for example, at the Achaemenid royal cemetery of Naqsh-e Rostam. Canepa makes three important observations on monumental inscriptions in the Persian world, which go beyond typical epigraphic-historical approaches. First, the texts were not meant to be read by viewers on the ground. Many were carved so high on cliff faces that their content could only be grasped through mediation (other copies on parchment or tablets). Second, whether or not they could be read, these texts converted normal places into politically and socially charged space. Third, these inscriptions "could tangibly collapse gulfs of time" between the Achaemenid past and Sassanian present.[14] Although late Roman individuals interacted with epigraphic material in very different

---

[12] For the diachronic power of inscriptions, see Barrett 1993; Yasin 2015; Van Dam 2018: 517. The edited volume *The Afterlife of Inscriptions: Reusing, Rediscovering, Reinventing & Revitalizing Ancient Inscriptions* (Cooley 2000) pioneered the investigation of later reception of inscriptions but does not treat late antiquity. For attitudes toward contemporary late antique inscribed text, see Eastmond 2015; Leatherbury 2020.
[13] Westerfeld 2019; Ben-Dov and Rojas 2021; Rojas In progress; Maranci 2015: 177–182; Moralee 2006.
[14] Canepa 2015: 13–14.

ways than did Sassanian kings, Canepa's second and third points in particular inform my approach to the afterlives of inscriptions in the late antique eastern Mediterranean.

Most previous studies, then, have dealt with inscriptions that were illegible to late antique or medieval viewers: Egyptian hieroglyphs, Urartian, Old Persian. The lack of previous attention to classical Greek and Latin inscriptions in the early Christian period is due in part to the limited evidence for later reading and copying: I will state from the outset that Megara is the exception rather than the rule. Our subsequent examples deal not with the republication of classical texts on stone, but with the fates of the ancient stones themselves as described (or invented) in written sources and as attested in the archaeological record. More than a lack of evidence, however, this dearth of scholarship on epigraphic afterlives is due to the substantial value that inscriptions have as sociohistorical evidence for their moment of inscribing—their subsequent object biographies are usually foggier and can offer less to traditional historical narratives.[15] But inscriptions (like all writing) are both artifacts and texts, and I aim to highlight their transtemporal nature in line with work on synchronic statue assemblages, aggregative cityscapes, and the classical *paideia* permeating late antique literature.[16]

The central claim of this book is that classical inscriptions in late antique contexts were not simply leftovers waiting to be discovered by a modern epigrapher and restored to their "original historical context," but instead were active agents in shaping late antique views of the (pagan) past. With "active agents" I am not implying that inscriptions had their own *animus* or will; rather, I use the notion of object agency in line with usage in material culture studies, archaeology, and anthropology over the past three decades.[17] Inscriptions could act on viewers, far beyond the original intentions of their carvers. They did this not only through their physical characteristics (orderly layouts, official scripts, architectural synergy) and contexts (reused to construct walls or churches, or left in their original places on monuments still standing in late antique cities or sanctuaries) but also through their *content*: dedications to gods and emperors, letters from kings or officials,

---

[15] Sitz 2019a: 644–645. I use the common metaphors of object "biographies" and "afterlives" in this book, while acknowledging the problematics of these terms in line with Hahn 2015.
[16] Smith 2007; Jacobs 2013; Kalas 2015; Larsen and Rubenson 2018. See also Berti et al. 2017 and Petrovic, Petrovic, and Thomas 2019 for inscriptions as material artifacts.
[17] Gell 1998; Latour 2005; Jones and Boivin 2010.

honorific texts, lists of priests/officials, or civic decrees. I am primarily concerned with epigraphic material in Greek, the *lingua franca* of the eastern Mediterranean since the Hellenistic period and still spoken (and read) by many individuals in the late Roman east, but other material, including that in Latin, in Semitic languages, in ancient Anatolian tongues, and in ancient Egyptian, appears in this study as well. Some of these writing systems could no longer be comprehended in late antiquity, and they worked on viewers differently than those that could.

I posit that the Greek inscriptions, which could be read (as we have just seen at Megara), projected an impression of a past that was *so very civic* in nature, providing a counterbalance to the more polemical, religiously charged views of bygone eras espoused by a number of late antique Christian apologists. These ancient inscriptions played their part at preventing more destructive repudiations of the pagan past in the context of the sometimes violent rhetoric of religious change that marked the transition from Greco-Roman cults to Christianity. I have chosen to explore the role of inscriptions particularly at former pagan sanctuaries because of the polarizing role that temples played in discourses of the late Roman empire, simultaneously decried from church pulpits as polluted spaces of pagan perversion and occasionally protected by imperial proclamations on account of their cultural and historical value. These sanctuaries were especially charged spaces for negotiating the upheaval of power relations between the subscribers of the traditional cults and those of the new religion, between emperors, civic leaders, ecclesiastical actors, and city inhabitants. Before we come to the late antique fate of ancient temples and their inscriptions, however, we will take a detour to the not so distant past.

Manufactured Violence

In August 2015, the Islamic State (ISIS) detonated explosives in the ancient temples of Bel and Baalshamin in Palmyra, Syria. The temples, which had weathered changes in cultures and contexts for two millennia (as we will see in Chapter 3), collapsed. ISIS had previously established their tendency for wanton destruction of cultural heritage when they released a video of smashed statues in the Mosul Museum in Iraq that same year. In each instance, news outlets and social media users around the globe responded with horror and outrage; this obliteration of irreplaceable artifacts and the

8 PAGAN INSCRIPTIONS, CHRISTIAN VIEWERS

destruction of the UNESCO World Heritage site of Palmyra served to underscore, yet again, the savageness of ISIS.

The narrative set forth by the international media saw these violent acts as evidence of ISIS's religious intolerance. The temples of Palmyra were dedicated to false gods; the destroyed statues were idols, the objects of polytheistic worship. As such, under an extremist interpretation of Islamic tradition, they must be destroyed. More astute observers, however, recognized that ISIS's actions were not so straightforward: it was the *viral video* of the Mosul Museum destruction, not the destructive act itself, that was the goal.[18] The video spread like wildfire through both social and mainstream media. ISIS's disturbing videos of violence against captive journalists, on the other hand, were heavily censored in the media and shared by few social media users in the West. The destruction by explosives of the two Palmyrene temples had a similar effect: ISIS was again in the headlines. The farce was given up when, after the two temples, the Arch of Septimius Severus in Palmyra (hardly a religious structure) was blown up. This was demolition for attention's sake, a dramatic statement against the value of the past, manufactured violence to spread a cause.

Let us consider another instance of violence against a temple:

> The columns [of the temple] were of great bulk. . . . In each of these the man made an opening all round, propping up the superstructure with olive timber before he went on to another. After he had hollowed out three of the columns, he set fire to the timbers. . . . When their support had vanished the columns themselves fell down, and dragged the other twelve with them. The side of the temple which was connected with the columns was dragged down by the violence of their fall, and carried away with them. The crash, which was tremendous, was heard throughout the town, and all ran to see the sight.[19]

This account describes not the destructive activity of ISIS, but the purported actions of Bishop Markellos against the Temple of Zeus Belos in Apamea (Syria), traditionally dated to 386 CE. Markellos wished to destroy the temple, and an anonymous workman conveniently appeared with the expertise to accomplish it. The plan was initially stymied by a demon, who would not allow

---

[18] Harmanşah 2015.
[19] Theodoret of Cyrrhus *Historia Ecclesiastica* 5.21 (trans. Jackson).

the timbers to catch fire, but Markellos chased it away with holy water. The episode was written by Theodoret of Cyrrhus in the mid-fifth century—some six decades after the alleged event—in his *Historia Ecclesiastica*, an account of church history that weaves together the verifiable with the miraculous. The passage has long been read as an archetypal exemplar of Christian destruction of a pagan temple and, through this architectural violence, the dissolution of the pagan religious traditions that had undergirded life in ancient cities from the earliest periods. By the fifth century, attacks on temples were a *topos* in hagiographies (saints' lives) as well as ecclesiastical histories.[20]

Violence against sanctuaries paired well with the fiery polemical rhetoric used by some Christian writers at the time to describe temples, pagan gods, and worship rituals.[21] Eusebius of Caesarea repeatedly referred to pagan gods pejoratively as "demons" and alluded to the illicit sexual activity happening at temples of Aphrodite at Baalbek/Heliopolis and Aphaka in Lebanon.[22] Clement of Alexandria recited a list of pagan gods who demanded human sacrifice, "glutting themselves to the full with human blood."[23] Pagans harvested the guts of murdered Christian children to make harp strings, according to the sixth- or seventh-century Coptic panegyric on Makarios of Tkôw.[24] The goddess Isis, or rather, the "demon which took her form," tricked members of the late antique philosophical circles of Alexandria in Zacharias' *Life of Severos, Patriarch of Antioch*.[25] Gregory the Great (pope from 590 to 604) tells a colorful tale of a Jew who overnighted at a temple of Apollo and witnessed there a gathering of demons reporting on the temptations they had afflicted on locals.[26] The trope that ancient sanctuaries housed demons appears epigraphically as well: at Zorava in Syria, a church dedication from 515 CE declares "The abode of *daimones* has become the house of God.... Where sacrifices to idols occurred, there are now choirs of angels."[27]

Late pagans such as Eunapios, Zosimos, and Libanios obviously did not go in for the demons, but they too paint sanctuaries as spaces of violence.[28] Libanios' *Pro Templis* claimed that monks were running rampant in the

---

[20] Saradi 2008: 114.
[21] Wiśniewski 2016 argues that Christian rhetoric about "demons" originated in part from ancient traditions styling temples as places of real encounters with the gods.
[22] Eusebius *Vita Constantini* 3.55; 3.58; for Baalbek, see Chapter 4.
[23] Clement of Alexandria *Exhortation to the Greeks* 3.7 (trans. Butterworth); Rives 1995.
[24] Westerfeld 2019: 107.
[25] Zacharias *Life of Severos* 22 (trans. Brock).
[26] Gregory the Great *Dialogues* 3.7.
[27] *IGLS* 15, 1.177 (trans. Trombley 1993: 104).
[28] Foschia 2005.

countryside of Antioch on the Orontes, pulling down temple walls and roofs, carrying away statues, and overturning altars, especially at rural temples. This led to a disruption of agriculture in the areas where temples were destroyed, since the farming poor had invested all their hopes in these buildings, the "soul (ψυχή) of the countryside."[29] Farmers lost the will to work the land and therefore contributed fewer taxes to the imperial coffers (perhaps the most relevant detail for Libanios' audience, Theodosios I).

For a long time, scholars took literary descriptions of violence against pagan temples in late antiquity at face value, as descriptors of real events with clear-cut motives. They simply exorcised the demonic actors and miraculous assistance from these textual accounts but regarded the essential narratives as true.[30] This has influenced not only the way in which the end of paganism has been written, but the interpretation of archaeological remains at sanctuary sites too. Friedrich Wilhelm Deichmann in 1939 produced a catalogue of churches built in ancient sanctuaries and stated that "die Wandlung des antiken Heiligtums ist das Symbol der *Ecclesia triumphans*" (the conversion of the ancient temple is the symbol of the church triumphant).[31] In this view, ecclesiastical authorities appropriated older sanctuaries to demonstrate the superiority of Christianity. A historical narrative was constructed in which temples were rapidly destroyed or made into churches in the decades of pagan-Christian competition after Constantine, which is precisely what many of our late antique Christian authors, such as Eusebius, wanted us to think. This paradigm of antagonistic replacement held for decades, and currents of it still run through some scholarship. But in the 1960s and 1970s, archaeologists pushed back: evidence for temple reuse suggests that the pagan buildings had been abandoned for decades or centuries before their conversion, which often can be associated with urban contraction rather than religious competition.[32] Even indications of a destruction event, such as burn marks, could be the result rather of invading forces or simply an accidental fire.[33] Luke Lavan questions whether even "clear" evidence of Christian interference with temples, such as crosses carved onto these structures, is actually indicative of anti-pagan sentiment: crosses were graffitied onto practically everything in late antiquity.[34]

---

[29] Libanios *Pro Templis* 9 (trans. Norman).
[30] Fowden 1978; Trombley 1993.
[31] Deichmann 1939: 114.
[32] Frantz 1965; Speiser 1976. For an updated overview: Lavan 2011a.
[33] Ward-Perkins 2011.
[34] Lavan 2011a: xxvii.

INTRODUCTION 11

Richard Bayliss's expansive 2004 study of temple destructions and conversions from the entire Mediterranean confirms a general pattern of long abandonments and later, pragmatic reuses. Most conversions in his catalogue date to the mid-fifth century or later and can be divided up into two distinct types: "direct transformations" (churches that reuse the still-standing temple structure, called the *naos*, including cella-churches, internalized cellas, and inverted transformations) and "indirect transformations" (those that are built within the temenos, but not actually in the temple building, or those built from the reused blocks of the disassembled/collapsed temple).[35] There were regional differences in the fates of temples, with comparatively more evidence for conflict and destruction in the Diocese of the Oriens (stretching from Isauria south to Egypt).[36] When destruction did occur, it was not solely the responsibility of church authorities; state actors were frequently involved.[37] Christians were also quite happy to reuse all sorts of buildings as churches, not only temples: villas, baths, basilicas, theaters, gymnasia, stoas, fortifications, and mausolea.[38] The superficial assumption that churches naturally sprang up in temples as a consequence of the "peace of the church" has not stood up to scholarly scrutiny.

In fact, Bishop Markellos' violence against the Temple of Zeus in Apamea, as narrated by Theodoret of Cyrrhus, may never have happened. The archaeological evidence is inconclusive, as few remains from the temple have been identified. In actuality the temple may have simply collapsed in an earthquake at some point, leaving behind columns and wall blocks strewn about. Aude Busine argues that these architectural remains inspired an aetiological tale giving meaning to the collapse, a narrative explaining the late antique cityscape in which people lived.[39] Or perhaps not. Perhaps Markellos really did engineer the temple's collapse—other examples of temple destruction, such as at the Serapeion at Alexandria around 391, are better documented by contemporary sources.[40] Either way, Theodoret's account, like ISIS's videos, is manufactured violence. Written long after the event it purports to describe, the story served to advance the Christian communal identity of Apamea

---

[35] Bayliss 2004: 35–47. "Cella" refers to the enclosed room at the center of a temple; "temenos" refers to the sacred precinct set aside for a god, usually marked by walls, stoas, or other architectural or epigraphic boundaries.
[36] Bayliss 2004: 67–68; Lavan 2011a: xxxvi–xxxvii.
[37] Hahn 2011b.
[38] Vaes 1986.
[39] Busine 2013: 329; Busine 2014.
[40] See Chapter 2, p. 47 and Chapter 5, p. 208.

and Theodoret's own narrative. He places this episode of temple destruction shortly before the destruction of the Alexandrian Serapeion: Syrian bishops had done it first, and Theodoret wanted to be sure that everyone knew it.

Histories and hagiographies were the social media of late antiquity, interactive platforms for the spreading of information, true or false, and for the crafting a particular persona, a particular worldview. Even the emperor Julian could fall victim to "fake news": prior to his visit to Ilion/Troy in 354, Julian had heard that the bishop Pegasios had destroyed the tomb of Achilles. But upon arrival he found the tomb perfectly preserved.[41] Libanios' pagan beliefs do not necessarily make him a more reliable narrator than Christians bent on narrating destruction: both Libanios and the monks he complained about competed to control temple spaces and their interpretations in the Antiochene countryside.[42] Like ISIS's destruction of the temples of Palmyra, violence against temples in late antiquity—or stories of violence against temples—must be contextualized as something more than straightforward attacks arising from religious animosity. The rhetoric of temple destructions offered hearers the interpretational framework through which to view their surroundings. For Christians, it created a logically consistent narrative of triumph from the scattered and strewn detritus of classical urban life, from the columns, ashlars, and architraves of past temples.

It hardly needs to be stated in this day and age that rhetoric is not reality.[43] We know better than to uncritically take textual accounts at their word. But fiery, antagonistic rhetoric has a way of inspiring action, regardless of whether its initiator only intended to curry favor with a particular group or genuinely wished to see her or his proclamations put into action. Why, then, do we find such a significant gap between the rhetorical celebration of temple demolitions, and the archaeological remains, which suggest that such activity was rare? Previous attempts to address this gap have pointed toward the *Codex Theodosianus* (hereafter *C.Th.*), the law code compiled under Theodosios II and first published in 438. Book 16 of the Theodosian Code contains various laws on religious matters, beginning with the time of Constantine. Sacrifices are repeatedly prohibited, with a particular enmity toward divination (which could be used against the emperor), but most imperial fiats regarding temples prescribe preservation of desacralized temples. It seems that initially, imperial interest in temples ran counter to the

---

[41] Julian *Epistle* 19; Sage 2000.
[42] Shepardson 2019: 193.
[43] See recently: Kahlos 2019: 1–11.

occasional ecclesiastical hope for a showy destructive event. In 342 (*C.Th.* 16.10.3), temples outside the city walls should be left untouched "although all superstitions must be completely eradicated."[44] By 356, Constantius II declared that all temples must be closed but did not specify what to do with them (*C.Th.* 16.10.4). Julian reversed this proclamation with his attempted pagan revival, but his premature death in 363 put the empire back on the path of Christian dominance. A 382 missive declared that a temple, probably at Edessa, was to be put to common use as a place to view statues, so long as there were no sacrifices (*C.Th.* 16.10.8).[45] By the 390s, imperial edicts warned people to stay away from temples (*C.Th.* 16.10.10, 16.10.11, 16.10.13), and in 399, the Praetorian Prefect of the East was commanded to tear down all temples in the countryside without disturbance (*C.Th.* 16.10.16). In 407/8, Arcadius, Honorius, and Theodosios II legislated that all altars should be destroyed but that temples should be put to public use (*C.Th.* 16.10.19). This series of regulations changed course in 435, when Theodosios II commanded that all shrines and temples should be destroyed and purified by a cross (*C. Th.* 16.10.25).

Obviously, not all temples were destroyed. We have many well-preserved examples that have stood in the eastern Mediterranean since antiquity. Theodosios may have intended only still-active temples to be taken apart (or just shut down?), but in any case, archaeological evidence attests that the laws were applied haphazardly at best; the *Codex*'s frequent imposition of fines on judges who do not follow its precepts hints that these regulations were often not enforced.[46] Nor can we assume that the laws motivated every action that was taken with regard to temples, whether for their preservation or destruction. The *Codex Theodosianus* is therefore of limited help in filling in the gap between destructive rhetoric and archaeologically attested reality. Rather than the mixed-messaging legal protections, this gap has also been attributed to practical considerations: deconstructing a temple was a difficult and expensive process that required specialized demolition know-how. What is more, many cities undoubtedly preferred to keep their temples intact, for reasons that had nothing to do with pagan sympathies: Helen Saradi has argued that temples, with their marble façades and careful carving, contributed to the *kalos* (beauty) of cityscapes even in late antiquity, and Ine

---

[44] Trans. Pharr.
[45] See further Chapter 3, pp. 82–83.
[46] Bayliss 2004: 117; Hahn 2011a.

Jacobs has documented the significant maintenance that was put into keeping up the classical aesthetics of late antique cities.[47] Rebecca Sweetman, on the other hand, has argued that churches were less interested in appropriating rhetorically charged temple structures than they were in appropriating structures of power and wealth. If churches were built at ancient temple sites in the Peloponnese, it was not because of the ideology of triumphalism so much as an attempt to control the same economic nodes and reinforce the same social hierarchies that temples had.[48]

Each of these explanations fills in *parts* of the gap between the rhetoric and reality of temples, but we can go further. What did late antique Christians (or Jews, or pagans) actually *see* when they approached ancient sanctuaries? Monumental marble façades composed of columns, entablature, and pediments; perhaps temenos (precinct) walls with an impressive propylon (entryway); stoas encircling sanctuaries and creating a temple courtyard; maybe even statues donated to the god(dess) or put up to honor individuals. Or, in many cases, they would have seen only the *inscribed bases* of these statues. In late antiquity, statues (including occasionally cult statues) became desirable decoration for both private homes and public venues, and many were transported out of sanctuaries and into these new display locations. Constantine famously decorated his new capital on the Bosphoros by "denuding almost all other cities," in the words of Jerome, and most statues were moved without their bases.[49] Inscriptions on bases, stelai, and architecture stayed where they were, and it is these text-monuments I wish to insert into the gap as a steppingstone between rhetoric and reality. When city councils, or ecclesiastical authorities, or imperial officers, or private individuals of means, or the local crowd viewed sanctuaries and contemplated what to do with them, they viewed a *heavily inscribed* built space. To those who were literate and willing, these inscriptions allowed temples to "speak for themselves," proclaiming in the inscribed words of donors and dedicators from centuries past what temples *were* and what they *did*. These texts wove together composite narratives of the civic, local, Hellenic, and/or Roman past—narratives that challenged the damning rhetoric late antique visitors may have been hearing from the pulpit.

---

[47] Saradi-Mendelovici 1990; Saradi 2006; Jacobs 2013.
[48] Sweetman 2010; Sweetman 2015.
[49] Jerome *Chronicon* Year 330: *Constantinopolis dedicatur paene omnium urbium nuditate*; Ma 2012.

Inscribed Sanctuaries

The famous epigrapher Louis Robert described the Greco-Roman world as a "civilisation de l'épigraphie," and perhaps no spaces were as densely inscribed as sanctuaries. Objects or buildings gifted to a deity bore dedicatory inscriptions from the individual, city, or association that paid for it; cities set up war monuments or honored citizens, their own or from elsewhere (proxeny decrees); the imperial family accumulated monuments in its honor; the *boule* and the *demos* (the council and the assembly) displayed their own decisions as well as interstate treaties; important documents from distant kings, emperors, or their proxies were on view; temples set up inventories of their goods/lands or accounts of construction activity; manumitted slaves could point to public inscribed copies of their freedom; and sanctuaries set up lists of subscribers, officials, or priests. So-called sacred laws, perhaps better termed cult regulations or ritual norms, made sure that everyone followed the rules: which animals to sacrifice to which god on which day, what to wear, which foods or activities to abstain from.[50] Besides these inscriptions on stone, there were written notices on more temporary materials such as wood, or on durable material that has a tendency to get melted down, such as bronze. Each of these inscriptions, whether permanent or ephemeral, projected a certain message about the nature of temples and the purposes they served. Even to the illiterate, this mass of text proclaimed "I am a monument," as in the famous sketch of Robert Venturi and Denise Scott-Brown in *Learning from Las Vegas* (the 1972 architectural study of how buildings use signage and decoration to convey meaning).[51] To those who could read, these texts could communicate more specific messages, as we will see in the many cited inscriptions in the chapters that follow.

It is worth pointing out here at the outset what was *not* inscribed at Greek and Roman sanctuaries. Ancient polytheistic Mediterranean traditions had no holy book to quote from, no set liturgy of sacred words, no unifying symbol that marked a space as "holy" in the same way that a cross or Chi-Rho came to mark spaces as "Christian" in late antiquity. The triumph of Christianity was, to an extent, a triumph of effective marketing, of building a clear and recognizable brand as opposed to poorly defined and porous paganism. Epigraphy has been a critical source for modern historians to

---

[50] Sokolowski 1969; Lupu 2005; Carbon and Pirenne-Delforge 2012; Harris 2015.
[51] Venturi, Scott-Brown, and Izenour 1972.

reconstruct Greek religious praxis (belief is harder to get at), but in actuality this usually entails reading *civic* decrees outlining sacrifices to be performed and processions to be organized within a bureaucratic framework. The "sacred laws" mentioned above comprise a scholarly, rather than ancient, category of text; the usual criterion for the inclusion of an inscription under this heading is that it has something to do with ritual.[52] Such texts were often introduced or concluded with the familiar phrase "the boule and the demos decided . . ." (*vel sim.*), just as in civic decrees erected outside of sanctuaries. "Sacred laws" could be broken, with the penalty specified often a monetary fine—not eternal damnation. Sanctuaries occasionally produce aretologies (lists of praiseworthy characteristics of a god), but these are comparatively rare. Perhaps most strikingly, the god him/herself rarely speaks on the carved stones at sanctuaries. As frequently as Apollo channeled his voice through the Pythia at Delphi, the god himself was rarely quoted on monuments of petition or thanksgiving. In short, the inscriptions at sanctuaries were not terribly different from those filling other public spaces in the ancient world, even if certain genres of texts (i.e., dedications) tended to congregate there.

There are of course exceptions. A verse inscription at Epidauros should probably be understood as a quote from the god himself; gods liked to speak in hexameters.[53] Epidauros has also produced a series of miracle inscriptions, in which stories of supernatural healings are presented.[54] Asklepios punished those who doubted his healing powers and rewarded those who affirm it. So too in the so-called confession inscriptions of central Asia Minor: these texts from the first to the third centuries CE record the sins of individuals and their punishments from the gods.[55] Other inscriptions indicate a genuine concern with internal moral purity, akin to but distinct from the Judeo-Christian concept of sinfulness and righteousness.[56] Cities occasionally put up honorary decrees passed for the gods themselves, outlining the benefits conferred by divine beings on the *poleis*.[57] By the fourth century CE, some pagans, like Helladios at Megara and Aidisios and Ploutarchos at the Heraion on Samos, began to record epigraphically their individual acts of sacrificing.[58]

---

[52] Gawlinski 2021: 22.
[53] Robertson 2013: 230.
[54] LiDonnici 1995.
[55] Chaniotis 1995; Chaniotis 2004.
[56] Petrovic and Petrovic 2016; see also Parker 1983.
[57] E.g., *I.Stratonikeia* 512, an honorific decree of the city for Hekate inscribed on the anta of the temple at Lagina.
[58] *IG* XII 6, 2.584i and ii.

Dedications to the gods were ubiquitous in sanctuaries as in other civic spaces. But even in dedications the gods get short shrift (or *Schrift*): such texts often opened with the name of the god (in Greek dedications) but proceed to spend much more text-space on the identity of the donor, her/his family and offices, and specifics, both architectural and financial, of the mortal's gift. Pay attention to such inscriptions throughout this book: how much do you learn about the god her/himself, and how much about the donor or city?

Inscriptions at ancient sanctuaries in the Greek east, then, were primarily what we might term "secular" in composition, the testaments and producers of the so-called polis religion that was transformed under Hellenistic kings and later Roman emperors but never lost its profound emphasis on human political affairs. My use of "secular" here is controversial: the separation of secular and religious subject matter is our division, not an ancient one. "Civic" might be a more apposite descriptor, and it is the adjective I frequently use in this book to describe these texts, but it is worth noting that for the ancients, the civic *was* the sacred. More to the point: even very secular-sounding ancient inscriptions were made sacred in antiquity by being set up in the ritual space of an active pagan sanctuary. Framed by the smoke of burnt sacrifices and echoing back the sound of sung hymns, recording wins in sacred athletic games and praising those victorious in religious musical competitions, kept tidy by sanctuary personnel and under the watchful gaze of the cult statue occupying the temple, even the most secular-sounding inscription was caught up in the intractable entanglement of cities, individuals, rulers, and gods. The epigraphic documentation of well-run cities, military triumphs, good relations with rulers or other states, and prosperous citizens affirmed the god's power and good will, just as the god in turn elevated treaties, contracts, and royal decisions to inviolable human-divine pacts. But stripped of this ritual context in late antiquity—bereft of sacrifices, no choirs singing hymns, priests and sanctuary personnel gone or converted, competitions falling by the wayside—these inscriptions lost their sacralizing frames. What was left was the civic texts carved into marble. This book is the story of what happened to these stones.

Literacy in Late Antiquity

But did anyone (other than the historically minded priest Helladios at Megara) actually read the epigraphic monuments marking cityscapes and sanctuaries in late antiquity? *Could* they read these older texts? Actual rates of literacy in late antiquity cannot be reconstructed with any confidence, but a growing body of evidence indicates that many individuals were literate within certain sectors or registers, that is, military or administrative documents, monumental dedications, or records of commercial transactions—even if they could not sit down and read poetry.[59] Women could be scribes in the employee of female members of senatorial families, while literature was sold in the marketplaces of sixth-century Constantinople.[60] True, most regions witnessed a decline in the number of newly made inscriptions from the third century onward, but many "average" people continued to be commemorated with inscribed gravestones through the sixth century, especially in inland Anatolia.[61] Sites such as Aphrodisias provide ample evidence of graffiti, at least some of it apparently from the middling to lower strata of society.[62] Religious graffiti, such as invocations and prayers for help (Κύριε βοήθει, "Lord, help"), are widespread. These examples represent only what has come down to us—surely a significant amount of material, written on perishable material, has not survived.

What is more, the modern conception of literacy encapsulating both reading *and* writing does not serve well. Learning to write requires substantial effort, whereas learning to read by sounding out words is much easier— the main benefit of an alphabetic system as opposed to a logogramic one. Even those who could not read, however, could still engage with inscribed texts. Only one literate person need be present to read for a gathered crowd or verbally epitomize the text for the benefit of others.[63] This de(in)scribing transferred the text from written to oral and substantially broadened its audience. Theoretically, an entire multitude of the illiterate could "read" an inscription based on this oral transmission and glean meaning from its actual content—to say nothing of the various associations invoked by the presence of writing itself.

But reading contemporary texts is one thing; reading much older ones something else entirely. In the *circa* thousand years separating the rise of

---

[59] For updates to Harris 1991 on literacy: Bodel 2015; Kolb 2018. For late antiquity in particular: Browning 1978; Everett 2009; Bagnall 2011: 75–94; M. M. Mitchell 2017.

[60] Haines-Eitzen 2000: 41–52; Lauxtermann 2003: 47.

[61] Mango 2015: 34; Bolle, Machado, and Witschel 2017, especially S. Mitchell 2017b for Anatolia. Mitchell has even proposed that peasants in that region composed funerary epitaphs themselves, drawing on a "repetitive repertoire of poetic expressions" (Mitchell 1993: 105).

[62] E.g., *I.Aphrodisias* 2007 1.19; see also Chaniotis 2011.

[63] Papalexandrou 2007: 162; Agosti 2010.

Archaic Greek inscriptions on stone from the beginning of Christian hegemony under Constantine, the appearance and content of inscribed texts were transformed many times over. The earliest inscriptions in Greek made use of alphabets still heavily dependent on the Phoenician letters from which they evolved. Certain letters, such as the digamma (F), largely fell out of use by the Classical period. In addition, different regions of the Greek-speaking world employed distinct epichoric scripts, which present significant difficulties for those more familiar with later standardized letter forms—just ask any beginning student of Greek epigraphy. Individual letters could be written backward or upside down; texts could run to-and-fro in *boustrophedon* inscriptions—left to right, right to left—or wind themselves around the base of a statue.[64]

Sometimes a text was not Greek at all: the eastern Mediterranean nourished an impressive array of languages. Ancient ethnolinguistic groups in Asia Minor such as Karians, Lykians, Lydians, and Phrygians all had their own languages and writing systems, in many cases superficially resembling the Greek alphabet but completely unintelligible. Although Greek gradually became dominant, especially after Alexander, local languages persisted in some cases into the Roman period and beyond. By late antiquity the old Anatolian languages had fallen out of use (at least in written form), but the texts themselves were certainly still on view along with the epigraphic *Nachlass* of even older cultures, such as the Hittites and the Urartians. Unintelligible inscribed texts on rock-cut monuments, tombs, and freestanding stones defined Anatolia in a way that was not the case in (largely) linguistically homogeneous Greece. In the Levant, Aramaic and Hebrew inscriptions continued to appear alongside Greek. Egyptian settlements and sanctuaries were defined by the prominent appearance of hieroglyphs covering buildings, as well as the late forms of the Egyptian language, Demotic and Coptic.

But except for Egypt, the epigraphic production of these other local language groups was small in comparison to the material in Greek, which spread from the Greek mainland and islands to coastal Greek colonies, then through the highways and byways, eventually arriving in even the smallest villages of the eastern Mediterranean. By the Hellenistic and Roman periods, the Greek alphabet had settled into its familiar form and various dialects had largely coalesced into *koine*. The state of preservation of the text would, of course,

---

[64] Dietrich, Fouquet, and Reinhardt 2020. Pausanias 5.17.6 describes boustrophedon texts as "written in winding turns difficult to figure out" (trans. Zadorojnyi 2018: 54).

have made the reader's attempt more or less difficult. The second-sophistic writer Julius Pollux (second century CE) described ancient inscriptions as "indistinct, unclear, blurred, faint, obscure . . . hard to understand, unknowable" (ἄσημα, ἀσαφῆ, συγκεχυμένα, ἀμυδρά, ἀμαυρά . . . δύσγνωστα, ἄγνωστα).[65] But this need not suggest that *all* older inscriptions were incomprehensible to (late) Roman viewers, only those that were poorly preserved.

Chapter Outline

That a significant number of individuals in late antiquity *could* read is clear. Did they *choose* to read older inscriptions? Or did these older texts fade into the background, visual "white noise" in crowded spaces? Chapter 2, "The Use of Real or Imagined Inscriptions in Late Antique Literature," gathers the literary evidence to assert that yes, people from a variety of backgrounds could and did read ancient inscriptions. What is more, different modes of reading ancient inscriptions in late antiquity can be gleaned from these texts. Late antique authors as varied as Agathias of Myrina, Prokopios, Kosmas Indikopleustes, Ammianus Marcellinus, Sokrates Scholastikos, and the anonymous writers of saints' lives and oracle compilations were quite capable of reading real, historical inscribed texts or incorporating fictitious, made-up inscriptions into their writings. But these authors have a tendency to interpret inscriptions based on local traditions and their own preconceived notions of the cosmos. Stones could either confirm something about the distant past or offer a prophesy with essential (though cryptic) information about the future. Put differently: people in late antiquity sometimes took on the role of epigrapher, but they read ancient stones from a very different perspective than do present-day specialists of epigraphy. Chapter 2 therefore accomplishes two main tasks: it proves that at least some literate individuals in late antiquity were able and willing to read even much older inscriptions, and it shows how inscriptions were often put to work in building a new Christian world. This chapter provides the necessary cultural contextualization for the archaeologically attested fates of the inscribed stones themselves in the following three chapters.

A mention of the "archaeologically attested fates of the inscribed stones" in late antiquity undoubtedly conjures up for many readers of this book images

---

[65] Julius Pollux *Onomasticon* 5.149–150 (trans. Zadorojnyi 2018: 51).

of *spolia*: column drums built into a fortification wall, a classical cornice set into a Christian church, first- and second-century reliefs mounted on the Arch of Constantine. The concept of spolia, that is, reused building material, has defined the field of late antique archaeology like no other paradigm—despite the fact that the term itself is not an ancient one and that it has no single accepted definition today (should only decorative marbles count, or all reused building material?). Indeed, the use of the word "spolia" has been called into question in several recent publications, with a new preference for the more neutral term "reuse." In my view, the main problem with the term "spolia" is not so much that it is potentially misleading and modern, as the way that this term has caused researchers to focus on reused material, often to the exclusion of material that was *not* reused. One of the goals of this book is to demonstrate that spoliated inscriptions (and spoliated stones more generally) can only be understood in light of what was *not* spoliated, but left in place: spoliation was a choice.

Before a chapter on spolia, therefore, Chapter 3, "Preservation: Tolerating Temples and Their Texts," documents inscribed stones preserved in place and still legible in active late antique city- and sanctuary-scapes. It raises the issue of preservation as an archaeological blind spot. In both biographies and what we might call archaeographies (the interpretation and writing of the archaeological record), certain agreed-upon milestones define lives and monuments. Birth, initiation to adulthood, marriage, war, new additions to the family, and death are viewed as the structuring elements of an individual's biography, just as monuments are founded, decorated, expanded, damaged, renovated, and finally collapse. In short, archaeological publications, like biographies, tend to be concerned with things that *happened*. Yet these milestones draw attention away from the long straight stretches of sameness: the years of persistence without which the milestones would not exist. Long periods of active use or passive tolerance without substantial alterations receive much less page space than the turning points in a monument's lifespan.[66]

Inscribed texts were no exception. An archaeological approach focused only on turning points—on moments of destruction or spoliation—misses this interstice, the decades or even centuries when people viewed, valued, and preserved older monuments without substantially altering them. Chapter 3 argues that toleration should not be confused with ignoring, nor should the continued existence of an ancient sanctuary with its inscriptions

[66] Dey 2015: 247.

necessarily be taken as an indicator of "pagan perseverance." Rather, I argue that the epigraphic messages projected by temples contributed to their suitability, or in some cases even desirability, in late antique contexts. I establish this by analyzing examples of temples that either were left standing in their original form into late antiquity (Ephesos, Priene, Mylasa, Magnesia on the Maeander, Delphi) or were converted into ecclesiastical spaces (perhaps Ankara, Aizanoi, and Palmyra; more certainly Diokaisareia-Olba, Sardis, Lagina, Medinet Habu, and Didyma). These sanctuaries maintained elements of sanctuary architecture alongside the texts that were inscribed on their architraves, antae, and walls. Chapter 3 clarifies that inscribed texts from pagan sanctuaries were most certainly on view in late antiquity and were the objects of occasional engagement.

With this awareness of preserved-in-place inscriptions, we next turn to spolia in Chapter 4, "Spoliation: Integrating and Scrambling tions-Inscrip." Much of the work on spolia has addressed the question of whether the reuse was practical or was intended to transmit a message about the (de)valuation of the past or the position of the present vis-à-vis the past. The limited previous research on *epigraphic* spolia has come down on the side of pragmatism: inscribed stones tended to be smoothed and conveniently shaped for reuse. But a close analysis of the archaeological remains at several sites points toward an awareness and engagement with ancient inscriptions. Moralee has argued convincingly for triumphalist use of inscribed spolia at Gerasa, and in this chapter, we will see how remarkable that church is by contextualizing it within broader habits of building, ranging from the spolia-built Christian structures at the Korykian Cave Clifftop Temple (Kilikia), Sagalassos, Aphrodisias, Klaros, and Baalbek to a synagogue at Sardis and an in-process spoliation attempt at Labraunda. Indeed, Chapter 4 chips away at the old dichotomy of practical versus ideological reuse by looking more closely at the building logic of several late antique spolia structures as it relates to reused inscribed stones, ultimately concluding that in some cases, late antique builders *did* take the content of inscriptions into account when they were repurposed, but the reasons behind this were often more complex and varied than straightforward Christian triumphalism.

After establishing the preservation of inscriptions and their spoliation, Chapter 5, "Erasure: [[Damnatio Memoriae]] or Conscious Uncoupling?," moves to the most tangible evidence for late antique interaction with ancient inscriptions: *rasurae* and obliterated texts. These stones underwent targeted chiseling, whether as a part of the process of spoliation or even while preserved in their original locations. As we will see at sites such as Aphrodisias, Labraunda, Aizanoi, Antioch ad Cragum, and the Korykian Cave Clifftop Temple, this habit was not random or indiscriminate but fixated especially on the names of pagan gods and their donors, resulting in their "unnaming" in line with wider attitudes toward pagan figures by some late antique authors. *Damnatio memoriae*, the Roman and Late Roman practice of enacting memory sanctions against disgraced emperors or officials by chiseling their names from inscriptions and destroying their images, has dominated discussions of epigraphic erasures, but I argue that the non-damnatio erasures presented here have aims distinct from those of damnatio memoriae. In order to establish this, I also review the evidence for the destruction of statues in the early Christian period, a subject that has been far more extensively documented and analyzed than the fate of ancient inscriptions. Indeed, statues will be our companions throughout this book, as a comparable medium of commemoration that also provoked the three responses to inscriptions identified here (preservation, spoliation, and destruction). Different ontologies, however, for statues and inscriptions in this period resulted in divergent treatments of the imaged and the inscribed. The Conclusion (Chapter 6) brings together these different facets of the fate of ancient inscriptions in late antiquity, with important implications for the field of epigraphy today.

The Fine Print

It should go without saying that this book cannot be comprehensive. I have selected a small subset of the tens of thousands of inscriptions that have come down to us from antiquity: those occupying a particular geographic and temporal context—the eastern Mediterranean, from Greece to Egypt, fourth to seventh century CE—and a particular architectural/ritual space—formerly pagan sanctuaries. My geographic constraints are contingent on the particular archaeological contexts available for study from late antiquity, here defined as roughly the period from the conversion of Constantine in 312 (or, if not conversion, at least his pivot toward church leaders) and the Arab incursions of the mid-seventh century, without taking either terminus as a hard stopping point. I have limited myself to the eastern Mediterranean because the trajectories of the eastern and western Roman imperial provinces diverged in this era, both gradually and in fits and starts. The eastern part of the empire with its capital at Constantinople largely maintained its prosperity (with periodic upsets, naturally) into the later sixth or seventh centuries. This is critical, as it means that cities of the east had the agency to make decisions about their built patrimony: many could, and did, embark on remodelings, maintenance programs, the construction of buildings with newly worked architectural elements, or the curation of public spaces. If an inscribed stone was reused, left in place, or erased, it was because a decision had been made to do this when other options were at least in theory available. This holds true for many sites in the western empire as well, especially Rome itself, but the picture in the west is more varied and requires exacting attention to changing cultural contexts (i.e., Vandal rule in North Africa, the Ostrogothic kings in Italy), to regional building habits and supply chains, and to local discourses on the (pre-) Roman, pagan past. Broad pronouncements on the fate of inscriptions empire-wide will not do, and even in the east, we will encounter a variety of interactions with epigraphic remains. Context is king.

Within the eastern Mediterranean, particularly fertile areas of investigation are determined by the nature and quantity of the epigraphic material itself, as it has come down to us (and as it has been published). There was no singular "epigraphic habit" of the Greek world; each region favored different genres of texts and different writing bearers on which to inscribe them.[67] The "forest inscriptions" of Lebanon (Hadrian's environmental-economic policy of carving imperial ownership of endangered trees into the natural stone) had different viewers and communicated different messages than did the door lintel of the Temple of Aphrodite at Aphrodisias—and met a different fate. The "forest inscriptions" remain largely undisturbed until today, offering no clues to how they were perceived in late antiquity, while the door lintel of the Temple of Aphrodite was spoliated and erased (Chapters 4 and 5).[68] The epigraphic landscape of late antique Egypt (Chapter 3) remained dominated by the monumental, colorful, enigmatic pharaonic hieroglyphs that covered so many ancient walls even as new Greek and Coptic graffiti were occasionally added, but this ancient writing system could be not be read by the vast majority of viewers. In the Levant (stretching from modern Syria to Lebanon, Jordan, Occupied Palestinian Territory, and Israel), good marble was scarce; lengthy civic decrees or inscribed royal/imperial letters were not frequently put up in cities (at least, not on durable materials).

---

[67] Bodel 2001; Nawotka 2020.
[68] Forest inscriptions: *IGLS* 8.3; *I.Aphrodisias* 2007 1.2.

The epigraphic praxeologies of these cities instead tended toward honorific declarations, as at Palmyra (Chapter 3), which kept its bilingual Aramaic-Greek texts on display long after Zenobia's dream of a Palmyrene empire had died. The entire region of Phoenicia has so far produced fewer (published) inscriptions than individual cities elsewhere.[69] Cities in Greece, on the other hand, blessed with abundant marble, inscribed prolifically: detailed decrees and inventories filled public spaces, and statue bases and dedications popped up everywhere. But Greece features less in this book than might be expected. The preference there for using freestanding stones rather than architectural writing bearers (except at certain sites, such as Delphi, Chapter 3) means that far fewer ancient texts have been found in situ. Freestanding blocks, such as stelai and bases, were susceptible to being taken down, moved, reused as building material, or outright broken up and burnt for lime; interestingly, late antique church builders in Greece do not seem to have availed themselves of this building material very often. Rather, in Greece, many a modern epigrapher has been delighted to find ancient inscriptions in *Byzantine* churches dating from the ninth century and later. These texts were displayed in walls or found new life as the altar table. I have the impression that late antique builders in Greece, of whatever religious persuasion, were reluctant to appropriate inscribed stones except when critical infrastructure (fortifications) called for it; their Byzantine descendants were later enthused by these semantically charged bits of the Hellenic past and made ample use of them—but this would be the topic of another monograph.[70]

The majority of the sites discussed in *this* book come from Asia Minor, the heavily Hellenized bridge connecting the new Roman capital at Constantinople with the prosperous cities of the Levant and the dangers and opportunities of Sassanian Persia farther to the east. Asia Minor is exceptional in terms of its epigraphic heritage for several reasons. First, a number of quarries provided good-quality marble, meaning that epigraphic output was high. In Roman Phrygia, even people who styled themselves as farmers and shepherds—salt-of-the-earth types—could afford decorated and inscribed marble gravestones. Second, there was a tendency to use the wall space of temples and public buildings as a blank canvas on which to inscribe lengthy Greek documents and short records. As it turns out, this willingness to inscribe texts directly onto architecture was enormously important and

---

[69] Głogowski 2020.
[70] Byzantine interaction with the Hellenic past: Papalexandrou 2007; Kaldellis 2008; Kaldellis 2009.

resulted in longer and more secure object biographies for these inscriptions.[71] Whether this habit arose independently in the Greek cities of western Asia Minor and the islands or can be related to pre-Greek Anatolian habits of inscribing texts directly on exposed rock and on monuments (as I suspect) cannot be proven either way.[72] Rojas has recently explored how such rock-carved monuments inspired speculation and local histories in the Roman period and, I would add, served to normalize writing on architecture, right up to late antiquity.[73] Third, the later history of Asia Minor has resulted in a wealth of late antique contexts available to archaeologists. Most cities of the region experienced a sharp decline in the early seventh century due to coinciding disasters; later Byzantine settlements at the same sites were often smaller and confined to limited areas, meaning that city centers and occasionally sanctuaries are well preserved in their late antique states. Finally, for whatever reason, the inhabitants of the west coast and inland Asia Minor in late antiquity seem to have been particularly eager to engage with the epigraphic material surrounding them and to have done so in particularly sophisticated ways, as we will see both in the literary sources (Chapter 2) and in the evidence for erasures (Chapter 5).

A few notes on terminology. I use the term "pagan" to refer to adherents of the traditional cults of the Greco-Roman world, despite the problematics of this word. There was, of course, no such thing as "the pagan religion," and indeed the idea of "paganism" was invented in late antiquity, as early Christians sought to label their competitors.[74] Some researchers prefer to abandon the term and rely instead on the designation "polytheists," but this label leaves out pagan monotheists. I therefore use "pagan" as an imperfect, etic shorthand to describe individuals or monuments of neither Christian nor Jewish origin. I also use another debated term, "Christianization," to refer in a general way to the changes taking place in late antiquity related to the rise of the new religion, without assuming that "Christianization" was an inevitable or impersonal process. The inscriptions and monuments we encounter in this book are themselves active agents in "Christianization," at times moderating and at other times contributing to it. I frequently refer to "the Hellenic or Roman past" on display in late antique contexts, while acknowledging the local limitations of these descriptors: did late antique viewers interpret the

[71] Roels 2018.
[72] Sitz 2019c.
[73] Rojas 2019: 64–67, 71–80.
[74] Jones 2012; Kahlos 2012.

Greek-style architecture built by Hekatomnid Karian dynasts at Labraunda as elements of the "Hellenic" past, or rather as something particularly local and Anatolian? I therefore use "Hellenic and Roman past" imperfectly and often chronologically. Other terms are defined as they arise in the following chapters. All translations are my own, unless otherwise noted. I have reproduced Greek epigraphic texts using the Leiden system; this occasionally results in minor alterations to previously published editions.[75] Throughout, I use Greek spellings, except in cases where the Anglicized form is more recognizable since, in the words of that pioneer of the exploration of ancient Asia Minor, George Bean, "to write Homeros or Alexandros or Eukleides seems somehow to make a stranger of an old friend."[76] In cases where we encounter new, not old, friends, I use the Greek spelling (so, Alexander the Great but Alexandros, son of Antonios, whom we will meet shortly in the next chapter).

---

[75] For the Leiden system, see Dow 1969. Note that, in order to communicate material aspects of the inscriptions, I occasionally use some signs differently (following other scholars); this is always indicated in the footnotes.

[76] Bean 1966: 6.

2

The Use of Real or Imagined Inscriptions in Late Antique Literature

The "Arch of Alexander" and the Ends of the Earth

Three Byzantine monks are on a quest: find the ends of the earth and with it the garden of Eden, earthly paradise. In the wilderness beyond the world of cities, the monks encounter an arch with the inscription:

> This arch was erected by Alexander king of the Macedonians when he pursued Darius the Persian from Chalcedon up to here. These are the dark <places> he traversed. Whoever wishes to penetrate further, let him go to the left . . . and he will arrive into light; to the right there be rocky mountains and great swamps full of snakes and scorpions.[1]

Even a casual student of epigraphy can recognize the fictitious nature of this inscription, recorded in the Greek versions of the *Life of St. Makarios of Rome*—triumphal arches usually do not give directions—and in any case, Alexander the Great did not build arches. The *Life* is part hagiography, part adventure tale; a similar inscription also appears in some versions of the expansive *Alexander Romance* tradition, which made the conquering Macedonian king into a legend in the middle ages and beyond.[2] After reading the inscription, the monks heed the arch's advice to go to the left and encounter St. Makarios, who warns them that no mortal can proceed

---

[1] ταύτην τὴν ἀψίδα ἀνήγειρεν Ἀλέξανδρος ὁ βασιλεὺς Μακεδόνων ὅτε κατεδίωκεν ἀπὸ Χαλχηδόνος Δαρεῖον τὸν Πέρσην ἕως ἐνταῦθα. Ταῦτα δέ εἰσιν τὰ σκοτεινὰ ἃ διῆλθεν. ὁ θέλων οὖν ἐνδότερον εἰσελθεῖν εἰς τὰ ἀριστερὰ μέρη περιπατείτω . . . καὶ εἰσελεύσεται εἰς φῶς, τὰ δὲ δεξιὰ μέρη ὄρη εἰσὶ καὶ κρημνοὶ καὶ λίμναι παμμεγέθεις ὄφεων καὶ σκορπίων μεμεστωμένα (trans. Zadorojnyi 2013: 365, ed. Vassiliev 1893: 141–142, recension B). This literary inscription parallels that at the beginning of Lucian's *True Story* ("Herakles and Dionysos reached this point") as the characters in that novel head west, beyond the Pillars of Herakles.

[2] Gero 1992: 86.

farther: angels guard the gates of Eden. The monks dutifully return to the world of men and make their way back to their monastery.

The "Arch of Alexander" inscription has clearly been made up by the author of the *Life* or by Alexander's storytellers, and it might be only a medieval addition to the Makarios tradition. The extant Greek recensions of the *Life of St. Makarios* are Middle or Late Byzantine, but the original version probably dates prior to the mid-seventh century, given that the monks traverse the whole east with nary a mention of Islam.[3] But whether the arch inscription represents a late invention or an original element of the story, the *Life of St. Makarios* indicates an awareness of ancient inscriptions and a willingness to instrumentalize this knowledge for the construction of a new, Christian topography. In what follows, we will see this attitude again and again, although not always from a Christian perspective, in the late antique literary evidence of engagement with inscribed texts, both fictitious (like Alexander's arch) and real. Although the subject has received little previous study for the late antique period, histories (both classicizing and ecclesiastical), chronicles, oracle compilations, and hagiographies demonstrate significant interest in ancient inscriptions. We can frame the relationship between these literary sources and inscriptions as one of "transtextuality," a term coined by literary theorist Gérard Genette to describe a text that quotes, plagiarizes, or alludes to another text.[4] Some of our texts are metatexts (writings about the written), offering implicit or explicit reflections on the inscribed stones to which they refer.[5] Others engage in intermedial quoting by adopting phrasing or terms common in epigraphy, a distinct medium, into literary contexts, as we just saw with the putative inscribed arch in the *Life of St. Makarios*.[6] The word ἀνήγειρεν ([he] erected) in the *Life*'s inscription is paralleled on a number of real inscriptions dating from the Roman and late antique periods, especially in Syria and the wider east; the *Life* has borrowed this epigraphic term to make its fictitious inscription sound authentic.[7] The Alexander inscription provides critical information to the monks through a particularly civilized medium at the very limit of human civilization; yet they are led by pious zeal even further, to a more authoritative source of information: the saint.[8]

---

[3] Vassiliev 1893: xxxviii; Gero 1992: 85, fn. 24.
[4] Genette 1982.
[5] Focken and Ott 2016.
[6] See Dinter 2013 for "intermediality."
[7] E.g., *SEG* 2.755 (Dura Europos, 159 CE): "ἀνήγειρεν τὴν ψαλίδα ταύτην" and *IGLS* 2.292 (Anasartha, 602–610 CE, regularized): "τόδε τὸ τεῖχος ἀνήγειρεν. ✝"
[8] Zadorojnyi 2013: 366.

The Hellenic past as distilled in the inscription provides crucial support for the Christian faith while being surpassed by it. Viewing late antique written sources through the lens of transtextuality clarifies that these authors did not simply *record* encounters (actual or fictitious) with older epigraphic material, but made statements on the continued potency of these inscriptions in the late Roman world. The evidence of written sources allows us to identify several modes of reading ancient inscriptions in late antiquity, which will inflect our onward journey through the archaeological evidence for the fate of inscribed stones in second part of this book. At the end of the chapter, we turn to the problematics of classical reception in the late antique world.

Writing the Past from Inscriptions

We will start at the beginning, with a topic that *has* received substantial attention: the uses of inscriptions in classical Greek and Latin literature. Inscriptions are critical sources for our present-day writing of classical history, but oddly enough, most ancient Greek and Roman historians did not mine the ample epigraphic material surrounding them for information. Arnaldo Momigliano said it best: ancient historiography contained "a maximum of invented speeches and a minimum of authentic documents."[9] Herodotos and Thucydides both make use of a number of inscribed dedications and documents, but by and large they privileged their own eyewitness accounts and oral histories; when inscriptions were cited, they served to reveal the character of figures appearing in these accounts or, on a deeper level, as metahistorical foils for these authors' own historiographic projects.[10] Most historians after Herodotos and Thucydides made only sparing use of epigraphic material; inscriptions were often paraphrased rather than quoted directly in order to fit seamlessly into the literary confections called histories.[11] The quotation of epigraphic material was instead left to ancient orators, who proved points by reading aloud from transcribed inscriptions (sometimes forged or heavily reworked) in court.[12] Travelers such as Pausanias and geographers drew extensively on epigraphic material, often explicated

[9] Momigliano 2012: 115.
[10] Allgaier 2022.
[11] For inscriptions in classical Greek and Roman literature: Stein 1931; Biraschi et al. 2003; Rhodes 2007; Liddel and Low 2013; Spielberg 2019. The evidentiary value of epigraphic texts was recognized by, e.g., Josephus (Pucci Ben Zeev 1995).
[12] Grethlein 2014.

by local *periegetai* (guides), both for raw data and to serve as "trigger-mechanism[s] for composing a narrative unit."[13] But not all inscriptions in literature were necessarily what they purport to be: Lucian of Samosata (second century CE) claimed that a pair of giant phalli at the temple of the Syrian goddess there bore a dedication from Dionysos to his stepmother Hera, thereby proving that the temple was built by the god.[14] This dedication may have been added to the phalli based on oral tradition or in a bid to increase the popularity of the sanctuary, if it was not simply a misreading of a faded older text. So far we have covered inscriptions that were at least putatively real, but the writers of Greek and Roman novels availed themselves of fully fictional dedications and epitaphs as plot devices and commentaries on the natures of writing and of men.[15]

In late antique historiography, no discernable break in attitudes toward inscriptions took place: most history writers rarely used epigraphic material. Ammianus Marcellinus (writing in Latin around 390) does not often quote either inscribed or archival documents; when he does mention inscriptions, he seems to write from memory rather than a precise record.[16] He references inscribed monuments attesting Herakleid descent in Gaul but ignores the inscribed base of an obelisk in the Circus Maximus at Rome, which states that Constantine first intended the Egyptian stone for his new capital on the Bosphoros; Ammianus reports that the emperor had always meant it for Rome without mentioning the epigraphic counter-history.[17] Eusebius of Caesarea, when birthing the new subgenre of ecclesiastical history, quoted directly and extensively from documents such as letters and from previous written accounts—but not from inscriptions, in which he shows little interest (or found little to support his project).[18] Pilgrims' accounts too do not engage extensively with epigraphic witnesses: Egeria in the 380s barely mentions the *titulus crucis* (the piece of wood on which Pontius Pilate ironically declared Christ the "king of the Jews" in Greek, Latin, and Hebrew) in her description

---

[13] Tzifopoulos 2013: 161.
[14] Lucian *De Syria Dea*, 16.
[15] Slater 2009; Zadorojnyi 2013: 368–370.
[16] Bersani 2003: 633.
[17] Ammianus 15.9.6 (Gauls); 17.4.13 (obelisk; *CIL* VI 1163); Bersani 2003: 634.
[18] Eusebius alludes to a few inscriptions in his *Historia Ecclesiastica*: the names of Paul and Peter in Roman cemeteries (2.25.5), a statue base dedicated to "Simon the Holy God" in Rome (2.13.1; cf. *CIL* VI 567), and a letter from Antoninus Pius prohibiting the unlawful persecution of Christians (4.13). These latter two he gleaned from the writings of Justin Martyr. Jones 2018 argues that the Antoninus document probably derived from a real letter inscribed at Ephesos. Eusebius and those like him were reading not only Greek and Latin texts but also the Hebrew Bible, which also makes use of documents: Tyrell 2020.

of the veneration of the True Cross in Jerusalem.[19] The church historians mention this *titulus* in the story of the invention of the cross, but it is inadequate to identify *which* of the three discovered crosses belonged to Christ—a miracle is a more effective indicator.[20] Late antiquity lacked a Pausanias, lawyers had no need of quoting from stone when the relevant laws were gathered in official codices, and the ancient novel lost out to other genres, such as hagiographies.

Even so, several written sources from our period do engage with epigraphic material, both contemporaneous and from centuries past. Ancient inscriptions are in the spotlight here but contemporary late antique ones occasionally make an appearance, because late Roman authors do not seem to have drawn a sharp distinction between past and present inscriptions—although carved stones from ages past could be imbued with particular prophetic potency, as we will see. Even Archaic Greek inscriptions were accessible to erudite individuals: the Latin grammarian Priscian, writing his *Institutiones Grammaticae* around 500 CE in Constantinople, recognized a digamma (F) on an ancient tripod dedicated to Apollo, imported to adorn the new Rome on the Bosphoros. The tripod, which Priscian includes in his discussion of digammas in Aeolian poetry, was inscribed "in the most ancient letters" (*litteris antiquissimis*) with the names Laocoon (ΛαϝοκόϝωΝ) and Demophoon (ΔημοφάϝωΝ), both from the Trojan War cycle.[21]

Priscian's tripod surely had a limited readership, but anthologies of ancient epigrams were more accessible to the average (educated) reader. Metrical texts composed from the fifth century BCE onward, including various Persian War epitaphs attributed to Simonides of Keos, were preserved in these anthologies, the best known of which is the tenth-century *Anthologia Palatina* (*AP*). The *AP* incorporated older epigram collections, including that of Agathias of Myrina (c. 530–c. 580 CE), published around 567.[22] We will return to Agathias momentarily. Epigrammatic writing was of course a literary genre and not all epigrams were actually inscribed, but some may have been copied into late antique anthologies from the inscriptions themselves. The dedicatory poem for Hagios Polyeuktos in Constantinople, composed around 527 (*AP* 1.10), was certainly viewed in its physical form: the *AP*

---

[19] Egeria 37.1.
[20] Sokrates *Historia Ecclesiastica* 1.17; Sozomen *Historia Ecclesiastica* 2.1–2; Rufinus *Historia Ecclesiastica* 10.7.
[21] Priscian *Institutiones Grammaticae* 6.69; see also 1.22. Cf. Papalexandrou 2008.
[22] Cameron and Cameron 1966; Cameron 1993; Lauxtermann 2003: 83–128.

includes marginal notations describing the location of different parts of the text within the architectural spaces.[23] As Denis Feissel has noted, "Byzantine savants were capable of serious—even scholarly—epigraphic work."[24] Early medieval western literary collections of inscriptions likewise indicate interest in the older inscribed stones, particularly the texts encountered by pilgrims to Rome (mainly early Christian metrical or building inscriptions, but some pagan dedications as well).[25] The Christian poet Prudentius around the year 400 drew on inscriptions in Rome describing the sacrifices and honors afforded to Augustus and Julius Caesar to prove his point that pagans foolishly venerated mere humans.[26]

At times we glimpse only the shadow of ancient inscriptions in later textual sources. Laura Nasrallah has made the (tendentious) argument that the collection and dissemination of the letters attributed to the apostle Paul in the second century was inspired by the letters of Hellenistic kings, Roman emperors, and officials visible in public inscribed dossiers: this process amounted in her view to the publicizing and universalizing of epistles originally sent to specific churches in specific situations.[27] In other instances, the toponyms used in late antique cities (e.g., the *thermae Diocletianae*, the *aqua Hadriana*, or the *basilica Constantiana*) were drawn from building inscriptions adorning these structures. Catherine Saliou has ingenuously argued that misreadings of the complex imperial nomenclature in construction inscriptions occasionally resulted in the replacement of "bad" emperors with "good" ones in these toponyms. For example, the literary-minded empress Eudokia (c. 401–460) composed an epigram in which she seems to have credited Antoninus Pius for the construction of water infrastructure at Hammat Gadar (in Greek Emmantha; in Arabic Umm Qais) in the province of Palaestina.[28] But a fragmentary Latin inscription found in the city suggests that the emperor in question was actually Commodus (Marcus Aurelius Commodus Antoninus Augustus).[29] By focusing on the name "Antoninus," Eudokia—or more likely her local guides—effectively erased the (assassinated) Commodus and replaced him with the highly regarded

---

[23] Connors 1999: 496, 516; Whitby 2006. *AP* 9.686 states that its epigram in praise of a prefect was located "on the eastern gate of Thessaloniki," implying that it may have been copied directly from stone (*I.Chr. Macédoine* 87).
[24] Feissel 2012: 4.
[25] Walser 1987; Handley 2000; Bauer 2004: 21–25.
[26] Prudentius *Contra Symmachum I*, 245–253.
[27] Nasrallah 2018: 282–284.
[28] *SEG* 32.1502, *l.* 10; Saliou 2019: 5, no. 21.
[29] Eck 2016: 124.

Antoninus Pius without lifting a chisel. The good emperor likewise received credit at Nikomedia for the epigraphically attested *thermae Antoninianae* in the sixth-century account of John Malalas, although the baths were likely built by Caracalla (Marcus Aurelius Severus Antoninus Augustus).[30] Public inscriptions both served and subverted the commemorative function of earlier imperial building projects.

Agathias and the Remarkable Afterlife of Chairemon

Finding an ancient inscription preserved both in textual copy and in physical, carved form is a rare treat. Most of the inscriptions mentioned by Herodotos, the statue dedications recorded by Pausanias, and Lucian's inscribed phalli have disappeared, serving today only as indicators of these authors' historical methods or "archaeophiliac" (in Rojas's terminology) tendencies.[31] In late antiquity, too, older inscriptions were sometimes known only through earlier literary records. The twenty-five inscriptions cited or alluded to in Malalas' *Chronographia* probably came from his textual sources, not from autopsy; so too with Zosimos' *Historia Nova*.[32] Some may no longer have been extant when these historians were writing, or may have been entirely fictitious. The two columns at Tigisis in Numidia, described by Prokopios as bearing a Phoenician text blaming the Biblical Joshua, son of Nun, for the Phoenicians' westward migration, supported the Hebrew Bible's account of the conquest of Israel and explained the ethnogenesis of the "Moors"; but it is doubtful that Prokopios had any firsthand knowledge of these stones, and even more so that they actually recorded what he said they did.[33]

But occasionally we get lucky and have both the stone itself and a literary account of it. Continuing his discussion of the Egyptian obelisks at Rome, Ammianus reproduced a Greek translation of the Egyptian hieroglyphs on the obelisk brought by Augustus to adorn the Circus Maximus in 10 BCE (now in the Piazza del Popolo). Although the translation by an otherwise-unknown figure named Hermapion makes use of the names of Hellenic, rather than Egyptian, gods and departs from the actual hieroglyphic text at certain places, it correctly names the pharaoh Ramesses (II, r. 1279–1213

---

[30] *TAM* IV,1.29; Malalas 11.25. Saliou 2019: 5–6, no. 13.
[31] Rojas 2017; Rojas 2019.
[32] Malalas: Downey 1935; Agusta-Boularot 2006. Zosimos: see the index of Stein 1931.
[33] Prokopios *Wars* 4.10.21–22. Schmitz 2007 and contra Frendo 2007.

BCE) and captures his imperialistic message: "The Sun to King Ramesses. I have granted to you to rule joyfully the whole inhabited world, you whom the Sun loves."[34] Ammianus could interact with the hieroglyphs only through the mediation of translation, but he nonetheless shows more interest in this inscribed text than any other in his lengthy history. Did he find the ancient Egyptian obelisk more stimulating than the standard Latin and Greek fare he encountered daily, or was this text particularly useful for his literary aims, in that it confirmed Rome's role as the new ruler of the entire inhabited world through its mastery even of pharaonic Egypt? In the next chapter, we will consider a different context for viewing hieroglyphs, in a setting where they were quotidian rather than exotic.

Agathias, the compiler of epigrams in the age of Justinian, too made use of an inscription to prop up his historiographic project when writing his *Histories* around 580 CE, and again we have the rare opportunity to check his reading against the stone itself (or rather a photo of it; the stone is now lost) (Figure 2.1). Detailing the devastation wrought by an earthquake that struck the island of Kos in 551, Agathias relates a story he has heard about a much earlier earthquake that devastated the city of Tralles in Karia during the reign of Augustus and describes his own encounter with an inscription from that period. Agathias had personally visited Tralles and made inquiries about the history of the city. The passage is worth quoting at length:

> The story goes that, when the city [Tralles] lay in a tragic heap of ruins, a certain rustic, a tiller of the soil (ἄγροικόν τινά ... τούτων δὴ τῶν γεηπόνων) by the name of Chaeremon was so deeply moved by the calamity that he could bear it no longer and ... went not just to Rome but to the land of the Cantabria [in Spain] on the very shores of the Ocean. For Caesar was there at the time conducting a campaign against some of the local tribes. When Chaeremon told him what had happened the Emperor was so touched that he straightaway designated seven of Rome's noblest and most distinguished ex-consuls and sent them with their retinues to the spot....
>
> These happenings are all vouched for by the official history of the city and corroborated by an epigram which I read when I went there. In one of the fields on the outskirts of the city, apparently the spot that Chaeremon came from (the name of the field is Siderus [Σιδηροῦς δὲ ὄνομα τῷ ἀγρῷ

---

[34] Ammianus 17.4.17: ἥλιος βασιλεῖ ῾ παμέστῃ: δεδώρημαί σοι ἀνὰ πᾶσαν οἰκουμένην μετὰ χαρᾶς βασιλεύειν, ὃν ἥλιος φιλεῖ. Westerfeld 2019: 134–142.

Figure 2.1 Tralles. Honorific base for Chairemon (*SEG* 61.880). Photo courtesy of Murat Aydaş.

ἐκείνῳ]) there stands the base (βωμός) of a statue. It is of great antiquity and on it it appears that a statue of Chaeremon must once have stood, though there is now no longer any trace of it. Nevertheless the dedication in verse inscribed on the base is still discernible and runs as follows:

"Once, when an earthquake razed his city to the ground, the gallant Chaeremon did straightaway take thought to rescue it and travelled till at length he found in far-away Cantabria the Emperor and his court. Now on this altar does his image stand and citizens by grateful fancy led greet as a second founder of their land the man who rescued Tralles from the dead."[35]

---

[35] Agathias *Histories* 2.17.2–8 (trans. Frendo 1975). Greek text of the epigram, as recorded in Agathias *Histories* 2.17.8:

Κλασθείσας πάτρας σεισμῷ ποτε, Κάνταβριν ἐς γᾶν
Χαιρήμων ἔπτα, πατρίδα ῥυσόμενος.
Καίσαρι δ' εἰλιχθεὶς περὶ γούνασι τὰν μεγάλαυχον
Ὤρθωσε Τράλλιν, τὰν τότε κεκλιμέναν·

Chairemon's story, as related by Agathias, is remarkable; even more extraordinary is the fact that the very statue base seen and copied by Agathias in the sixth century was found in 1978 in a village thirty-five kilometers outside of present-day Aydın, Turkey (ancient Tralles).[36] Agathias implies that the base was freestanding "in one of the fields on the outskirts of the city" (ἔν τινι γὰρ τῶν ἀμφὶ τὴν πόλιν ἀγρῶν) but the actual stone was found in the ruins of a "Byzantine chapel" (undated) built onto an older Roman structure near one of Tralles' aqueducts.[37] The fact that pieces of an ambo were found in the chapel points to a late antique date for its initial construction, as ambos were no longer installed in Middle Byzantine churches.[38] Had the inscribed base been built into the chapel as spolia already in Agathias' day (a detail he left out)? Or was it brought to the chapel only later?

Regardless, we can imagine that Agathias was interested in the base not only as evidence for his history writing but also because of his own predilection for composing and collecting epigrams. The stone offers only a few minor corrections to the version of the text that has come down to us in manuscripts of Agathias' *Histories*. Clearly he was able to read, reproduce, and use the inscription, more than half a millennium old in his day. Yet he had certainly been misled by the "official history of the city" (ἡ πάτριος τοῦ ἄστεος ἱστορία), presumably a written account, but one perhaps related to Agathias through the oral traditions of sixth-century residents of Tralles. The historical Chairemon could hardly have been merely a farmer, a rustic "tiller of the soil" (ἄγροικόν τινά . . . τούτων δὴ τῶν γεηπόνων): he and his family (known from other inscriptions) were from the upper echelons of Trallian society and perhaps even Roman citizens.[39] The real Chairemon fulfilled his traditional euergetic duty after the earthquake by using his privilege and connections to intercede on behalf of his city before the emperor. But the fiction of him being only a farmer motivated by exceptional love of his city

Ἀνθ' ὧν συγγενέες τοῦτο βρέτας, ὄφρ' ἐπὶ βωμῷ,
Οἷα δίκα κτίσταν, τάνδε φέροιτο χάριν.

For the epigram as it appears on the stone (which varies somewhat from the literary copy given here), see Jones 2011: 114. The stone opens with a decree recording that the statue of Chairemon was dedicated by the *koinon* of the Siderians (τὸ κοινὸν τῶν Σιδ[ηρ]είων), also corresponding with Agathias' assertion that he saw the base in a field (perhaps actually an estate or village) called Siderus.

[36] SEG 61.880; Jones 2011; Tül and Aydaş 2011. By 1997, only a small fragment of the stone could be located: Blümel 1999: 405–406.
[37] Dinç 1998: 213–215; Dinç 2003: 9.
[38] Ousterhout 2019: 310.
[39] Jones 2011: 111.

makes for a better story. Agathias drew on a much older inscription as confirmation of the tale he had already heard, rather than as independent historical evidence, in the service of his historiographic project modeling the proper actions of patriotic citizens and benevolent rulers.

Kosmas Indikopleustes: Hellenistic History in Late Antique Ethiopia

Kosmas Indikopleustes (voyager to India) too was quite capable of copying and comprehending older inscriptions, even from as early as the Ptolemaic period, but like Agathias, he was probably misled by local tradition. The Alexandrian merchant-turned-monk completed his *Christian Topography* around 550 CE as a record of his prolific travels and a geographic description of the world intended to promote Kosmas' belief in a flat earth (the minority opinion then as now).[40] His goal in the work was to paint the widespread understanding of a spherical earth as an absurd pagan philosophical fallacy and provide an alternate Christian cosmography based on scripture and his own observations from his many years of travel. Around 520, he and a fellow merchant named Menas had sailed the Red Sea down the coast of Africa to Adulis (Zula, Eritrea), at that time part of the Christian Aksumite kingdom in a region called Ethiopia in late antiquity. King Kaleb Ella Asbeha of Aksum was preparing to launch a war against the Arab-Jewish kingdom of the Himyarites in southern Arabia, on the opposite coast of the Red Sea.[41] As it happens, two Greek inscriptions at Adulis described successful conquests by ancient kings, and Kaleb requested that the governor at Adulis send him a copy of these texts (apparently already having some notion of what they contained). Whether the king sought propaganda or a prophecy (see below) we cannot know. To fulfill the king's request, the Aksumite governor at Adulis employed the two Greek merchants, Kosmas and Menas, to copy the inscriptions, one on a marble throne, the other on a stele next to it. Neither stone has made its way down to us, but Kosmas relates that they stood by the road leading into the town—and that the chair had found a grisly new function in his day, serving as a place of execution. Fortunately, Kosmas and

---

[40] I here present the traditional view of Kosmas, but the attribution of the text to a "Kosmas Indikopleustes" is late in the manuscript tradition.
[41] Bowersock 2013.

Menas sent one copy of the texts to the governor but "we kept also like copies for ourselves which I shall here embody in this work."[42]

The merchant begins by giving an extraordinary description of the materiality of the stones themselves that puts some modern, text-focused corpora to shame. The throne, referred to as the "Ptolemaic chair" or the "chair of Ptolemy" (δίφρῳ τῷ πτολεμαϊκῷ), was a monolith of fine white marble "but not of the sort which comes from Proconnesus."[43] The support pillars, sides, and back are described, as well as its size and general shape, "like the chair we call the Bishop's throne."[44] The stele too is described:

> three cubits in height and of quadrangular form, like a tablet, which at the centre of its upper portion rises to a sharp point whence the sides slope gently down in the form of the letter lambda (λ), but the main body of the slab is rectangular. This tablet has now fallen down behind the Chair, and the lower part has been broken and destroyed.[45]

Any student of epigraphy immediately recognizes the description of a pedimented stele. Kosmas helpfully adds that only a small part of the stele was broken, and so the text he copied is nearly complete. He not only described the stele and the chair: he drew them. "Here is the form of the Chair and of the marble, and Ptolemy himself."[46] All three extant manuscripts of Kosmas (Vaticanus gr. 699, ninth century; Laurentianus Pluteus 9.28, eleventh century; Sinaiticus gr. 1186, eleventh century) provide copies of what was presumably the original sixth-century illustration of the Adulis inscribed monuments (Figure 2.2).[47] The pedimented stele is clearly recognizable in the drawings, down to the broken-off lower right corner. Kosmas, or his Byzantine copyists, struggled with the 3D form of the chair, but several elements from the text's description are integrated in the image. These illustrations are remarkable. Kosmas and Menas apparently sketched these

---

[42] *Christian Topography* 2.56 (trans. McCrindle): κατασχόντες ἑαυτοῖς τὰ ἴσα, ἃ καὶ νῦν θήσω ἐν ταύτῃ τῇ συγγραφῇ.
[43] *Christian Topography* 2.56 (trans. McCrindle).
[44] *Christian Topography* 2.54 (trans. McCrindle).
[45] *Christian Topography* 2.55 (trans. McCrindle): ὡσεὶ πηχῶν τριῶν, τετράγωνον, ὡς εἰκών, ἧς ἡ κεφαλὴ τὸ μέσον μὲν ὀξὺ ἄνω, τὰ παρ' ἑκάτερα δὲ μικρὸν χαμηλότερα, ὡς τύπον τοῦ στοιχείου τοῦ λάμβδα, ὅλον δὲ τὸ σῶμα τετράγωνον. Νυνὶ δὲ αὐτὴ ἡ εἰκὼν πεπτωκυῖά ἐστιν ὄπισθεν τοῦ δίφρου, τὸ κάτω πάνυ μέρος αὐτῆς κλασθὲν καὶ ἀπολεσθέν.
[46] *Christian Topography* 2.57 (trans. McCrindle).
[47] Kominko 2013: 24–35. Vaticanus gr. 699, f. 15v; Laurentianus Pluteus 9.28, f. 38r; Sinaiticus gr. 1186, f. 28r. For the description of the Laurentianus illustration, see Anderson 2013: 35–36.

40 PAGAN INSCRIPTIONS, CHRISTIAN VIEWERS

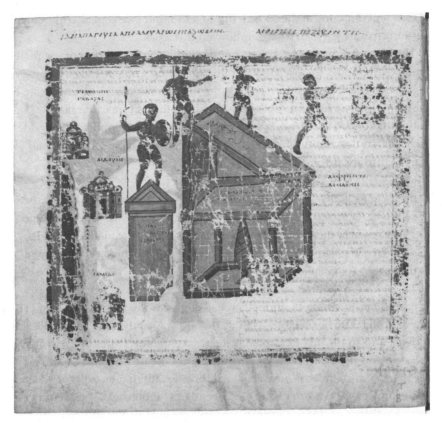

Figure 2.2 Manuscript of *Christian Topography* by Kosmas Indikopleustes. Illustration of the inscriptions of Abdulis. Ninth century. Vatican Library, Vat. Gr. 699, Folio 15v. © 2023 Biblioteca Apostolica Vaticana, all rights reserved.

two inscribed monuments on the spot; the attention to detail indicates an intimacy with the much older stones and a profound interest in their physical characteristics.

The inscription on the stele dates from around 244 BCE and records the successful campaign of Ptolemy III Euergetes against Seleukos II Kallinikos in the Third Syrian War.[48] The Hellenistic text, as transcribed by Kosmas, begins:

---

[48] Bowersock 2013: 34–43.

The great king, Ptolemy, son of King Ptolemy and Queen Arsinoe, twin gods, grandson of the two sovereigns King Ptolemy and Queen Berenice, gods *sôtêres* (savior), sprung from Hercules the son of Jupiter on the father's side, and on the mother's side from Dionysus the son of Jupiter, having received from his father the Kingdom of Egypt and Libya and Syria and Phoenicia and Cyprus, and Lycia and Caria, and the Islands of the Cyclades, made an expedition into Asia.[49]

The text goes on to describe the capture and training of elephants for Ptolemy's war effort and his successful conquest of Asia as far as Bactria (which may be an exaggeration). Although the merchant Kosmas was hardly one of the "Byzantine savants" evoked by Feissel, his reading of the stele appears to faithfully reproduce the Hellenistic royal document—approximately 750 years old in his day—so carefully that the inscription is sometimes quoted by scholars of the Hellenistic period as a key witness of Ptolemaic self-representation without even mentioning its late antique transmission history.

The second text copied by Kosmas Indikopleustes was inscribed on the marble throne at Adulis, but despite his careful copying, he probably misunderstood its nature.[50] The chair text also describes conquests by a king (unnamed in the text), in this case successful campaigns against various tribes of east Africa with detailed geographic descriptions of the regions where each group resided: "I reduced ... the Semênoi, a people who lived beyond the Nile on mountains difficult of access and covered with snow, where the year is all winter with hailstorms."[51] The inscription continues with an expedition across the Red Sea into Arabia (a particularly felicitous detail for King Kaleb preparing his own incursionary force) and ends with a dedication to Ares. The text is therefore a treasure trove both for present-day researchers working on the military-political history of east Africa and for Kosmas himself, who clearly delighted in the geographic details, which confirm (he tells us) what he saw with his own eyes and what he had heard from others. The

---

[49] *Christian Topography* 2.58 (trans. McCrindle). *OGIS* 54, *ll*. 1–8: Βασιλεὺς μέγας Πτολεμαῖος, υἱὸς βασιλέως Πτολεμαίου | καὶ βασιλίσσης Ἀρσινόης θεῶν ἀδελφῶν, τῶν βασιλέω<ς> | Πτολεμαίου καὶ βασιλίσσης Βερενίκης θεῶν σωτήρων | ἀπόγονος, τὰ μὲν ἀπὸ πατρὸς Ἡρακλέος τοῦ Διός, τὰ δὲ ἀπὸ μη|τρὸς Διονύσου τοῦ Διός, παραλαβὼν παρὰ τοῦ πατρὸς | τὴν βασιλείαν Αἰγύπτου καὶ Λιβύης καὶ Συρίας | καὶ Φοινίκης καὶ Κύπρου καὶ Λυκίας καὶ Καρίας καὶ τῶν | Κυκλάδων νήσων ἐξεστράτευσεν εἰς τὴν Ἀσίαν. The line breaks presented in the *OGIS* are hypothetical.

[50] Bowersock 2013: 44–62.

[51] *Christian Topography* 2.64–65 (trans. McCrindle; *I.Ethiopie* 277).

inscription functions for him as a sort of late antique GIS (geographic information system), allowing Kosmas to calculate the "breadth of the earth from the hyperborean regions down to Sasu and Barbaria" in support of his flat-earther beliefs, and indeed the illustrations in all three manuscripts superimpose the image of the chair and stele on a stylized map of the region with figures walking between the cities.[52] But Kosmas was wrong (not only about the flat earth): he states that the inscription on the chair is a continuation of the other text by Ptolemy, despite the fact that the chair text is written in the first person and the other is not. The chair was more likely dedicated by a local African king and dates much later (probably the third century CE) than the Ptolemaic text.[53]

Where did Kosmas get the idea that the throne text was a continuation of the Ptolemaic stele? Although he does not state it, it is likely that the throne was already known as the "Ptolemaic chair" in local parlance—he introduces it with that nomenclature and records that the spot was used to execute criminals (that is, the throne was a local landmark, and therefore likely to have had a name). As mentioned, King Kaleb clearly had some familiarity with the contents of the inscriptions prior to his request for a copy, so the connection of Ptolemy with the stele at the least had likely been made already by a Greek-reader or (perhaps) persisted as a continuous local oral tradition. The belief that the chair should be associated with a Greek/Macedonian king may have been supported by the Hellenic imagery on it: Kosmas describes two figures carved on the back of the throne, whom he identifies as Herakles and Hermes. His companion Menas interprets Herakles as a symbol of power and Hermes of wealth, but Kosmas himself remembers a passage in *Acts* (14:12) in which Paul was called Hermes in Lykaonia because he was the main speaker of his missionary band. Kosmas therefore identifies Hermes as a symbol of speech. The biblical text opens a window onto its original Greco-Roman context for Kosmas, becoming a more authoritative source for that culture than other ancient stories and myths.

Kosmas' inquisitive and incisive mind is on display in this episode with the inscriptions; it is unfortunate that he committed so much of his energy to deconstructing ancient understandings of the spherical earth, but,

---

[52] *Christian Topography* 2.64 (trans. McCrindle). Kominko 2013: 29–34.
[53] For the date: Bowersock 2013: 55. Liuzzo 2019, however, has recently proposed that the inscription may in fact have been Ptolemaic: perhaps Kosmas was correct.

in any case, despite his generally anti-pagan attitudes, he apparently had no concerns about the pagan gods and deified kings and queens described in the Ptolemaic text, nor the carved figures of Herakles and Hermes on the chair. After the passages relating to the inscribed texts, he proceeds with a more general discussion of "those Ptolemies who reigned after Alexander the Macedonian," linking them with the prophesies in the book of Daniel.[54] For Kosmas, ancient history *was* biblical history. In another episode, the merchant describes his travels through the wilderness of the Sinai, where he claims to have seen many stones inscribed with "Hebrew letters"; Jews who had supposedly read the inscriptions informed him that they recorded the names of individuals who departed in such and such a year in such and such a month, similar to the graffiti of travelers at inns with which Kosmas was familiar.[55] He writes that the Hebrews had only learned letters when God sent down the Ten Commandments: they spent the forty years in the wilderness practicing on these stones, before transmitting knowledge of writing to the Phoenicians, who shared it with the Greeks. In reality Kosmas was likely viewing Nabatean, not Hebrew, inscriptions in the Sinai, but for him the biblical narrative of wandering in the wilderness was confirmed by the historic landscape and its many carved texts.[56] The engagement of Kosmas Indikopleustes with the two inscriptions at Adulis indicates the potential for careful (and accurate) late antique readings of even much older texts and discussions of their writing bearers—even if, in this case, the engagement was instigated by a non-Greek king for his own purposes. But despite his close readings, Kosmas privileged a probably local understanding of the chair as the "throne of Ptolemy," further linked in his mind with the biblical past, rather than offering a critical interpretation of the text.[57]

Prokopios' Inscribed Ships

Prokopios, a contemporary of Agathias and Kosmas, on the other hand, was willing to present an epigraphic counterargument to an oral tradition.

---

[54] *Christian Topography* 2.66 (trans. McCrindle).
[55] *Christian Topography* 5.53 (trans. McCrindle).
[56] Rojas and Ben-Dov 2021: 22.
[57] Cf. John Lydus' interpretation of the Latin inscription (*I.Byzantion* 15) on the Column of the Goths in Constantinople: he (wrongly) attributes the victory monument to Pompey (*De mensibus* 4.132), perhaps because of a local tradition identifying in that way?

He described a ship carved from stone on the island of the "Phaeacians" (Kerkyra/Corfu), which some believed to be the one that carried Odysseus home to Ithaka: the *Odyssey* tells how Poseidon in anger turned the Phaeacian vessel to solid stone after it had deposited the hero.[58] But Prokopios, who seems to be writing from his own observations, noted that the ship on Kerkyra is not a monolith (as one would expect if it had been petrified in an act of divine wrath) and, more important, it bears an inscription testifying that "some merchant in earlier times set up this offering to Zeus Casius."[59] The multi-stone ship construction reminded the historian of another inscribed ship at Geraistos on Euboea: hexameters declared that Agamemnon had set it up before sailing to Troy. Prokopios adds that the Homeric king had dedicated the ship to Artemis because of the suffering of Iphigenia. He presumably learned this from oral stories or an earlier written account of the ship. Although Prokopios seems to trust Agamemnon's inscription (like the merchant's dedication to Zeus Casius), he does note that it "was engraved either then [at the time of the Trojan War] or later," and the ship excursus comes in the context of Prokopios' musings on "where in the world the island of Calypso was."[60] There is no island close to Kerkyra (the land of the Phaeacians) that could possibly have housed Calypso, as told by Homer. Prokopios writes, "it is not so easy to reconcile the actual facts precisely with the very ancient records, since the long passage of time is wont very generally to change the names of places and the beliefs concerning them."[61] The historian thereby introduces a hint of uncertainty to Agamemnon's stone ship with its possibly later inscription. Time could corrupt both names and beliefs; oral traditions and inscribed text alike were open to criticism. In Chapter 5, we will again encounter Prokopios as he notes how an ancient toponym had changed by his day, in that case due not to the passage of time but to the shifting sacred canopy.

---

[58] *Odyssey* 13.153–169.

[59] Prokopios *Wars* 8.22.25 (trans. Dewing).

[60] Prokopios *Wars* 8.22.28; 8.22.19 (trans. Dewing). These two stone ships follow shortly after his description of the remarkable wooden ship of Aeneas in Rome. Prokopios also viewed erased inscriptions in Rome and connected them with the damnatio of Domitian: *Anecdota* 8.14 (see also Chapter 5, p. 257).

[61] Prokopios *Wars* 8.22.22 (trans. Dewing 1928): τοῖς γὰρ παλαιοτάτοις ἐς τὸ ἀκριβὲς ἐναρμόσασθαι τὸν ἀληθῆ λόγον οὐ ῥάδιον, ἐπεὶ ὁ πολὺς χρόνος τά τε τῶν χωρίων ὀνόματα καὶ τὴν ἀμφ' αὐτοῖς δόξαν ἐκ τοῦ ἐπὶ πλεῖστον μεταβάλλειν φιλεῖ.

Prophesying from Stone: Invented Oracles

Epigraphic Omens at Chalcedon, Alexandria, and Carthage

Not all late antique readers were as historically minded as Agathias, Kosmas, and Prokopios: some were more concerned with the future. Both the classicizing historian Ammianus and the ecclesiastical historian Sokrates Scholastikos (writing in Greek in the mid-fifth century) claimed that an inscription was discovered during the disassembly of the walls of Chalcedon at the command of the emperor Valens circa 375, carried out in order to reuse the stones for a bath in Constantinople. This inscription prophesied a barbarian invasion, if ever Byzantium had plentiful water and the stone was built into a bath. The two versions of the oracle (both in Greek) differ at several points, but the gist is the same. Here is part of the oracle recorded in Sokrates:

> When nymphs their mystic dance with wat'ry feet
> Shall tread through proud Byzantium's stately street;
> When rage the city wall shall overthrow,
> Whose stones to fence a bathing-place shall go:
> Then savage lands shall send forth myriad swarms.[62]

Spoliating the stone walls of Chalcedon to build a bath was risky business. The exasperated Valens initially refuses to heed the warning, but is prevailed upon by representatives of nearby cities and abandons the demolition of the walls, leaving them in the derelict state that Sokrates sees in his own day. We can doubt the story and relegate the prophecy to the category of "pseudo-oracle" or rather prophecy *ex-eventu*, but the narrative nonetheless indicates attitudes toward inscriptions: it was credible to the readers of Sokrates and Ammianus that ancient stones could impart critical information about the future, and (to the readers of Sokrates) that city leaders would petition an emperor to act on such presages. Sokrates states that the prophecy was in fact

---

[62] Sokrates Scholastikos 4.8.6 (trans. Zenos):
 Ἀλλ' ὅτε δὴ νύμφαι δροσερὴν κατὰ ἄστυ χορείην
 τερπόμεναι στήσονται ἐυστεφέας κατ' ἀγυιάς
 καὶ τεῖχος λουτροῖο πολύστονον ἔσσεται ἄλκαρ,
 δὴ τότε μυρία φῦλα πολυσπερέων ἀνθρώπων,
 ἄγρια, μαργαίνοντα, κακὴν ἐπιειμένα ἀλκήν.
 Cf. Ammianus 31.1.5. Coates-Stephens 2002: 280–281.

fulfilled after Valens built the famous aqueduct bearing his name (nymphs with wat'ry feet in Byzantium's streets): the Goths attacked the city in 378.

Valens was particularly unlucky with epigraphic omens. Ammianus reports that attempted usurpers used a divinatory tripod to predict who would be the next emperor (an illegal act, of course). A plate placed on the tripod functioned like a Ouija board: a ring dangled by a thread swung toward the letters of the alphabet engraved on the plate, forming hexameters "like the Pythian verses [from Delphi] ... or those given out from the oracles of the Branchidae [at Didyma]."[63] The last of these verses mentioned the plain of Mimas, and Valens correspondingly avoided Mt. Mimas in the territory of Erythrai in Ionia. But after his death at Adrianople in Thrace, an ancient burial mound was found on the battlefield with an inscribed tablet identifying it as the grave of one Mimas. Julian too was warned by an epigraphic omen (among many others) before his death in Persia: Ammianus alludes to the emperor's public inscriptions at Antioch, which gave his full regnal name, Flavius Claudius Iulianus Pius Felix Augustus. After the death of two officials, named Julian and Felix, the people of Antioch read these inscriptions as Julian, Felix, *and* Augustus: the emperor himself was next on the chopping block.[64] Zosimos claims that when the general Stilicho (c. 359–408) stripped the gold leaf from the doors of the Capitolium at Rome, an inscription was revealed reading "These are preserved for a wretched tyrant"; Stilicho later met his wretched end (execution).[65] News from the future was not always bad: at a village near Zeugma in the province of Syria, a goose laid an egg embossed with crosses and the message that "the Romans will conquer," according to the early sixth-century Syriac chronicle of Pseudo-Joshua the Stylite.[66] Epigraphic miracles could also serve to confirm "orthodoxy": in the late fifth-century *Miracles of St. Thekla*, an Arian bishop's attempt to chisel away a mosaic inscription proclaiming the consubstantiality of the Trinity ended with a nasty fall for the workman commissioned to do the deed. Thekla protected the inscription because it was "the foundation and safeguard of the whole faith, of this very church, and of human nature itself."[67]

---

[63] Ammianus 29.1.31 (trans. Rolfe). See also Bersani 2003: 634–638.
[64] Ammianus 23.1.5; see the commentary of Boeft et al. 1998. Cf. for example *I.Mus. Iznik* 1019: *D(omino) n(ostro) Fl(avio) Cl(audio) Iuliano P(io) F(elici) semper Aug(usto)*.
[65] Zosimos 5.38.5 (ed. Paschoud): *misero regi seruantur*, ὅπερ ἐστίν "ἀθλίῳ τυράννῳ φυλάττονται."
[66] Pseudo-Joshua 68 (trans. Watt and Trombley).
[67] *Miracles of Saint Thekla* 10 (trans. Talbot and Fitzgerald Johnson).

Another passage in Sokrates Scholastikos confirms the prophetic role played by inscriptions for many individuals in late antiquity—although in this instance, Sokrates himself is a skeptic. At the time of the destruction of the Serapeion in Alexandria by bishop Theophilos around 391, hieroglyphs in the form of crosses were uncovered—presumably the actual ancient Egyptian hieroglyphic ankh.[68] The Christians present at the Serapeion insisted that the sign was a symbol of Christ, while the pagans took a more postmodern stance: the symbol could mean one thing to Christians, and another to themselves. This "lit crit" reading was unconvincing to the Christians. But some individuals present claimed to be able to actually read the ancient hieroglyphs and (correctly) identified the ankh as a sign meaning "life." Further decipherment resulted in a prophecy: when the cross (ankh) appears, the Temple of Serapis will be destroyed (which in fact had already happened in the narrative). A great number of pagans were said to convert based on the apparent veracity of the hieroglyphic prediction.

But Sokrates himself admits his doubts. How would the ancient Egyptian priests who inscribed the hieroglyphs have known about the coming of Christ? The advent of the savior had been a mystery hidden even from the devil. Rather, for Sokrates the miracle was the *discovery* of the cross symbol at the critical moment of debate between pagans and Christians, leading to mass conversion. The ankh was a God-sent weapon in the arsenal of Christian proselytizing; Sokrates compares this incident to St. Paul's instrumentalization of the altar of the unknown god in Athens to convert the Athenians (*Acts* 17:23). This passage in Sokrates serves as a note of caution: individuals in late antiquity could come to different conclusions about inscribed texts based on their background beliefs and individual process of reasoning. The current study can only paint in broad strokes the range of attested modes of reading ancient inscriptions.

A later author, Pseudo-Cyril (seventh/eighth century), did not share Sokrates Scholastikos' skepticism (or at least had a different literary aim). In an encomium perhaps in part inspired by stories of the Serapeion hieroglyphs, Pseudo-Cyril describes how the same Theophilos of Alexandria and his nephew came upon a "Temple of Alexander" with three thetas carved on the door lintel (ancient Egyptian winged sun disks?).[69] Theophilos

---

[68] Sokrates Scholastikos 5.17; followed by Sozomen 7.15. A version of the story was first told by Rufinus *Historia Ecclesiastica* 11.29, writing around 402 CE, and by Eunapios *Lives of the Philosophers* 472, around the same time. Westerfeld 2019: 142–152; see McKenzie, Gibson, and Reyes 2004: 107–110 for the archaeological evidence of the Serapeion's Christian use.

[69] Pseudo-Cyril *Encomium on the Three Youths*; Westerfeld 2019: 158–159.

interprets the letters as standing for Theos, Theodosios, and Theophilos. Jackpot: the doors of the temple open and gold pours out. Theophilos writes to the emperor Theodosios, who instructs him to use the gold to construct new churches. Here the inscribed thetas/sun disks functioned as a riddle that could be solved only by the right man at the right time. The temple was constructed by pagans, but its true purpose was to fund the Christianization of Alexandria.

This view of inscription as prophetic *Mitarbeiter* in the process of conversion is apparent in the west as well. Quodvultdeus, bishop of Carthage from c. 437– 450s, offers a personal account from his youth. After the Temple of Caelestis in Carthage had been closed for some time, the local Christian population wanted to reuse it, despite the protests of remaining pagans (who warned that snakes in the underbrush would protect the temple). The bishop at the time, named Aurelius, set his chair in the place previously occupied by the cult statue of the goddess. Lo and behold, Quodvultdeus and his friends spotted on the façade of the temple a dedicatory inscription in bronze from another Aurelius: "Aurelius the priest (*pontifex*) dedicated [it]."[70] The original dedication was most likely from an emperor with Aurelius as part of his nomenclature (Marcus Aurelius, Commodus, Caracalla, etc.): numerous such building dedications from North Africa are known.[71] Quodvultdeus was selective in his reading, since we can expect an imperial name to have been accompanied by full imperial titulature and the designation, not just as *pontifex*, but as *pontifex maximus*. This has not diminished Quodvultdeus' view of the inscription's prophetic ability: the Christian bishop (and *pontifex*) Aurelius now sits in the temple, as providence had long ago ordained.

The *Tübingen Theosophy*: Converting Temples

The inscriptions "read" in late antiquity need not always be genuine ancient texts. A collection of oracles epitomized in a manuscript called the *Tübingen Theosophy*, based on an earlier *Theosophia* compiled in the late fifth/early sixth century CE most likely by an Alexandrian Christian, indicates the importance of inscriptions to Christians when interacting with formerly pagan

---

[70] Quodvultdeus *Liber promissionum et praedictorum* 3.38.44: *Aurelius Pontifex dedicavit*; Kahlos 2019: 62–63.
[71] Horster 2001: 415–439.

sites.[72] The *Tübingen Theosophy* includes a number of real late pagan, "theological" oracles delivered from Apollo's sanctuaries at sites such as Klaros and Didyma. These abstract, monotheistic-trending verses were reinterpreted by followers of the new religion as prophesies of the coming of Christ.[73] One oracle of Apollo Klarios has been found in inscribed form on a wall at Oinoanda in Lykia, dating from the second or third century CE, as we will see in Chapter 5. The original compiler of the *Theosophia* may therefore in some instances have copied Christianize-able texts from actual inscriptions still on display.

The *Tübingen Theosophy* also contains "fake" oracles, such as one attributed to Apollo at Kyzikos, on the southern coast of the Sea of Marmara in Asia Minor.[74] In a brief summary of what was presumably originally a longer story, we are told that in the time of the emperor Leo (457–474), the inhabitants of Kyzikos were contemplating transforming an unspecified temple in their city into a church of the Theotokos, when they found an oracle (χρησμός) inscribed on the side of the temple. The oracle had been given to a previous generation at Kyzikos, who, when building the temple, had asked Apollo to whom the sacred structure should be dedicated. Phoebus Apollo responded with a rhythmic, though not metrical, oracle:

Do whatever calls forth virtue (ἀρετὴν) and order (κόσμον). I, at any rate, announce a single triune (τρισένα) God on High, whose imperishable *logos* will be conceived in a virgin (ἀδαεῖ). And he, like a fiery arrow, will streak through the world, gather up everything and bear it as a gift to his Father. This house will be hers, and her name is Maria.[75]

The pre-Christian inhabitants of Kyzikos are told to act in accordance with *arete* and *kosmos*, presumably the maximum that could be expected from

---

[72] For the work and its context: Mango 1995; Beatrice 1995; Busine 2005: 396–431; Freund 2006; Carrara and Männlein-Robert 2018.

[73] For the continued functioning of oracular sites in late antiquity: Athanassiadi 1991 and Athanassiadi 1992 (with reservations about some of the archaeological interpretations); Robertson Brown 2016; Heineman 2018.

[74] Our designation of these oracles as "fake" is problematic. Can we more charitably imagine a late priest(ess) at an oracular shrine, either personally converted, commanded by local authorities, or sensing the new social needs of the late antique *populus*, attempting to smooth the transition from old cult to new?

[75] *Tübingen Theosophy* 54.1–6 (trans. Kaldellis 2009: 48):Ὅσα μὲν πρὸς ἀρετὴν καὶ κόσμον ὄρωρε, ποιεῖτε· ἐγὼ γὰρ ἐφετμεύω τρισένα μοῦνον ὑψιμέδοντα θεόν, οὗ λόγος ἄφθιτος ἐν ἀδαεῖ ἔγκυμος ἔσται· ὅστις ὥσπερ τόξον πυρφόρον μέσον διαδραμὼν κόσμον ἅπαντα ζωγρήσας πατρὶ προσάξει δῶρον· αὐτῆς ἔσται δόμος οὗτος, Μυρία δὲ τὸ ὄνομα αὐτῆς.

those living under the old gods. The author(s) of the story have imagined here virtuous, not debauched, pagans, and their inscriptions could correspondingly give good advice. Apollo continues with his proclamation of a single Triune God and predicts that the temple will one day belong to Mary. Although the shortened version in the *Tübingen Theosophy* does not state it, the finding of the oracular text in the process of transforming the temple would make the most narrative sense in the original story if the Kyzikans were debating the fate of the temple—perhaps some thought that it should be destroyed outright, others wanted to convert it, while other "crypto-pagans" wanted it preserved as is. Or perhaps conflicting Christological views had resulted in uncertainty regarding to whom the new church should be dedicated.[76] The oracle of Apollo thus served to justify both the conversion of the temple into a church *and* its specific dedication to Mary, the mother of the *logos*.

A parenthetical note in the text of the *Tübingen Theosophy*, possibly added later, states that the same oracle was "found in Athens, on the left side of the temple by the door"; despite this precise location, no trace of such an inscription at the Parthenon has been found, though the meaning of "by the door" does not exclude the possibility of a freestanding stele, base, or altar.[77] Fascinatingly, on the island of Ikaria, a variant of this oracle was physically carved on a wall block.[78] It is dated to the fifth or sixth century CE and was found in the countryside, near an early Christian basilica at Oinoe, perhaps formerly the site of a temple. This inscription indicates that the oracle of the *Theosophy* was not only a literary device, but was put into action epigraphically in the process of Christianizing the late Roman landscape. The block on which this oracle is inscribed also holds a hymn to an archangel and the Theotokos, as well as a gnomic saying directed against Jews, or, in Georgios Deligiannakis's view, against a heterodox Christian sect on the island disparagingly labeled as "Jews."[79] These neighboring texts on the stone from Ikaria hint that the oracle may have served to encourage community consensus on the role of Mary as the Theotokos, in opposition to "heretical" groups. Busine notes that in other textual sources, this same oracular text is said to be engraved in specific locations, for example on the altar to the unknown god

---

[76] For monophysite leanings in another oracle in the *Tübingen Theosophy*: Beatrice 1997: 11–13.
[77] Κατὰ τὴν πύλιν (trans. Kaldellis 2009: 48). The Parthenon did, in fact, become a church dedicated to the Theotokos at some point before 693, the earliest dated graffito: Xenaki 2016; Xenaki 2020.
[78] *IG* XII 6, 2.1265a; *I.Ikaria* 31; Deligiannakis 2011: 325–326; Deligiannakis 2015: 195–198; Deligiannakis 2017: 524–529.
[79] The hymn is *IG* XII 6, 2.1265b; the anti-Jewish saying is *IG* XII 6, 2.1263.

in Athens (the one described by Paul in *Acts*).⁸⁰ Based on the two mentions of Athens in the written sources, the oracle was probably inscribed somewhere in the city in late antiquity; an elegant solution would be an altar inscribed with the oracle set up near the Parthenon. The evidence indicates the wide circulation of this spurious oracle in the Eastern Mediterranean and the probability of multiple engraved copies set up in various places.

A variation on the *Tübingen Theosophy*'s story of the temple at Kyzikos is also found in the *Chronographia* of Malalas. In this version, Jason and the Argonauts received the oracle but misunderstood Apollo's prophesy. They dedicated the temple not to Mary (Maria, Μαρία/Μυρία), but rather to the ancient Greek goddess Rhea (Ρέα), "mother of the gods," written (we are told) in bronze letters on the door lintel.⁸¹ The names are aurally close. Many years later, under Zeno, the temple finally was rededicated to the "right" divine figure, the Theotokos Maria. In antiquity, Rhea was often associated with Kybele, an Anatolian mother goddess, and the symbolism of the shift from the old divine mother to the new mother of Christ is clear. If a temple to Rhea-Kybele existed at Kyzikos (as is likely), an actual inscribed dedication to Rhea may have been located on the temple door lintel or architrave.⁸² When read in conjunction with the spurious oracle, it would have provided powerful confirmation that the temple of Ρέα μῆτερ θεῶν (Rhea, mother of the gods) should instead be dedicated to Μαρία μῆτερ θεοῦ (Maria, mother of God).⁸³ Such a text may even have inspired the invented oracle in the first place, in particular the use of the personal name Mary/Maria rather than Theotokos or a more poetic circumlocution for the mother of Christ. In its many variants, the story of "Apollo's" oracle indicates that pagan inscriptions, real or fabricated, in stone or in papyri, could be put to work in constructing consensus around the building of new Christian structures at former polytheist sites.

It is this prophetic mode of reading inscribed text that distinguishes the late antique habit of using inscriptions in literature from the Greek and Roman tradition of doing so. The ancient world obviously had its own robust system of oracles, auguries, and omens, and there are a few examples of an inscribed

---

⁸⁰ Busine 2012: 247.
⁸¹ Malalas 4.8.21–2: καλέσαντες τὸν οἶκον Ῥέας μητρὸς θεῶν. The text of the oracle in the *Tübingen Theosophy* spells Mary's name as Μυρία.
⁸² For the textual evidence for a cult of Kybele at Kyzikos: Xagorari-Gleißner 2008: 132.
⁸³ One could even wonder whether the change was carried out epigraphically: "ΜΗΤΡΙ ΘΕΩΝ" could be modified to read "ΜΗΤΡΙ ΘΕΟΥ"—perhaps as easily as closing the *omega* and erasing the first bar of the *nu*.

text offering a prophecy: Plutarch claims that during Alexander's invasion of Asia Minor a spring near Xanthos in Lykia produced "a bronze tablet bearing the imprints of ancient letters" (Greek or Lykian?) foretelling Greek victory over the Persians, while in the same author's *De Genio Socratis*, an inscribed bronze plate found in the tomb of the mythical Alcmena commanded Greeks to live in peace with each other and to introduce a new cult of the Muses.[84] According to Suetonius, Julius Caesar's assassination was foretold by the discovery of an inscribed tablet at a tomb in Capua, while a lightning strike presaged Augustus' death: the "C" of Caesar was obliterated from one of his inscriptions, indicating that he had only one hundred (C) days to live and would then become a god (*aesar* meaning "god" in Etruscan).[85] In other cases the mysterious appearance of books (scrolls) occasioned the (re)introduction of a cult, as at Andania in Messenia.[86] But stone inscriptions in particular became more charged with a numinous energy in late antique literature. Rather than viewing this as an indicator of increasing "superstition" at the end of antiquity, we should note that other avenues of investigating the future were more restricted in our period, and those seeking knowledge of the future had to resort to new forms of divination.[87] The usurpers plotting against Valens had to rely on the Ouija board–like plate to spell out hexameters *like* those from Delphi or Didyma, presumably because they could not (or should not) consult the old oracles. Soothsayers came under increasing suspicion from church and state authorities; the reading of animal entrails was no longer an easy avenue to divinely sanctioned advice. It was into this gap that prophesying inscriptions were occasionally inserted in our texts. As we will now see, not only this attitude toward inscriptions, but the genres into which they were embedded, evolved in late antiquity.

Plagiarizing for the Saints: The *Life of Abercius*

When Papias, the bishop of Hierapolis (Pamukkale), compiled his *Account of the Logia about the Lord* between circa 90 and 120 CE, he incorporated material straight from the horse's mouth—or as close to it as he could get,

---

[84] Plutarch *Life of Alexander* 17.4: δέλτον . . . χαλκῆν, τύπους ἔχουσαν ἀρχαίων γραμμάτων; Plutarch *De Genio Socratis* 7.

[85] Suetonius *Life of Julius Caesar* 81; *Life of Augustus* 97. See Busine 2012: 242.

[86] Pausanias 4.26.8. As Busine 2005 has documented, the "discovery" of inscribed text was used throughout the ancient world to justify the introduction of a new cult.

[87] Wisniewski 2020.

anyways. Papias interviewed individuals who had personally known Christ's disciples, including, for example, the daughters of St. Philip (either one of the twelve disciples or a deacon mentioned in *Acts* 6:5), who had settled at Hierapolis later in his life.[88] Papias' goal with this oral history of Christianity was to uncover the "truth": Jesus' very commandments to the faithful. A passage in his *Account* reveals his epistemological bias: "For I did not consider what came from books to be of as much value as what came from a living and abiding voice."[89] Papias was fortunate in his age: he had access to individuals only one or two degrees of separation from Christ himself. Later writers were connected by ever thinner threads to these earliest days of Christianity and had to expand their evidentiary basis substantially: reading and quoting from earlier written accounts (as Eusebius and other authors quoted from Papias), visiting and viewing the monuments associated with early Christian figures (such as the martyrium and tomb of Philip at Hierapolis), and learning from the written *Lives* of holy men and women, whose miracles confirmed that they were living Christ's truth. But not every saint had a contemporary, or near contemporary, biographer, so in order to reconstruct these lives, late antique writers of hagiographies, just like history writers, turned to various other sources of information about the past—including inscribed stones.

These hagiographical texts present yet another mode of reading ancient inscriptions: the selective lifting of epigraphic material from its original context and planting it into saints' lives to authenticate the tales. Here the older inscription may, or may not, be explicitly referenced in the narrative. The most striking example of this literary spoliation is the *Life of Abercius* (*Vita Abercii*). Abercius is said to have lived in Hier(o)polis in Phrygia Salutaris, modern-day Koçhisar in the Afyonkarahisar province, not the more famous Hierapolis where Papias lived.[90] It has long been recognized that the *Life of Abercius*, whose original composition is dated to the fourth or fifth century, incorporates the actual text from the saint's late second/third century CE tombstone, discovered in a stroke of exceptional good luck by Sir William Ramsay at an abandoned village bathhouse in 1883 (Figure 2.3).[91]

---

[88] McKechnie 2019: 46–57.
[89] Papias *apud* Eusebius *Historia Ecclesiastica* 3.39.4 (trans. Schott): οὐ γὰρ τὰ ἐκ τῶν βιβλίων τοσοῦτόν με ὠφελεῖν ὑπελάμβανον ὅσον τὰ παρὰ ζώσης φωνῆς καὶ μενούσης.
[90] Although the city names are spelled the same in literary use, the local form at Koçhisar seems to have been Hieropolis; I therefore use Hier(o)polis to refer to the Koçhisar site and to avoid confusion with Hierapolis (Pamukkale). For the city name: Ramsay 1897: 680–681.
[91] *ICG* 1597 = *SEG* 30.1479, Musei Vaticani no. 31643. Originally published Ramsay 1883: 424–428, no. 36.

Figure 2.3 Hier(o)polis. Inscription of Abercius (*SEG* 30.1479). Late second/early third century. Vatican Museum no. 31643. © Governorate of the Vatican City State-Directorate of the Vatican Museums, all rights reserved.

The fragments of this tombstone made their way to the Vatican's Museo Pio Cristiano via Ramsay and the Ottoman sultan Abdul Hamid. The clear, carefully carved Roman letters stand out on the white marble funerary *bomos* (a stone in the shape of an ancient altar), which is broken at the top, right, bottom, and back from its reuse in later structures; a wreath occupies the preserved left side of the stone.[92] The anonymous author of the *Life of Abercius* tells us that the bishop Abercius (Aberkios, Ἀβέρκιος) prepared a tomb for himself and had inscribed on it a lengthy epitaph in hexameters. The epitaph as given in the *Life* can be divided into three parts, prose opening and closing

---

[92] For additional images of the stone: Wirbelauer 2002: 361–363; Mitchell 2008: 328–334.

sections and the central section in verse.[93] Much of the epitaph is known exclusively from the *Life of Abercius*; the stone itself preserves only the central lines. This is important, as we will see shortly.

Most of the *Life* is set during the reign of Marcus Aurelius (r. 161–180), and the saint's death has traditionally been dated to c. 190 CE (in any case before 216 CE). This makes the Abercius inscription one of the very earliest Christian inscriptions known anywhere; the letter forms are compatible with a late second or early third century date. The epitaph does not disappoint with its heady, veiled Christian symbolism, about which much ink has been spilled.[94] In the opening, Abercius tells us that he is the "citizen of a chosen city," that he made this tomb while living, and that he is a "disciple of the holy shepherd . . . whose eyes are great and all-seeing." In the central part, there is a first-person narrative full of elusive language describing a trip "to Rome" to see a "Queen with golden robes and golden shoes" as well as a "a people with a shining seal," followed by a visit to Syria, where Abercius tells us he has "brothers" and is accompanied by a "Paul." "Faith" (πίστις) led him and provided fish from a "holy maiden," as well as wine mixed with bread. In the concluding section, Abercius asks that "all who understand and approve these words pray for Abercius." The epitaph then concludes by instituting a grave fine to prevent anyone from burying someone else in his tomb: whoever breaks this regulation will have to pay two thousand gold pieces (*aurei*) to the Roman treasury and one thousand to his native city of Hier(o)polis. Such fines, although usually in much smaller amounts, are known from other tombstones of Roman Asia Minor.

It is easy to find the early Christian symbolism in this epitaph. The "holy shepherd" is Christ, the "Queen" in Rome is the Church. "Paul" is perhaps a copy of the apostle's writings, which Abercius carried with him to visit fellow Christians in Syria.[95] The fish is a well-known marker of Christian identity; wine and bread recall the eucharist. Despite this collage of Christian-associated imagery, early scholarship was split on whether the historical Abercius, as represented in the epitaph, was actually an early Christ follower

---

[93] *Life of Abercius* 77 for the text of the epitaph. The most recent edition of the *Life of Abercius* is Seeliger and Wischmeyer 2015; the *Life* has recently been translated into English: McKechnie 2019: 263–287. For the vast earlier bibliography: McKechnie 2019; Vinzent 2019.

[94] See most recently Baslez 2020.

[95] The line with the name "Paul" is damaged on the stone (*ICG* 1597, l. 11), and the manuscript variants likewise show confusion. The author of the *Life of Abercius* was presumably working from an already-damaged stone and did not quite know what to do with Paul. He also makes no mention of a "Paul" in the narrative part of the *Life*.

(as predominantly Catholic and some Protestant scholars maintained) or a member of another Phrygian pagan mystery cult that used similar veiled imagery (with several prominent Protestant scholars favoring the latter position).[96] The bulk of recent scholarship favors a Christian identity, even if the epitaph was originally intended to project a dual Christian-civic persona.[97]

Ramsay discovered a second, fully preserved gravestone also displaying several lines from Abercius' epitaph ("citizen of a chosen city," "disciple of a holy shepherd," and the grave fine) in the same village, except that instead of the name "Abercius," the name "Alexandros, son of Antonios," appears in the opening section (Figure 2.4). This text is dated precisely to "the year 300, month 6," which in the local era is equivalent to 216 CE.[98] This stone seems to indicate that, within a few years of the Abercius' death, his grave was considered worthy of epigraphic emulation by other Christians in the city of Hier(o)polis—although as we will soon see, the relationship between the Alexandros gravestone and the Abercius inscription has recently been called into question. The Alexandros stone has only the opening and closing portions of Abercius' epitaph (not the first-person travel narrative to Rome and Syria), with some modifications.

Upon Ramsay's publications of these two inscriptions, it was understood that the author of the *Life*, living in Hier(o)polis in either the later fourth or fifth century, had copied the epigram directly from Abercius' own second-/ early third-century Roman tombstone. What is more, much of the narrative of the *Life of Abercius* (which is not among the more credible saints' lives but is replete with demons, miraculous healings, intergenerational curses, and a flying altar) has clearly been built from the text of Abercius' epitaph, or rather, from misunderstandings derived from it: in the story, the saint travels to Rome, sees there not the Church but a physical queen (the empress Faustina the Younger, c. 130–175/6 CE, wife of Marcus Aurelius), and performs an exorcism on her daughter, the princess Lucilla. The devil exits Lucilla and agrees to go back to his ancestral haunt, but Abercius first commands him to "carry this altar . . . bring it safely to my city of Hier(o)polis, and set it up near the South Gate."[99] We are told in a subsequent passage that this is the very altar on which Abercius' epitaph is carved.[100] This note was probably an

---

[96] Mitchell 2008 gives a concise overview of this debate.
[97] Mitchell 2011: 1752–1759. Brent 2019 has recently revived the question of whether the tombstone was actually Christian.
[98] *ICG* 1598 = *IGR* IV 694. Originally published Ramsay 1882: 518–520, no. 5, now in the Istanbul Archaeology Museum (Mendel 1914: 569–570, no. 778).
[99] *Life of Abercius* 64.
[100] *Life of Abercius* 77.

Figure 2.4 Hier(o)polis. Inscription of Alexandros, son of Antonios (*IGR* IV 694). 216 CE. Istanbul Archaeology Museum. Ramsay 1897, 721.

attempt by the *Life*'s author to explain to his readers why the early Christian saint's epitaph was placed on a stone in the shape of a pagan altar, as were many Roman grave stones. After the exorcism, the grateful Faustina builds a bath at a hot spring miraculously created by the saint in his home region. This passage may explain for its contemporary readers the presence of a bath at a nearby, documented hot spring with a hypothetical inscribed dedication to or from Faustina.[101] Although the author of the *Life* was capable of reading the words on the Abercius tombstone, he either willingly appropriated or unwittingly misunderstood its content and used it to build a fantastical narrative.

This copying of a second-/third-century Roman grave epitaph into a hagiography, along with a narrative expansion on it probably colored by local stories about the saint, is similar to how Agathias interacted with the Chairemon base in his *Histories*. In this case, the pious author of the *Life of Abercius* did not aim to reconstruct historical *events* from the Abercius stone or (hypothetical) Faustina inscription, but rather to explain the cityscape around him from a Christianizing perspective and to offer a stirring narrative of a local hero of the new faith. We (post)moderns may find the hagiographer's methods reductive, but his material has not been doubted. Despite the contentious scholarly debates about the meaning of the symbolism, the quibbling over particular variants in the manuscripts of the *Life*, and the arguments about the significance of the epitaph for early Christian theology and the primacy of Rome, Abercius' grave text as a whole has not been called into question. As Paul McKechnie wrote in 2019, "the correspondence between the text on the stone and the text as handed down in the manuscript tradition of the *Life of Abercius* is exact," so that the *Life* can be used to complete the lines on the fragmentary inscribed copy.[102] But there is just one problem with this conflation of the *Life*'s lengthy epitaph and the inscribed version: the text preserved on the Vatican stone represents only a small portion of the full epitaph of the *Life*. The name Abercius never appears on this marble, nor, for that matter, does any part of the opening or closing sections, known only from the *Life* and the Alexandros inscription.

In 2019 Markus Vinzent made a shocking accusation: the *Life of Abercius*' late antique author had fabricated the "Abercius" epitaph in his hagiography from two separate older Roman inscription he found in Hier(o)polis: the Alexandros stone and the fragmentary base now in the Vatican (conventionally called the "Abercius inscription").[103] Vinzent points out that these two engraved texts do not overlap anywhere on the stones: he proposes that the author of the *Life* took the opening and closing sections of his lengthy epitaph from the Alexandros stone (simply substituting in the name of Abercius) and then adopted the central section (the travel narrative to Rome and Syria)

---

[101] Thonemann 2012a: 275; Busine 2013: 341–342.
[102] McKechnie 2019: 150.
[103] Vinzent 2019: 77–160.

from the other, anonymous stone, while adding in a few extra-Christian lines on his own initiative (the ones referencing the eucharistic bread and wine), which are not preserved on either stone. Vinzent places the composition of the *Life of Abercius* around the time of the Council of Chalcedon in 451, at which the bishop of Hier(o)polis (*also* named Abercius) took a strong anti-Nestorian stance.[104] If the ancient saint was important enough to be invited to Rome at the behest of the empress Faustina, then the present imperial powers should also take heed of the fifth-century bishop Abercius from the small backwater city of Hier(o)polis in Phrygia. Vinzent notes that the grave fine recorded on both the Alexandros inscription and in the *Life* is an extraordinarily high amount of money (six times higher than any other grave fine in Asia Minor).[105] He proposes that Alexandros had been one of the leading men of the city with one of the most expensive grave monuments in all of Roman Asia Minor, resulting in the high valuation of his grave's inviolability; the author of the *Life* had simply copied the amount into his composite Abercius epitaph. In Vinzent's view, the Abercius epitaph, conventionally called the "queen of Christian epitaphs," is a Frankenstein text, stitched together from two Roman (second-/third-century) inscriptions with additions made by the zealous author of the *Life* in the fifth century.

Vinzent's argument will undoubtedly reignite debates about the Abercius epitaph, and the stone in the Vatican is certainly in need of a full epigraphic reevaluation in light of recent work on Roman Christian tombstones of Phrygia and other regions of Asia Minor, rather than as the first teleological step leading to the triumph of the Church.[106] Scholars would do well to avoid conflating the text of the epitaph in the *Life* with that on the stone. But a few preliminary criticisms of Vinzent's thesis can be made. First, the words actually preserved on the stone in the Vatican include the following: Rome, queen, people, sealed, Syria, Paul, faith, fish, virgin/maiden. It is theoretically possible that an adherent of a *different* cult in Roman Phrygia just happened to value these very Christian-sounding places/things and have a non-Christian companion named Paul—Paul(l)os was a regular Roman name in Asia Minor—but a simpler explanation is that the original inscription in the Vatican is in fact an early Christian text. Phrygia boasts a number of pre-Constantinian Christian tombstones, so the Abercius stone would be

---

[104] Vinzent 2019: 108, 130–131, following Seeliger and Wischmeyer 2015: 466–467.
[105] Vinzent 2019: 134.
[106] On coeval Anatolian tombstones: Mitchell 1993; Huttner 2013; Chiricat 2013; Breytenbach and Zimmermann 2017; Pilhofer 2018; McKechnie 2019: 210–245.

in good company.[107] Second, it is quite plausible that there was a man named Abercius (Aberkios; the Greek form of the Latin name Avircius) living in Hier(o)polis in the late second century. Eusebius in his *Historia Ecclesiastica* quotes from an earlier anonymous treatise against Montanism (referred to as the "Phrygian heresy"), which is dedicated to a man named Avircius Marcellus and was written around 192 CE.[108] The anonymous author also mentions "our fellow presbyter, Zotikos of Otrous."[109] Otrous (Yanıkören) was a small city neighboring Hier(o)polis, about thirty kilometers distant. Although the home of Avircius Marcellus is not given in this anonymous treatise, he was probably a Phrygian and quite possibly a Hier(o)politan (and perhaps even the very Abercius whose inscription is under discussion here). Another Abercius is known from a grave stone dated circa 330–350 and probably originating from Prymnessos, also in Phrygia and about fifty kilometers from Hier(o)polis.[110] The later Hier(o)politan bishop at the Council of Chalcedon in 451 was also called Aberkios. The Latinate name had a long history in this region. Vinzent's argument requires that there be another individual epigraphically commemorated in Hier(o)polis in the late second/early third century with a Christian-sounding inscription describing a journey to Rome and Syria; but that he not be the early Christian holy man about whom stories were told at Hier(o)polis two centuries later. An easier explanation is that there was in fact a historical Christian man (not necessarily a bishop) named Abercius in Roman Hier(o)polis who left behind the tombstone now in the Vatican, even if the stories about him in the *Life* are largely made up.

Another element of Vinzent's argument is unfounded: the very high value, three thousand gold coins, of the penalty for disturbing the grave (as seen on both the Alexandros stone and in the *Life*'s version of the Abercius epitaph) can better be explained by local circumstances of the burgeoning Christian community at Hier(o)polis, rather than Vinzent's scenario in which Alexandros had one of the most deluxe graves in all of Roman Asia Minor and assigns an absurd penalty for disturbing it. Alexandros' grave stone (a base topped by a fluted column) is nice but not opulent; it is comparable to other third-century grave monuments in the region of the "pine cone" *bomoi* type (an inscribed base topped by a pine cone- or omphalos-shaped

---

[107] Destephen 2010; S. Mitchell 2017b; S. Mitchell 2017c.
[108] Eusebius *Historia Ecclesiastica* 5.16.3. McKechnie 2019: 113.
[109] Eusebius *Historia Ecclesiastica* 5.16.5.
[110] Wischmeyer 1980: 26–27. This Abercius may have been born in the mid to late third century.

marker).[111] Such graves have fines in the 500 *denarii* to 100 aurei range.[112] There is no apparent reason why there should be such a high value extracted as a penalty for opening Alexandros' grave. More likely, Alexandros was simply copying from Abercius' earlier epitaph; Alexandros' description of himself as a follower of a "holy shepherd" makes it probable that he was also an early Christian. The opening and closing sections of the Abercius epitaph (including the grave fine) recorded in the *Life* were presumably inscribed on part of the broken-off bits of the grave stone now in the Vatican (either on the top and bottom, as on the plaster reconstruction on display in the museum, or on the now-missing back of the stone).[113] The amount is certainly high, given that most other grave fines were calculated in denarii (silver coins), rather than gold ones.[114] Perhaps Abercius and Alexandros wanted to ensure that their bodily remains would be left in place for the coming resurrection: already around 210, Tertullian of Carthage wrote a defense of the bodily resurrection, indicating that this was a topic of concern among early Christians.[115] Or perhaps Abercius was worried that his enemies (pagan, Montanist, etc.) planned to desecrate his grave.[116] Perhaps he had quite an inflated opinion of himself, what with his network of Christian associates in Rome and Syria. The amount of three thousand gold pieces is paralleled by another stone from the *other* Hierapolis (Pamukkale), which assesses a fine of 3,300 *silver* coins.[117] Abercius has simply adopted a familiar formula and ramped it up by specifying gold rather than silver. The problem with penalizing someone who would open and reuse (or rob) a grave with a substantial fine of any denomination is that the individual was probably too poor to pay such a penalty. The amounts therefore do not really matter. They are simply an indication of the illegality of disturbing the dead—and in fact many early Christian and Jewish tombstones of Anatolia instead relied on curses ("it will be a matter between him and God") to dissuade would-be tomb openers.[118] Alternatively, both

---

[111] Photos of the Alexandros tombstone in the Istanbul Archaeology Museum were first published in Mitchell 2008, Figs. 9.9 and 9.10.
[112] 500 denarii: *MAMA* XI 123; 100 aurei: *MAMA* XI 145.
[113] Margaret Mitchell has traced the history of the plaster reconstruction and considers various possibilities for the placement of the texts: Mitchell 2011. The wreath on the left side of the stone does not, contra Vinzent 2019: 96, necessarily "indicat[e] that the stone previously was used as a Roman altar." Wreaths as a sign of victory could adorn dedications, civic honors, gravestones (especially military ones), and athletic inscriptions (Yegül 2014: 205–210).
[114] Iluk 2013.
[115] Tertullian *On the Resurrection of the Body*.
[116] If Abercius was not himself a Montanist: Pepuza, the Montanist headquarters, was about a two-day walk from Hier(o)polis.
[117] *ICG* 1595 = *CIJud II* 779.
[118] McKechnie 2019: 211.

Abercius and Alexandros may have directed their grave fine specifically against family members who hoped to have a spot in the grave. The funerary monuments of Phrygia are overwhelmingly family-oriented: the inscriptions specify certain family members with permission to share in the tomb. Karin Wiedergut has recently argued that grave fines (and their varying amounts) were directed against future descendants who did *not* have permission to use the grave.[119] Alexandros and Abercius were therefore very strange in their exclusion of *everyone* from their graves, and they may have wanted to emphasize to family members that they were serious about their solo-burials. There are, moreover, metrical questions regarding Vinzent's assertion that the author of the *Life* added lines to the Abercius stone; but I will leave that analysis to others. In my view it is likely that the author of the *Life of Abercius* in the fourth or fifth century had in front of him at Hier(o)polis the fully preserved, three-part tombstone of a Roman Christian named Abercius, only fragments of which are currently preserved in the Vatican.

But even if Vinzent's hypothesis about the Abercius inscription is correct, it is clear that the author of the *Life of Abercius* was quite capable of reading and appropriating older Roman inscribed texts for his own ends. Anyone left doubting the Christian faith in general or St. Abercius in particular could be referred by the author to Abercius' grave stone, either still in situ (presumably outside the South Gate, mentioned in the hagiography) or perhaps built as spolia into late antique city walls in the same area (as was the fate of so many Roman grave stones). The inscribed monument and the saint's *Life* worked in tandem, providing reciprocal etiologies for each other in a Christianizing view of history. Tombstones were especially common fonts of inspiration for early Christian hagiographers.[120] The *Life of Porphyry of Gaza* incorporates the precise date of the death of the bishop Porphyry, making an intermedial quote from funerary epigraphy (whether drawn from an actual tombstone or not): "he fell asleep in peace with the saints, on the second day of the month Dystros, in the year 420 [CE] according to Gazan reckoning. He had been a bishop for twenty-four years, eleven months, and eight days."[121]

But other genres of inscriptions could also be mined for material by hagiographers. Whereas the author of the *Life of Abercius* was explicit in

---

[119] Wiedergut 2018.
[120] Wischmeyer 1980: 23; Rapp 2011: 294–299.
[121] Mark the Deacon *Life of Porphyry* 103 (trans. Rapp): ἐκοιμήθη ... μηνὶ Δύστρῳ δευτέρᾳ ἔτους κατὰ Γαζαίους ὀγδοηκοστοῦ τετρακοσιοστοῦ, ἐπισκοπήσας ἔτη κδ καὶ μῆνας ια καὶ ἡμέρας η. See also Busine 2013: 339.

citing Abercius' tombstone as a source, he did not draw attention to other epigraphic material he probably used in composing his narrative: some inscriptions were "undercover," that is, disguised as something they were not. Peter Thonemann in 2012 argued that the *Life of Abercius* draws not only on the tombstone of Abercius (for him the full epitaph text as recorded in the *Life*) but also on a hypothetical secular, imperial inscription at Hier(o)-polis.[122] The narrative includes a letter purported to be from Marcus Aurelius to Euxeinianos Pollio, a citizen of Hier(o)polis whom Abercius had engaged in a Platonesque dialogue in the first part of the *Life*.[123] In the supposed letter, the emperor heartily thanks Pollio for his largesse in helping the people of Smyrna after the earthquake of 177 CE. Such praise for a local citizen from the emperor himself would certainly be a worthy candidate for inscribed public display in second-century Hier(o)polis; compare the letter of Antoninus Pius in praise of a local citizen of Aizanoi, inscribed on that city's main temple (Chapter 3). This passage functioned as pseudo-historical evidence boosting the veracity of the hagiography while lending it an attractive, authentic ancient aura through intermedial quoting. The text of the letter in the *Life of Abercius* gives the correct honorific titulature of the emperor and names historical officials in Asia Minor known from other sources to have lived during the second century. A Pollio, son of Euxenos, is likewise attested in another inscription; he may very well have sometimes been called Euxe(i)nianos Pollio (with Euxeinianos being a patronymic, "son of Euxe(i)nos").[124]

As Thonemann posits, these lines with second-century officials and titulature were likely poached by the fourth- or fifth-century author of the *Life* from a real inscribed letter of Marcus Aurelius dated to 177/8, presumably still on display in Hier(o)polis at the time. After thanking Pollio in the letter, the emperor asks him to send Abercius to Rome in order to perform the exorcism on Lucilla, because he has heard that this bishop is skilled at chasing out demons. These prose lines *are* actually fabrications of the author of the *Life of Abercius*, shrouded in a veneer of historicity by being embedded within the text of the authentic letter of Marcus Aurelius. The letter concludes with a farewell to Pollio in accurate second-century style. The inclusion of the imperial letter achieved the double aim of showcasing a proud civic moment

---

[122] Thonemann 2012a: 265.
[123] McKechnie 2019: 170–175. The two men debate free will in a dialogue with allusions to the *Book of the Laws of Countries* by the Syrian Bardaisan (154–222 CE).
[124] Thonemann 2012a: 272.

of the Hier(o)politan past and refashioning that largely pagan history into a proto-Christian one.

The *Martyrdom of Ariadne of Prymnessos* likewise made use of intermedial quotes from an older civic inscription within its narrative.[125] This hagiographical text dates from the fourth or fifth century and takes place in a small city (modern Sülün near Afyonkarahisar) also situated in Phrygia Salutaris, like Hier(o)polis. Ariadne is the slave of a man named Tertullos; he is accused of sheltering a Christian in his house. During a trial before the provincial governor, a kinsman of Tertullos gives a lengthy oration praising his relative in terms and phrases lifted (sometimes inelegantly) from second-century Roman civic honorary inscriptions. Several textual elements point to a Pamphylian origin for the original inscribed honors; Pamphylia lies to the south of Phrygia. Although such a text has not been found at Prymnessos, a recently published honorary decree from Perge in Pamphylia for a Tertullos (a historical imperial official in the second century CE) bears many similarities to the encomium delivered in the *Martyrdom*—beyond the obvious use of the name "Tertullos."[126] Either the *Martyrdom* was originally composed at Perge, before the story migrated to Prymnessos, or Prymnessos may have erected a copy of the honors bestowed on the historical Tertullos, perhaps because he was a citizen of that city, as suggested by Thonemann. Alternatively, the author of the *Martyrdom* may have traveled to Perge and, while in the area, copied down a text suitable for his narrative.

The *Life of Abercius* and the *Martyrdom of Ariadne* indicate the sophisticated appropriation of earlier inscriptions to situate Christian saints among the authentic figures, titles, and historical events of the Roman past. The genre of hagiography was new, but the use of inscriptions (real and imagined) to authenticate narratives took place already in ancient biographies.[127] Fake honorific decrees were trotted out to show how highly the Athenians valued the philosophers Aristotle and Zeno, while Sokrates was absolved of the charge of bigamy by a made-up Athenian decree permitting the practice during a population crisis.[128] The biographical habit of drawing on epigraphic material was still in full bloom in the late fourth or fifth century, as seen in the *Historia Augusta*: this imaginative account of second- and third-century emperors quotes frequently from (often fabricated) inscriptions, especially

---

[125] Robert 1980: 244–256; Thonemann 2015.
[126] *I.Perge* 193; Thonemann 2015: 158–165.
[127] Low 2016: 150–151.
[128] Haake 2013.

epitaphs, which are usually made to confirm some detail of the emperor's death, as told in the *Historia*. At the beginning of this chapter, we saw how a fictitious arch inscription in the *Life of St. Makarios* went even further, not only authenticating the monks' journey (everyone knew that Alexander had reached practically the ends of the earth), but demonstrating the superiority of the Christian holy man over even the most storied of ancient kings.

Conclusion: The Literary Afterlives of Ancient Inscriptions

The cornucopia of textual evidence gathered in this chapter indicates that literate individuals in late antiquity were both able and willing to read older Greek and Roman inscriptions and appropriate them for their own purposes. Late antique historians could draw on older inscriptions to corroborate events recorded in written or oral histories, while oracles delivered by "Apollo" or mysterious supernatural forces justified the new religion and effected community consensus on the reuse of older pagan temples. These habits were not new—ancient Greeks and Romans already used inscriptions in historical narratives and let oracles iron out difficult political and religious decisions—but they have received far less attention in late antique scholarship than they have in the literature on, say, Herodotos or the Second Sophistic. Indeed, the sources gathered here suggest that the prophetic role of literary inscriptions increased in our period. New genres were likewise nourished by a steady diet of older inscribed tidbits. Ancient inscriptions could be baked into hagiographical narratives, lending an aura of historic authenticity to the stories. These transtextual allusions assured that the late antique author used the appropriate "old-fashioned" style of language and correct paratextual addresses while anchoring the narrative to significant moments in imperial or civic history. As we have seen, these ancient inscriptions were put to work in the world-building of the new Christian era; this finding offers insight into the potential modes of reading real, reused inscribed stones, found in the archaeological record and described in the subsequent chapters. Cities and sanctuaries were full of pagan-era inscribed texts capable of directly communicating to late antique viewers in the process of making decisions about their built environment, whether constructing an aqueduct or a church, or deconstructing a temple. The ancient inscriptions still on display at pagan sanctuaries were not simply in limbo until their rediscovery by modern archaeologists, but had the potential to be direct sources of information to late antique viewers about the past history of the sacred space and, potentially, its foreordained Christian future.

As we have established, there is ample evidence for the late antique reading of ancient inscriptions; this chapter is essentially a study of the reception of older epigraphic material in late antique texts. Yet reception studies tend to hop over late antiquity and proceed directly to the medieval, Renaissance, or early modern reception of classical antiquity. The late antique viewer, or the early Byzantine viewer, or whatever we artificially wish to label her or him, existed between two worlds: both unambiguously Roman and increasingly Christian (not at all a contradiction), propagator of the classical tradition and yet fully aware that the world was changing, maybe even acting as an agent of that change her- or himself. Late antique viewers therefore approached ancient inscriptions from somewhere between an emic and an etic perspective. The pasts of the late Roman east were both startlingly local and deeply interwoven with broader cultural groups and kingdoms, whether Hellenic, Roman, Karian, Lydian, Phrygian, Galatian, Persian, Syriac, Samaritan, Jewish, Nabatean, Hebrew, Egyptian, Ethiopian, and even "Asianic," a catchall term for the generic eastern ancestors claimed by some cities in Anatolia, to name only a few of the cultural identities at play in late antiquity.[129] It is difficult to know how late antique individuals would have positioned themselves with relation to ancient texts: did older inscriptions in Greek "belong" to their identity group (however defined)? Did they recognize texts in epichoric languages as their own cultural heritage, or were these the remains of a mysterious "Other?" How great a role did a viewer's self-identification as Christian play in her/his attitude toward older texts? Our sources do not provide comprehensive answers. The well-educated history-writer Agathias seems to recognize in Chairemon the traditional polis-oriented euergetic activity he would like to see more of in his own day: Chairemon was a "good ol' boy." The pious, anti-pagan Kosmas had no difficulty identifying Ptolemy as a historical king and treated his inscription as a record of the familiar Hellenic past. But in other instances, the past is framed as a "foreign country." Sokrates Scholastikos depicts the (presumably fictional) oracle stone built into the city wall at Chalcedon as a mysterious force from an unspecified past that defies even the most earnest attempt at decipherment and compliance: the prophecy of a barbarian invasion eventually came true despite

---

[129] For "Asianic" ancestors: Sergueenkova and Rojas 2017; Rojas 2019: 110–116.

USE OF REAL OR IMAGINED INSCRIPTIONS   67

Valens' heeding of the inscribed warning. The text was written in Greek, but from another world, one that produced oracles and left them lying around for hapless readers until the fullness of time had come.

A later source from Constantinople projects an increasingly "foreign" view of the past and the gradual constricting of both the modes of reading ancient inscriptions and the group of readers themselves. The eighth-century *Parastaseis Syntomoi Chronikai* records the efforts of a group of "statue investigators" who canvassed the Byzantine capital's neighborhoods for statues, in part brought there by Constantine himself. These statues were part of the cultural patrimony of Constantinople and provided a link with the classical past. Yet knowledge about this past was imprecise. Statues could act as "wildcards," revealing mysterious messages or even macabre finds: in the telling of the *Parastaseis*, a bronze elephant in the Forum of Constantine contained an entire human skeleton and a tablet with the words "Not even in death am I separated from the holy maiden Aphrodite."[130] Why "Aphrodite" should be found inside of a bronze elephant is not explained in this (seemingly fictitious) story: ancient writing had the potential to surprise and inspire speculation about a past that ranged from mysterious to bizarre.

Many sculptures would have arrived in Constantinople without their bases, but some ancient artifacts, like the tripod with the digamma inscriptions seen by Priscian, had texts integrated onto the object itself. The three-headed Serpent Column in the Hippodrome, snatched from Delphi where it had been set up as a victory monument after the Persian War in 479/8 BCE, bears on its bronze coils the names of the thirty-one cities that had taken part in the Battle of Plataia. The *Parastaseis* records that a group of philosophers from Athens visited the Hippodrome in the time of Theodosios II (r. 402–450) in order to read the inscriptions, perhaps including the Serpent Column. One philosopher begins to laugh upon reading a text, but we (the readers) are not let in on the joke—or was he simply unable to make any sense of the inscription at all?[131] In another episode, a statue fell and killed one of the investigators while he was debating its identity, perhaps indicating the danger of misreading an ancient text, or of separating the statue from the crucial identifying information contained on its base.[132] Benjamin Anderson argues that the *Parastaseis* represents the efforts of a group of blueblood Constantinopolitan families

---

[130] *Parastaseis* 17 (trans. Cameron and Herrin): Ἀφροδίτης παρθένου ἱερᾶς οὐδὲ θανούσης χωρίζομαι. Does "Aphrodite" here refer to the goddess or to a mortal woman (or to the elephant)?
[131] *Parastaseis* 64.
[132] *Parastaseis* 28.

to assert their expertise in interpreting ancient statues, expertise that was lacking among the *novi homines* of the imperial bureaucracy coming from far-off regions of the empire.[133] "Correctly" interpreting the city's patrimony required esoteric knowledge that newcomers to the city lacked. The past became an ever more foreign country.

---

[133] Anderson 2011.

3

Preservation

Tolerating Temples and Their Texts

Touring Temples

When Constantius II visited Rome in 357 CE, he toured the eternal city's monuments, as so many tourists do today. Pagan temples were must-see attractions, despite the strong Christian tendencies of the emperor. In the telling of the staunchly pagan senator Symmachus (c. 345–402), writing nearly thirty years later, the emperor:

> viewed with a mild expression the sanctuaries, he read the names of the gods inscribed on their upper parts, he asked about the origins of the temples, he admired their founders and, although he himself followed other religious traditions, he preserved these (traditions) for the empire.[1]

Symmachus was writing to the young emperor Valentinian II in the midst of a debate between himself and Ambrose, bishop of Milan, over the removal of the Altar of Victory from the Curia in Rome. The altar had stood in the senate house since the time of Augustus, and was, according to Symmachus, a talisman of Roman victory. The altar had been removed first by Constantius II himself, before being reinstated by Julian and removed again by Gratian in 382, but Symmachus used Constantius' allegedly admiring attitude toward temples to suggest that the emperor had not really been so anti-pagan after all. *Caveat lector*: Symmachus' memory of the erstwhile emperor's visit to Rome may be selective in the interest of rhetorical effect. Valentinian in the end found Bishop Ambrose's threats of ecclesiastical abandonment and eternal damnation more persuasive, and the Altar of Victory was not

---

[1] Symmachus *Relatio* 3.7 (383/4 CE): *vidit placido ore delubra, legit inscripta fastigiis deorum nomina, percontatus templorum origines est, miratus est conditores cumque alias religiones ipse sequeretur, has servavit imperio.* Ammianus Marcellinus (*Res Gestae* 16.10.14) lists several temples among the sites on the emperor's itinerary.

reinstalled in the senate house. But whether or not Symmachus' account of Constantius' tour is wholly accurate is immaterial. It was at least conceivable that an individual would read the names of gods on temple entablatures while walking through Rome and that these texts would provoke contemplation of the origins of these structures. Constantius' purported admiration for the founders of temples may have been precipitated by seeing their dedicatory inscriptions on the architraves; his own father, Constantine, had more irreverently referred to Trajan as "Wall Ivy" because of how he covered buildings with his name.[2] Viewing the great monuments of the past, reading the names inscribed on them, and asking about their origins was possible not just in Rome but in late antique cities throughout the Mediterranean. Architectural remnants of the pagan past—not only spoliated ones, but also those left in place—remained front and center.

In Chapter 2, we saw that Constantius II was not the only one engaged in reading the older inscribed texts dotting late antique cityscapes. Various individuals, from the highly educated Agathias to the demolition team charged with spoliating the walls of Chalcedon (were said to have) read, comprehended, and used ancient inscriptions. These blasts from the past were believed to communicate something about the contemporary late antique world: prophecies of invasions, right conduct for late Roman citizens, a deep local Christian history, and proof of divine providence. Given these modes of reading, we now turn our gaze to the archaeological evidence. The present chapter examines the preservation of inscribed texts dating from the Classical through the Roman period at still-standing monuments within, even at the heart of, vibrant late antique cities and rural sites. Some of these spaces were appropriated for Christian use, but others were not. In each instance, the inscribed texts remained on display even as the contexts around them changed.

And were they actually read? It is, for the most part, impossible to confirm archaeologically the written accounts in Chapter 2. What physical evidence of a process so ephemeral as reading could we expect? In fact, the stones themselves do occasionally provide indications of late antique engagement with the *content* of ancient inscriptions, proving that reading took place. Inscribed altars to various gods at the sanctuary of Asklepios at Epidauros in Greece were marked, probably in the fourth century CE, with pictographs

---

[2] More precisely, "wall plant" (*herbam parietariam*): *Epitome de Caesaribus* 41.13. Cf. Ammianus 27.3.7.

symbolizing the god named in the dedication, accompanied by a number. For example, altars to Poseidon were marked with a trident and a dolphin. As Christopher Pfaff has argued, these marks were added by the pagan cult personnel to organize the altars for regular sacrifices.[3] Some of the original dedicatory texts date as early as the fifth century BCE: even much older texts were still comprehensible, at least when as brief and straightforward as dedications. In at least one instance, the reader misunderstood the inscribed text: a dedication to Demeter was marked with the symbol for Asklepios, an error deriving from the name of the mortal dedicator of the altar, Asklepas.[4] This case of mistaken identity underscores the need for the pictographs in the first place—they were a more reliable means of identifying the god than the potentially confusing, perhaps fading older script.

But late pagans were not the only ones marking ancient inscriptions. New Christian symbols and words could be added to older texts in order to neutralize or update them. A recently published brick with a dedication to Zeus Keraunios (Ζεὺς Κεραύνιος) from Stratonikeia had a cross etched on top of the text when it was reused in a church.[5] At Aphrodisias, an inscription on the Northeast Gate of the city was Christianized in perhaps the seventh century; we will discuss this gate further in Chapter 5. A spoliated honorific inscription for Augustus from Pergamon had a rough cross scratched onto the stone at precisely the part of the text referring to him as the "son of god" ([θ]εοῦ υἱὸν).[6] A second-century CE inscribed plaque reused at a former nymphaeum at Laodikeia (Asia Minor) carried a brief text in large, clear letters: "When L. Antonios Zenon Aurelianos held the office of prophet," which, as Louis Robert noted, was a dating formula.[7] A Chi-Rho with alpha and omega was painted in black over this text at some point, leaving the background text visible yet difficult to read. Writing *on top of* an ancient text was rare in late antiquity, but, given that inscribed ancient stones were attributed with prophetic powers (e.g., foretelling the ignoble end of the emperor Valens), might the presence of the name of another, later emperor (Zeno, r. 474–491) on this plaque, combined with the reference to prophecy, require an act of Christianizing negation? A votive column of ca. 150 CE at Sagalassos dedicated to the "pure goddesses who listen" (Θεαῖς Ἁγναῖς ἐπηκόοις) was

---

[3] Pfaff 2018: 420–421.
[4] *IG* IV² 507; Pfaff 2018: 396.
[5] Söğüt 2018: 438, Fig. 5.
[6] *I.Pergamon* 381, l. 1; Pergamonmuseum no. IvP 381 A–E.
[7] *I.Laodikeia Lykos* 67: Προφητείας | Λ(ουκίου) Ἀντωνίου | Ζήνωνος | Αὐρηλια|νοῦ. Robert 1969: 289, no. 6, Pl. CV.1.

reused as a drain cover slab in the Upper Agora in the fifth or sixth century.[8] A relief of the goddesses on the upper part of the column was broken off—intentionally or not is difficult to determine—and an εἶς θεός (one God) graffito was scratched on the base. The graffito may have been added before or after the relief was broken, but in any case, the *eis theos* is written closer to the older inscription than to the visual depiction of the goddesses. It can be understood as a written retort to the older text. This archaeological evidence, besides the reinscribed ancient texts we saw at Megara in Chapter 1 and a number of erasures we will come to in Chapter 5, proves that reading inscriptions took place in actuality and not only in literature, even at still-standing (non-spoliated) monuments, as described below.

This is the most archaeological chapter of the book. At several sites, a review of the archaeological contexts surrounding temples is necessary in order to establish how buildings were used in late antiquity and even that they were still standing. The final collapse of these structures was of little interest to early archaeologists, who expended their energies on pinpointing original construction dates through stylistic analysis of carved decoration, stratigraphic evidence based on ceramic finds, and yes, dedicatory inscriptions. The finer points of carved moldings or ceramic typology were surely lost on the late antique viewer, but the texts carved in marble could continue to speak. Even with the most up-to-date archaeological methodology, however, and the publication of full building biographies spanning from construction to collapse, it is not always easy to establish the late antique phase of a structure. Nonetheless, clues exist: Ine Jacobs has highlighted the archaeological evidence (sometimes difficult to spot) for the maintenance and repair of older buildings from the fourth to the seventh century in the eastern Mediterranean.[9] The monuments selected for inclusion in this chapter can all be said with confidence to have stood into the period of "Christianization" (even if they collapsed at some point in late antiquity). Some were still largely standing into the early modern period or even today; others underwent architectural conversion to churches while maintaining core architectural features of the pagan sanctuary. The unconverted generally show no late antique structural modifications, but that does not mean that they were bereft of visitors, of whatever religious preferences: I have selected only temples with solid archaeological evidence for late antique activity, either on the

---

[8] *SEG* 47.1761 (3). See also Waelkens 1997, Fig. 67; Talloen and Vercauteren 2011: 352.
[9] Jacobs 2013. She discusses the evidence for temple maintenance or reuse at Aizanoi, Ephesos, Sardis, Hierapolis, Aphrodisias, Sagalassos, Side, and Selge.

sanctuary's fabric itself (in the form of newly carved texts or crosses), or in its immediate vicinity (newly built structures or the encroachment of housing). Most inscriptions presented in this chapter cannot offer *unequivocal* proof that they were read in late antiquity, but their surrounding contexts within frequented areas of cities or rural sites, as well as the addition of new texts or graffiti to the structures, point toward the viewing of, and conceptual engagement with, these ancient texts. By dint of remaining visible, they reveal which written records of the classical past were acceptable to late antique viewers, even which texts may have been desirable and useful. Tolerating is not the same thing as ignoring.

This tolerance applied to ancient sculpture as well, even that depicting pagan gods or mythological figures.[10] Late antique cities were crowded with carved figures of centuries past, as well as occasional newer late antique additions; pagan mythological figures continued to be produced in Asia Minor in the round in the fifth century and on mosaics or metal objects in the seventh.[11] At Ostia, funerary portraits couched as mythological figures were resurrected from the Roman necropolis and brought into the city from the mid-third century CE onward as decoration for both public and private buildings: an inscription in the forum declared that a statue had been moved "out of desolate places" (*ex sordentibus locis*).[12] Such claims (*ex* or *de sordentibus locis*; *de abditis locis*, "from hidden places") became tropes on bases throughout Italy and in Cherchel (North Africa).[13] Although inscriptions in the Greek east did not make explicit the reused nature of the statues on display, statues were nonetheless moved around. Both public and private statue collections in Constantinople featured images of pagan gods; at the senate house, the figures of Zeus of Dodona and not one but two Athenas could be seen.[14] The private collection of Lausos, *praepositus sacri cubiculi*, was assembled at Constantinople around 420 and contained no less a specimen than Pheidias' chryselephantine Zeus of Olympia, who lived out his late antique afterlife among the Knidian Aphrodite, the Samian Hera, and the Lindian Athena[15]—at least, until the fire of 475 CE brought this blessed assemblage to an end.

---

[10] Saradi-Mendelovici 1990; Bauer and Witschel 2007; Lavan 2011b; Jacobs 2013: 395–445; Kristensen 2013; Kristensen and Stirling 2016.
[11] Jacobs 2010: 270–271; Smith and Ward-Perkins 2016.
[12] *CIL* XIV 4721; Murer 2016: 183–195; Murer 2019: 119–121.
[13] Cooley 2012a: 324.
[14] Bassett 2004: 74–90, 188; Kaldellis 2016: 738.
[15] Stevenson 2007: 72–79.

Not every ancient statue was tolerated or collected, as we will see in the coming chapters, and the same is true of inscriptions. There is one sticking point, however, in this matter of the continued display of ancient inscriptions in late antiquity: what about plaster? Could the inscriptions presented in this chapter simply have been covered with a layer of plaster, thereby hiding them even as structures stood otherwise unharmed? Perhaps. But given the lack of archaeological evidence for plaster at the temples presented here—no plaster caught under a fallen block, none stuck deep in the crevices of carved letters—there is every indication that these texts remained visible. The erasures in Chapter 5 further support the hypothesis that inscriptions were not covered.

Inscribed Text and Figural Imagery at Unconverted Temples

Ephesos: Embodying Emperors on the Embolos

In late antiquity, the Embolos (Curetes Street) of Ephesos was an eclectic mishmash of classical and contemporary monuments, advertising the city's prestigious past and present both architecturally and epigraphically.[16] The street was redesigned as the main commercial and social thoroughfare of the provincial capital of Asia in this period, and statues of different periods crowded its length. One such bronze figure was Aelia Flaccilla (r. 379–386), the wife of Theodosios I, who was accompanied by at least eleven reused Nike (Victory) bronzes and their inscribed agonistic bases from the second or third century CE.[17] The inscriptions began "to Good Fortune" (ἀγαθῇ τύχῃ) or "to the sweetest fatherland" (τῇ γλυκυτάτῃ παρίδι). These bronzes *and* their texts were not only tolerated in Ephesos, but actively sought out as desirable street décor. We find similar statue migrations at other late antique urban sites, such as Sagalassos, whose temples feature in the next chapter. The Embolos at Ephesos ended at the Library of Celsus, repurposed as a fountain around 400.[18] It kept its original façade inscriptions, including a lengthy dedication by the eponymous Celsus, labels for statue personifications, and an

---

[16] Bauer 1996: 284–290, 424–425; Thür 1999; Feissel 1999: 125–126; Ladstätter and Auinger 2009; Roueché 2009; Waldner 2020: 174–175.
[17] Roueché 2002: 529–536.
[18] Jacobs and Richard 2012.

Figure 3.1 Ephesos. Façade of the "Temple of Hadrian" with *I.Ephesos* 429. Quatember 2017 Pl. 22. Used by permission.

imperial letter concerning the founding of the library.[19] It also gained a new, late antique dedication in lofty poetic diction commemorating the euergetic relationship of an official named Stephanos with the city of Ephesos.[20]

The so-called Temple of Hadrian (actually a small shrine for both Hadrian and Artemis) was one among many structures that maintained its classical looks with a highly decorative façade along the Embolos (Figure 3.1). Most of the original dedicatory inscription dated to 117/118 CE remained on view on the architrave, reading in part:

> [To Ephesian Artemis and to the emperor Caesa]r Augustus Trajan Hadrian, and to the neokoros demos of the Ephesians, Publios Quintilios [Valens Varios,] son of Publios, of the tribe Galeria [... with his wife ...] and his daughter Varilla, erected the temple from the foundations with all its decoration and the statue in it from their own money.[21]

The western section of the architrave, including the portion mentioning Artemis, was damaged and repaired at some point in the fourth century; a newly inserted replacement block was not reinscribed with the older text,

---

[19] *I.Ephesos* 5113, 5108–5111, and 5114. 5110 is a later addition or replacement label.
[20] *I.Ephesos* 5115.
[21] *I.Ephesos* 429, ll. 1–2: [Ἀρτέμιδι Ἐφεσίᾳ καὶ Αὐτοκράτορι Καίσα]ρι Τραιανῶι Ἁδριανῶι Σεβαστῶ[ι] καὶ τῶι νεωκόρωι Ἐφεσί[ων δήμ]ωι Πόπλιος Κυιντίλιος Ποπλίου υἱὸς Γαλερία | [Οὐάλης Οὐάριος — σὺν — τῇ γυναι]κὶ καὶ Οὐ[α]ρίλλῃ θυγα[τ]ρὶ τὸν ναὸν ἐκ θεμελίων σὺν παντὶ τῶι κόσμωι καὶ τὸ ἐν αὐτ[ῷ ἄγαλμα ἐκ] τῶν ἰδίων ἀνέθηκεν. See Quatember 2017: 28–30.

but the remainder of the entablature remained in place and on view.[22] Presumably, this repair work could have extended to chiseling off the entire dedication, but there was no reason to remove the name of a good emperor and the city's proud patrons.

The façade of the "Temple of Hadrian," crowned by a nude *Rankenfrau* on the tympanum, functioned as a backdrop for imperial statues from at least the Tetrarchic era onward. Statue bases of Diocletian, Maximian, Galerius, and Constantius Chlorus were set up in front of the temple; that of the disgraced Maximian was removed. He was replaced later by a statue of Theodosios I's homonymous father between 379–387, indicating the longevity of the temple as a space for imperial commemoration, even under a devout Christian emperor.[23] Diocletian and Galerius were remembered by Christian authors, such as Lactantius and Eusebius, as persecutors, but no memory sanctions were imposed by subsequent emperors: the Tetrarchic bases (and their statues?) were left in place even as construction began on the first church of St. Mary nearby (probably near the end of the fourth century).[24] This church created a new monumental focal point for the city, and change was apparent elsewhere at the site as well. Statues of Augustus and Livia found buried in fill under a sixth-century floor near the State Agora were marked with small, simple crosses on their foreheads; the motivations behind this marking are unclear (exorcising a demon? posthumous baptism through a seal of faith? making a territorial claim?).[25] Carved imagery on the "Temple of Hadrian" on the other hand was tolerated without modification, despite its technically pagan content (tempered by imperial associations). A figural frieze in the pronaos (the temple's porch) depicts the founding of the city by the mythological Androklos, as well as a "who's who" lineup of pagan gods and a sacrificing Roman emperor. This frieze was previously interpreted as a late antique addition to the structure based on the style (with the sacrificing emperor identified, remarkably, as the anti-pagan Theodosios I), but recent investigations indicate that the relief is an original second-century component of the temple.[26] Theodosios would be relieved.

The particular construction decisions made during the fourth-century renovation of the "Temple of Hadrian" at Ephesos indicate that neither the

---

[22] Quatember 2017: 83–89, no. 029A. See Chapter 5, p. 256.
[23] *I.Ephesos* 305.1–3 (Tetrarchs); *I.Ephesos* 306 (father of Theodosios I).
[24] Karydis 2019: 185 for the construction date of the church.
[25] Hjort 1993: 109–111; Jacobs 2010: 280; Kristensen 2013: 94–98; Jacobs 2017.
[26] Quatember 2017: 114–125. The shrine collapsed at an uncertain date post-fourth century.

Roman-era dedicatory inscription to the emperor nor the figural imagery needed editing at that time, when hired hammers were in the vicinity and could have carried out whatever changes were required. The same holds true for most other monuments along the Embolos—but not every inscription in Ephesos was so lucky, as we will see in Chapter 5. Given the willingness to use older inscriptions in the world-building of late antiquity, as detailed in the literary sources collected in Chapter 2, the text of the dedication to Hadrian from local euergetes, read in conjunction with the new statue bases in front of the temple, provided viewers with a clear message of continuity that goes beyond simple aesthetic appreciation: the present imperial rulers were just as good and successful as Hadrian had been, and local benefactors were as able and willing to beautify the city as their predecessors. If the sacred canopy was shifting, the monuments along the Embolos let it slip only so much, but no farther. This narrative of continuity built from inscribed and molded marble would develop cracks eventually, but during the fourth century, at least, Ephesos still lived up to its classical patrimony.

Museumification at Priene's Temple of Athena?

Not all temples received archaeologically identifiable repairs in the fourth century, making it difficult to situate them within evolving late antique cityscapes. The Temple of Athena Polias at Priene is famous as a prime architectural specimen of the late Classical/Hellenistic periods, funded by Alexander the Great. But it had a dramatic late antique afterlife as well, in a city with a population declining in numbers but active in constructing new Christian and Jewish structures.[27] Like the "Temple of Hadrian" at Ephesos, this temple may have functioned as an inscribed space for imperial and historical commemoration, before a fire event, followed by an earthquake, brought about its demise at an uncertain date. In the following, I consider the evidence that Priene's Temple of Athena may have been at least partially standing into the first half of the fifth century and present a snapshot of the shrine (its architecture, contents, and inscriptions) in its last days.

What messages did the Temple of Athena project as it was still standing? A dedicatory inscription from Alexander the Great stood in large letters on

[27] Burkhardt and Wilson 2013: 173–174; Fildhuth 2017: 33–65; various essays in Raeck, Filges, and Mert 2020.

Figure 3.2 Priene. Dedication of Alexander the Great (*I.Priene B—M* 149) and following documents on the front of the northeast anta of the Temple of Athena Polias. British Museum no. 1870,0320.88. © The Trustees of the British Museum.

the northeast anta (the projecting pier that terminates the cella wall): "King Alexander erected the temple for Athena Polias" (Figure 3.2).[28] The rest of the anta and its exterior wall was packed with an extensive dossier of Hellenistic edicts, decrees, and *senatus consulta*, which related to the city's

---

[28] *I.Priene B—M* 149: Βασιλεὺς Ἀλέξανδρος | ἀνέθηκε τὸν ναόν | Ἀθηναίηι Πολιάδι.

territory, privileges, and identity.[29] During the reign of Augustus, a rededication was added to the architrave of the *peristasis* (the colonnade surrounding a temple's cella): "The demos [dedicated it] to Athena Polias and to emperor Caesar Augustus, god, son of a god."[30] The blocks of the architrave and the anta with the dossier were found where they had fallen in the temple ruin; the texts would have been visible in their in situ locations prior to the collapse.[31] When did this collapse happen? Housing began to encroach into the sacred precinct as early as the late third century CE, but the later use of the temple and its end is obscure because of the early date of the excavations, which began in the 1760s (Figure 3.3).[32]

Nonetheless we have evidence for the last days of the Temple of Athena at Priene. Broken statues found in situ in the cella and pronaos show signs of burning and were uncovered in a matrix of dark soil.[33] Bases were also found; any inscriptions that may have been on them were not recorded.[34] The acrolith cult statue of Athena was standing inside the cella at the time of the fire; she held in her hand a Nike with gilded bronze wings.[35] It seems that Athena kept her head until the fire: fragments of her lips were recovered. The other fire-damaged statues from the cella include a head identified as the Hekatomnid ruler Ada (adopted mother of Alexander the Great), a bust of the emperor Claudius, another probably of Julius Caesar, and a headless imperial cuirassed torso (Figure 3.4).[36] Bases and sculpture fragments were recovered in the pronaos and throughout the temenos of the sanctuary.[37]

The presence of the cult statue of Athena in the cella need not indicate that pagan worship was ongoing at the time of the fire. Despite Eusebius of Caesarea's inflated account, it is likely that Constantine's delegates visited only select sanctuaries and appropriated only suitable statues for his new capital.[38] Constantinople's urban aesthetic tended toward blingy bronzes of

---

[29] The documents were inscribed from c. 285 BCE into the second century BCE: Sherwin-White 1985; Thonemann 2012b.
[30] *I.Priene* B—M 153: Ὁ δῆμος Ἀθηνᾶι Πολιάδι καὶ | [Αὐ]τοκράτορι Καίσαρι Θεοῦ υἱῶι Θεῶι Σεβαστῶι [καθιέρωσεν].
[31] Pullan 1881: 29.
[32] Hennemeyer 2013: 197; Fildhuth 2017: 71–72.
[33] Pullan 1881: 29; Carter 1983: 13; Koenigs 2015: 158.
[34] Carter 1983: 251.
[35] Carter 1983, no. 72–83.
[36] Carter 1983, no. 85 (Ada), 91 (Claudius, nose missing), 90 (Caesar, with nose), 94 (cuirassed torso; findspot not secure). As we will see in Chapter 5, heads (especially noses) were frequent objects of iconoclastic violence. None of the fragments from the sanctuary at Priene shows marks of intentional damage, although some are missing heads.
[37] Carter 1983: 260–265.
[38] Eusebius *Vita Constantini* 3.54.

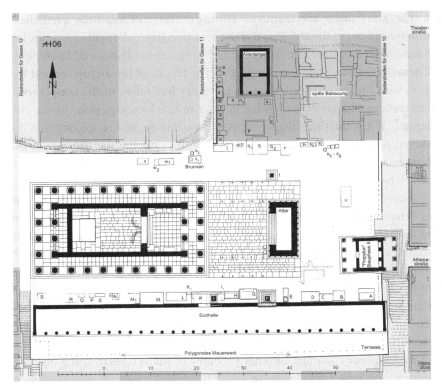

Figure 3.3 Priene. Plan of the sanctuary of Athena Polias. Hennemeyer 2013, Fig. 4. Used by permission.

Hellenic mythological figures; the staid marbles of Hekatomnid and Roman historical personages found in the temple at Priene would have been of less interest. At least some cult statues remained in place until the second half of the fourth century: Serapis in the Serapeion at Alexandria was hacked to bits only in 391; Allat at Palmyra was attacked in her temple around the same time; Apollo, Artemis, and Leto fell in the temple at Klaros during or after the mid-fourth century; Zeus at Magnesia on the Maeander tumbled from his pedestal most likely after the reign of Julian (361–363).[39] The statues inside the cella of the Temple of Athena in Priene cannot offer a clear indication of the date of the temple's first destruction event; it need not be third or even

---

[39] For Alexandria and Palmyra, see Chapter 5, C5P14 and C5P17, respectively; for Klaros, see Chapter 4, C4P56; for Magnesia, see below.

Figure 3.4 Priene. Marble female head identified as Ada, found in the Temple of Athena Polias. British Museum no. 1870,0320.138. © The Trustees of the British Museum.

fourth century. There is the possibility that the fire was deliberate. But setting a massive blaze in the midst of a densely built city was risky: Diocletian, eagerly embarking on the Great Persecution, declined to burn a church at Nikomedia due to fear that the fire would spread.[40]

After the fire at Priene, the roof tiles of the Temple of Athena (few of which were found) and a few wall blocks were removed.[41] The full collapse of the structure and its peristasis seems to have taken place in a later earthquake, also of uncertain date. The "Byzantine Basilica" (also called the *innerstädtische Basilika*) was built nearby, south of the theater, in probably the first half of the fifth century (with later renovations). It did not appropriate any architectural elements from the temple itself, although columns

---

[40] Lactantius *De mortibus persecutorum* 12.
[41] Koenigs 2015: 159.

from the south stoa of the temple temenos were used in the first phase of this church, along with numerous inscribed *stelai* from the sanctuary laid as paving (discussed in Chapter 4).[42] Spolia was clearly welcome in this ecclesiastical building project, and if the temple had already collapsed or had been damaged by fire, we might expect its marble elements to have been reused in the church's building fabric. But most pieces of the temple were found where they had fallen.[43] Jesko Fildhuth broadly dates the fire and collapse of the temple between the third century and the third quarter of the fourth century, and in any case prior to the fifth-century construction of the basilica, based on a section of *trochilus* (the upper part of a column base) from the temple reused as a table in a bath, which should be contemporaneous with the construction of the basilica.[44] But the spolia table was not necessarily an original feature of this building. Wolf Koenigs suggests that the final collapse of the temple may have been in the 467/68 earthquake that struck Ionia, in which case it would have been still standing when Priene's central basilica church was built.[45] Whatever the date of the temple fire (the first destruction phase) may be, a post-Constantinian date for the collapse of the temple's peristasis and its architraval dedication to Athena and Augustus finds support in the Christian graffiti etched on the stylobate and the *pteron* floor, which confirms the continued visiting of the temple. The graffiti includes an alpha and omega with a Chi-Rho and a text with two Christian-associated words: Ἀμβρόσις ἀναστάσις, which may either be two masculine names, Ambrosi(o)s and Anastasi(o)s, or, as the previous editors have taken it, the name Ambrosios agrammatically accompanied by the word "resurrection."[46]

If the statues in the cella were still on display in late antiquity, this assemblage could take on a new meaning within the Christianizing city. Like the "Temple of Hadrian" at Ephesos, the Temple of Athena may have served as a space for imperial commemoration through the display of statues and the inscribed architrave dedication to Augustus. Here, however, the exhibition was retrospective: no new imperial figures were introduced. The assemblage of ancient statues had perhaps already stood within the temple from the first century CE.[47] Or, some may have been collected in the cella only in

---

[42] Westphalen 1998: 292–294; Fildhuth 2017: 33–37, 70–72.
[43] Koenigs 2015: 158.
[44] Fildhuth 2017: 70.
[45] Koenigs 2015: 159.
[46] *I.Priene B—M* 227.2 (alpha and omega); *I.Priene B—M* 227 (Ambrosios). Koenigs 2015: 157 and supplementary plan 2 (for the locations of the graffiti).
[47] Carter 1983: 265.

a late period; the "mixed company" hints that the temple functioned as a sort of museum, displaying important figures from Priene's past (imperial Romans, a Hekatomnid satrap) alongside the cult statue of Athena, perhaps reframed as a work of art rather than of worship. The metal grating originally separating the cult statue from viewers had been removed before the fire; only the dowel holes in the floor remained at the time of excavation.[48] A law of 382 recorded in the *Codex Theodosianus* encouraged the reinterpretation of temples as museums: Gratian, Valentinian, and Theodosios describe a temple, probably at Edessa (Şanlıurfa), where "images are reported to have been placed which must be measured by the value of their art rather than by their divinity."[49] The use of a small number of temples as museums in late antiquity is supported by archaeological evidence: at the Temple of Apollo at Bulla Regia (Tunisia), diverse statues of pagan gods were brought together and displayed in the courtyard, while at Olympia (Greece), bronze statues took their places in between the columns of the Temple of Zeus.[50] A colossal toe was found within the cella at Priene; its full-size figure would have been too large for that space, so the toe must have been brought into the temple at some point, perhaps an object of wonder on account of its great size.[51] Remains of the altar of Athena were uncovered in front of the temple, but much of the structure was gone, meaning that the most potent pagan apparatus of the sanctuary was neutralized.[52]

This potential "museumification" of the Temple of Athena at Priene may have been enhanced by the historic texts engraved on its walls. The architrave dedication to Athena and Augustus and the original dedication of Alexander on the temple's anta, as well as the civic documents carved near it, were in situ until their collapse. Augustus was still famous in late antiquity (see the section on Ankara below); so too was Alexander, as can be seen inter alia in the *Life of Makarios of Rome*, the *Alexander Romance* tradition, and Kosmas Indikopleustes' discussion of Ptolemy.[53] Given the extensive writings praising these two legendary rulers, the inscriptions on the Temple of Athena at Priene may have been particular points of local pride and a motivating factor in the temple's preservation, as opposed to its spoliation, prior to its twofold destruction. The city's full history and engagement with

---

[48] Carter 1983: 230; Mylonopoulos 2011: 280–281.
[49] *C.Th.* 16.10.8 (trans. Pharr).
[50] Lavan 2011a: xxxviii; see also Lepelley 2020 (for the west).
[51] Carter 1983: 41.
[52] Hennemeyer 2013: 11.
[53] Alexander in late antiquity: Stoneman 2008; Djurslev 2019.

superpowers, from Hekatomnids to Roman emperors, was on display both epigraphically and in figural marbles at a time when the late antique settlement was living in the shadow of its classical glory days.

Performative Bureaucracy at the Temple of Augustus and Roma at Mylasa

Not far from Priene, the Temple of Augustus and Roma at Mylasa (Milas) in Karia, built between 12 and 2 BCE, most likely follows the pattern of preservation, unconversion, and imperial display outlined above. Although largely lost today, the temple building was almost perfectly preserved up to the mid-eighteenth century, when Robert Pococke made a detailed drawing of the structure in 1740 (Figure 3.5).[54] Conversion to a church in late antiquity cannot be ruled out given the paucity of archaeological findings, but two inscriptions of the fifth century CE (discussed below) carved on the temple podium hint that the building functioned for a bureaucratic, rather than ecclesiastical, purpose. The entablature's frieze of carved *bukrania*, tripods, and *phialai* (all of which had pagan cultic associations) remained in place, as did its architrave dedication: "The demos (dedicated it) to the emperor Caesar Augustus, son of a god, high priest, and to the goddess Roma."[55] This text was on view during our period and long after.

Late antique Mylasa is not well known archaeologically, but epigraphic attestations for the foundation of churches and the *Life of Eusebia* (also called Xene), written at Mylasa in the fifth or sixth century, indicate the continued vitality of the city.[56] The main conflict in the *Life* is not between pagan and Christian elements, but between "worldly" and "heavenly" concerns: Eusebia refuses to marry, absconds from her homeland, and changes her name to Xene before founding a convent in Mylasa. The narrative implies that the entire city participates in Christian festivals—although this is probably hagiographical exaggeration. The recent exciting excavation of the Uzunyuva complex at the city center from 2010 to 2016 uncovered the remains of a monumental Hekatomnid tomb of the fourth century BCE (a "twin" of the famous Maussolleion in nearby Halikarnassos); its surrounding area was redeveloped in late antiquity, with a colonnaded street built over a

---

[54] Pococke 1745: 61; see also Rumscheid 2004: 131–137, Figs. 1–7.
[55] *I.Mylasa* 31: Ὁ δῆμος Αὐτοκράτορι Καίσαρι Θεοῦ υἱῷ Σεβαστῷ ἀρχιερεῖ μεγίστῳ καὶ Θεᾷ Ῥώμῃ.
[56] *I.Mylasa* 621, 622, 625, 628. Ruggieri 2005: 86–87; Ruggieri 2011.

Figure 3.5 Mylasa. Temple of Augustus and Roma. Inset detail of the inscribed architrave (*I.Mylasa* 31). Pococke 1745, Pl. 55, with modifications.

deconstructed altar.[57] Numerous ancient inscriptions were used as spolia in surrounding structures, some of which bore Christian and Jewish graffiti.[58]

And what was the fate of the Temple of Augustus and Roma in Mylasa? Cyriacus of Ancona, who visited Mylasa in 1446, recorded that the temple was used as a church of St. Nicholas by the town's Greek population, but the detailed drawings of the early modern travelers indicate that the building had not undergone any structural alterations usually seen in late antique temple-churches.[59] There is no evidence of an apse added to the temple, the

---

[57] Publications of the excavation finds at Uzunyuva are still in preparation, but for preliminary remarks see Rumscheid 2010; Henry 2017: 358–365; Işık 2019.
[58] Jewish graffiti and texts: Marek and Zingg 2018 no. 48 and 78; Christian graffiti: no. 48, 60, 61, 63, 101, 105, and 117. For context, Marek and Zingg 2018: 189.
[59] Rumscheid 2010: 131–132.

orientation of which (roughly north to south) was not ideal for a church. The temple's peristasis, entablature, and gable (at the very least the front one) remained in place, and statue bases stood next to the temple's entrance at the time of Pococke's drawing.[60] Most significantly, at only approximately six meters wide and seven meters deep, the cella could have served only a very small congregation (Figure 3.6). If the reuse had taken place in the still-active late antique city, we might expect the walling up of the temple's peristasis to create a more sizable church, as happened at Diokaisareia in Isauria, or the disassembly of the temple's blocks to build a larger basilica, as at Aphrodisias, also in Karia. The conversion may have been fairly recent in Cyriacus' day, as Mylasa's Greek Christian population adjusted to reduced circumstances under Muslim rule. The neighborhood around the Temple of Augustus became the "Rum" district, that is, the Roman (Greek) quarter of town.[61]

A final piece of evidence points toward a secular function for the Temple of Augustus in late antiquity, while confirming that it remained part of an active neighborhood: new texts were added to the podium wall in the fifth century.[62] These were not Christian graffiti, but letters from government officials concerning taxation, a late example of the centuries-old Anatolian practice of inscribing important documents on temple walls, as we have just seen with the Priene dossier. Letters of Theodosios II (in both Latin and Greek) and his *comes sacrarum largitionum* Flavius Eudoxius were inscribed around 427 CE, bestowing tax-free status on Mylasa's harbor.[63] This was a major economic boon and a privilege Mylasa was no doubt eager to broadcast—especially as the document was from the emperor himself. Then, in 480 CE, the praetorian prefect Flavius Illus Pusaeus Dionysius declared that his *Forma generalis* (resolving a tax dispute) should be inscribed in every Karian city; it was added to the Temple of Augustus.[64] The inscription breaks with older epigraphic habits by being inscribed in lengthy lines (c. 4.5 m), rather than divided into columns, as was customary in the Hellenistic and Roman periods. This was not an antiquarian attempt to imitate past epigraphic practice but rather an

---

[60] Pococke 1745, Pl. 55.
[61] Usta 2018: 45.
[62] Rumscheid 2004, Figs. 9, 10, and 11. There may have been additional inscriptions: Pococke 1745: 61 says that he saw "several defaced inscriptions, with the cross on them" on the stones of the temple. But none of the published texts shows cross graffiti.
[63] *I.Mylasa* 611, 612. Note, however, that bureaucratic documents could also be inscribed on church walls: see Kasai below. But they were more likely to be set up along public streets: Feissel 2009; Feissel 2010.
[64] *I.Mylasa* 613; Feissel 1994.

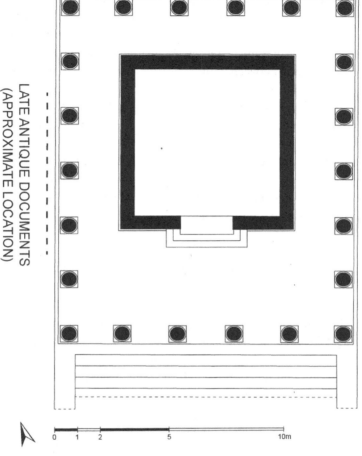

Figure 3.6 Mylasa. Plan of the Temple of Augustus and Roma. Approximate locations of *I.Mylasa* 613 on the podium indicated. Author and Yasmin Nachtigall, after Rumscheid 2004, Fig. 17.

up-to-date means of (performatively) communicating official rulings—even if the lengthy text was actually rarely read.

Several factors, then, speak against the ecclesiastical conversion of the Temple of Augustus in Mylasa in late antiquity: the depaganized temple may have served an administrative or archival function, in line with Libanios of

Antioch's recommendation that temples be converted into tax offices.[65] On the other hand, this temple may have served a bureaucratic function under the auspices of local ecclesiastical leaders: at Laodikeia on the Lykos, the vaulted subterranean room of Temple A apparently became a church archive. A door was opened between it and a nearby church, and many lead seals of the late antique period were excavated there.[66] Regardless, the temple's dedication to Augustus, son of a god, and to the goddess Roma on the architrave remained on display for Mylasa's late antique inhabitants: it is clearly legible in the eighteenth-century drawing.[67] This historic dedication may have added legitimacy to the bureaucratic documents now inscribed on the temple. There would, of course, have been no reason to remove this inscription: imperial names, like imperial statuary, were not often damaged or erased, save for damnatio memoriae.

A Fallen God at Magnesia on the Maeander

Mylasa was not the only city to use the wall space of a temple as a billboard for official documents in late antiquity. Not far away, at Magnesia on the Maeander, the small Temple of Zeus Sosipolis in the agora gained an administrative document (a lengthy tax register) on its exterior cella wall, even as the god Zeus continued to sit on his throne in the cella (Figure 3.7). The inscription dates either to the early fourth century (shortly after Diocletian reorganized the tax system) or more likely to the mid-fourth.[68] Inscribed in columns across seven meters of the wall, this document recorded properties in the territory of Magnesia belonging to both small-scale landholders and large estates. The text joined an earlier one (second century BCE) on the temple anta, which outlined cult regulations for the public worship of Zeus, Artemis Leukophryene, and Apollo.[69] Again, the ancient inscription provided a precedent of what we might call "visual bureaucracy" for the late antique document, lending this later text the legitimacy of a long tradition of

---

[65] *Oratio* 30.42. See also Talloen and Vercauteren 2011: 358–363 and Jacobs 2013: 293.
[66] Şimşek 2018: 93–94.
[67] Duggan 2019: 151–152 argues that the architrave inscription never existed but was a fiction added by early modern artists to identify the structure. But given its consistent presence in representations (including Pococke's drawing) on the uppermost fascia of the architrave (exactly where we would expect it), there is no reason to doubt.
[68] *I.Magnesia* 122; Thonemann 2007: 438, 441; Harper 2008: 86–88; Huttner 2018: 10–11, 21–31.
[69] *I.Magnesia* 98.

Figure 3.7 Magnesia on the Maeander. Temple of Zeus Sosipolis, section reconstruction. Humann 1904, Fig. 165.

documentary display. The wall of the stoa immediately opposite the Temple of Zeus was itself the setting of an extensive Hellenistic dossier concerning the festival of Artemis Leukophryene.[70]

Although the settlement at Magnesia in late antiquity remains obscure, the city's agora was still active in the 360s, given a base dedicated to the emperor Julian (later erased) near the temple's opisthodomos and the presence of at least one Christian graffito.[71] The cult statue of Zeus was found in pieces on the floor of the temple cella, including fragments of the head- and beard-hair.[72] He may perhaps have been pulled from his perch and shattered on the floor as an intentional act of religious violence, but it is more likely that the collapse of the entire structure (at an uncertain date) did the deed. We can assume that the temple was in good order when the land register was inscribed on it in the fourth century and when the base dedicated to Julian was set up nearby. Even if the Magnesians did not necessarily share Julian's pagan sympathies (and they may have), it could hardly have been appropriate to set up a dedication to any emperor next to a ruined structure. A "merel

---

[70] *I.Magnesia* 16–87.
[71] *I.Magnesia* 201 (Julian); *I.Magnesia* 239b (graffito). For the location of the base to Julian (Humann's "fünfte Basis," 158) see the excavation plan of the agora (Humann 1904 Blatt III). Büyükkolancı 2018: 401–402 argues that the "Byzantine walls" encircling Magnesia on the Maeander more likely date to the 260s.
[72] Humann 1904: 155, Fig. 167.

game" graffito (a circle divided into equal portions by spokes, resembling a millwheel) is inscribed on the cella floor of the Temple of Zeus Sosipolis, perhaps indicating the shrine had lost its sacrality probably even as the statue of Zeus sat in place and certainly prior to the collapse of the entire building (Figure 3.8).[73] Another game circle of the same type is carved on the pronaos paving. We may tentatively propose that at least until 363 (the year of Julian's death), the temple, its texts, and cult statue remained on display as the use of the space shifted.

Congregated Graffiti at Delphi

The inscribing of documents on the walls of structures, whether in the ancient or late antique periods, was primarily a phenomenon of Asia Minor (leaving aside here the text-saturated walls of ancient Egyptian pharaonic temples, which we will come to in due course). Crete too had an early tradition of inscribing buildings.[74] The blocks of the famous Law Code of Gortyn, first carved on a curved structure in the first half of the fifth century BCE, were reused in the first century BCE to construct an odeon in the city's agora, with the blocks carefully numbered to preserve their original order.[75] The text presumably remained on display in late antiquity as the settlement at Gortyn transformed into a major episcopal site. Other regions of the eastern Mediterranean were not likely to inscribe lengthy documents at all (at least not on permanent materials). Few civic, royal, or imperial decrees are known from the Levant; the epigraphic habit there tended more toward short honorific dedications. There are of course some exceptions. At Baitokaike (Hosn Soleiman, Syria), a retrospective dossier of privileges for the sanctuary of Zeus was engraved in the mid-third century CE on a wall block to the right of the monumental entrance to the temenos. It included both Greek and Latin components: a Seleukid letter, a civic decree sent to Augustus, and the confirmation of royal privileges by Valerian and Galienus. In the Hellenistic

---

[73] Humann 1904: 157 and Fig. 152. Heimann and Schädler 2014 question whether "merel game" circles really were board games: the play gets into a "loop" without any way to win unless a player makes a significant mistake. Jacobs 2013: 618–619 argues that they are actually Christian symbols, or may have been read as such—yet they only appear on horizontal surfaces, as other game boards. Clearly, a more comprehensive study is needed, but I remain with the traditional view that they are game boards.
[74] Perlman 2004.
[75] *I.Cret.* IV 72. Marginesu 2014: 210–211; Zavagno 2017: 143.

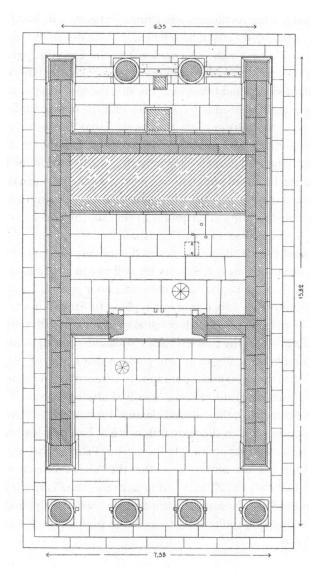

Figure 3.8 Magnesia on the Maeander. Temple of Zeus Sosipolis, plan. Humann 1904, Pl. 18.

text (in Greek), King Antiochos was amenable because he had heard about "the activity of the god Zeus of Baitokaike."[76] This dossier joined dedications at the site, including a well-preserved one to the Θεῷ Βαιτοχειχει (god of Baitokaike) in clear letters over another entrance.[77] By the sixth, a monastery with attendant village had taken over the site; the sanctuary was given over to agriculture and the production of lime, with the dossier and dedications left on display.[78] Mt. Hermon (Jabal al-Shaykh/Jabal Haramun), which sits at the meeting point of modern-day Syria, Lebanon, and the Israeli-occupied Golan Heights, housed numerous sanctuaries constructed in the Roman imperial period by its mixed population of Jews and pagans. Pagan cult seems to have continued into the fifth or sixth century; in any case, numerous temples and dedications/building inscriptions (primarily in Greek) continued to stand even as some villages turned Christian.[79]

In mainland Greece, dedications and documents were more likely to be written on stelai or bases, which, as we will see in the following chapter, were commonly reused as building material in our period. But on occasion, inscribed monuments were preserved in place. In Athens, many statues and their bases seem to have kept their original spots into the fifth century, at least those standing within the Post-Herulian Wall, although significant changes in the city's built fabric began to take place in that century.[80] Athens leveraged its classical monumental topography to attract affluent young men to its philosophical schools until Justinian finally shuttered them in 529 CE. Even the Athena Promachos, the colossal classical bronze on the Acropolis, may have still been in place in the early fifth century, based on an inscription of 408–10 CE for a statue set up "next to Promachos Pallas (Athena) of the city of Kekrops."[81] It is unclear, however, whether the Pallas Promachos referred to was the original statue of Athena, but in any case, Lena Lambrinou has now argued that the Parthenon underwent an extremely careful, and conservative, restoration using spolia after it was burnt, probably by the Herulians in

---

[76] *IGLS* 7.4028, l. C18b: περὶ τῆς ἐνεργείας θεοῦ Διὸς Βαιτοκαικης.
[77] *IGLS* 7.4031, 223/224 CE.
[78] Ahmad 2018: 48.
[79] Gregg and Ûrman 1996; Aliquot 2008; *IGLS* 11.
[80] If this wall does indeed date to the decades after the Herulian attack in 267 CE, and not much later: Baldini and Bazzechi 2016. Regardless, the Agora, which lay outside of the Post-Herulian Wall, has produced very few inscriptions in situ: nearly all were reused as spolia, some already in antiquity. For Athens in late antiquity: Saradi and Eliopoulos 2011: 265–281; Bazzechi 2016; Tanaseanu-Döbler and von Alvensleben 2020; Deligiannakis 2021.
[81] *IG* II/III² 5, 13284, l. 4: παρὰ προμάχῳ Παλλάδι Κεκροπίη[ς] (my trans. after Klaus Hallof); Burkhardt 2016: 123–133.

267 CE: older monuments were still highly valued.[82] The Palace of the Giants, constructed in the Agora around the same time as the Promachos Pallas statue dedication, likewise made use of older marble figures of Giants and Tritons as supports for the façade, indicating again a tolerant approach to the city's patrimony. The choragic monument of Lysikrates famously still stands at the heart of Athens today, bearing its inscribed commemoration of a musical contest in 335/334 BCE.[83] Elsewhere in the city, the Arch of Hadrian bears a text on each face: that toward the Acropolis declares "This is Athens, the ancient city of Theseus"; the other reads "This is the city of Hadrian, not of Theseus."[84] Hadrian, like Augustus and Alexander, was well known in late antiquity; although often criticized, his construction activity across the empire was remembered.[85] Cross graffiti and traces of Christian painting suggest that the arch was a living monument, updated as the sacred canopy shifted.[86]

The sanctuary and city of Delphi in central Greece seem to have had a quicker decline than Athens. The sanctuary shows little identifiable construction or renovation activity in late antiquity: there was, so far as we can tell, no attempt to curate the ancient monuments or inscriptions at the core of the sanctuary, as we saw in the interventions on the Embolos in Ephesos. Instead, many of Delphi's ancient structures, such as the heavily inscribed Treasury of the Athenians, stood in place until they collapsed, mostly at uncertain dates. The oracle—the site's main draw in earlier periods—was in decline already from the second century onward, as it failed to adapt to the new desire for more theologically oriented divine pronouncements, such as those delivered by Didyma and Klaros.[87] Three churches were constructed, although not in the Temple of Apollo itself.[88] Also to the south, the so-called Roman agora revitalized the fringe of the sanctuary. One Christian tombstone was found. At some point, the metopes of the Tholos standing in the sanctuary of Athena Pronaia at a short distance from the main sanctuary were chiseled, apparently in an act of Christian iconoclasm.[89] The polis of Delphi, which surrounded the sanctuary, was suffering by 424: a rescript in

---

[82] Lambrinou 2015; see also Tanoulas 2020: 104–106.
[83] *IG* II/III² 3,1.3042.
[84] *IG* II/III² 3,1.5185.
[85] Destephen 2019.
[86] Kouremenos 2022: 354–355.
[87] Heineman 2018.
[88] For Christian Delphi: Laurent 1899; Déroche 1989; Robertson Brown 2016.
[89] Pollini 2013: 7.

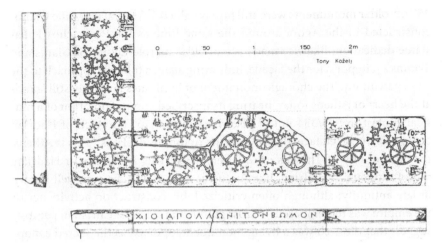

Figure 3.9 Delphi. Altar of the Chians. Amandry 1981, Fig. 60. Courtesy of the École française d'Athènes. © Hellenic Ministry of Culture and Sports / Archaeological Resources Fund.

the *Codex Theodosianus* cryptically stated that the city "has often been exhausted by new kinds of losses" and absolved it of other duties.[90] A limited number of imperial dedications were set up at the sanctuary in the fourth century, including to Constantine, who had in fact snatched a number of Delphi's ancient treasures for his new capital. These late antique dedications at Delphi took their places among the thousands of freestanding inscriptions and inscribed monuments, but unfortunately the precise situation of much of the site in this period is unclear because of later Byzantine disturbances and the *"grande fouille,"* which cleared a great deal of the stratigraphy between 1893 and 1903.

Only at one spot in the heart of the main sanctuary did the new religion leave prominent marks. The upper surface of the Altar of the Chians, standing directly in front of the Temple of Apollo, is positively *covered* with cross graffiti and carved circles with spokes (Figure 3.9).[91] Cross graffiti is not common at the site, but here the Christian symbol is present in such numbers that many crosses overlap each other. The circles resemble the "merel game"

---

[90] *C.Th.* 15.5.4.
[91] Amandry 1981: 739, Fig. 60.

graffiti (discussed above), but a number of them appear to imitate Chi-Rhos overlaid on crosses, suggesting a specifically Christian meaning in this context. Were these symbols meant to desacralize or purify the most prominent altar to Apollo? Did the spot take on a Christian significance? We have no way of knowing. But in any case, the altar was not destroyed. While its flat top was covered in Christian graffiti, the dedication on the crowning molding, reading, "The Chians (dedicated) the altar to Apollo" in clear, well-spaced lettering of the Classical period, is untouched, even the prominent name of Apollo.[92] So far as I am aware, none of the thousands of inscriptions at Delphi shows erasures attributable to Christian editing. The late antique inhabitants of Delphi were apparently quite comfortable with the written dedications, treaties, decrees, and manumissions surrounding them.

Secular or Sacred? Imperial Documents on Temples of Uncertain Use

It is clear from the above examples that unconverted temples could preserve their ancient inscriptions—even dedications to pagan gods and emperors—during the period of "Christianization." But what about temples converted to churches? Were their pagan-era inscriptions tolerated? In some instances, yes: a number of sanctuaries went over to Christian use but preserved ancient, even pagan texts, as we will see. The dating of this Christian appropriation can be difficult to establish, as in the following two enigmatic cases. The Temple of Augustus and Roma at Ankara and that of Zeus at Aizanoi were both excavated by Daniel Krencker and Martin Schede in the 1920s; by chance, these two temples also exhibit many of the same ambiguities in their Christian-era afterlives. Long assumed to have been converted into churches in late antiquity, it has recently been suggested that both temples were transformed only in the seventh century or later. It is therefore fruitful to consider these two sites together. I ultimately argue that the conversions make the most sense in the context of late antiquity, but regardless, both continued to display Roman documents of local and transregional significance during this period.

---

[92] *F.Delphes* III 3.212.

The *Res Gestae divi Augusti* in Late Antique Ankara

The *Res Gestae divi Augusti*, crowned the "Queen of Inscriptions," is still visible in Ankara (ancient Ancyra or Ankyra) today in both Latin original and Greek copies, carved on the walls of the Temple of Augustus and Roma (constructed in the decades before Augustus' death in 14 CE). This lengthy, autobiographical account of the first Roman emperor details his remarkable political achievements, foreign and civil wars won, and impressive array of buildings built. The heading of the Greek copy reads in large letters: "The deeds and gifts of the god Augustus, which he left behind engraved on two bronze stelai at Rome, translated and written below."[93] The Greek text is written in nineteen columns on the exterior southeastern wall of the temple's cella; the Latin text flanks the entrance to the temple on the north and south pronaos walls, three columns apiece.

Like the other inscriptions discussed in this chapter, the *Res Gestae* shows no intentional damage, though it has been scarred by digging for metal clamps and by the building of later walls abutting the temple. In continuously populated Ankara, the capital of Turkey, no other epigraphic monument of antiquity survived in situ to the present. The majority of inscribed blocks from within the ancient polis ended up as spolia in Byzantine and later construction projects, or collapsed and were buried under subsequent buildings. But the Temple of Augustus and its texts weathered the changes over the centuries. At some point, the temple seems to have become a church: an inscription of the ninth/tenth century on the north interior wall of the temple's opisthodomos records the burial of the *hegoumenos* of a monastery. Other Byzantine inscriptions from the ninth and tenth centuries on the inner and outer walls of the cella likewise record Christian burials. The decisive turning point in the building's preservation history came in late antiquity. What was the status of the building in that period? Whether or not the temple was converted into a church impacts how the *Res Gestae* may have been read.

The Temple of Augustus' biography requires contextualization within the polis of Ankara, the capital of the late Roman province of Galatia (Prima) and a critical node on the land route connecting Constantinople with the east, used by military troops and pilgrims headed toward the Holy Land.[94]

---

[93] *I.Ancyra* 1, heading (ed. Mitchell and French 2012): Μεθηρμηνευμέναι ὑπεγράφησαν πράξεις τε καὶ δωρεαὶ Σεβαστοῦ θεοῦ, ἃς ἀπέλιπεν ἐπὶ Ῥώμης ἐνκεχαραγμένας χαλκαῖς στήλαις δυσίν (trans. after Cooley 2009: 28–29). For the display of the *Res Gestae* at Ankara: Hesberg 2009: 20–22; Mitchell and French 2012: 144–150; Roels 2018: 221–223; Botteri 2018a.

[94] Foss 1977: 30–31; French 2016, Map 3a. Belke 2017: 28–38.

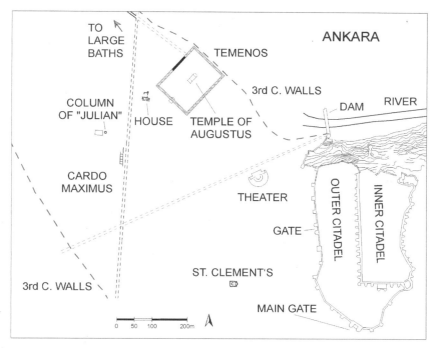

Figure 3.10 Ankara. Plan of the archaeological remains of the city. Author and Yasmin Nachtigall, modified from Kadıoğlu, Görkay, and Mitchell 2011.

The city was almost the seat of the 325 church council, before it was moved to Nicaea. Constantine's criteria for selecting the council's location seem to have been both convenience (for him) and the need for a festive and impressive setting for his *vicennalia* celebration, perhaps meant to woo bishops into imperial cooperation; Eusebius of Caesarea at least was duly impressed by Constantine's dinner party.[95] Ankara was clearly considered a suitably imposing imperial gathering place, and several emperors in the fourth century intermittently resided there (Figure 3.10). The city maintained its status in late antiquity as a Christian center, albeit one with a large proportion of heterodox congregations, particularly Montanists.[96] Ankara's luck turned in the seventh century, as in so many proud poleis of Anatolia. A Persian incursion devastated the city—if a highly rhetorical epigram from the period of

---

[95] Eusebius *Vita Constantini* 3.15.
[96] Mitchell 2005: 1–12; Serin 2018: 338; *I.Ancyra* 411.

98 PAGAN INSCRIPTIONS, CHRISTIAN VIEWERS

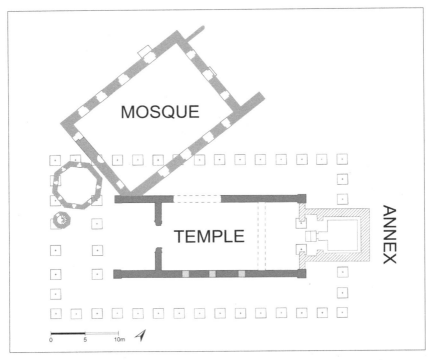

Figure 3.11 Ankara. Temple of Augustus, current state plan. Author, after Krencker and Schede 1936, Pl. 2.

Michael III (r. 842–867), referring to a city "stained with blood of old by the hands of the Persians," can be taken at face value.[97] The city was briefly taken by Arab forces in 838 before returning to Byzantine control and undergoing a massive program of fortification, dedicated in 859.

Krencker and Schede's 1920s excavations of the Temple of Augustus and Roma identified a rectangular, vaulted annex built off of the temple's northeastern termination as a late antique church apse, constructed from reddish and whitish stones after the rear cella wall had been completely removed (Figure 3.11).[98] They designated the hollow substructure of the annex as a crypt for the relics of a saint. Although crypts underneath church apses were not a feature of the architectural vocabulary in Anatolia, several late antique churches in Constantinople, such as the Studios basilica and Hagios

[97] *I.Ancyra* 325, *ll*. 1–2 (trans. Mitchell and French).
[98] Krencker and Schede 1936: 32–35.

Figure 3.12 Ankara. Temple of Augustus, view of the annex from the exterior (permit no. 64298988-155.02E.218252). Author, courtesy of the Turkish Ministry of Culture and Tourism.

Polyeuktos, did have them.[99] But the central access stairway facing into the nave at Ankara is not paralleled in the capital. Moreover, the red-and-white-striped masonry (double-faced with a rubble core) of the annex superstructure only resembles the late antique construction technique of alternating red brick with stone but is structurally dissimilar (Figure 3.12). The architecture of the annex is vexed by irregularities, to the point that its identification as a church apse is now, in my view, untenable. Stephen Mitchell laid out its problematic elements in 2008 and proposed that the annex is instead an Ottoman *iwan*, an open-air room in a medrese (the building was called the Ak Medrese in the Ottoman period); another possibility, given that the annex sits above a crypt/cellar, is an *iwan*-form tomb, as suggested by Kutalmış Görkay in 2012.[100] The matter is not closed, however. Urs Peschlow maintained the identification of the annex as a church apse in 2015, but dated it to post-838.[101] He admitted, however, that the "apse" has no parallels in

---

[99] For these and further examples, see Mathews 1972: 27; 32–33; 54; 57–60.
[100] S. Mitchell 2008: 30; Görkay 2012: 205; Sitz 2019a: 655–657.
[101] Peschlow 2015: 37–46.

that period either. Ufuk Serin likewise identifies the annex as a church apse, dated to the seventh century or later, when in her view enemy attacks caused the residents of Ankara to abandon more distant churches and take over the temple.[102] In each of these scenarios, the temple remained unconverted prior to the seventh century.

With the redating, if not reinterpretation, of the annex, essentially no evidence for the late antique period at the Temple of Augustus remains. According to Peschlow, a hypothetical earthquake of the fifth century brought down the peristasis of the temple (now completely missing; even most of the foundations have been stripped).[103] Or, according to Mitchell and David French, the peristasis may have been intentionally removed to depaganize the structure by making it look less like a temple.[104] They furthermore propose that the temple of the imperial cult was reconceptualized as a secularized shrine of empire in late antiquity. In their view, it was the presence of the *Res Gestae* itself, essentially the founding document of the Roman empire, that motivated the careful preservation of the monument. Intentionally removing the peristasis to alter the temple's pagan appearance, however, would require a major restructuring of the roof; Peschlow's hypothesis of an accidental collapse is more economical. Perhaps at the time of the peristasis' disappearance, much of the uppermost two courses of the cella walls (the courses above the frieze) were removed; presumably a new trussed timber roof was made.[105] The floor was lowered within the cella at some point before the ninth or tenth century, when a Byzantine grave inscription was carved low down on the interior wall of the cella, near the level of the Roman floor.[106] The excavators found only scant traces of a secondary floor at the western end of the cella, associated with a threshold set into the Roman door (lower than the missing Roman threshold).[107] In another sondage (G) in the center-rear of the cella, no remains of any floor, even the substratum, were found; nor was evidence of the epigraphically attested graves in the cella/opisthodomos uncovered.[108] We can perhaps attribute this total removal of

---

[102] Serin 2011: 1274; Serin 2018: 344–347, 357.

[103] Peschlow 2015: 45, 77 proposes a fifth-century earthquake because of a steep drop-off of coins at Ankara's Large Baths in that period; an earthquake would also explain an inscription recording the restoration of various buildings (*I.Ancyra* 334), though this interpretation is not without its difficulties (Mitchell and French 2019: 85).

[104] Mitchell and French 2019: 247. See now also Mitchell 2022.

[105] Peschlow 2015: 37–38; see also Görkay 2012: 214.

[106] *I.Ancyra* 501 (see further below).

[107] Krencker and Schede 1936, Pl. 33c; Sondage F on Plate 3.

[108] Both Sondage F and Sondage B should have hit the graves, based on the epitaphs on the wall: Krencker and Schede 1936: 32. The sarcophagus visible in Krencker and Schede's section (Plate 6) in

the cella's secondary floor and its bedding to the period of the medrese; it may have been imperative to be sure that no Byzantine bodies were hiding just out of sight. Despite the lack of archaeological data for the date of the transformation of the Temple of Augustus, I maintain that the conversion to a church may well have taken place in late antiquity. The reasons for this dating are three: the topography of Ankara, broader architectural trends in building reuse, and the city's highly Christianized atmosphere in the sixth century.

First, the urban topography. The neighborhood around the Temple of Augustus was vibrant in the sixth century: a monument known as the Column of "Julian," located approximately two hundred meters from the temple (about three minutes' walking distance), was probably (re)dedicated to Justinian, based on its carefully carved sixth-century capital, and a few meters away, shops lining the city's *cardo maximus* received a rich pavement of *opus sectile* in the late fifth or early sixth century.[109] After the 838 Arab attack of the city, however, Ankara seems to have abandoned its third-century CE city walls and contracted to a newly fortified area on the city's natural acropolis, comprising an inner and an outer citadel, both apparently built by Michael III and dedicated in 859 (although some have proposed an earlier, seventh-century phase to these walls, motivated by the Persian and early Arab incursions in that century).[110] The citadel fortifications make extensive use of ancient marble, with particularly fetching spolia arranged for decorative effect.[111] The Temple of Augustus itself is likewise surrounded by a thick defensive wall also built of spolia, which follows in the preserved section the original Roman temenos wall. Although this fortification wall cannot be dated, it may be coeval with the citadel walls.[112] The temple lies at a substantial distance from the main gate of the outer citadel; the only other Byzantine monument known from Ankara, the cruciform Church of St. Clement, probably of the ninth century, is located closer to the gate (and therefore closer to safety).[113] If the Temple of Augustus were simply an abandoned structure in

---

a disturbed placement had a water hole carved into it, suggesting that it had been repurposed before being moved into the cella.

[109] Kadıoğlu, Görkay, and Mitchell 2011: 225–238. The "Column of Julian" was moved from its original position in 1934 and now stands even closer to the temple.
[110] Ninth century: Peschlow 2015: 139–186; Mitchell and French 2019: 1; seventh century: Foss 1977: 74–75; Serin 2018: 355–356.
[111] Pallis 2019: 61–65, Fig. 1.
[112] Serin 2018: 358–362; Peschlow 2015: 245–249.
[113] For this church, see Peschlow 2015: 187–232; Serin 2014: 65–92.

this period, its shining white marble blocks could have provided an attractive source of spolia or lime for the new citadel walls. Moreover, converting the building into a church that would immediately require a program of extensive fortification is impractical. The effort put into constructing this thick wall (with a probable total length of more than four hundred meters) may have been easier to justify if the structure was already a significant ecclesiastical presence in the beleaguered city.

Second, and more significant than Ankara's local topography, are wider trends in the reuse of buildings in Byzantine Anatolia. Reuse was, of course, widespread in every period. But ecclesiastical reuse was *sui generis*. Whereas in late antiquity, churches could be installed in all manner of older buildings (temples, baths, bouleuteria, etc.) in addition to being built *ex novo*, this was not the case in the medieval period. The ideal of a church had fossilized to the point that certain architectural types or a degree of ecclesiastical continuity were expected. Post-seventh-century churches either were typically built within the ruins of late antique basilicas (indicating continuity of sacred space), or were constructed on a new site from the ground up (in which case a distinctive ecclesiastical building form was created, as with St. Clement's in Ankara). Examples for buildings newly converted in the Middle Byzantine period are lacking. The closest candidate in Anatolia is a twelfth- or thirteenth-century chapel installed in the tepidarium of a Roman bath at Sinope, known as the Balatlar Kilisesi.[114] But the caldarium next door was probably already a church in late antiquity, so the structure as a whole may have been understood as sacred space. Bayliss's catalogue of temple destructions and conversions provides no example of a temple in the east Christianized later than the seventh century.[115] The decision to take a previously unconverted temple and transform it into a church in the ninth century would be exceptional—excluding the tenuous late date of the conversion of the Temple of Zeus at Aizanoi, discussed below.

At Ankara, converting the temple into a church entailed either removing completely the rear cella wall (it is now missing) or at least carefully carving through this wall in order to open onto an apse, perhaps located in the opisthodomos. The location of three windows carved into the southeastern cella wall favors the later possibility: the windows were carved when the rear cella wall was still in place, because they are roughly centered within the cella.

---

[114] Köroğlu et al. 2019: 22–23; Köroğlu, İnanan, and Alper 2014.
[115] Excluding an eighteenth-century conversion at Deir al Kalaa in Lebanon. In the west, temple conversions continued unabated into the Middle Ages.

The windows are surely post-construction additions to the building, rather than an original design feature of the Temple of Augustus, since they are carved through horizontally laid ashlar blocks, rather than being delineated by headers and footers or by blocks set as an arch, as was typical in Roman building practice.[116] Even the grates were hewn, impressively, directly from the ashlars of the temple wall. An arched opening onto an apse may have likewise been carved directly from the temple rear cella wall using the same technique of cutting through the preexisting ashlars. This would have been a major project requiring a building team with the requisite engineering "know-how"; so too would the construction of a new trussed wooden roof, common in late antique basilicas but less so in the Middle Byzantine period, when vaulted roofing of ecclesiastical spaces was the norm.[117] Given the paucity of comparable building projects in the Middle Byzantine period, the construction techniques needed to convert the Temple of Augustus into a church fit better in late antiquity.

Thirdly, Ankara was by the sixth century a thoroughly Christianized city. While in the fourth century, Ankara's elite remained part of a larger network of traditional *paideia* and Hellenic culture, as attested in the letters of Libanios of Antioch, by the sixth century, the self-representation and euergetic activity of Ankara's upper class was explicitly Christian.[118] The epigraphic material from both elite and common graves, such as those recently excavated in the city's Maltepe neighborhood, indicates the importance of projecting a Christian identity.[119] Even a late fifth-century grave stone belonging to a woman named "Aphrodite" is emblazoned with crosses and the phrase "servant of god"; paganism was so passé that Aphrodite could bear not just a theophoric name, but the very name of the former goddess herself.[120] The city's public spaces were likewise marked by Christian messages: the emperors Arcadius and Honorius set up a sizable inscription with a prayer, accompanied by a cross, between 395 and 402.[121] Probably during the reign of Justinian, the entire city was publicly dedicated to the

---

[116] Krencker and Schede 1936: 32. Contra Mitchell and French 2019: 247–248, who suggest that the window may be an original feature of the temple architecture.

[117] Ousterhout 2019: 93–99.

[118] Foss 1977: 51–58; S. Mitchell 2017a: 129; Mitchell and French 2019: 11–12; 15.

[119] Aydın and Zoroğlu 2016: 295–328.

[120] *I.Ancyra* 431. Although pagan theophoric names continued to be common among Christians (Mazzoleni 2015: 451), the direct use of a goddess's name (Aphrodite, Artemis, Hera, etc.) was rare after the third century, according to searches of the *Inscriptiones Christianae Graecae* and *Lexikon of Greek Personal Names* databases.

[121] *I.Ancyra* 333.

Theotokos in an unusual text inscribed on an architrave, in which the city's traditional designation as Ἡ μητρόπολις τῆς Γαλατίας (The metropolis of Galatia) is supplanted by its new Christian designation: [† Ἡ πό]λις † | [† τῆς Ἁγίας] Θεοτόκου † | [† Ἄγκ]υρα. † (The polis of the holy Theotokos, Ankara).[122] The surviving material represents only a tiny portion of Ankara's patrimony, and surely some individuals maintained traditional beliefs. But to all appearances, Ankara was by the sixth century a fully Christian city. The conversion of the Temple of Augustus would be on brand.

But what about the imperial import of the building? Might this not have functioned as a deterrent to ecclesiastical appropriation? Perhaps—in the fourth and early fifth centuries, when the imperial cult continued in one form or another, and several cities displayed monuments to the imperial family. But imperial cult temples and other monuments were not immune to decay, deconstruction, and appropriation even before emperor worship had fallen fully by the wayside. The Temple of Antoninus Pius at Sagalassos was in ruins by the late fourth/early fifth century, its blocks divvied up for domestic construction; Aphrodisias' Sebasteion was used for shops from the mid-fourth century onward and the imperial cult temple itself taken apart in the late fifth or sixth century; the Great Church at Miletos replaced the imperial cult temple in the second half of the sixth century; at Pessinus, in Ankara's neighboring province of Galatia Salutaris, the architectural elements of a probable imperial cult temple found their way into various late antique and Byzantine construction projects.[123] Farther afield, the Temple of Augustus and Roma at Caesarea Maritima in Palaestina was built over by an octagonal church between 525 and 550.[124] In late antiquity, emperors were honored through statue monuments, acclamations, and ephemeral processions—not in large-scale, single-use imperial cult structures. In the sixth century, cityscapes as a whole took on a distinctively Christian appearance, with churches now articulating city centers; poetic descriptions of cities increasingly focused on their Christian associations, rather than the classical monuments of old.[125] Imperial processions in Constantinople maintained imperial fora along the Mese as stopping points, but it was the chapels located there that defined the path; Hagia Sophia became the terminus of triumphal parades.[126]

---

[122] I.Ancyra 323.
[123] Sagalassos: see Chapter 4, p. 166; Aphrodisias: Ogus 2018: 174–177. Miletos: Niewöhner 2016: 5–35; Pessinus: Verlinde 2015: 246, 303–326.
[124] Patrich 2011: 104–105.
[125] Saradi 2006: 47–70.
[126] Bauer 1996: 380–382; Bauer 2001: 46–61.

If the Temple of Augustus in Ankara was still standing as an unconverted monument of empire in the sixth century, it would have been literally out of place: increasingly left out of religious or political processions, and perhaps dropped from rhetorical descriptions of the city as well.

But what about the *Res Gestae* itself, written on the walls of the temple? Might such an explicitly imperial, political, and even pagan text from the "god Augustus" have precluded the building's use as a church? Not necessarily. While Augustus himself continued to be the object of pagan cult in late antiquity and was commemorated by writers such as Eutropios (fl. c. 360) as the first ruler to bring together the entire Roman empire (and was even occasionally criticized as a tyrant), the first emperor was increasingly regarded as an integral part of Christian history.[127] The Gospel of Luke states that "a decree went out from Caesar Augustus that all the world should be registered," which ensured Augustus' perpetual association with the birth of Christ.[128] Late antique legends added to this association: in one widely spread tale, Augustus receives an oracle in which Apollo proclaims that a "Hebrew child" has come to rule the heavens; the emperor subsequently erects an altar to the "firstborn god" on the Capitoline Hill.[129] Early Christian thinkers took this connection further: Octavian's unification of the entire Mediterranean had paved the way for Christ's apostles to proselytize broadly. As Origen (c. 185–253 CE) wrote, if there had been constant warfare in the decades after Christ's resurrection, his disciples would not have been able to spread the "good news."[130] Melito of Sardis (d. ca. 180 CE) took correlation as causation: he attributed the remarkable flourishing of the Roman empire in the first and second centuries after Christ precisely *to* the birth of the savior and the growing Christian community.[131] The empire was not simply the context for the rise of Christianity, but was the *result* of it. Kosmas Indikopleustes, rounding off his long excursus on the Ptolemies, their inscription(s) at Adulis, and the prophecies of *Daniel* (Chapter 2), concluded that the Old Testament did not foretell the Roman empire because it "participates in the dignity of the Kingdom of the Lord Christ, seeing that it transcends ... every other power, and will remain unconquered until the final consummation."[132]

---

[127] Eutropios *Breviarum* 7.1–10. Augustus in late antiquity: Fishwick 1990: 475–477; Simić 2018; Sloan 2018; Tougher 2018; Augustus as tyrant: Roberto 2015.
[128] *Luke* 2:1, English Standard Version.
[129] Moralee 2018: 99–102; Boeye and Pandey 2018.
[130] Origen *Contra Celsum* 2.30.
[131] Apud Eusebius *Historia Ecclesiastica* 4.26.7–8.
[132] *Christian Topography* 2.71 (trans. McCrindle).

It was therefore possible to read the *Res Gestae*, like the figure of the first emperor himself, from two different perspectives in late antiquity, tied to broader historiographic trends and divergent worldviews: that of classicizing history and that of ecclesiastical history. From the point of view of a reader with an interest in classicizing historiography, the *Res Gestae* was a critical witness to the rise of the empire and the greatness of Rome, which could also function as a "book of princes," offering a positive example for later emperors. Indeed, references to Augustus as an imperial prototype increased during the reign of Justinian, who attempted to reunite the Mediterranean under his rule.[133] From the perspective of ecclesiastical history, however, the *Res Gestae* was not simply a historical record of empire; Augustus' "accomplishments" attested God's providence. This was a document integral to the rise of the church.

But was the *Res Gestae* actually read in our period? The evidence tentatively points toward the affirmative. Suetonius, who referred to the *Res Gestae divi Augusti* in his biography of that emperor, was certainly still read and may have had a significant influence on Ammianus Marcellinus, who wrote his own history simply called the *Res Gestae*.[134] Ammianus was a military man and probably passed through Ankara, perhaps in the accompaniment of Julian, who paused at the city in 362 on the way to his fateful encounter with the Sassanians.[135] Julian seems to have stayed in Ankara a couple of weeks, and both the emperor and a man of historical interests, such as Ammianus, must have surely visited the Temple of Augustus. Was the title of Ammianus' classicizing history a transtextual adoption from his reading of the *Res Gestae divi Augusti* in Ankara? Another indication that the *Res Gestae* inscription was read is a Latin dedication to Julian made at Ankara by the praetorian prefect Saturninius Secundus in 362, which reads in part: "For the master of the whole world, Iulianus Augustus, having traversed in a single season the span from the British Ocean to the river Tigris."[136] As Mitchell and French note, this hyperbolic claim (Julian had not in fact yet reached the Tigris) seems inspired by the Latin text of the *Res Gestae divi Augusti*, in which Augustus describes territorial expanses (or at least territorial ambitions), spanning from west to east.[137] Another hint of the *Res Gestae*'s afterlife can be found

---

[133] Simić 2018: 128–130.
[134] Suetonius *Life of Augustus* 101; Wood 2014.
[135] For Julian's stay at Ankara: Ammianus Marcellinus 22.8; Mitchell and French 2019: 5.
[136] *I.Ancyra* 332, *ll.* 3–10.
[137] Mitchell and French 2019: 77–78; Latin *Res Gestae* sec. 26.

in the panegyric delivered by the rhetor Themistios before Constantius II in Ankara in 347 or 350. Themistios refers vaguely to "one of the kings of the past" who thought he "shared in a certain divine power (θείας τινὸς δυνάμεως) . . . and compelled men to dedicate temples and statues to him as to a god (θεῷ)."[138] The identity of this past king has been debated, but, with the speech localized in Ankara, the king may in fact be the first emperor: the "god Augustus" (Σεβαστὸς Θεός) of the Greek heading of the *Res Gestae*.[139] An exceptional series of inscriptions from Ankara of the mid-to-late sixth century, known as the *exempla biblica*, offer further evidence that the *Res Gestae* was read—and its layout imitated. Three panels, densely inscribed, retell biblical stories and reference Abgar's supposed letter to Christ; the goal was to exhort readers to a godly, virtuous life.[140] Inscriptions of this genre are unparalleled in late antiquity, and the format—long, dense texts presumably mounted on a wall—may have been adopted from the *Res Gestae*.

A more tangible indication of Christian engagement (if not reading) of the *Res Gestae* on the Temple of Augustus is found in the form of inscriptions and graffiti etched below the Greek copy on the exterior cella wall. Short grave texts from the years 825, 834, and 997 CE are located below column 1, column 9, and columns 10–11 of the *Res Gestae*, respectively, while at least four crosses can be seen on the orthostate below columns 15 and 16 of the Greek text (Figure 3.13).[141] The crosses are difficult to date, and although they have been previously published as isolated graffiti, their relation with the *Res Gestae* directly above was not noted.[142] This dislocation has been precipitated by published images of the *Res Gestae*, which zoom in on the text to the exclusion of its surrounding wall space. Engagement with the *Res Gestae* (at the least its visual aspects) is attested in some of the Byzantine-period texts, whose letter forms show an affinity for the Roman-era inscription. A burial record of 834 is carved directly below column 9 of the Greek *Res Gestae*, in line with it and written in capital letters that, in the words of Mitchell and French, "imitate the primary text" (Figure 3.14).[143] Note in particular the flat-bar alpha in comparison with other Middle Byzantine texts from Ankara, which have triangular alphas (*I.Ancyra* 500) or broken-bar alphas (*I.Ancyra* 501 and 502). The grave texts and crosses congregating under the Greek text

---

[138] *Oration* 1.3d, *ll.* 1–5 (trans. Heather and Moncur).
[139] Sitz 2019a: 660.
[140] *I.Ancyra* 347, 348, and 349.
[141] *I.Ancyra* 497–499.
[142] Krencker and Schede 1936: 34, Fig. 42. Peschlow 2015: 44.
[143] *I.Ancyra* 2 498; Mitchell and French 2019: 249.

108 PAGAN INSCRIPTIONS, CHRISTIAN VIEWERS

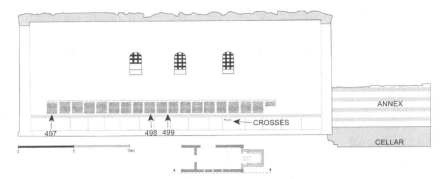

Figure 3.13 Ankara. Temple of Augustus, section of the exterior southeastern façade. Cross graffiti and Byzantine inscriptions (*I.Ancyra* 497–499) below the Greek *Res Gestae* are marked. Author and Yasmin Nachtigall, modified from Krencker and Schede 1936, Pl. 6.

Figure 3.14 Ankara. Temple of Augustus, detail of cast of the exterior southeastern façade. Greek *Res Gestae* with Byzantine grave text *I.Ancyra* 498 below. Mommsen 1883, Pl. 9.

of the *Res Gestae* suggest that the presence of the earlier inscription attracted these Middle Byzantine texts: the remainder of the temple exhibits only two crosses (on the interior walls of the opisthodomos) and two grave texts.[144] Within the cella, on its north wall, the ninth-/tenth-century grave epigram

---

[144] Cross: Krencker and Schede 1936, Pl. 23; grave texts: *I.Ancyra* 500 and 501.

of Eustathios, a *tourmarches* (a military leader), is written in clear, majuscule letters that are "stark antikisierend," in the words of Andreas Rhoby.[145] The letter forms may draw visual inspiration from the Greek *Res Gestae*, despite being located farther away from it. None of these literary and epigraphic indications is proof that the *Res Gestae* was read in later periods, but they point in that direction.

That the figure of Augustus could be read through a Christian lens has been argued above; but what to do about the pagan references within the *Res Gestae*? Although the *Res Gestae* names several gods whose temples Augustus has restored, and refers to Augustus as a "god," none of this per se would preclude its presence on the exterior wall of a late antique church. At Lagina (discussed below), pagan dedications on the temple's walls remained on display, even as a church was built directly across from it; a dedication from the *theos Sebastos* graced the sanctuary's propylon.[146] Pagan content was problematic only under certain circumstances, as we will see in Chapter 5, and despite all the hullabaloo surrounding the imperial cult, emperors were not confused for "real" pagan gods in late antiquity. Emperors were treated in both Roman and late antique historiographic tradition as men, and the imperial cult itself required substantial, sustained effort on the part of elite actors in provincial cities to "render the divinity of the emperor plausible."[147] Deified emperors were subjected to much less Christian vitriol than figures such as Zeus and Aphrodite. The windows carved into the southeastern wall of the cella of the temple at Ankara are located directly above the Greek text of the *Res Gestae*—meaning that workmen with scaffolding and chisels were employed on the wall. Had the erasure or symbolic defacement of the "pagan" text been wanted, it could have easily been carried out.

Another pagan inscription on the Temple of Augustus may initially seem to present greater difficulties. A list of priests of the imperial cult from the years 5 BCE to 18 CE was carved on the front face of the left anta as one entered the building, with a Trajanic addition on the right anta.[148] Despite their polytheistic credentials, the emphasis of the list is on the priests' local, Galatian identity and their civic benefactions. The first lines, in the largest lettering, reads [Γα]λατῶν ο[ἱ] | [ἱε]ρασάμενοι | θεῶι Σεβαστῶι | καὶ θεᾷ Ῥώμηι (Those of the Galatians serving as priests of the god Augustus and goddess Roma); several

---

[145] Rhoby 2014: 546–548 TR18; *I.Ancyra* 501.
[146] *I.Stratonikeia* 511; see Lagina section below.
[147] Rüpke 2018: 289.
[148] *I.Ancyra* 2. Mitchell and French 2012: 144–150; Coşkun 2014.

Celtic names occur in the list (Brigatos, Albiorix, Ateporix, etc.).[149] While at its construction, the temple was ostensibly about the pan-empire veneration of Augustus, it was actually a monument of local elite history; this Galatian-specific overtone may have been apparent to late antique readers as well.[150] Jerome in the late fourth century recorded that Celtic continued to be spoken in Galatia, and a sixth-century story of a Galatian monk who awoke from a demon possession able to speak only his native tongue indicates that this local language was still used.[151] A sixth-century church's *horos* stone from the region refers to a location with a Celtic-Greco toponym, Ἀτοροιστοχωρίω (Atoroistoxorion).[152] Continuing prejudice against the Galatians as an ethnic group may have served to strengthen this local identity: Jerome refers to their "ancient stupidity" in his commentary on *Galatians*.[153] Augustus himself was strongly associated with Galatia in the late antique and Byzantine periods because the province had been created under his rule and because of the (false) association of the name Galatia with the emperor's Gaulic troops.[154] Neither the *Res Gestae*'s reference to the "god Augustus" nor the presence of the list of Galatian priests of the imperial cult was an immediate disqualifier for the temple's potential use as a church.

Nor was its imperial subject matter. By the late fifth and sixth centuries, there was significant inter-permeation of imperial and ecclesiastical themes in literature, art, and architecture. The aptly named Yazıtlı Kilise (Inscribed Church) at Kasai in Pamphylia has a lengthy series of letters between an emperor (probably Zeno, r. 474–491) and the *magister officiorum* regarding a military affair carved on its exterior apse wall.[155] Justinian's *Novel* 8 (535), which attempted to curb corruption among imperial officials, was to be kept within churches or, better yet, to be set up "in the porticoes of the most holy church, rendering the reading and comprehension of the laws ready for all."[156] Depictions of the imperial family were placed in church apses already in the fifth century (as at San Giovanni Evangelista in Ravenna), and Justinian and Theodora made prominent appearances on the apse walls at San Vitale (also in Ravenna) and on the embroidered altar cloth of Hagia

---

[149] *I.Ancyra* 2, ll. 1–4.
[150] Güven 1998; Chiabà 2018: 117–122.
[151] Cyril of Scythopolis *Vita S. Euthymi* 55; Freeman 2001: 11–12.
[152] *I.Ancyra* 346 bis, l. 5.
[153] Jerome *Commentary on the Letter to the Galatians* 2.3; Cassibry 2017: 9–34; Sitz 2019a: 667.
[154] Eutropios 7.10; Malalas *Chronographia* 9.13; *Etymologicum Magnum* 220, l. 8; Tzetzes *Chiliades* 1.131–136. Sitz 2019a: 666.
[155] Feissel 2016: 672–684; Onur 2017: 143.
[156] *Novellae Constitutiones* 8 (trans. Toth and Rizos 2016: 912).

Sophia.[157] A recently excavated church complex in Beth Shemesh in Israel features a side room off of the main nave, donated according to an inscription by the emperor Tiberius II (r. 574–582 CE). The room has the position of a side chapel, and four holes in the floor indicate an altar. It lacks an apse, however, and the mosaic floor depicts a bird, probably the imperial eagle, with the text: Χ(ριστὸ)ς νικᾷ, (Christ conquers).[158] The "chapel" through its iconography and inscription seamlessly fuses imperial and religious veneration; this muddying of sacred and secular can be seen throughout late antique cities.

And as for the Latin copy of the *Res Gestae* on the Temple at Ankara? This text flanking the door to the temple was likely illegible to all but a few in late antique Ankara, but even so, the presence of Latin may have evoked the empire more broadly, and imperial bureaucracy in particular: Latin continued to be the official administrative language into the sixth century and was used in the military even later.[159] Yet again, this testament of empire may have had a more local significance. Ankara in the Roman period had an unusually large number of public and funerary inscriptions written in Latin, thanks to its administrative and military roles; many were undoubtedly still on display in late antiquity. Dedications were made to Constantine and Julian in that language.[160] The exquisite gravestone of a marble worker of Ankara named Kyrilos, of the late fifth or sixth century, is written in Greek but uses a Latin-form delta (presaging the later Greek minuscule).[161] Kyrilos' workshop may be showing off an epichoric style. The noticeable presence of Latin texts distinguished Ankara from the more parochial cities of inland Anatolia, highlighting its long-standing importance to the Roman empire and trans-Mediterranean connections.

To sum up, the *Res Gestae* on the walls of the Temple of Augustus and Roma at Ankara could be read from a variety of viewpoints in late antiquity and was likely a motivating factor in the temple's preservation. Temple and text protected each other: the other known copies of the *Res Gestae* (Greek on a long base at Apollonia, modern Uluborlu, and Latin at the imperial cult center in Pisidian Antioch, modern Yalvaç) did not survive intact, and few temples in Asia Minor can compete with the Temple of Augustus' superb

---

[157] Carile 2018: 59–66.
[158] Schuster 2017. Last accessed May 28, 2020.
[159] Dmitriev 2018.
[160] *I.Ancyra* 330 and 331.
[161] *I.Ancyra* 424.

integrity—certainly none within densely populated modern cities.[162] The *Res Gestae* did not preclude the building's use as a church; the conversion of the temple would be consistent with what we know of the religious atmosphere of late antique Ankara.

If the temple was ever a church, that is. With the annex assigned to the post-Byzantine period, not a shred of evidence for a church remains, except for the grave inscriptions of individuals such as Hyphatios, hegoumenos of a monastery (ninth or tenth century).[163] These burials are not, however, certain evidence of the building's use as a church. It was not mandatory for Byzantines to be buried in or immediately adjacent to a church; a derelict building or desolate field would do, especially if a chapel was located somewhere in the vicinity.[164] At Ankara, a chapel may perhaps have been located on the site now occupied by the Hacı Bayram mosque, with the defunct temple functioning as an associated burial ground. Crosses could be graffitied on all manner of walls, not only on churches. Even the grave inscription of a hegoumenos is not a sure indication that a monastery was located at the site: poor Hyphatios may have died while traveling and been buried far from his own monastery. His grave epithet is not certain evidence for a church or monastery at the Temple of Augustus. Whatever the case may be, the temple must have had a compelling function in the fifth and sixth century to have avoided spoliation in a still-active city. Late antique urban planning was by necessity practical, and such a building could have survived intact only if it fulfilled a necessary role, or if the quarter was quite abandoned—which it clearly was not, given the column probably dedicated to Justinian (the Column of "Julian") and the richly paved shops from around the same period. If the temple was not converted from an imperial monument into a church by the sixth century, perhaps it instead was given over to the military. The most verbose and visible grave epithet from the temple is that of the *tourmarches* Eustathios, of the

---

[162] For the three preserved copies of the *Res Gestae*: see Scheid 2007: xi–xiii; see also Chapter 5, pp. 250–253.

[163] *I.Ancyra* 500.

[164] See Moore 2013: 86–88, 167 for "field cemeteries." Ninth-/tenth-century Byzantine burials took place at the *Thermengymnasium* of Aizanoi, which was spoliated beginning c. 400 but not converted: Naumann 1980: 131; Naumann 1982: 381–382. At Antioch ad Cragum, Byzantine graves were found in the cella of the unconverted Northeast Temple: see Chapter 5, p. 242. Recent fieldwork at Labraunda has uncovered graves dating from around 1000 CE in an open field, to the northwest of the West Church: Sitz and Delibaş 2022. In Greece, Middle Byzantine graves at Parapotamos were dug into a preexisting tumulus (Poulou-Papadimitriou, Tsavelli, and Ott 2012: 407–408), while at Thebes, the temple to Apollo Ismenios was robbed out by the fifth century CE, when Christian graves were dug within the cella; around the same time a church was built 150 meters away (pers. comm. Stephanie Larson, August 6, 2020).

ninth or tenth century, and the area was clearly the beneficiary of defensive investment.[165] Or perhaps the temple fulfilled different functions over the years. In any case, the *Res Gestae divi Augusti* was almost certainly still on display and subject to viewing in late antiquity, in a city that was simultaneously imperial and highly Christianized.

A Tale of Two Temples at Aizanoi: Zeus at Church

I have presented the Temple of Augustus at Ankara as a sort of Schrödinger's cat; it may, or may not, have ever been a church, and we may never know for sure. At the Temple of Zeus at Aizanoi (Çavdarhisar) in Phrygia II Pakatiana, traces of a semi-circular apse opening at the temple's east can hardly be interpreted as anything other than evidence for a church—only its dating is disputed (Figure 3.15). Aizanoi offers the rare opportunity to study the fate of inscriptions at two temples, which show distinct impulses: tolerance, preservation, and conversion at the Temple of Zeus; erasure, spoliation, and "unnaming" at the Temple of Artemis, discussed in Chapter 5. These were not random or contradictory reactions but were specific responses to the content, context, and layout of the texts.

The Temple of Zeus at Aizanoi, like the temple in Ankara, is one of the best-preserved temples in all of Asia Minor; it stood as a monumental complex at the heart of the Roman city (Figure 3.16). Significant stretches of the peristasis and the cella walls tower above the present-day village, while its impressive vaulted substructure is in pristine condition. The east-west oriented temple is located in a large, paved *Tempelhof* (temple courtyard) bordered with porticoes. The dedicatory text to Zeus and Domitian on its architrave was formed in bronze letters, an indication of the prestige-factor of the structure at the time of its dedication (92–95 CE).[166] The bronze is long gone, but given the inherent value of the material, this is hardly surprising—or perhaps the city hastily removed the dedication after Domitian's death and damnatio in 96 CE.

Traces of an apse at the Temple of Zeus were seen by Léon de Laborde in 1826 and again in Krencker and Schede's excavations in 1926–1928; it

---

[165] Cf. the use of the sanctuary of the Muses at Antioch on the Orontes as the *praetorium* (official residence) of the *Comes Orientis* in the 330s: Malalas *Chronographia* 13.4.
[166] *SEG* 58.1492; Jes, Posamentir, and Wörrle 2010: 83.

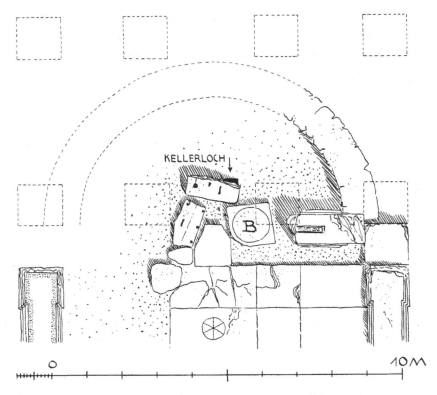

Figure 3.15 Aizanoi. Apse in the proanos of the Temple of Zeus. Rudolf Naumann 1979, Fig. 44. Used with permission.

was subsequently removed.[167] The apse was sizable (circa nine meters wide) and opened off of the antae, in the area formerly occupied by the temple's pronaos; the church's entrance was now at the west, where the narrow opisthodomos became a narthex (the church's entry vestibule; later collapses have completely destroyed much of the cella walls). During the church phase, the temple's east cella wall was still intact, as indicated by severe fire damage evident in the cella, which stops short of the pronaos at the line of the wall. Given the severity of the damage, it is unlikely that the building was subsequently used. Prior to the fire, the original Roman doorway into the temple was probably simply left open, forming an architectural barrier between the

---

[167] Laborde 1838: 55; Naumann 1979: 76–77, Fig. 44; Rheidt 2001: 247–253; Niewöhner 2007: 153–156. The excavations also found a bronze sheet emblazoned with a *Maria orans* and a bronze processional cross (both undated); the findspots of these objects were not published (Naumann 1979: 77).

Figure 3.16 Aizanoi. Temple of Zeus. Author, courtesy of the Aizanoi Excavations.

church's nave and an extended *bema* (the sanctuary of a church, where the altar was located).

It was precisely in this sacred area of the church that documents in Latin and Greek from the second century CE are preserved on the north anta wall, beginning approximately two meters above ground level. On the interior of the anta wall, Hadrian adjudicated a dispute over the temple's rental income from its landholdings with a proconsul of Asia around 125 CE.[168] Above, higher on the interior anta, a letter from Septimius Severus (dated to 195 CE) praised Aizanoi in response to a festival held in the emperor's honor, declaring, "you are a famous city and long of great service to the Roman Empire."[169] The exterior of the same wall displays letters in Greek from Antoninus Pius and the renowned council of the Areopagus in Athens in praise of the local notable Markos Oulpios Eurykles and his time as a member of Panhellenion, dated around 157 CE.[170] While the land dispute had likely faded from memory in

---

[168] *OGIS* 502; *MAMA* IX, xxxviii–xxxix; Laffi 1971; Nörr 2012.
[169] *CIG* III 3837 (trans. Oliver 1989: 432, no. 213). The inscription is not lost, contra Oliver.
[170] *OGIS* 504–507.

Figure 3.17 Aizanoi. Exterior wall of the Temple of Zeus with graffiti, below the Eurykles dossier (*OGIS* 504–507). Courtesy of the Deutsches Archäologisches Institut Istanbul (D-DAI-IST-R31242).

late antiquity, the documents show the personal involvement of Hadrian in local affairs; in the other texts, Aizanoi comes off rather well.

Christian graffiti, including crosses (undatable), were etched on the orthostates of this exterior wall along nearly its whole length, including below the Roman inscriptions (Figure 3.17). Two crosses are below the Eurykles dossier, while others congregate on the west wall, near the entrance to the church.[171] Two Middle Byzantine texts have also been published: a renovation inscription dated to 1004/5 on the north cella wall and an admonition to enter the church gladly, aptly located near the entrance.[172] Two small crosses are located on the interior anta wall (i.e., within the church sanctuary), again on an orthostate below the Roman texts. It is natural that the Christian graffiti was located closer to eye level rather than encroaching on the Roman inscriptions higher up, but height was no obstacle to those with a mind to

---

[171] Beyazıt 2016; Beyazıt 2018: 32–38, 200–223. On this west wall of the temple, there is also an ancient or late antique painted red wreath: Beyazıt 2018: 224. See also Naumann 1979, Figs. 9, 15, 16; Mergen 2016.

[172] *MAMA* IX 557 and 558.

deface (or enhance?) the older inscriptions, as demonstrated by later graffiti from the Çavdars (a non-Christian group that took over Aizanoi in the medieval period as Byzantine hegemony in Anatolia collapsed). Horses and riders were carved on top of the ancient texts in the inscription field, as well as even higher up on the temple walls.[173] This Çavdar graffiti offers a powerful contrast to the Christian symbols: leaving the ancient Roman texts untouched was a cultural attitude, not a default.

The excavators assumed that the Christian reuse of the Temple of Zeus at Aizanoi took place in late antiquity; the construction around 400 CE of a new porticoed street (the *Säulenstraße*, built with spolia from the Temple of Artemis) brought increased access and attention to this central sector of the city and may indicate an early date for the temple's revitalization as a church, although there is no indication that this street connected directly with the temenos. Philipp Niewöhner more recently proposed that the conversion of the temple did not take place until later, perhaps the eleventh century.[174] This date is based on his reappraisal of the *Tempelhof*'s stratigraphy and an analysis of the architecture of the church, which he argues fits poorly into late antiquity: a single-apsed structure lacking aisles, galleries, and windows. The church is admittedly atypical in plan, but this is a feature of reusing a preexisting structure. Several other late antique temple-churches had only one apse, and for a cella transformed into a single nave, the Aizanoi temple-church finds its closest parallels in the Hephaisteion in Athens, the Bêt Djaluk temple in Phoenice (Syria), and a small heroon at Notion, near Klaros on the west coast of Ionia (although this conversion is not dated).[175] Transitional period and Middle Byzantine churches likewise usually had tripartite sanctuaries, so the plan fits no better in those periods. Windows carved into the now-missing southern wall of the cella (as at Ankara) could have provided adequate lighting.

Niewöhner's concerns about the stratigraphy of the temenos are more difficult to assess due to the substantial later interventions in the temple court, which was used for burials probably from the seventh to ninth centuries before being transformed into a fortified Byzantine settlement in the eleventh century.[176] The altar to Zeus east of the temple was stripped to its

---

[173] At least one cross (Beyazıt 2018: 195–197) was also carved high up on the exterior north wall, two courses above the level of the inscriptions, indicating that crosses could have been carved next to or on the Roman texts, had it been desirable.
[174] Niewöhner 2007: 153–155.
[175] Bayliss 2004, Fig. 16 (Athens) and Fig. 18 (Bêt Djaluk); Notion: Büyükkolancı 1996: 372–373.
[176] Rheidt 2001: 252.

lowest courses at some point and seems to have been used as an oven by the Byzantine period, as indicated by a bread stamp emblazoned with a cross.[177] Niewöhner proposes that the entire *Tempelhof* first underwent a period of spoliation, followed by burials, then the collapse (probably in an earthquake) of the temple's east peristasis. Debris from this façade was rearranged as foundations for houses of the eleventh century, and he raises the possibility that the 1004/5 inscription recording the renovation of the naos may use this term in the pagan sense, indicating the conversion of the pagan naos into a church for the first time.[178] But naos was the standard word for a Christian church by the Middle Byzantine period, and the Byzantine author surely would have prefaced any reference to a pagan naos with a qualifier, such as "false naos" *vel sim*. What is more, the eastern façade need not have collapsed before the apse could be built in the pronaos. The circuit of the apse stops short of where the peristasis columns stood, suggesting that these were still in place when the apse was built.[179] The missing prostyle columns may have been intentionally removed in order to construct the church apse, as seen, for example, at the Hephaisteion in Athens, where great care was taken to preserve the temple's columns, frieze, and even both gables at the point of conversion, recently tentatively redated from the sixth/seventh century to the fifth.[180] Niewöhner notes that much of the flooring of the pronaos was missing before the construction of the apse. But this need not indicate centuries of abandonment and spoliation. The paving under the apse may have been removed intentionally during the church construction process: given that the original cella floor level was higher than that of the pronaos, the inner space of the apse needed to be elevated.[181]

Niewöhner's assertion that the temple court was dug down two meters below the Roman ground level prior to the construction of the eleventh-century houses (and in his view prior to the installation of the church) applies to only sections of the temple's surroundings, not the entire *Tempelhof*.[182] In

---

[177] Köroğlu 2016; see also Naumann 1979: 39–40, Pl. 62 a and b.
[178] Niewöhner 2007: 153, *MAMA* IX 557.
[179] Naumann 1979: 76. One architrave block from the temple (excavation Inv. A11.TMP.01) has game boards graffitied on its soffit; the didactic plaque on site suggests that these boards may have been carved by Çavdars or Byzantines.
[180] Sturm 2016: 814–819, Fig. 17. The first epigraphic evidence for the Christianization of the Hephaisteion are obituary texts of the ninth century: McCabe 2020. The gables at Aizanoi seem to have been intact, as many of their collapsed elements were excavated: Schulz 2010: 92–95.
[181] A "merel game" graffito was carved on the pronaos floor, on the building's central axis. It may represent an intermediate phase prior to the construction of the apse.
[182] Niewöhner 2007: 153; Rheidt 2001: 249.

the drawings of the 1920s excavation, the temple court's original paving slabs can be seen in situ in several locations, so the change in ground level was not the result of systematic stripping. It may have been the digging of graves (probably in the seventh to ninth centuries) that precipitated the removal of some paving slabs and the subsequent erosion of the soil/fill (aided by the natural slope of the temple mound, which is in fact a tell created by a Bronze Age settlement underlying the area). Excavations in 2009 revealed that the Byzantine settlement continued south of the *Tempelhof*; human bones were found there mixed in soil, "transferred together with the surrounding earth during construction works."[183] It may have been only in the eleventh century that soil of the temple court was dug and moved nearby during construction activity.

In short, the lack of surviving evidence makes it impossible to securely date the conversion of the Temple of Zeus at Aizanoi; Niewöhner is understandably skeptical of an early date, given the lack of late antique finds within the *Tempelhof*. But this dearth of finds in an area that was substantially disturbed in later periods does not immediately rule out conversion in the fifth or sixth century. The lack of substantial alterations to the temple's built fabric need not indicate, as Niewöhner suggests, that the builders were limited to minimal construction measures, but may rather reveal the impulse to preserve as much of the temple as possible. No newly built churches have been uncovered in the city of Aizanoi proper, which was a bishopric by 325, in opposition to the many *ex novo* ecclesiastical structures in the hinterland: the metropolis's habit for reusing buildings was a preference rather than a necessity. A small late antique chapel was added to the city's stadium/theater complex, a church was built into the Mosaic Bath perhaps in the fifth century, and the round macellum building became a chapel in the sixth.[184] If the conversion of the Temple of Zeus was carefully carried out in late antiquity, preserving as much of the temple (and its texts) as possible while the paving of the *Tempelhof* was still intact, what evidence could we expect? As discussed at Ankara, the lack of comparanda for structures first converted to ecclesiastical use later than the seventh century tips the scales in favor of a late antique date. Regardless, the inscriptions on the walls of the Temple of Zeus at Aizanoi were still on display in late antiquity and proclaimed Aizanoi's connections with the popular Roman rulers Hadrian and Antoninus Pius and its long proud history of

[183] von den Hoff 2011: 126, Figs. 2–5.
[184] Niewöhner 2007: 144–148; Niewöhner 2010: 146–153.

successful elites. As at Ankara, the messages projected by these still-visible texts spoke both to local civic identity and to wider connections with the Roman world.

Tolerance at Palmyra

In Chapter 1, we explored ISIS's manufactured violence against the temples of Bel and Baalshamin at Palmyra in 2015. These temples had already experienced changes in use and prestige over the centuries. The Temple of Bel became a church or chapel probably in the fifth century with minimal architectural modification: a baldachino (but no apse) was installed, and Christian figures were painted on the walls, replacing whatever statues or figural imagery of the old gods had been on display at the sanctuary.[185] A brief Christian text hailing the Theotokos in Greek was added to the eastern interior wall of the cella, while various Roman-era inscriptions honoring individuals in both Greek and Palmyrene Aramaic continued to dot the surrounding temenos portico.[186] The Temple of Baalshamin too was reused in our period, but it is not clear whether this constituted a church or a meeting house.[187] Three rectangular, non-communicating annexes (apses?) were built off of the temple's pronaos; the cella remained intact, functioning either as the nave or a hall. The Roman temple included lateral windows in the cella (with proper headers, footers, and jambs), which allowed light into this central space. Whatever the function of the structure in late antiquity, modifications did not extend to removing a bilingual text dating to 130–131 CE inscribed on a console of a pronaos column (facing into the "apses"). This inscription commemorated the (re)builder of the sanctuary:

> The council and the demos honored Male called Agrippa, son of Iaraios, son of Raaios, secretary for a second time, who, during the visit of the divine Hadrian, offered oil to foreigners and to follow citizens, provided in every way for the reception of the soldiers, and built the temple of Zeus, the pronaos, and the other [things] at his own expense.[188]

---

[185] Intagliata 2018: 51.
[186] *IGLS* 17, 1.47.
[187] Intagliata 2018: 51–53.
[188] *IGLS* 17, 1.145: [ἡ βουλὴ καὶ] ὁ δῆ[μος] | Μαλην τὸν καὶ Ἀγρίππα[ν] | Ιαραιου τοῦ Ρααιου, γραμμ[α]|τέα γενόμενον τὸ δεύτε|ρον ἐπιδημίᾳ θεοῦ Ἀδρ[ι]|ανοῦ, ἄλιμμα παρασχό[ν]|τα ξένοις τε καὶ πολείτα[ις], | ἐν πᾶσιν ὑπηρετήσαντα | τῇ τ[ῶν] στρατευμάτων | ὑπο[δοχ]ῇ καὶ τὸν ναὸν | τὸν [τοῦ] Διὸς σ[ὺ]ν τῷ π[ρο]|ναίῳ [καὶ σὺν τ]αῖς ἄλλα[ις —]τ[— ἐξ] ἰδ[ίων —].

The Aramaic version of the text states that the temple is dedicated to Baalshamin *and* Durahlun, an associated god: this information was not available in Greek. Although Aramaic ceased to be written in Palmyra shortly after Zenobia, it may have still been spoken and was perhaps legible. The names of Zeus/Baalshamin and Durahlun were permitted to remain in this reused space.

The ubiquitous Greek-Aramaic bilingual texts (Greek usually in the first position) around the city of Palmyra gave a local flavor to this epigraphic landscape. Honorific texts, some quite short, others longer, are dominant among the city's inscribed remains, both at sanctuaries and in other public spaces. The Great Colonnade, with its many bilingual honorific console texts bestowed by the city on deserving individuals, was the main thoroughfare of late antique Palmyra; some columns were also marked with Christian graffiti.[189] Even Zenobia, erstwhile queen of Palmyra, maintained her epigraphic honors along the Great Colonnade: never mind that she had been captured by Aurelian after carving up much of the Roman east to form her own empire from 270 to 272.[190] This and other texts were accepted elements of the late antique urban image of Palmyra and perhaps reminded viewers of the city's unique history up until its sharp contraction after the fall of the Umayyad dynasty in the mid-eighth century.[191] As we will see in Chapter 5, tolerance toward the epigraphic remains of the pagan past did not extend to the figural representation of another famous Palmyrene female figure, the goddess Allat-Athena.

Priests, Talking Columns, and Unreadable Texts at Christianized Temples

Diokaisareia-Olba: A Careful Conversion

If the temples at Ankara, Aizanoi, and Palmyra were converted to ecclesiastical use in late antiquity, they indicate the preservation of texts on temples reused wholesale as churches, with the cellas left intact ("direct transformation" in Bayliss's terminology).[192] Other "direct transformation" temples,

---

[189] *IGLS* 17, 1.105–108.
[190] *IGLS* 17, 1.57.
[191] Intagliata 2018: 107–108.
[192] Bayliss 2004: 79.

such as the Parthenon, Hephaisteion, and Erectheion in Athens, lacked inscribed ancient texts, though as we have seen in the previous chapter, a "pseudo-oracle" may have been set up near the Parthenon to smooth its transition to a church of the Theotokos. In other instances, temples were deconstructed and rebuilt as churches, or churches were constructed adjacent to still-standing temples. At Diokaisareia-Olba (Uzuncaburç) in the province of Isauria (western Kilikia), the Temple of Zeus Olbios was converted into the city's main church in the second half of the fifth century, after the Hellenistic temple had been closed for decades and its building fabric partially robbed out.[193] Its western temenos wall displayed a Hellenistic dedication to Zeus Olbios from the "great archpriest Teukros, son of Zenophanes" (of the ruling Teukrian dynasty), facing the temple.[194] This temple-church was no makeshift Christian space; the blocks from the cella were painstakingly removed, and the intercolumniations of the temple's still-standing peristasis were walled up, creating an impressively large church that probably required as much construction labor as simply building *ex novo*. If the erasure of the priest inscription on the Temple of Zeus Olbios had been desirable, it would have been easy to carry out. Nearby, the façade of the city's Tychaion likewise maintained its Roman architrave dedication from a private couple on display, indicating a generally tolerant attitude toward ancient pagan dedications alongside the energy expended on creating a new Christian topography at Diokaisareia-Olba.[195]

"Archaeophilia" at Sardis's Artemision

Architectural proximity too can indicate interaction between late antique Christian communities and the pagan past. The small Chapel M at Sardis, capital of the late antique province of Lydia, is dwarfed by the monumental columns of the Temple of Artemis, begun in the Hellenistic period on an Archaic cult site and never finished; the Christian structure is built so close to the peristasis that they are practically touching (Figure 3.18). The first phase of Chapel M was constructed in the late fourth/early fifth century CE,

---

[193] Bayliss 2004: 144–149; Elton, Equini Schneider, and Wannagat 2007: 6–23; Westphalen 2006: 399, Fig. 9.
[194] *SEG* 51.1852, *ll.* 1–2: Ἀρχιερεὺς μέ[γ]ας Τεῦκρος Ζηνοφάνους . . . Διὶ Ὀλ[β]ίωι. *MAMA* III, Fig. 71.
[195] *MAMA* III, 56.

Figure 3.18 Sardis. View toward Temple of Artemis and Chapel M. Author, courtesy of the Archaeological Exploration of Sardis.

based on a hoard of coins dated to circa 400 CE.[196] The nearby Church EA was probably built in the mid-fourth century, indicating an early push for visible Christianization at Sardis.[197] New archaeological evidence confirms that the sanctuary of Artemis was a busy place in late antiquity: the temple with its double cella was subject to "a deliberate remodeling."[198] The eastern columns *in antis* seem to have been removed, the pronaos was covered by a fill containing numerous sherds of the late fourth or early fifth century CE, and water pipes were installed over the defunct and deconstructed western cella (Figure 3.19). Colossal heads of Antoninus Pius and Faustina the Elder remained inside the eastern cella during these renovations, prior to its collapse in the seventh century; Commodus' was intentionally mutilated and buried, while a defaced head tentatively identified as Marcus Aurelius was found on the south pteroma of the temple (the walking space between the cella wall and the columns of the peristasis).[199] The area around the sanctuary was active as well, with buildings repaired and a potential Christian

---

[196] Bell 1916: viii; Foss 1976: 48; Cahill and Greenewalt Jr. 2016: 504–506.
[197] Buchwald 2015: 9.
[198] Cahill and Greenewalt Jr. 2016: 504–505; cf. Yegül 2020: 180–184.
[199] Yegül 2020: 193–199.

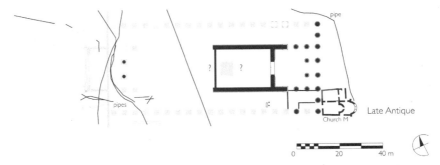

Figure 3.19 Sardis. Plan of the Temple of Artemis area in late antiquity. © Archaeological Exploration of Sardis/President and Fellows of Harvard College.

martyrium constructed to the north. At the former entrance to the eastern cella, near Chapel M, myriad crosses and the common late antique phrase "light, life" (φῶς, ζωή) were etched on the door jamb (Figure 3.20).[200]

Figure 3.20 Sardis. Christian graffiti on the southeastern door jamb of the Temple of Artemis. Courtesy of the Howard Crosby Butler Archive, Department of Art and Archaeology, Princeton University.

[200] For the later antique and medieval history of the site, see Yegül 2020: 12; for the locations of the graffiti, see his Pl. 17.

These Christian markers joined earlier texts on the temple. At the opposite end of the temple, on the western pronaos northern anta, a wordy contract of the early Hellenistic period between a man named Mnesimachos and the sanctuary was carved (Mnesimachos had defaulted on a loan from the sanctuary and had to mortgage his land).[201] Closer to the church (at the east end of the temple), an unusual verse inscription wraps around one of the fillets of a monumental column base in the peristasis, about four columns to the north of Chapel M and in front of the entrance where Christians were busy scribbling. The column itself speaks, albeit enigmatically: "One stone forms my torus and my lower portion, but I rise first of all the others, not from the public stones, but 'on the house' (i.e., from the temple's own funds)."[202] The vocabulary used is unusual, but the gist is clear: the column's base is impressively carved from a monolith, while the funding came, not from the demos, but "domestically," probably from the sanctuary itself. Nearby, graffiti on unfinished surfaces of two separate columns likewise spoke to the viewer: "finish me!"[203]

Whether anyone in late antiquity read the Mnesimachos contract or "listened" to the talking columns is questionable. The Mnesimachos text was already partially erased during the raising of the floor level in the Roman renovation of the Temple of Artemis; the western cella and pronaos fell into ruin as Chapel M was constructed at the east.[204] The dense contract is hardly engaging reading (to anyone who is not an epigrapher, anyways). The speaking columns, located near the entrance to the church, had a better chance of being read, but these texts were not visually prominent due to their constricted writing spaces and the more eye-catching carving of the column base *tori*. But other inscriptions in the area of the temple may have been more attention-grabbing, if less legible. Multiple stelai written in the ancient Lydian language were found around the sanctuary, especially in the area of the Archaic Lydian altar to the west of the temple. This Anatolian language with its distinctive alphabet would have been incomprehensible. Brief dedications in Lydian were also inscribed on at least some of columns of the temple, following the old Anatolian habit of writing donor dedications

---

[201] *I.Sardis* I 1.
[202] *I.Sardis* I 181: Ἡ σ[π]εῖρα χὠ [ῥ]ιζαῖος εἷς ἐστιν λίθος, πρῶτος δὲ πάντων ἐξ ὅλω ἀνίσταμαι οὐ δημοτεύκτων, ἀλλ᾽ ἀπ᾽ οἰκείων λίθων (trans. after Yegül 2014: 204).
[203] *I. Sardis* I 182.1, 3: μὲ σκεᾷς, on columns 17 and 16. Petzl 2018; Yegül 2020: 106–107.
[204] Yegül 2020: 163.

Figure 3.21 Sardis. Nannas Bakivalis monument. Courtesy of the Howard Crosby Butler Archive, Department of Art and Archaeology, Princeton University.

directly on columns.[205] In the following chapter, we will encounter another unreadable inscription at Sardis, built into a late antique synagogue.

Literate viewers at Sardis would have had more luck with a bilingual Lydian-Greek inscription to the north of the Temple of Artemis. The short votive text in Lydian, running right to left, reads "Nannas Bakivalis to Artemis"; the Greek right below it rendered this message intelligible to Sardis's (late) Roman population.[206] The texts are inscribed on a base forming part of a statuary monument with a decidedly Archaic appearance: two stylized lions and a headless eagle, all dating from the sixth or fifth century BCE (Figure 3.21).[207] The eagle-eyed viewer, however, might have noticed that the bases

---

[205] Gusmani 1964: 259, no. 21.
[206] Gusmani 1964: 259, no. 20: *nannaś bakivalis artimuλ*. The Greek reads Νάννας Διονυσικλέος Ἀρτέμιδι (Nannas Dionysikleos to Artemis). The inscription on another base in this statue group has been erased at an uncertain date.
[207] For the dating, see Hanfmann and Ramage 1978, no. 236; 235; 238.

were reused and that the zoomorphic statuary did not form a coherent group. The "Nannas Bakivalis monument" was rather built in the Roman or late Roman period from older spare parts. Rojas has identified this motley assembly as one symptom of the "archaeophilia" gripping Roman Sardis, where traces of the distant past were intentionally sought out, experienced, and interpreted within a wider set of beliefs and myths about pre-Roman local history.[208] The monument may have been assembled as late as the fourth century CE: the archaeophilia of late pagans mixed with "passive resistance" to Christianization. The late fourth-century historian and sophist Eunapios, himself a native of Sardis and an ardent pagan, described the religious atmosphere of the city: the traditional shrines were in ruins and at times there were no altars available.[209] During the reign of Julian, the pagan high priest of the province of Lydia, a philosopher named Chrysanthios, managed to thread a fine needle by restoring temples in such a way that his efforts "almost escaped notice" and did not prompt a Christian backlash after Julian's death.[210] Was the redeployment of older monuments Chrysanthios' preferred method of restoration?

Regardless of the date of the "Nannas Bakivalis monument," the Artemision at Sardis was probably a contested space in late antiquity as worship of the goddess was gradually snuffed out, despite the efforts of Chrysanthios and others. Imperial cult statues became obsolete; Christians etched crosses at the temple threshold. The construction of Chapel M immediately in front of the former temple introduced an entirely new aesthetic into the archaeophiliac temple-scape: the late antique–built fabric of the chapel must have stood out in the same way that ultra-modern glass buildings do in historic districts today. Finally, it was not only human agents, inscriptions, statue monuments, and architectural styles that participated in this struggle to control the sacred canopy of Sardis: Rojas has noted that Mt. Tmolos itself (or rather himself) was understood in the ancient period to be a "mountain-person," an animate individual with his own will and power.[211] We can only guess how this mountain-person would (have been believed to) have felt about the latest competition to the old cult of the goddess. In spite of this long history of pagan worship and a local ontology linking landscape and myth, Christianity won the day and worship shifted from Artemis to a new sacred figure at the

---

[208] Rojas 2019: 36–43.
[209] Eunapios *Vita Sophistarum* 23.4.3.
[210] Eunapios *Vita Sophistarum* 23.2.8 (trans. Rojas 2019: 42).
[211] Rojas 2019: 96–102.

diminutive Chapel M, even as the sanctuary's epigraphic patrimony was left untouched. But the ultimate winner in this contested space was the sands of time, literally: both temple and church were eventually buried by erosional soil deposits coming down the slope from the acropolis. Perhaps Mt. Tmolos had the last laugh after all.

Lagina: Early Christian Economics

Lagina, the extra-urban sanctuary connected with the city of Stratonikeia (Karia) via a Sacred Way, offers particularly rich evidence for tolerance shown toward an inscribed temple during the period of transformation from pagan sanctuary to Christian site. The Temple of Hekate was exceptional in the Hellenistic and Roman periods for its sheer density of wall inscriptions: approximately one hundred fifty discrete texts ranged from lengthy to laconic. These included a decree of the city honoring the goddess, letters attesting Stratonikeia's loyalty to Rome during the Mithraidatic wars, a list of cities recognizing the sanctuary's *asylia*, lists of priests, and brief records of individual priests (added to the temple at the end of each priesthood probably into the third century CE).[212] These texts participated in a particularly Karian tradition of using temples as writing-bearer, contributing to a broader process of regional identity formation through a local aesthetic of inscribed sacred space.[213] And in late antiquity? Stratonikeia's pagan sanctuaries experienced a final flourishing in the early fourth century when the Tetrarchic ruler Maximinus Daia sought to revitalize traditional pagan cults in the midst of his conflict with Licinius and the (freshly converted) Constantine. As Maximinus traveled with his army through Karia, two wealthy siblings from Stratonikeia financed a spectacular festival at the sanctuary of Zeus Panamaros and provided olive oil to the entire army. Such a display of euergetic piety toward the pagan gods was rare by this period. As Peter Brown quipped, "the third century, as we know it, does not appear to have happened at Stratonikeia."[214]

But time did not stand still. Recent excavations at Lagina, conducted from 1993 to the present, have uncovered a poorly preserved structure identified as a Christian basilica occupying the space between the Temple of Hekate

---

[212] *I.Stratonikeia* 505, 512, 507, 508, and 601–741.
[213] Sitz 2019a.
[214] Brown 1978: 51. *I.Stratonikeia* 310. See also Söğüt 2018.

and its altar (Figure 3.22). The church is three-aisled, with a narthex almost abutting the temple's stereobate. The basilica was built in alignment with both the temple and the altar, which are on two different axes; it therefore required unusually curved walls. The basilica's apse, now completely missing,

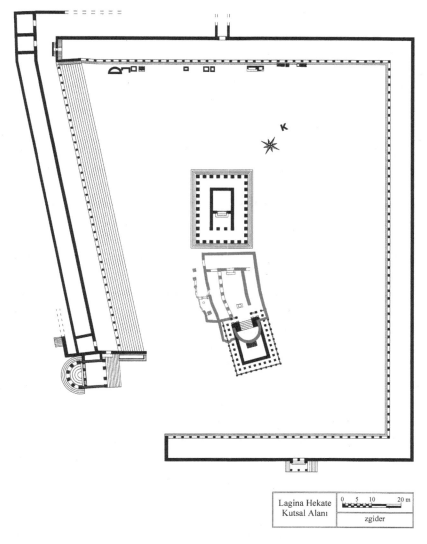

Figure 3.22 Lagina. Plan of the sanctuary of Hekate with the basilica in grey. Gider 2012, Fig. 1. Used with permission.

Figure 3.23 Lagina. General view of propylon, the Temple of Hekate, and the area of the basilica. Author, courtesy of the Stratonikeia Excavations.

was presumably built on the remains of the altar. The church is difficult to date but lies directly on the paving of the temple's courtyard, suggesting that no long period of sedimental accumulation or vegetal growth had taken place between the active usage of the courtyard and the construction of the basilica. An early date for the structure is consistent with the presence of two fourth-century coins found in the excavations.[215] The walls of the basilica are roughly built of spolia, which came mainly from the Doric stoa surrounding the temple precinct but also included the tympanum of a second-century CE *naiskos* bearing a bust of Serapis, as well as the pediment and architrave of another *naiskos* with a dedicatory inscription to Augustus.[216] It is not clear how these blocks were incorporated into the ecclesiastical architecture, but they are well preserved, without intentional damage.

The temple was most likely still standing at the time of the construction of the church. The ruins of the collapsed temple, with its inscriptions and exquisitely carved frieze depicting gods and mythological scenes, were found largely undisturbed where they had fallen in the 1891–1892 excavations by Osman Hamdi Bey; approximately 80 percent of the temple's blocks can be accounted for (Figure 3.23).[217] So far as I am aware, none of the spolia used

---

[215] Tırpan and Söğüt 2010: 507–510; Söğüt 2019: 251; 267–269; 317.
[216] Gider 2005: 68–78; Söğüt 2008; Söğüt 2011; Gider 2012.
[217] Tırpan and Söğüt 2005: 24. See also Newton 1862, Pl. 77–80. The only portion of the temple that may have been disturbed is the interior of the cella, which was probably never fully floored and had an open pit where offerings to Hekate could be made (Büyüközer 2018: 20–24); disturbances in this pit and the finding of "some late Roman inscription fragments" (Şahın 2010: 20) suggest activity in this space.

Figure 3.24 Lagina. Graffiti on the stylobate of the Temple of Hekate. Author, courtesy of the Stratonikeia Excavations.

to build the church can be definitely attributed to the temple.[218] The temple's cult statue had been evicted before the temple's collapse: no fragments of Hekate were found. The recent excavations suggest that the 365 CE earthquake, which devastated several monuments in Stratonikeia nearby, may have caused the damage visible on Hekate's altar and even the collapse of the temple, but a later earthquake might also be the culprit.[219] A second Christian chapel was constructed near the propylon.

Christian graffiti etched on the temple's crepidoma (the stepped platform on which the columns and cella sit) confirm that the structure was still standing during our period: the temple's *ptera* (the walking spaces between the cella walls and the colonnade) were accessible, and no graffiti was etched on fallen elements from the superstructure (Figure 3.24). Graffiti in the form of crosses is also found on the paving at the sanctuary's propylon, which has stood since antiquity and marks the entrance to the large peribolos with an inscription from the "god Augustus, son of a god."[220] Additional

---

[218] Baumeister 2007: 232–238 attributes frieze blocks built into the church to a Hellenistic altar; contra Tırpan, Gider, and Büyüközer 2012: 196. The spolia-rich chapel visible to the immediate west of the altar may be a later addition to the church.
[219] Söğüt 2019: 261.
[220] *I.Stratonikeia* 511, l. 1: Αὐτοκράτωρ Καῖσαρ θεοῦ υἱὸς θεὸς Σεβαστὸς.

graffiti congregates on a wall near the propylon and on the paving between the temple and altar (that is, the floor of the basilica), including one indicative of *scriptus interruptus*: the carver began the usual "Lord, help your servant so-and-so" formula but only got as far as the tau: Κ(ύρι)ε Βοήθ<ε>ι τ... (ΚΕΒΟΗΘΙΤ on the stone, without any traces of a letter, damage, or erasure after the tau). On a spoliated fragment of a round altar inside the church is written Κύριε ἐ[λέησον?] (Lord, h[ave mercy?]).[221]

Other graffiti at Lagina, however, are ambiguous or even pagan: *topoi* inscriptions (next to the propylon) and *plantae pedum* (outlines of feet, on the propylon's paving and on the temple's crepidoma). *Topos* inscriptions (place of so-and-so) could designate locations of ceremonial, craft, or service personnel in both the Roman and late Roman periods.[222] The habit of outlining feet was common in Egyptian cults, but *plantae pedum* can also be found at the sanctuaries of traditional Greek and Roman gods; at the nearby oracle of Klaros both hands and feet were carved on the temple crepidoma at an uncertain time.[223] Based on this mixture of Christian and traditionally pagan motifs, Vincenzo Ruggieri has argued for a continued habit of pilgrimage at the site in the late fourth century and early fifth century, as the goddess Hekate was replaced by a new, uncertain Christian saint.[224] He points to an invocation text (Κύριε βοήθει) immediately adjacent to a *planta pedum* on the temple's stereobate and takes them as a single graffito: early Christians simply adopted and propagated this originally pagan symbol. In actuality, the Christian text may have been added to the carved feet only later. The particular context at Lagina encouraged graffiti (whether late pagan or Christian): the walls of the temple were already *covered* in text. The priests' records were increasingly informal in appearance; this gradual "graffiticization" of the official records paved the way for actual graffiti. As is often noted, writing attracts more writing; the majority of the graffiti occurs at the temple's southwest, where the lengthy documents celebrating Stratonikeia's relationship with Rome were inscribed on the cella wall centuries earlier.[225] In any case, there is no clear-cut separation of pagan and Christian graffiti at Lagina. Perhaps some of the *plantae pedum* are in fact Christian imitations of earlier pagan graffiti, without specific religious

---

[221] Aydaş 2009, no. 26.
[222] Saliou 2017.
[223] Moretti et al. 2016: 308–309, Fig. 2.1. Cf. also Takács 2007.
[224] Ruggieri 2008: 95–99.
[225] For the location of the dossier on the temple, see Van Bremen 2010: 494–495.

intentions. Why shouldn't someone simply copy a motif already on view on the temple? Especially one as imminently reproducible as the outline of a foot?

Labeling the graffiti of the Temple of Hekate at Lagina as "Christian" or "pagan" is largely a moot point; the texts and images filling the temple's blank spaces drew the viewer into a conversation across time.[226] But Ruggieri's essential point of continuous use of the site in the fourth century CE is likely valid: there is no evidence for a break in activity (although the ceramic and numismatic finds at the site may eventually clarify the matter). It is not necessary to attribute this to religious pilgrimage and the seamless replacement of goddess with saint, however. Rural sanctuaries and their ancient festivals, such as Lagina's annual *kleidophoria* (the carrying of Hekate's key from sanctuary to city) and the Hekatesia-Romaia (an international festival occurring in four-year cycles), served essential economic and social purposes as well.[227] Pausanias in the second century CE described a festival at a rural shrine near Tithorea in central Greece: "the small traders make themselves booths of reeds or other improvised material ... they hold a fair, selling slaves, cattle of all kinds, clothes, silver and gold."[228] Both legal and literary sources indicate that rural festivals of pagan origin were permitted to continue in the fourth century and beyond, so long as no sacrifices were performed.[229] If an evolved version of the old festivals continued at Lagina, the sanctuary's location on a road leading from Stratonikeia northward would make it impractical to move; Stratonikeia was two hours farther south and would have created hardships for those coming from the territory of Alabanda, a robust day's walking distance (approximately forty-five kilometers) north of Lagina.[230] Moreover, the sanctuary was presumably inhabited continuously by cult personnel and agricultural workers farming the goddess's land and husbanding her livestock. Stephanos of Byzantium (sixth century CE) refers to Lagina as a πολίχνιον, a small town, and lists ethnics for both men and women from there, drawing on a Hellenistic source.[231] Although the information was centuries old in Stephanos' time, there is no indication that the area around

---

[226] Cf. Yasin 2015: 44–54.
[227] McInerney 2006: 43–55; Jördens 2018. For the festivals of Lagina: Williamson 2013: 212–219.
[228] Pausanias 10.32.15 (trans. Jones).
[229] C.Th. 16.10.17: "amusements shall be furnished to the people, but without any sacrifice or any accursed superstition, and they shall be allowed to attend festal banquets" (trans. Pharr). Cf. also Libanios *Oration* 30.17–19. See Graf 2015: 306–322.
[230] Hild 2014: 20, Fig. 56.
[231] *Ethnica* 11.6.8.

Lagina was ever fully abandoned. A "merel game" graffito is also carved on the Temple of Hekate's stylobate, perhaps indicating that the *pteron* became a gathering place. An Antonine inscription attests the presence of an "agora for food" (βιοτικὴ ἀγορα); a natural spring is located at the site.[232] Lagina was not only a sanctuary, but also a *locus amoenus* in the countryside, a pleasant excursion out of the polis. Already before the fourth century CE, Lagina possessed the infrastructure necessary for habitation and a long tradition of rural festivals, presumably supported by a wide agricultural network.

In sum: it is likely that the Temple of Hekate at Lagina and its texts were on display, at least up until 365, and possibly later—even as a church was built immediately opposite the temple in perhaps the fourth century. The site goes against the usual pattern, wherein temples were left dormant for decades or centuries before the space was reused for Christian worship. The continuous use of Lagina may have been primarily economically, rather than religiously, motivated, and Christians added graffiti to the temple and to the propylon without any attempt to deconstruct or disfigure either. The temple's texts recording local history, Stratonikeia's illustrious connections with Rome, and the euergetic activity of Lagina's priests, as well as its frieze depicting pagan gods, were still on view.

Everyday Hieroglyphs at Medinet Habu

This tolerance toward texts of a pagan nature is apparent in Egypt as well—but here, much of the writing covering temples was completely incomprehensible. Egyptian hieroglyphs were in their death throes, with the latest attestation of hieroglyphic script dated to 394 CE—and the author of that graffito felt the need to write his message in Demotic as well (also in its final use phase by that period).[233] The *Hieroglyphica*, a fifth-century (?) treatise written by one Horapollo, purports to translate hieroglyphs but fails to grasp that most functioned as logographic, phonographic, or determinative signs, instead offering allegorical interpretations that are nonetheless rooted in a long Egyptian tradition.[234] This manner of interpretation was common among Roman and late Roman authors.[235] Horapollo's treatise was known

---

[232] *I.Stratonikeia* 668; Söğüt 2019: 266.
[233] *I.Phil.Dem.* 436, at the sanctuary of Isis at Philae; Dijkstra 2008.
[234] Westerfeld 2019: 6.
[235] E.g., Plotinos *Ennead* 5.8.6.

already in the fifteenth century, but failed to help early modern European scholars understand the hieroglyphic writing system—the Rosetta stone was necessary for that (and in fact medieval Arabic writers perhaps came closer to solving hieroglyphs).[236] But the sort of reading comprehension that would please a modern Egyptologist was only one possible means of interpreting ancient Egyptian writing. We have seen in the previous chapter how the ankh was put to work in the Christianization of the Serapeion at Alexandria in the late fourth century. This act of interpretation was one episode in a much broader late antique discourse on hieroglyphic writing, the contours of which were set already in Roman period. Indeed, literary discussions of hieroglyphs peaked in the fourth century.[237] The "sacred script" had long been associated with priests and the mysteries of Egyptian religion. As Ammianus Marcellinus wrote concerning the rock-cut tombs of western Thebes:

> it is said, those acquainted with the ancient rites, since they had foreknowledge that a deluge was coming, and feared that the memory of the ceremonies might be destroyed, dug in the earth in many places with great labour; and on the walls of these caverns they carved many kinds of birds and beasts, and those countless forms of animals which they called hierographic writing.[238]

The belief that ancient pharaonic writing predated the flood aided early Christian authors seeking to establish the antediluvian chronology of mankind.[239] Hieroglyphs were believed to encode the "wisdom of the Egyptians" (*Acts* 7:20), which had been studied, and ultimately surpassed, by Moses; they were therefore convenient tools in the early Christian construction of world history and the superiority of Christian epistemology.

While Egyptian knowledge could be useful for universal histories, it could be a bad influence theologically: Gregory of Nyssa blames Arianism's belief in the dual nature of Christ on the Egyptian tradition of hybrid gods, such as the wolf-headed Anubis. He states that "their theory draws all its strengths from the riddles of the hieroglyphics."[240] The abbot Shenoute of Atripe (c. 347–465 CE) at Sohag in Upper Egypt too declared the ancient writing system

---

[236] El Daly 2005; for a more cautious view, see Sundermeyer 2020.
[237] Winand 2020: 164.
[238] Ammianus 22.15.30 (trans. Rolfe). See also Ammianus 17.4.8.
[239] Westerfeld 2019: 81–87.
[240] Gregory of Nyssa *Contra Eunomium* 12.4 (trans. Moore and Wilson).

a source of danger, referring in one of his Coptic writings to hieroglyphs as "laws for murdering men's souls . . . written in blood and not in black ink alone."[241] He goes on to decry "the likeness of snakes and scorpions, and the dogs and the cats, and the crocodiles and frogs . . . being laughable and false things." We should note, however, that Shenoute actively cultivated his persona as an anti-pagan extremist determined to smoke out the last vestiges of old ritual in the surroundings of his monastic federation at Sohag; his rhetorical proclamations about hieroglyphs were certainly not shared by all. In actuality, discourses about Egyptian hieroglyphs varied in late antiquity, as Westerfeld has demonstrated; she has pointed out the need for a study of the physical fate of hieroglyphs at pharaonic sites to complement her research on their discursive role in the texts.[242]

I do not present such a study, but I can make a few observations. First, even Shenoute's smear of hieroglyphic writing did not prevent his monks from utilizing ancient stones bearing hieroglyphs as spolia in the construction of the White Monastery at Sohag, some of which came from a nearby temple site.[243] The monks who made ancient tombs their abode throughout Egypt seem for the most part to have been unperturbed by the enigmatic texts carved all around, occasionally adding their own writing to the walls.[244] Churches were inserted into numerous pharaonic sanctuaries in Egypt, yet hieroglyphic writing is largely left untouched by the iconoclast's chisel, which instead struck figural images of gods carved on walls.[245] The interplay of reuse, destruction, and tolerance can be seen especially at a town called Jeme (now Medinet Habu), located at the mortuary sanctuary of Ramesses III on the western bank at Thebes (Luxor) in Upper Egypt. This monumental pharaonic sanctuary was constructed circa 1150 BCE and is most famous for its relief depicting Ramesses' victory over the "Sea Peoples" at the end of the Bronze Age. But already in the Ptolemaic and Roman periods, the cultic focus of the site was diminished as a town sprang up within the sanctuary's perimeter walls. This town continued to flourish through late antiquity and after the Arab conquest, until circa 800 CE; copious papyri and ostraca written in Coptic from the seventh and eighth centuries suggest that Jeme reached its zenith in that period. The nineteenth-century excavations

---

[241] Shenoute of Atripe *Acephalous Work A6* (trans. Westerfeld 2019: 105). See also Winand 2020: 165, who takes a more negative view of Coptic interactions with ancient hieroglyphs.
[242] Westerfeld 2019: 173.
[243] Klotz 2010.
[244] Westerfeld 2019: 1–3.
[245] See Chapter 5 p. 216. Some iconoclastic actions in Egypt may date from much later.

Figure 3.25 Medinet Habu. View of church in the temple, before 1903. Antonio Beato, Yale University Art Gallery.

regrettably swept away most post-pharaonic remains, but it is clear that by late antiquity, people were living inside the mortuary temple of Ramesses III and in mudbrick houses around it.[246]

At the heart of the settlement, a large church was built inside the second courtyard of the pharaonic temple; it is most likely the church referred to in papyri as the "Holy Church of Jeme." The structure made use of the full courtyard: closure walls between the gargantuan piers and columns of the original structure created a five-aisled basilica (Figure 3.25). The ground level of the central court was raised to be level with the entryways, and a monumental column in the east portico was removed (no mean feat) in order to build an apse. The columns on this side were also shaved down, presumably to create a flat plane for a wall. The engaged pharaonic statues along the north and south of the courtyard were chiseled away, creating pilasters on the ground level but leaving rough blocks protruding into the (less visible) gallery. The entire church interior may have been plastered and painted in the vibrant tones and rich faux marble seen at other sites, such as the Red Monastery at Sohag (also

---

[246] See Hölscher 1954 Pl. 44. Fournet 2020 highlights papyri sources mentioning the renting out of temple spaces by the state for domestic habitation.

part of Shenoute's federation), but the total deconstruction of the church at Jeme by early archaeologists makes it difficult to move beyond speculation.

The appropriation of a temple courtyard, the removal of the engaged ancient statues, and the caustic rhetoric of monks such as Shenoute may suggest an antagonistic relationship between the "Holy Church of Jeme" and its pharaonic predecessor, but this is not necessarily the case. Most temple reuse in Egypt exhibits practical, rather than polemical, motivations.[247] It is unclear whether the people of Jeme recognized the monumental structure at the center of their town as a temple: it had been built approximately a millennium and a half earlier, and the settlement is sometimes referred to in the papyri as a "Kastron" (military encampment), perhaps because of the sizable perimeter wall and the martial scenes carved on the exterior of the temple.[248] The sanctuary of Ramesses III at Medinet Habu was only one of many pharaonic monuments lining the western bank of the Nile at Thebes, from the Valley of the Kings to the Temple of Hatshepsut; neither the monumentality of Ramesses' temple nor its carved decoration was as striking to local individuals as it is to those of us approaching this material from the "outside." Conceptions of the deep past in (late) antiquity differed from those of historians today: the colossal statues of Amenhotep III standing near Jeme were identified as the mythological Memnon already in the classical period. Memnon was the "king of Ethiopia" in the Trojan War, and various Greek and Roman visitors left records of their visits on these colossi, one of which was famous for emitting a loud sound in the mornings.[249] The inhabitants of Jeme may therefore have had a radically different understanding of the ancient ruins in which they lived, situating them not in historical narratives of the end of the Bronze Age but within a transregional mental landscape of Greek myths. The alteration to the second court of Ramesses' temple during the process of transformation may have aimed not so much at covering up the pharaonic past, but at creating an interior space in line with the architectural vocabulary current in ecclesiastical spaces around the Mediterranean.

But a single step outside the door of the church at Jeme would have brought a viewer into a space that was undeniably Egyptian. Behind the late antique walls stood massive columns and pillars covered with pharaonic imagery and hieroglyphic texts. Red, blue, and green paint continues to decorate some of these architectural elements. That these walls were not covered

---

[247] Grossmann 2002.
[248] Wilfong 2002: 8.
[249] Rojas 2019: 157–161.

by plaster is indicated by the multiple figural images that underwent rough defacement and by graffiti in Coptic applied directly onto the pharaonic decorative program. This graffiti is congregated especially in the southwestern corner of the original courtyard's portico, and most include crosses and/or *nomina sacra*. For example, one in this area, written within a *tabula ansata*, begins ι̅c̅ x̅c̅ ⲡⲛⲟⲩⲧⲉ (Jesus Christ God).[250] In another instance, a cross within a wreath is painted next to the southern entrance into the courtyard. The hieroglyphs and surrounding carved imagery were clearly on view and subject to updating.

How did these Coptic-speaking Christians position themselves vis à vis the pharaonic past? These brief graffiti give us few insights, but textual sources suggest that they may have seen themselves simultaneously as part of the "in-group" (descendants of ancient, hieroglyph-writing Egyptians) and as a distinct community, given the loss of knowledge of the ancient writing system. The Arabic tradition of the seventh century and later records that Coptic monks were aware that their language was the latest phase of the ancient Egyptian tongue, as recorded in hieroglyphs, even if there is no convincing evidence that they could actually read them.[251] In any case, the graffiti on the ancient Egyptian reliefs wrapping around the "Holy Church of Jeme" at Medinet Habu indicate that hieroglyphs remained on display and did not provoke erasure or destruction, Shenoute's mockery notwithstanding. The illegible Egyptian past blended seamlessly into the Christian present.

Reading Nonsense at Didyma

One final Christianized temple with inscribed texts—of a sort—requires our attention. The city of Miletos in western Asia Minor was full of well-preserved ancient buildings, including temples. The façade of the propylon of a sanctuary of the imperial cult was preserved intact and built into the entryway of the Great Church, constructed adjacent to the agora in the late sixth century.[252] Meanwhile, the pronaos of the city's Serapeion was incorporated into Miletos' new fortifications in the seventh century.[253] The temple façade maintained its distinctive pedimental architecture as it became the main gate

---

[250] Edgerton 1937 no. 352.
[251] El Daly 2005: 66.
[252] Niewöhner 2016: 5–35.
[253] Niewöhner 2019: 197.

into the Byzantine city; only the bust of Serapis was partially removed (an alteration that may have taken place earlier; we will encounter other smashed statues from Miletos in Chapter 5). The fates of these two sanctuaries are paralleled by that of the Temple of Dionysos, which was converted into a chapel in the late Roman period with little architectural intervention beyond the addition of an apse, at least before the complex's complete rebuilding as the Church of Michael in the early seventh century.[254] Philipp Niewöhner has argued that the preservation of ancient structures at Miletos was not the result of abandonment, neglect, or inertia, but rather was the product of the particularly antiquarian, conservationist attitude of the Milesians toward their cultural patrimony, also apparent in newly carved architectural decoration in churches at the site. Rather than an indication of pagan sympathies, this antiquarian attitude hints at local patriotism and a continuing desire for urban autonomy.[255]

The Milesians had the opportunity to view ancient structures not only in their city, but at the nearby oracular sanctuary of Didyma (the Didymeion), bound to Miletos by a centuries-old sacred way. The Temple of Apollo there was so large that a sizable basilica could simply be built within its *adyton* (essentially an open-air cella), leaving the rest of the temple walls largely untouched (Figure 3.26). The church, documented in the excavations of 1906–1913 before its removal, was built of spolia in probably the fifth century, including blocks from the *naiskos*, a small shrine to Apollo that stood within the adyton. It was in this period that the so-called *Gotenmauer* carefully cordoning off the front columns of the temple was most likely constructed.[256] Even before the construction of the church, the Didymeion had had a colorful late antique afterlife: Lactantius claimed that an oracle from "Apollo at Miletos" triggered Diocletian's persecution of Christians in 303; by the period of Julian there were allegedly Christian martyria crowding the ancient temple, which the emperor-priest ordered removed.[257] But the god would soon fall silent for good. The church was built, Christian graffiti peppered the temple, and habitation crowded the sanctuary. In the sixth century the sanctuary site became the city Justinianopolis.[258]

---

[254] Niewöhner 2016: 37–57.
[255] Niewöhner 2019: 198–204.
[256] Bumke 2009: 78–79.
[257] Lactantius *De mortibus persecutorum* 11; Julian's letter was summarized by Sozomen in the mid-fifth century: *Historia Ecclesiastica* 5.20.7.
[258] Feissel 2004: 268–269.

Figure 3.26 Didyma. Church in the adyton of the Temple of Apollo. Wiegand 1924, Pl. 2.

The sanctuary of Apollo at Didyma was filled with inscriptions on stelai and on the *Prophetenhaus*, while the Temple of Apollo itself lacked the usual decrees, letters, or dedications gracing temples in Karia and surrounding areas. This is perhaps due to the temple's long construction history and unfinished state. But a quick glance at the exterior walls and steps of the crepidoma in fact reveals a wealth of texts: masons' marks on practically every block (Figure 3.27).[259] These are composed of various letters, some as ligatured monograms: for example, one block on the south wall reads ΓΛΑΥ ΙΑ; a stereobate block on the same side has ΙΕ ΘΕΟ ΙΦ. The mark ΙΕ accompanied by other letters is the most common; it probably refers to blocks paid for by the ἱερόν (sanctuary) from its own funds. Because each block of the crepidoma bears a mason's mark, the letters string together into a lengthy, nonsensical

---

[259] *I.Didyma* 68–78, Figs. 47–51.

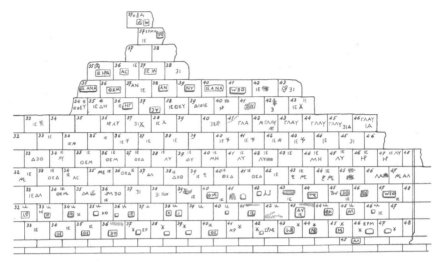

Figure 3.27 Didyma. Masons' marks on wall (south wall, eastern part). *I.Didyma*, Fig. 51. Used with permission.

text running across each step, composed of the recognizable alphabet and monogrammatic symbols. Whether the late antique community was able to recognize the markings as a part of the construction process or made up their own meanings for these mysterious texts is unknown. It may, or may not, be a coincidence that the theater at Miletos bears an inscription dated to the fourth or fifth century CE, which opens with an entire row of nonsensical letters underneath *charakteres* (magical symbols, some of which resemble ligatured monograms) (Figure 3.28). This text, called the "archangel inscription" (*Erzengelinschrift*) because of its invocation of angels to protect the city, has been fruitfully connected with wider apotropaic habits in Greco-Roman-Judaic-Christian magical practice, documented primarily in papyri and on amulets.[260] But for this text's specific format—publicly carved on a stone wall at the city's theater—and some of its specific content, the Milesians may have also drawn on a local prototype of publicly displayed, nonsensical strings of letters and symbols. The archangel inscription on the theater begins with the letters IE.

---

[260] *I.Milet* 943; Cline 2011b; Horsley and Luxford 2016: 170–175.

Figure 3.28 Miletos. *Erzengelinschrift* ("archangel inscription") on a wall of the theater. Photo: E. Steiner. Courtesy of the Deutsches Archäologisches Institut Istanbul (D-DAI-IST-Perg.86/311-1).

Conclusion: Kings of the Past on Display

In the end, Symmachus' rosy portrayal of Constantius II as a tolerant ruler failed to save the Altar of Victory in the Roman Curia in 384 CE. Within a few years, the empire's remaining pagans were under increasing legal and social pressure to abandon their traditional practices: the sacred canopy had decisively shifted. Nonetheless, many of the crown jewels of pagan cult—the storied temples of old—were preserved within cities and in the countryside. Throughout this chapter, I have argued that not only numerous temples, but also their Classical, Hellenistic, and Roman texts—even some mentioning pagan gods—were tolerated, subject to viewing without attack or censoring. These inscribed stones, many of which were still legible to Greek (and in a few instances, perhaps Latin or Aramaic) readers in the eastern Mediterranean, provided weights holding bits and pieces of the old sacred canopy in place, not so much keeping older beliefs alive but keeping cities, sanctuaries, gods, rulers, and euergetes front and center.

Unconverted inscribed temples continued to stand in still-active cities with growing Christian populations, some as spaces for the display of statues alongside ancient inscriptions, others for the public performance of imperial bureaucracy. Ancient inscriptions could even be tolerated even when churches were installed in, or adjacent to, the pagan structures. These texts might mention pagan priests and their dedications to the gods or benefactions to the cities, or display fossilized administrative documents of bygone eras. Even the illegible texts (or "texts") on display at Sardis, Jeme, and Didyma confirm the literary accounts we read in the previous chapter: ancient inscriptions were not inherently problematic in late antiquity.

A common factor at many of these monuments, whether converted or unconverted, is the epigraphic presence of famous "kings of the past," to quote again the rhetor Themistios. Augustus, still a well-known figure in late antiquity, appears in bold letters on architraves; the Temple of Augustus at Ankara almost certainly maintained its association with that emperor in late antiquity, given his epigraphic presence in the *Res Gestae*. Augustus will make another appearance in an important inscription from Aphrodisias in the next chapter. At Ephesos, it was rather Hadrian whose name persisted at the shrine on the Embolos, while Aizanoi could boast of documents from Hadrian, Antoninus Pius, and Septimius Severus inscribed on the Temple of Zeus. Alexander the Great himself, the stuff of legends then as now, appeared at Priene in his dedication to Athena. The names of these rulers are found in several instances in Greek in prominent locations at or near the beginnings of dedicatory texts on architraves or antae—that is to say, they were inherently *noticeable*, even to a casual (literate) viewer. As we have seen, a late antique reader with historical interests, such as Agathias of Myrina, was quite happy to read about a patriotic citizen's intercession with an emperor, while Kosmas Indikopleustes recorded royal documents for an Aksumite king looking for suitable precedents for his own late antique war plans. The author of the *Life of Abercius* reworked an imperial letter to elevate his city's profile in his hagiographical project. While we cannot prove that the sanctuary texts discussed in this chapter were read with a view to ancient rulers, it is likely that some individuals looked at monuments and linked these famous figures with civic histories. The effect of the regal names was to keep alive the ancient connections between cities and rulers, to embed these cities within the much larger webs of empire and, potentially, into new Christian sacred networks.

Not only rulers, but also the gods, were tolerated in certain spaces. Athena was present both in the architrave and anta dedications at Priene, as well as "in person" in the form of her statue within the cella, possibly into the early fifth century. The goddess Roma was commemorated in prominent inscriptions at Mylasa and Ankara, continuously on epigraphic display for centuries. The name of Zeus appeared in the documents located on the inner and outer wall of the temple-church at Aizanoi, at the entrance to the sanctuary-turned-monastery at Baitokaike, as well as on the wall opposite the magnificent temple-church at Diokaisareia-Olba; Zeus (or, if one read Aramaic, Baalshamin and Durahlun) remained on the façade of the Temple of Baalshamin at Palmyra. Apollo was not struck from his altar at Delphi, even as crosses crowded on the structure's upper surface. Praise of Hekate was not censored at the Christianized sanctuary of Lagina. Both mortal and divine rulers maintained their epigraphic presence in these cities and sanctuaries.

These ancient texts have been completely left out of discussions of "Christianization"; even narrower studies of the fate of pagan temples or statuary have focused quite diligently on their proclaimed topic, to the exclusion of epigraphic material. But the preservation of these inscribed monuments was not an accident. Late antique cities in the eastern Mediterranean were often busy places engaged in large-scale construction projects, such as city walls and churches, or repairs to earthquake-damaged buildings. These structures required a mass of building material: squared blocks, glossy marble revetment, sizable marble columns, or carved architectural decoration—all of which could have been harvested from defunct monuments. Yet even former temples frequently seem to have lived out their natural lifespans, preserved in place up until an earthquake or gradual collapse brought them to an end, or until they metamorphized into a church. This preservation, this non-spoliation, was a decision, one choice among many—albeit the easiest of the available options, the path of least resistance. Legal prescriptions about temples, as recorded in the *Codex Theodosianus*, likely played a role in these decisions, but, given the inconsistent messaging from imperial powers, with temples sometimes slated for destruction and at other times under protection, the semantic burden (what, exactly, counted as a "temple," what was meant by "closed" or "destroyed") and decision-making process rested with local actors, who, I argue, were themselves acted upon by the inscribed monuments surrounding them. As stated at the outset of this chapter, tolerating is not the same thing as ignoring.

The same applies to ancient statues. It is impossible to quantify the percentage of ancient statues around the Mediterranean that were simply left in place, or moved to a new display location within cities still concerned with their urban *kalos*, beauty, but it is likely high. In Chapter 5, we will see that not all statues survived late antiquity unscathed, but much of the damage apparent on statues in museum collections today may postdate our period: Michael Greenhalgh argues that many statues remained quite intact through the Byzantine and Muslim eras, until the early modern influx of western European travelers set off a statue-collecting frenzy (the decapitated heads were the easiest to transport) and may have encouraged the belief among local populations that ancient statues contained hidden treasure, to be uncovered only through breaking them open.[261] Moreover, the nineteenth-century drive for the modernization of cityscapes, constructed of the decidedly unmodern building materials stone and lime mortar, consigned numerous statues to a fiery death in lime kilns.

Although both ancient statues and ancient inscriptions were widely tolerated in late antique cities, they were valued and treated differently: inscriptions do not seem, for the most part, to have been moved around, collected, or intentionally put on display. But whether as sought-out elements of a carefully curated cityscape or as holdovers from a bygone era—part of the furniture, as it were—both statues and inscriptions made cities comfortably outfitted living spaces for late Roman individuals. The instances of preservation outlined in this chapter were certainly inflected by chance, but were not exclusively the product of it. Preservation was not the only fate awaiting pagan-era inscriptions and statues in late antiquity. It was one choice among many, as we will see in the subsequent chapters.

---

[261] Greenhalgh 2016: 334–348.

4
Spoliation
Integrating and Scrambling tions-Inscrip

(T)reading the Past: Epigraphic Spolia Underfoot

The *Life of Porphyry of Gaza* gives a dramatic account of the destruction of the Temple of Zeus Marnas at Gaza in ancient Palestine, traditionally dated to 402 CE. Porphyry, the bishop, embarks on a program of temple destruction with imperial permission. The monumental Marneion presents a challenge, so a child of seven offers some divine advice:

> "Burn the inner temple to the ground. For many terrible things have been done in it, especially human sacrifices . . . bring raw pitch, sulfur, and pork fat, and mix the three, and apply this to the bronze doors, and set them on fire, and thus the whole temple is going to burn . . . purify the place and build a holy church there." And he also said this: "I testify to you before God, it will not happen in any other way. For it is not me who speaks, but Christ who speaks in me." This he said in the language of the Syrians.[1]

After threatening the child with scourging to ensure that it really was Christ speaking, Porphyry carries out the recommended demolition procedure. The Marneion is destroyed, a church is built, and the old temple's architectural marbles are used to pave the street in front of the temple, "so that they would be trampled upon not only by men, but also by women, dogs, pigs, and beasts. This caused greater grief to the idol worshipers than the burning of the temple."[2]

Like pitch and sulfur, this account in the *Life of Porphyry* has fueled debates on late antique architectural spoliation, that is, the practice of reusing ancient building material. Should archaeologists read triumphalist appropriation

---

[1] Mark the Deacon *Life of Porphyry* 66 (trans. Rapp).
[2] *Life of Porphyry* 76 (trans. Rapp).

into the spoliation of stones for new constructions, as the *Life* suggests, or were older marbles simply convenient and cheap building material? The designation as "spolia" may already inflect our interpretations of the motive behind the reuse: "spolia" implies the looting of older materials as booty (as the term was meant to convey in the Renaissance). Many scholars now prefer "reuse" as a neutral and transcultural alternative.[3] I continue to use the term "spolia" as a convenient shorthand for building a scholarly dialogue, without making a priori assumptions about reuse having a certain meaning or intention. Whatever term is used, debates about spolia have been front and center in late antique archaeology because of an explosion of the visible reuse of older materials from the fourth century CE onward, in comparison with the preceding Roman period. This phenomenon has provoked many questions. Was the lack of newly carved elements a question of quarries, of stone carvers, or simply of taste? Did the spoliation of older material *actually* save time and money, or did it create serious challenges for building teams? Were the spoliated elements meant to be noticeable, and if so, was the viewer supposed to "read" them as a (positive or negative) appropriation of the past? In short, much of the debate has centered on the dichotomy of practical versus ideological reuse. In this chapter, we will see that the particular ways that inscriptions were built into late antique structures points toward a middle path: reuse can be both practical and reveal the cultural preoccupations of the builders.

Despite the ever-expanding bibliography on spolia, the spoliation of inscriptions is rarely discussed, in part because of the old divide of epigraphers from material culture researchers. A few brave souls have bridged this divide. Robert Coates-Stephens argues that the copious ancient inscriptions found in the late antique and medieval churches of Rome were largely ignored by builders, serving simply as conveniently shaped, smooth paving stones.[4] It was only much later that these stones were pried from floors and promoted to display locations on church walls.[5] On the island of Aegina in Greece, the heavily inscribed stones from a dining structure were reused to repair a fortification wall in probably the early fifth century CE, but Jon F. Frey has argued that they were placed without regard to their inscribed face.[6] Throughout late antique North Africa, Roman inscriptions were downgraded to building

---

[3] Dumser 2018 prefers "reuse;" Rous 2019 proposes "upcycling."
[4] Coates-Stephens 2002: 295–296.
[5] Yasin 2000.
[6] Frey 2015b: 45–84.

material, their inscribed faces variously hidden, on display, upside down, or sideways: as Stefan Altekamp notes, the way Latin inscriptions were reused by the Latin-speaking population hardly differs from the way they were used later by Arabic-speakers.[7] Georgios Pallis has recently documented several instances of epigraphic spoliation in Asia Minor and concluded that the stones were reused for practical purposes and occasionally decoratively; in his view, many inscriptions are placed with their inscribed face on view simply because this was the smoothed face, as opposed to the roughly hewn backs.[8] Although I do not follow Pallis's interpretation in every context, it is clear that builders in late antiquity were much less enthused about epigraphic spolia than were those in later periods. We do not have any late antique monument rivaling the Middle Byzantine (or later) "Little Metropolis" (Panagia Gorgoepikoos) church in Athens, constructed from various marbles both ancient and medieval, resulting in an extreme, almost kitsch, eclecticism.[9]

But in some contexts, the desire by the Christian community of Gaza to desecrate the Marneion's marbles underfoot, as described in the *Life of Porphyry*, has presented a framework for viewing spolia found in late antique floors—including ancient inscribed stones. This paradigm of Christian triumphalism produces fascinating results when applied to Gerasa (Jerash) in Jordan. Several ancient inscriptions, including those from pagan contexts, were reused in the construction of the city's Cathedral, built on a pagan cult site in the fourth century, and in the neighboring church of St. Theodore in the fifth. Both new late antique inscriptions and older reused ones were found near the entrances of the ecclesiastical complex, and Moralee argues that they should be read together in a diachronic dialogue that ends in Christian dominance. The late antique inscriptions explicitly drew attention to the former pagan use of the site, describing the "stomach-turning stench" of slaughtered animals and contrasting it to the pleasant fragrance of the church.[10] Some of the ancient texts were intentionally defaced: a reused column with a dedication to a local god shows chisel marks that only partially obscure the original text, while another text honoring three priestesses was cut up into narrow strips and used in paving; the inscription's message was visually scrambled.[11] These texts (both ancient and late antique) articulated a triumphalist

[7] Altekamp 2017: 46.
[8] Pallis 2019.
[9] Kiilerich 2005.
[10] *I.Gerasa* 299. Moralee 2006: 192–193; see also Leatherbury 2020: 168–169.
[11] *I.Gerasa* 20 and 25.

narrative through the physical defacement of the pagan past, generating a "historically based rupture" in fifth-century Gerasa.[12] The power of the new Christian sacred canopy was constructed through these stones.

In Asia Minor, Saradi interprets the inscriptions found at Priene in the paving of the city's main church (the "Byzantine Basilica") similarly, as an indication of Christian triumphalism.[13] These stelai dating from the fourth century BCE to the first century CE are attributed to the nearby sanctuary of Athena. They are largely Hellenistic honorific decrees, as well as a few interstate letters and a number of dedications to members of the imperial family. As documented in Chapter 3, the Temple of Athena was still standing at least in part into late antiquity, although housing slowly encroached into the temenos. The spoliated inscriptions were laid in the floor of the first phase of the basilica in probably the first half of the fifth century, mainly in the area of the narthex (the center of the nave was mosaicked), but unfortunately, their precise findspots were not recorded in the early excavations, nor whether they were found face up or face down.[14] Several, however, are worn on their inscribed face, so they were most likely face up. For Saradi, the critical factor in interpreting this reuse is the stones' location in the *floor*. At other sites, she views spolia, particularly architectural ornament, as evidence that ancient carving was still positively valued in late antiquity, within a wider thoughtscape of continuing classical *paideia* and aesthetics.[15]

Given the explicit reference in the Gerasa inscriptions to pagan cult, Moralee is justified in reading Christian antagonism and triumphalism into the epigraphic spolia found there. Gerasa's Temple of Artemis continued to be the visual center of the city in late antiquity, and pagan cult may have been ongoing as the churches were constructed.[16] But at other sites, including Priene, such an interpretation is not warranted. Spoliation began long before late antiquity; inscriptions too could be spoliated in ancient times.[17] Herodotos claims that the people of Byzantium used inscribed stelai of Darius I to build the altar of Artemis Orthosia in the fifth century BCE, while at Herakleia Latmia in Karia, inscribed antae blocks from the

---

[12] Moralee 2006: 204.
[13] Saradi 1997: 403. See Chapter 3, p. 81.
[14] Fildhuth 2017: 36; Westphalen 2000: 276. The ancient inscriptions found in the basilica are *I.Priene B—M* 7, 15, 16, 17, 19/20, 27, 28, 39, 98, 112, 115, 145, 189, 212, 215, 217, 268, 288, 331, and 340.
[15] Saradi-Mendelovici 1990; Saradi 2006.
[16] Wharton 1995: 65–73.
[17] Frey 2015a; Ng and Swetnam-Burland 2018; Duckworth and Wilson 2020.

Temple of Athena were reused as statue bases in the Roman period.[18] The practice of spoliation undoubtedly increased in late antiquity, but as we saw, scholars who have examined the subject of epigraphic spolia in our period have concluded that the motivations were largely practical, not polemical. That does not mean this holds true for every site, and in this chapter, I present some instances where I argue the content of inscriptions *was* taken into account during the act of spoliation. But at Priene at least, there is no indication that embedding of ancient stelai in the basilica floor was an ideological statement of Christian triumphalism. Although several certainly originated from the sanctuary of Athena based on publication clauses in the texts, not all necessarily came from there: public documents could also be displayed in the city's agora, and at least one of the stones is actually a grave marker, probably from the eastern necropolis.[19] The sale of a priesthood of Meter Phrygia—an explicitly pagan text—was found not in the floor, but covered by plaster in a wall of the church, while a cylindrical base with a fragmentary reference to a priest of Augustus was reused in the area of the basilica's altar—hardly a space of desecration.[20] Another honorary inscription from the sanctuary of Athena became paving not in the church but in a house.[21] The inscriptions within the basilica show none of the physical manipulation that the texts at Gerasa do, nor does the brief late antique dedicatory text in the Priene church make any reference to paganism.[22] The epigraphic spolia at Priene has every indication of being largely practical reuse—reuse that reveals the general tolerance displayed toward older texts and, given the large number of stelai found within the basilica floor in a city full of spoilable ruins, perhaps a particular aesthetic of inscribed spolia decoration.

The same lack of hostile intention can be seen in Church C at Knidos (Karia), built from blocks of a temple of Dionysos probably in the fifth or sixth century; a few stelai were reused, face up, near the entrance of the church. But these were honorific decrees of the demos for private individuals.[23] Surely there had originally been actual pagan dedications available for appropriation; the fact that those stones were *not* put on display in the floor indicates a lack of explicit antagonism. Likewise, at Ephesos, a large number of inscriptions in both Greek and Latin were incorporated into the atrium

---

[18] Herodotos 4.87. Posamentir 2020: 456.
[19] *I.Priene B—M* 288.
[20] Meter Phrygia: *I.Priene B—M* 145; Wiemer and Kah 2011: 3; Altar: *I.Priene B—M* 212.
[21] *I.Priene B—M* 18.
[22] *I.Priene B—M* 223.
[23] *I.Knidos* 83–85. Özgümüş 1992: 9–11; Bruns Özgan 2013: 75–118.

paving of the Church of Mary, either at the time the second-century Roman stoa was converted into a church in the decades before the 431 Council of Ephesos, or later.[24] Some of the texts (particularly those in Greek) have been quite visibly erased; in other cases, the stone has been cut into halves or quarters and the segments laid noncontiguously, similar to the "scrambling" that happened on the floor at Gerasa. But these inscriptions at Ephesos are primarily grave markers, not stones from the adjacent Olympeion or Ephesos' other sanctuaries; the floor in this atrium is overall heterogeneous, made up of both epigraphic spolia and rough structural blocks with *anathyrosis* and pouring channels visible. One has the impression of a floor made with haste, not hatred. At Didyma, the fifth-century basilica built within the adyton of the sanctuary of Apollo incorporated several inscriptions, including stelai, bases, and wall blocks. These texts were on display but for the most part untouched. An exception is a base (a statue dedication by Diocletian and Maximian) incorporated into the floor and damaged when a groove for a parapet was carved into it.[25] This was the result of the practical needs of construction and indicates that inscriptions were not immune to damage. Ancient texts were not put on a pedestal (although they were literally pedestals, in some cases), but they were for the most part tolerated when used as spolia in late antique ecclesiastical spaces.

This archaeological evidence suggests that the polemical paradigm of the *Life of Porphyry of Gaza* does not map on to spoliated stones at other sites. After all, biblical passages, *nomina sacra*, and donor inscriptions frequently appear on ecclesiastical floor mosaics; there was nothing inherently degrading about treading over texts.[26] As discussed in Chapter 1, the Levant and Egypt seem to have had a higher rate of violence against monuments of the pagan past. We will come back to this point when discussing statuary in Chapter 5. But at Gerasa, where Moralee has convincingly argued for the polemical use of ancient inscriptions in the Cathedral and the Church of St. Theodore, a third church makes use of very limited epigraphic spolia, and none of it provocatively. The Church of Bishop Isaiah was built in the sixth century, perhaps when pagan-Christian competition was no longer front and center in the minds of the donors and builders; contemporary mosaic inscriptions in the space focus on the salvation of the founders.[27] At Abila

---

[24] Karydis 2019: 181–185. For the inscriptions: Knoll, Reisch, and Keil 1932, no. 16–23.
[25] *I.Didyma* 89.
[26] Leatherbury 2020. Cf., however, *Codex Justinianus* i.8.1 (427 CE), which forbade depicting crosses on floors.
[27] Clark and Bowsher 1986: 319–321.

(Qweilbeh, Jordan), a city of the Decapolis, the five-aisled Church E of the fifth or sixth century probably reused a second-century CE granite column from a man named Dischasdeinionos: "to good Fortune (Tyche), on behalf of the safety of the rulers"—hardly a controversial sentiment.[28] Nearby, at Paneas (Caesarea Philippi/Banias, in the Golan Heights), excavations have recently uncovered a votive dedication to Pan on a second- or third-century CE basalt altar built into the wall of a church in such a way that the inscription was out of sight in the middle of the wall.[29] Even using the *Life of Porphyry of Gaza* as the interpretive paradigm for spolia at Gaza itself is suspect. The *Life* may date as late as the sixth century, more than a hundred years after the supposed destruction of the temple. Porphyry himself is not otherwise attested. As Busine argues, this text, like so many other hagiographies, functions as an etiology seeking to explain aspects of the late antique cityscape, such as a collapsed temple, and endow them with Christian meaning.[30] The *Life* gives a glimpse of Christian triumphalism from a single viewpoint, at a single time (the sixth century) and place (Gaza). What may have initially been simply a pragmatic building choice—if the marbles on the street actually originated from the Marneion at all—could later be used to enhance the city's Christian history.

Yet even when reuse is largely practical, it does not mean that the inscribed stones were value-neutral. Reused inscriptions were laid bare to reading and reinterpretation, both at the point of construction (when decisions were made about what to do with them) and later in their use phase. Frey has explored how spoliation is a process, carried out by scavengers and builders during a discrete period of time; spolia is the product that remains visible and open to evaluation, appreciation, interpretation.[31] This distinction is critical, as it differentiates the decisions made during construction from the result, which may have been viewed in ways not intended or anticipated by the builders. Texts like the *Life of Porphyry of Gaza* had the potential to shape how some individuals viewed spolia. The story told by Sokrates Scholastikos and Ammianus Marcellinus of a prophetic inscription uncovered at Chalcedon during an attempted spoliation, which foretold (or precipitated?) the Gothic attack on Constantinople in 378 (Chapter 2), may have inflected attitudes toward spoliated ancient inscriptions elsewhere. In the following,

---

[28] Menninga 2004: 45; Chambers 2009: 119. The column was found to the west of the church.
[29] Brown 2020.
[30] Busine 2013. See also Frey 2019: 267–268.
[31] Frey 2015b: 128–178. See also Lehmann and Gutsfeld 2013; Barker 2018.

I consider both decisions about inscriptions made during the construction process and final product available to viewers visiting spolia-built spaces.

This is the shortest chapter of the archaeological part of this book, but it ought to be the longest. The use of spolia was ubiquitous in late antique cities. Marble was both expensive and limited; cities therefore harvested it from redundant or damaged structures, including temples. The stone was valuable for its display factor and ability to be carved; as an ingredient of lime mortar, it was fundamental to many building projects. A great many inscriptions were probably burnt for lime, leaving behind no trace; many others were built into later walls and structures. This fate—to be the raw material for wall construction—especially awaited freestanding bases and stelai, which could be extracted and transported more easily than disassembling a wall or moving the resulting large ashlars. For example, at the great Panhellenic sanctuary of Olympia in Greece, multiple inscribed statue bases made their way into the late antique fortification, into the church in the workshop of Pheidias, and into the so-called *Spolienhaus*, even as other monuments were left in place.[32]

It would be fascinating to track assemblages of freestanding dedications and honorific texts from sanctuaries as they became dispersed around city- or village-scapes, as we have just done in a limited way for the above sites, but I have not pursued that avenue further for one primary reason: the dreaded "late wall." All too often, early epigraphic corpora and excavation reports list the findspots of inscriptions simply as being in a "late wall," without further detail, description, or potential date of this structure. Upon discovery, the inscribed stones were often swiftly freed from these material prisons (usually to the betterment of the inscription, which could be properly studied, squeezed, and stored, and to the detriment of the wall). Even when architectural reports and corpora offer further information on the find contexts of stones, the dates of such later constructions cannot always be ascertained. At Pergamon, numerous inscriptions, along with the reliefs of the Pergamon Altar, were found within Byzantine and Turkish walls; whether these walls themselves cannibalized earlier, late antique spolia structures or incorporated loose-lying blocks is not always clear.[33] At Bostra (Syria), the epigraphic remnants of the Greco-Roman past were fully integrated into the built fabric

---

[32] Lehmann and Gutsfeld 2013: 97–100; Robertson Brown 2016: 316–318.
[33] Fränkel 1890; Otten 2010.

of the Islamic-era town, as is the case in many other continuously occupied sites.³⁴

Because of these difficulties, the case studies presented in this chapter are primarily architectural: inscribed stones originating from temple walls, architraves, and antae, which made their way into securely dated late antique churches and, in one case, a synagogue. My focus is on the inscriptions, but these spolia blocks must be considered within their surrounding building program. As we will see through a close consideration of construction logic and the range of reuse possibilities, ancient inscribed texts in many cases were not simply ignored by building teams, even if the stones were used in a largely practical way.

Constructing Churches with Inscribed Text

The Korykian Cave: Building with Inscriptions

On a cliff high above the Korykian Cave (Κωρύκειον ἄντρον) in the region of Rough Kilikia (Isauria), a temple was disassembled in late antiquity and its blocks—including inscribed ones—were rebuilt as a church. The Korykian Cave itself (not to be confused with the homonymous cave near Delphi in Greece) is one of the most impressive natural features of Asia Minor and produced a "religioscape" stretching across millennia. The term "religioscape" has been used by anthropologists to denote the "distribution in spaces through time of the physical manifestations of specific religious traditions and of the populations that build them."³⁵ It is a useful term because it takes into account the synchronic experience of viewers at any point in time: late antique Christians saw not only their own churches, but also still standing, collapsed, or spoliated temples; remaining pagans likewise experienced their religious topography as it intersected with the new Christian structures. All the sanctuaries discussed in this book are religioscapes because they manifest a religious tradition (and its gradual demise), but the term is particularly potent at the Korykian Cave because of the massive cavern system linking the awe-inspiring natural world inextricably with anthropogenic worship spaces.

---

[34] *IGLS* 13.1.
[35] Hayden et al. 2019: 19.

Religioscapes are formed not just through built structures, but through the stories people tell, and at the Korykian Cave, those stories were very, very old. The massive cave system is visible on the surface in the form of two yawning abysses (karst sinkholes), now known colloquially as Heaven (Cennet) and Hell (Cehennem). While the Cehennem depression is inaccessible, the Cennet sinkhole can be visited today as in antiquity by a path leading into this lush gorge, which terminates at the gaping opening of the Korykian Cave itself. In the words of the Latin geographer Pomponius Mela, writing around 43 CE, the cave

> terrifies those who enter with its miraculous roar of cymbals and the great uproar of things rustling around. . . . It draws deep down anyone who dares, and it lets them in deep as if through a rabbit hole. . . . Inside, there is a space too hair-raising for anyone to dare to go forward, and for that reason it remains unknown. The whole cave, however, being narrow and truly sacred, both worthy of being inhabited by gods and believed to be so, reveals nothing that is not venerable, and it reveals itself as if with some kind of numinous power.[36]

Pomponius goes on to identify another nearby opening into the cave system as the lair of Typhon, the hundred-headed monster who struggled against Zeus. In a version of the myth, Typhon defeated Zeus, cut out the tendons of his hands and feet, and stashed them along with Zeus himself in the Korykian Cave. Zeus was saved only by the efforts of Hermes and Pan, who lured Typhon out of the cave with the promise of a fish dinner and then patched up Zeus.[37] This association of Typhon with the cave system predates Pindar (fifth century BCE) and probably finds its origins in the Hittite period, with Zeus playing the role of the storm god Tarhunt and Hermes that of the Luwian god Runt.[38] Typhon was a late echo of the Hittite monster Illuyankas, one of a number of dragon-monsters inhabiting Anatolia.[39] At the mouth of the cave, a section of polygonal wall and a cult structure perhaps of the Hellenistic period have been found; although this feature did not prevent visitors from going down Pomponius' rabbit hole, it was a barrier between the world of men and the cave of monsters. The remains of this structure

---

[36] Pomponius Mela 1.72–75 (trans. Romer).
[37] Apollodoros *Bibliotheka* 1.6.3; Oppian *Halieutica* 3.1–28.
[38] Pindar *Pythian Ode* 1.17. MacKay 1990: 2104.
[39] Rojas 2019: 80–92; 131–135.

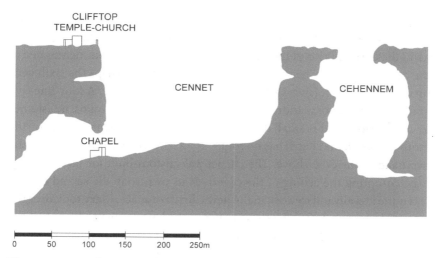

Figure 4.1 Korykian Cave (Kilikia). Section showing the sinkholes and the opening of the cave system, as well as the chapel and the temple-church. Author and Yasmin Nachtigall, after Bayliss 2004, Fig. 109.

have recently been identified as a shrine to Hermes on the basis of a dedication to that god and to Pan inscribed on the wall of the cave (which also suits the myth).[40]

Far above the cave mouth, set a few meters back from the cliff edge, stood a late Hellenistic Doric temple *in antis*, within the territory of the city of Korykos (Figure 4.1). This sanctuary was initially identified as a Temple of Zeus Korykos, based on the mistaken attribution of a graffito to that deity to this temple. But Hamdi Şahin has now clarified that the graffito is actually located at a different sanctuary at Göztepesi some kilometers away; the temple at the edge of the Korykian Cave was most probably dedicated to Hermes, like the shrine at the mouth of the cave below.[41] In order to avoid confusion, I follow Bayliss in calling the temple simply the "Clifftop Temple."

We do not know what stories people in late antiquity told about the Korykian Cave; it warranted a mention in Stephanos of Byzantium in the early sixth century only as an "ἀξιάγαστον θαῦμα," a must-see attraction.[42] But the area was certainly an active religioscape, perhaps drawing both locals

---

[40] Şahin 2012: 70; *I. Westkilikien Rep.* Korykion Antron 3.
[41] Şahin 2012.
[42] *Ethnica* 10.313.2.

living in houses (now ruins) to the south of the temple, those traveling along the paved road from the coast inland, and anyone wanting to experience firsthand the dark interior of the cave.[43] The divine protector commemorated at the cave changed: a Christian chapel was inserted in perhaps the sixth century on top of the former shrine at the entrance to the cave. A four-line epigram above the door is addressed from a Paulos to the Theotokos: he asks her to come gladly to this small dwelling.[44] But this is no normal house for the mother of God: the chapel has no roof.[45] It was protected from rainfall by the overhang of the cave above. The chapel was custom-built for its surroundings, co-opting the ceiling of the cavern as its own roof: the sacred canopy was quite literally put to work in the new Christian space. Mary took over the role of Hermes and Pan: she stood between the hair-raising unknown of the cave and the new Christian world above.

This process of transformation happened at the temple on the cliff above the cave as well. The cella of the Clifftop Temple, built of ashlar limestone blocks a single skin thick, was fully deconstructed and put back together as a three-aisled basilica, probably in the late fifth century (Figure 4.2).[46] The northern and eastern walls are the best preserved. Most of the blocks from the temple were used as raw building material in the northern wall of the church (the wall closest to the cliff edge) wherever they were needed; this is most clearly visible in the case of a stylobate block built into a course otherwise composed of orthostate blocks. The church far exceeded the size (and therefore the available blocks) of the temple, so parts of the structure were built instead from *Kleinquaderwerk* (rubble masonry of small stones). The spolia walls of the Clifftop temple-church therefore have an uneven, hodgepodge look—except for the northeast corner. Here, and only here, the blocks from the temple were re-erected in their original, Hellenistic configuration.

These blocks formed the ancient temple's anta, inscribed on its front face (east) and side face (south) with a long list of names and patronymics, probably representing priests of the sanctuary (Figure 4.3).[47] The approximately one hundred sixty-five names preserved on the front of the anta (face A)

---

[43] For the road and settlement: Eichner 2011: 162–185.
[44] *I.Westkilikien Rep.* Korykion Antron 5. *MAMA* III, 218–219.
[45] Feld and Weber 1967: 102–103; Bayliss 2004: 85; Rojas 2019: 132–135.
[46] Hild and Hellenkemper 1990: 314; Feld and Weber 1967: 277; Bayliss 2004: 84. According to recent analyses of the stones used to construct the church, none came from the Göztepesi sanctuary, as previously suggested: Şahin, Yüksel, and Görücü 2010.
[47] *I.Westkilikien Rep.* Korykion Antron 1. The text numbering is subdivided in this corpus by section corresponding with row (wall course) and column of text. The southern corner of the anta has suffered significant damage since the publication of Heberdey and Wilhelm 1896: 73–76.

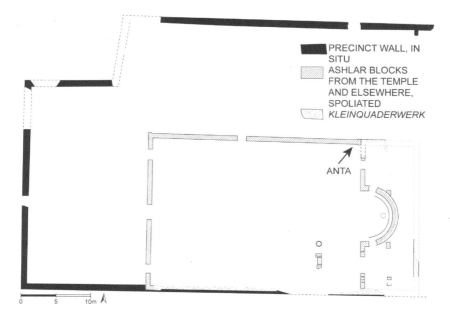

Figure 4.2 Korykian Cave (Kilikia). Clifftop temple-church plan. Author and Yasmin Nachtigall, after Bayliss 2004, Fig. 110.

were engraved retrospectively most likely in the Augustan period; those on the side wall were added over time, first on the setback of the anta (face B) and later, in the third century CE, on the anta wall next to the set back (face C) (Figure 4.4). The earlier names on faces A and B offer little information beyond evidence for local onomastics. Some are marked with the Greek letter beta, probably indicating that they held the priesthood twice.[48] The final name on face A, at the bottom of the anta, may perhaps be associated with Archelaos I, king of Kappadokia (d. 17 CE), who had been given territory in Kilikia in 25 BCE. At some point after Archelaos, more priests were listed on face B, the side of the anta; the palaeography here is less precise than in the Augustan list, but still orderly, becoming less so toward the bottom of the anta (the lower names are more difficult to read because they have been partially erased—we will come back to this in Chapter 5). On this face, Roman names

---

[48] The beta may rather indicate that the men had given twice a prescribed amount to the god or perhaps that they were the second of their name (i.e., "junior"), but, given similar lists of priests initiated in the Augustan era at sites such as Ankara, a list of priests seems most likely.

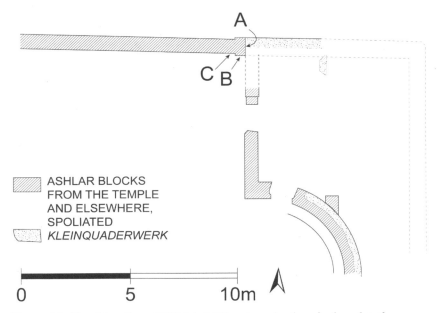

Figure 4.3 Korykian Cave (Kilikia). Clifftop temple-church plan, detail. Inscribed faces (A, B, and C) of the anta marked. Author and Yasmin Nachtigall, modified from Bayliss 2004, Fig. 110.

mix with Greek, and some individuals chose to include both aspects of their identity: "Zenophanes (twice), also called Romulos, priest of the Nemeses for life" (Ζηνοφάνης Β | ὁ καὶ Ῥωμύλος | ἱερεὺς διὰ βίου | τῶν Νεμέσεων).[49] When this setback of the anta was filled, names began to be inscribed on the inner wall of the anta (face C), to the left of the previous names.

Face C is an object lesson in the rupture and crisis of the third century: the poor quality of the script stands in stark contrast to the relatively regular inscribing on face B (Figure 4.5). A date of post 212 CE is suggested by the presence of numerous "Marcus Aurelius" names starting with the second name on face C; this nomenclature likely derives from the emperor Caracalla and his Antonine Constitution granting Roman citizenship throughout the empire.[50] From the very first names inscribed on the highest block of face C, letter forms are irregular in shape and size, and the writing is in some cases tilted. We may perhaps identify a mixture of "DIY" entries (where the priest

---

[49] *I. Westkilikien Rep.* Korykion Antron 1, section B2, *ll.* 10–12 and B3, *l.* 1.
[50] *I. Westkilikien Rep.* Korykion Antron 1, section C1, *l.* 4.

Figure 4.4 Korykian Cave (Kilikia). Clifftop temple-church, anta, inscribed faces A, B, and C. Author, courtesy of Hamdi Şahin.

himself, rather than a professional stone carver, recorded his name) and more professional additions on blocks II and III. "Marcus Aurelius" names continued to appear in the epigraphy of Anatolia until the mid-third century and then drop out; the approximate number of names on face C, forty-eight, and the fact that some served the god for two or even three years, agrees with a date of circa 273 CE for the last record (a Markos Aurelios [—]ios

162 PAGAN INSCRIPTIONS, CHRISTIAN VIEWERS

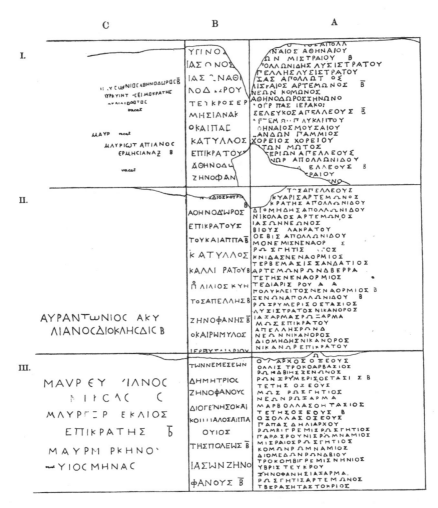

Figure 4.5 Korykian Cave (Kilikia). Drawing of the three uppermost courses of the inscribed faces of the Clifftop temple anta (A, B, and C, *I. Westkilikien Rep. Korykion Antron* 1). Heberdey and Wilhelm 1896, 73, Fig. 10.

Athenodoros).[51] The list of names reached the lowest block of the anta wall and concluded at precisely the period of even greater rupture in Asia Minor.

[51] *I.Westkilikien Rep.* Korykion Antron 1, section C8, *ll.* 6–7. Dating of M. Aurelius names in Anatolia: Mitchell 1977: 71. The latest dated inscription combining Markos and Aurelios from Asia Minor known to me also dates (coincidentally?) to 272/3: Αὐρ. Μᾶρκος Ποπλίου (*I.Ephesos* 3856). "Markos Aurelios" (or "Aurelios Markos") occurs in a number of difficult-to-date Christian inscriptions, according to the *Inscriptiones Christianae Graecae* database.

As the Sassanian king Shapur marched through Kilikia in 260, Goths sacked the cities of the coast and nearby Cyprus in 269, and the rebellious Palmyrene queen Zenobia annexed territory in this region in the early 270s, the social fabric of Korykos may have been rent so that the annual priesthood at the Korykian Cave Clifftop temple fell by the wayside or operated with less fanfare—to say nothing of the rising number of Christian converts who would soon leave their mark with a series of spectacular churches around Korykos.

Given the prosopographical potential of this list on the anta of the Clifftop Temple at the Korykian Cave, it is not surprising that epigraphers have focused on the historical contexts for these names (especially those in the Augustan list) at the expense of their physical setting within the late antique temple-church, which is in fact critical for the preservation of the list itself. As mentioned, the blocks of the northern anta wall, and *only* this wall, were re-erected in their original configuration when the church was constructed in the late fifth century; the anta wall became the north wall of the church. The result was that the names on the front of the anta (face A) were hidden behind the transverse wall of the north aisle (i.e., the wall running from the edge of the main apse to the north wall of the church). The Augustan-era list was therefore preserved out of sight for centuries: it was rediscovered only in the 1890s when J. Theodore Bent recorded that "quite accidentally, by pulling down a wall, we came across a list of 162 names."[52] What to make of this reconstruction of the temple's northeast anta as part of the church? Bayliss argues that it made construction sense to use the anta blocks all together, since they were already dressed to the same size and shape.[53] But this decision to rebuild the anta is questionable from a construction perspective: the result was that the east wall of the church was not bonded with the north wall, hardly an ideal situation from a structural point of view. Other heterogeneous blocks (including from the south anta) were incorporated into the walls elsewhere; clearly, spolia blocks did not all need to be originally dressed to the same size to find a home in the church walls.[54]

Acknowledging the presence of text on the anta of the Clifftop Temple offers a new explanation for the anta's re-erection as the church's north

---

[52] Bent 1890: 448.
[53] Bayliss 2004: 83.
[54] A few of these blocks, including one from the south anta, bear fragmentary inscriptions, but their original contexts and content are not clear. Feld and Weber 1967: 257.

wall: the inscription itself motivated this construction decision. When confronted with the lengthy inscribed list on the north anta's front and side, the attitude of the late antique builders tended toward preservation, even if most of the inscribed names would be hidden behind a wall. The inscribed blocks functioned like the pictures printed on puzzle pieces, making it possible to reassemble them in the correct order. The decision to reconstruct the anta in this way was clearly the product of planning: two of the blocks (the fourth and fifth blocks from the top) are placed upside down in the re-erected anta. This occurred not because the workmen were illiterate (they may have been), but in order to conceal large, rough cavities carved into the original outer lateral face of these blocks.[55] By turning the anta blocks upside down, these cavities now faced the interior of the church (specifically, the northern side aisle); the outer façade of the church wall was therefore smooth.

The Clifftop temple-church builders were concerned with creating a smooth, regular outer façade of the church, while the inner wall—in a dark, windowless side aisle—was less of a priority.[56] Otto Feld and Hans Weber assert that the interior wall was covered with plaster (some traces may still be visible on this wall, though without closer study it is difficult to distinguish plaster from natural accretions on the limestone), but there is no trace of plaster within the cavities, where we might expect it. As we will see in Chapter 5, there is an additional indication that the names were visible within the church, namely, that some of them have been roughly erased. The windowless side aisle would have been dark enough that plastering this section of the building may not have been a priority. The exterior aesthetic of building took precedence: the two anta blocks that were turned upside down have been subject to much more thorough, careful erasures of the names carved on faces B and C (which were initially on the inner wall of the temple pronaos and would now, after the inversion of the anta blocks, be on the exterior wall of the church). I could not find any traces of names on the outer face of these two limestone blocks, indicating the care with which they were removed. This church therefore bucks the trend of most other late antique ecclesiastical spaces, which lavished more attention on the interior of churches than their outer faces. A series of construction decisions made in the course of the spolia building project resulted in the preservation (and simultaneous

---

[55] Feld and Weber 1967: 257; Bayliss 2004: 83.
[56] Cf. the concern with a smooth outer face on the so-called inscription wall on the island of Aegina, built from spolia in probably the early fifth century: Frey 2015b: 80.

hiding) of some inscribed names, while others were left in place, and still others removed.

On the edge of the abyss—literally—between pagan past and Christian future, between the primordial evil trapped in the cave below and God's well-ordered world without, the blocks of the former Clifftop Temple above the Korykian Cave wove the new church inextricably into a long-standing religioscape. The late antique church builders thought beyond pragmatic concerns and acknowledged that the stones of the anta were simultaneously epigraphic record and building material in the way they reused these blocks. Curiously, their priorities seem to have been, in the following order: aesthetics (the smooth outer north wall of the church), preservation (of the list of names), and only finally, structural. The intentional, partial preservation of the ancient list of names from the temple in fact continued a tradition of memorializing older religious spaces at the site. The Hellenistic temple was built in a temenos closed by a wall of polygonal masonry, potentially of the Archaic period.[57] This polygonal wall was left in situ as a ready-made atrium for the new church. We have seen already this impetus for preservation at several sites in Chapter 3, where entire temples (and their texts) were maintained as features of Christianizing cityscapes. At the Korykian Cave Clifftop Temple, the manner of using epigraphic spolia suggests that this impulse toward preservation was at play here as well.

Scrambling Apollo Klarios at Sagalassos

Church builders at Sagalassos in Pisidia used epigraphic spolia differently. Although the city lost its status as "first city" of Pisidia in the provincial reforms around 311 CE, it remained a vibrant cityscape until the third quarter of the sixth century. Sagalassos took particular delight in the display of ancient statues throughout the late Roman period, even those of pagan gods. In the Upper Agora, Dionysos was left in his place when the Antonine nymphaeum was rebuilt in the sixth century; he was joined on the fountain's façade by a series of recycled statues, mainly those related to pagan healing cults (Asklepios, his mother Koronis, Hygeia, and possibly Apollo).[58] At the west side of the Upper Agora, a nude statue continued to stand in front of

---
[57] Feld and Weber 1967: 263.
[58] Jacobs 2010: 274; Jacobs and Waelkens 2017: 186–187.

the North West Heroon until an earthquake of the early seventh century brought it down. These statues were on display concurrently with the appropriation of the city's bouleuterion for the construction of a church, recently redated to the sixth century.[59] Farther south, colossal acrolithic cult statues of second-century imperial figures remained on display in the sizable Roman Baths.[60] Nearby, the north-south colonnaded street—the city's main thoroughfare—was redecorated with under-life-size figures of Apollo, Hygeia, and Aphrodite in the second quarter of the sixth century; these figures likely originally came from a private house, but were repurposed for the beautification of the colonnaded street.[61] Pagan gods were in some cases actively sought out and shown off.

But the sculptures originally from cult contexts were now homeless: Sagalassos' temples were desacralized in the course of late antiquity and found other uses. The imperial cult Temple of Antoninus Pius was abandoned by the late fourth century, its *disjecta membra* used to construct domestic structures that encroached into the former temenos of the emperor-god.[62] Only fragments of the temple's inscribed architrave were found on site.[63] Other pieces of this temple were used in a fortification wall and in Basilica E1, constructed smack in the middle of the city's old stadium, which fell out of use by the fifth or sixth century. This church was itself built largely from the stones of another temple, that of Dionysos; its blocks were numbered to facilitate rebuilding, indicating a careful and organized de- and reconstruction. The Dionysian carved decoration from the temple was left on display: the exterior wall of the north transept shows masks of maenads and Silenus, while dancing satyrs (!) graced the interior of the church.[64] Another temple in the city, the Doric Temple next to the Upper Agora, became a watchtower in the late fifth-/early sixth-century fortification wall.[65] The Sagalassians were not about to let their perfectly good classical monuments go to waste.

This enthusiasm for recycling—and tolerance for pagan subject matter—is also apparent at Sagalassos' other temple-church, Basilica E. Constructed on the site of the Temple of Apollo Klarios from its architectural pieces, Basilica

---

[59] Talloen and Poblome 2016: 142–145.
[60] Cf. Mägele 2017, who proposes that the statues were moved into the baths in late antiquity.
[61] Jacobs and Stirling 2017.
[62] Talloen and Vercauteren 2011: 355–356; Jacobs and Waelkens 2014: 111–121.
[63] *I.Sagalassos* 19.
[64] Lanckoroński 1892: 141, 151–152; Talloen and Vercauteren 2011: 366.
[65] Talloen and Vercauteren 2011: 361; Jacobs 2013: 292–293. The date of the late antique fortification wall has recently been dated later than in the preceding publications (pers. comm. Peter Talloen, April 2, 2022).

Figure 4.6 Sagalassos. Façade reconstruction of the Temple of Apollo Klarios with *I.Sagalassos* 20. Lanckoroński 1892, Pl. 25.

E incorporated the temple's original inscribed architrave into its interior (Figure 4.6).[66] The three-line text recorded the refurbishment of the temple by local euergete Titos Flavios Kollega, a high priest of the imperial cult, and his family members in 119/120 CE. The text begins, as is typical, with the name of the gods to whom the sanctuary was dedicated: "To Apollo Klarios and to the emperors"; it continues by detailing exactly which architectural features were added or renovated, which family members were responsible for the various parts, and how many denarii had been spent.[67] Nowhere on the architrave is intentional damage to the inscription evident; it is well preserved (though broken), except for the fourth block, which is missing. Even given the atmosphere of late antique tolerance outlined in the previous chapter, as well as the apparent respect for spoliated carved texts shown at the Korykian Cave Clifftop Temple, the prominent epigraphic presence of Klarian Apollo *inside* the church at Sagalassos is unexpected and warrants a closer consideration of the building's construction history and the inscription's findspot.

[66] Locations of various spoliated temple blocks in the church walls: Bayliss 2004: Fig. 52.
[67] *I.Sagalassos* 20:

  1 Ἀπόλλωνι Κλαρίῳ καὶ θεοῖς Σεβαστοῖ|ς καὶ τῇ πατρίδι Τ(ίτος) Φλ(άουιος) Κολλήγας, μετὰ Φλ(αουίας) | Λονγίλλης τῆς γυναικὸς αὐτοῦ, τὸ περίπτερον | [— μετὰ — καὶ —]|λάου τῶν Διομήδους καὶ [Ἰ]αδος, πατρὸς
  2 καὶ μητρὸς τοῦ Κολλήγα ἐκ τῶν ἰδίων καὶ ἐκ δηναρίων μυρί|ων τῶν ἐπιδοθέντων ἐν χρόνῳ τῆς ἀρχιερωσύνη|ς τοῦ Κολλήγα κατασκευάσας ἀνέθηκε καὶ καθιέρωσε[ν] . . . . ἐπὶ? . . . .]| Πρόκλου τοῦ σεμνοτάτου ἡγεμόνος. *vacat*
  3 *vacat?* τὴν δὲ σκούτλωσιν τῶν τοίχων τ|[ο]ῦ ναοῦ ὁ αὐτὸς Φλ(αουιος) Κολλήγας καὶ Τ(ίτος) Φλ(άουιος) [Οὐ]|ᾶρος Δαρεῖος, ὁ ἀδελφὸς αὐτοῦ, διὰ Φλ(αουίου) Διομ[ήδ]ους . . . .]
  "To Apollo Klarios and to the *theoi sebastoi* and to the fatherland, Titos Flavios Kollega, with Flavia Longilla his wife, furnished, erected, and dedicated the colonnade together with [so-and-so and so-and-so], the sons of Diomedes and Ias (?), father and mother of Kollega, from their own funds and from the ten thousand denarii which were donated in the time of Kollega's imperial priesthood, [. . .] in the tenure of [. . .] Proklos, the most venerable governor [. . .]. The wall revetment of the temple Flavios Kollega himself and Titos Flavios Varos Dareios, his brother, through Flavios Diomedes [. . .]" (trans. after Eich, Eich, and Eck 2018: 73). Here, I use bars (|) to indicate the original block breaks of the architrave (not line breaks, as usual), because it is important to see how text was distributed across the blocks. NB: the editors of *I.Sagalassos* use the bars to indicate rather the breaks of the at-present broken blocks.

Although Basilica E is not yet comprehensively published, research by Peter Talloen in 2005 and by Ine Jacobs, Koen Demarsin, and Marc Waelkens from 2006 to 2008 suggests that this spolia church was constructed in the second half of the fifth or early sixth century, based on the sherds found in a substrate of the floor in the northern aisle and transept, as well as underneath the slabs of the atrium.[68] Overlooking the city's Lower Agora, the Temple of Apollo Klarios had been a focal point of civic life in Sagalassos from its founding under Augustus; the sanctuary hosted the Klarian festival as well as the imperial cult in the Roman period. Memories of the agonistic festival were kept alive in late antiquity on a nearby street through the statue bases celebrating victors in these games, which, along with other early imperial honorific monuments, appear to have kept their spots when the road was rebuilt around 500 CE.[69] The temple was transformed by taking apart the cella walls, as well as the blocks of the podium, and then rebuilding them as the external walls of a basilica; the columns from the peristasis were moved inside and re-erected as the colonnade separating two side aisles from a nave, resulting in a three-aisled transept basilica. It was at this juncture between nave and transept that the inscribed architrave blocks were discovered in 1885/6 by Karl Lanckoroński, who recorded the excavation of the architrave in felicitous detail, given the early date of his publication.[70] After a block with Greek letters was spotted near the east end of the temple-church rubble, Lanckoroński began digging and found four architrave blocks (out of the original five that graced the temple's façade). He believed that the architrave and the columns supporting it were in their original, in situ location from the façade of the temple—that is, even though the cella walls and lateral peristases had been taken apart and repositioned to create the church, the six columns from the east façade of the temple, along with the architrave, were left untouched. In his view, the architrave dedication remained intact and pointed toward the apse of the church, where it would have been legible to the officiants. Lanckoroński's assertion that the words would have been visible to those in the apse implies that no traces of plaster were found on the architrave when he uncovered it, or he surely would have mentioned this in his careful account.

This configuration of the Apollo Klarios architrave blocks in the church, however, is not entirely satisfactory. It would be unusual to have a colonnade

---

[68] Talloen 2007: 328; Jacobs and Waelkens 2014: 109–113.
[69] Lavan 2015: 325–334.
[70] Lanckoroński 1892: 131–132.

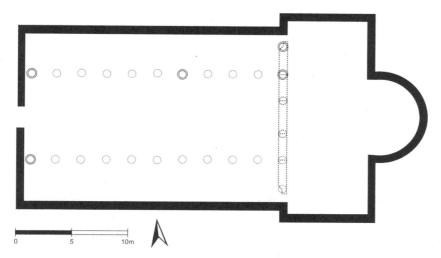

Figure 4.7 Sagalassos. Plan of the temple-church with Lanckoroński's proposed placement of the architrave (dotted lines). Author and Yasmin Nachtigall, modified from Lanckoroński 1892, Fig. 123.

running transverse at the termination of the nave. The gaze of congregants at Sagalassos would be greeted by the (roughly worked) reverse of the architrave blocks, partially blocking a view of the apse (which was probably mosaicked, given the glass tesserae found in the church) (Figure 4.7).[71] Moreover, the putative middle two columns of this supposed six-column configuration in the church were not found by Lanckoroński or subsequent excavations. Even if foundations from the temple lie at precisely this juncture between nave and transept, it does not follow that columns and architrave remained in place in the church.[72] These architrave blocks may have been incorporated in other parts of the structure instead. One possibility is that they were reused as architraves on the lateral colonnades of the north and south aisles, two blocks apiece. The varied lengths of the architrave blocks, however, with the central third block longer than the others, would require the columns of the church colonnade to be appropriately spaced. Another possibility is that the blocks were set into the walls of the north and south aisles or transept, forming an internal cornice. In either of these reconstruction

[71] Talloen 2007: 328.
[72] Jacobs and Waelkens 2014: 116.

possibilities, two blocks on the south would most likely face two blocks on the north across the nave.

Such a placement would solve the conundrum of an architrave running across the end of the nave and blocking the view of the apse—but it would put the original dedicatory inscription to Apollo Klarios on view in the church, now split into halves across the nave. Would a prominent pagan dedication be displayed in such a way? The problem has no easy solution, assuming that plaster was not used for the above-mentioned reason, but another possibility presents itself. Lanckoroński describes finding the four blocks in the middle of the nave, "etwas durcheinander gefallen."[73] This implies that the blocks were reused in the temple-church out of order: Block 1 was not followed by Block 2 but instead by Block 3, etc. The effect would be that the original dedication of the architrave would be "scrambled" through the non-joining of the text, similar to the way that the Gerasa priestesses text was sliced into discrete strips or the Ephesos Church of Mary inscriptions were cut up in the atrium floor. Another example of "scrambling" can be seen at the Church of Christ-in-Jerusalem on the Greek island of Kalymnos: only the middle block of a three-block dedication to Caligula and Apollo Delios was reused vertically as a door jamb.[74] The name of Apollo was on display in large letters, but the beginning and end of the line (on the absent first and third architrave blocks, respectively) are missing. By breaking up the syntax of these inscriptions, the text became either actually, or symbolically, disjointed and illegible. In Basilica E at Sagalassos, even if the blocks were not scrambled in this way, the dividing of the text into two halves facing each other across the nave may have been enough to visually distort the original pagan text. The extreme wordiness of the Roman dedication, with all three fasciae of the architrave crammed with *scriptio continua*, would have done its part to hide the name of Apollo (probably the only potentially offensive part of this inscription, which focused on Kollega's convoluted family relations and specific contributions to the temple building). This dividing up and potential scrambling of the inscription is comparable to the occasional use of epigraphic spolia upside

---

[73] Lanckoroński 1892: 132.
[74] *Tit. Calymnii* 108 (here I use vertical lines to indicate architrave block breaks, and have arranged the text so that the block breaks line up on lines 1 and 2):

[Γαΐωι Καίσαρι Γερμανι]|κῶι καὶ Ἀπόλλωνι Δαλίωι Κρησίωι |[Καλύμνας μεδέοντι]
[Καλυμνίων ὁ δ]|ᾶμος ἐκ τῶν τοῦ θεοῦ προσόδων. v.|

(To Gaius Caesar Germanicus and to Apollo Dalios [=Delios] Kresios ruling over Kalymna, the damos [=demos] of the Kalymnians [dedicated it] from the revenues of the god.)

down, as at Sardis, where in the "Byzantine shops" a letter honoring a man named Polybios was mounted on its head and overcut by a cross, or as at Lagina, where an inscribed statue base reused as a water basin at the entrance to the church was upside down.[75] Any impediment to reading could serve to advertise the object's status as spolia while undermining its content.

Another instance of epigraphic spolia within Basilica E at Sagalassos likewise suggests that the presence of prominent pagan text required some form of mediation. A Roman-period *perirrhanterion* (a basin for water) was repurposed for Christian holy water, standing next to the door opening into the transept from the east.[76] The dedication to Apollo on the *perirrhanterion* was, however, partially erased: only the terminal -ος of Ἀπόλλωνος (of Apollo) is now readily legible. This text was laconic enough to be easily intelligible and visually inescapable; it therefore required erasure within the church. The visible removal of text advertised the basin's reuse and the religious transformation it had undergone. On the other hand, a block honoring a priest of Apollo and *agonothete* of the Klarian games was built into a wall of the temple-church, where it was most likely covered by revetment.[77] This manner of reuse indicates practical motivations, given that similar bases remained on display on the street nearby.

The exact late antique context of the Apollo Klarios architrave in Basilica E at Sagalassos will probably never be certain, given the early date of Lanckoroński's excavation and the fact that the church was damaged in a seventh-century earthquake and repaired in the Middle Byzantine period. What is clear is that, when the Temple of Apollo Klarios was rebuilt as a church, a decision was made to reuse the architrave, rather than simply discarding or reworking the stones. The architrave may have been arranged in such a way that the full text could no longer be continuously read, or it may have simply faded into the opulent late antique church interior. The reuse of the temple is consistent with Sagalassos' general willingness to recycle the remains of the pagan past. Besides the pagan statues standing on Sagalassos' streets and *agorai*, two more pagan images were not only accepted, but purposefully built into the late fifth-/early sixth-century city walls: Roman busts of the two gods of war, Ares and Athena, flanked the entrance into the city at the Upper Agora gate.[78] So too at Basilica E: the inscribed temple architrave

---

[75] *I.Sardis* II 319–320; Aydaş 2009: 120, no. 17.
[76] Talloen 2015: 295.
[77] Lanckoroński 1892: 227, no. 201.
[78] Jacobs 2010: 277.

was not only tolerated at Sagalassos, but actively selected to be built into the church.

Gods and Angels in the Temple-Church at Aphrodisias

The converted Temple of Aphrodite at Aphrodisias, the provincial capital of Karia, likewise integrated epigraphic material into its building fabric and shows a range of responses to those texts, including hiding, displaying, and erasing. This temple-church is a *rara avis*: fantastically well documented archaeologically, epigraphically, and contextually (by which I mean the urban changes in the surrounding late antique city), and it is therefore one of the most cited examples of temple conversion. As we will see, the actual factors at play in the process of reconstruction are more complex than simply "Christianization." The church was one among many monumental structures in thriving late antique Aphrodisias, most of which date from centuries earlier but were maintained (sometimes with new uses) until the seventh century (Figure 4.8). The bouleuterion was repurposed as a *palaistra* (a space for wrestling competitions) by the late fifth century, while the population could also be entertained at the theater with its Augustan stage building, or in the stadium, which was renovated into an arena.[79] The imperial cult center of Aphrodisias, the Sebasteion, saw its richly sculptured porticoes turned into a market place in the mid-fourth century.[80] The recently excavated urban park, called the Place of Palms (formerly the "South Agora"), featured a massive pool at its center; sixth-century graffiti and gameboards are scrawled on the surrounding seating, indicating that the space was frequented by all levels of Aphrodisian society.[81] Inhabitants of late antique Aphrodisias had access to all the major amenities one could hope for in a late antique city, despite the challenges of a rising water table and various earthquakes—at least, until the city seems to have collapsed physically and socially in the seventh century, possibly as a result of a Persian attack circa 615.[82]

---

[79] Bouleuterion: *I.Aphrodisias* 2007 2.19. The word *palaistra* in the inscription has been taken as a poetic reference to public debates but probably literally meant a wrestling space: Hallett 2018: 355–356; Quatember 2019: 79–81. Theater: de Chaisemartin and Theodorescu 2017: 46–47. Stadium: Welch 1998: 565–569.

[80] Ogus 2018: 174–177.

[81] Wilson 2019: 203–205.

[82] Dalgıç and Sokolicek 2017: 274–275; Wilson 2019: 197–217.

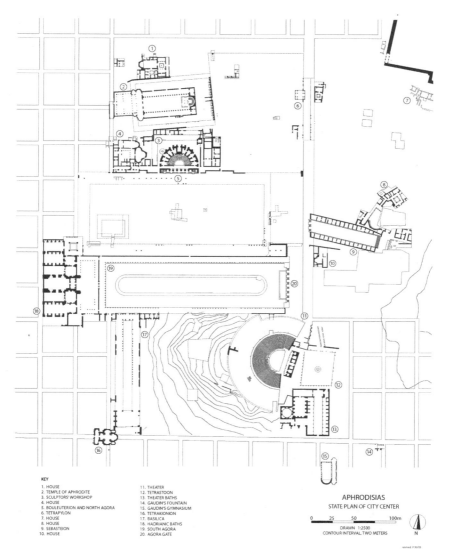

Figure 4.8 Aphrodisias. Site plan. Courtesy of NYU Excavations at Aphrodisias (Harry Mark).

And where was the church among all the fun and games in late antique Aphrodisias? The impact of Christianity on the city seems to have initially been slight: occasional defaced images of Aphrodite, crosses at the incipits of official inscriptions, a few erasures here and there (discussed in Chapter 5).

174 PAGAN INSCRIPTIONS, CHRISTIAN VIEWERS

At least one sculptor felt the new religion should be making more of an impact: the Christian abbreviation ΧΜΓ (probably meaning Χριστὸν Μαρία γεννᾷ, "Mary bore Christ") is carved on the top of the head of the governor Oikoumenios.[83] The Tetrapylon to the east of the Temple of Aphrodite was taken apart and rebuilt also circa 400; a cross replaced what was presumably an image of Aphrodite on the keystone of the arch.[84] Despite these signs of the times, Aphrodisias' mixed population of Christians, Jews, and pagans coexisted—and competed—for much of late antiquity.[85] The city was a center of traditional *paideia*: the pagan Asklepiodotos of Alexandria moved to Aphrodisias and founded a philosophical school, co-run with his father-in-law (a local man also named Asklepiodotos), in the second half of the fifth century. When the Alexandrian Asklepiodotos and his wife could not conceive a child, they traveled to the shrine of Isis at Menouthis in Egypt, obtained (somehow) a baby, and, in the telling of the Christian Zacharias' *Life of Severos*, caused quite a scandal in philosophical circles when it could not be proved that Isis had really performed this miracle.[86] An honorific inscription found at Aphrodisias for a prominent citizen named Asklepiodotos probably refers to the father-in-law.[87] Zacharias (writing in Constantinople around 520) told of the conversion of a young philosophy student, Paralios, whose brothers in the Karian metropolis "used to appease the demons with invocations, sacrifices, incantations and magic spells."[88] We can permit Zacharias some rhetorical and hagiographical leeway, but there is no reason to doubt that Aphrodisias' elites were in part still pagan in the later fifth century. Epigraphic evidence fills out the picture of a thriving pagan population—although a tendency toward ambiguity may indicate increasing discomfort with overt display of the old religion.[89] Regardless, the classical appearance of the city did not change significantly in the fourth or fifth century. The appropriation of the temple—the city's ancestral shrine—appears as a dramatic escalation of the process of "Christianization," a forceful insertion of the new religion into the built fabric of the city.

---

[83] *I.Aphrodisias* 2007 3.8.ii; Smith and Ward-Perkins 2016 no. 150; Smith 2002: 150–153.
[84] Wilson 2018: 476.
[85] Roueché 1989; Chaniotis 2002a; Chaniotis 2002b; Chaniotis 2008.
[86] Damascius *Life of Isidore*, apud Photios *Bibliotheke*, Frag. 117; Zacharias, *Life of Severos*, Roueché 2004: v. 1–18; Watts 2005: 442–443.
[87] *I.Aphrodisias* 2007 11.68.
[88] Zacharias, *Life of Severos*, 13 (trans. Brock).
[89] Chaniotis 2008: 249–255.

When did this conversion take place? A coin find of Leo I (r. 457–474) under the narthex indicates a *terminus post quem* for the construction of that part of the building; a date of circa 500 has been generally accepted.[90] The conversion has at times been viewed as a response to the 484–488 failed rebellion of Illos and the pagan philosopher Pamprepios against the emperor Zeno, based again on Zacharias' *Life of Severos*, which has Paralios claim that his pagan brothers in Aphrodisias sought oracles in support of the rebellion.[91] If we project from this that prominent pagans in Aphrodisias had supported the revolt, it follows that the conversion of the temple was a punitive measure. In actuality, the political smear in the *Life of Severos* (that pagans were wont to support usurpation) need not indicate the political reality at Aphrodisias nor a vindictive appropriation of the temple. The latest research on the temple-church suggests that the narthex and atrium were later additions; the conversion may have taken place earlier in the fifth century.[92] An alternative is that the temple may have been damaged in an earthquake at some point. The most logical renovation option for an obsolete or damaged temple at the heart of the city was the building's conversion, especially as Aphrodisias lacked a prominent urban church.

Another motivation behind the conversion has recently been proposed by Hugh Jeffery: rather than pagan-Christian competition, the appropriation may have been an ecclesiastical attempt to tame a popular cult of angels, given that the church was most likely dedicated to the Archangel Michael.[93] Angels were popular among pagans, Jews, and Christians and played roles in both magic and mystagogy; perhaps an angel cult in Aphrodisias was attracting a far too mixed clientele for the ecclesiastical authorities' tastes and had to be firmly Christianized (and orthodoxized).[94] Jeffery points to the great lengths the builders went to in order to incorporate the older well of Aphrodite (a salt water well, according to Pausanias) into the church apse, which necessitated raising the level of the wellhead (Figure 4.9).[95] This placement of a well in the middle of an apse is unparalleled, so far as I know, and presumably its waters were thought to be holy or healing. Whether or not Jeffery's hypothesis about an out-of-control cult of angels holds water, the well was clearly both indispensable and in need of direct ecclesiastical control. Only the clergy had

---

[90] Smith and Ratté 1995: 44–46; Hebert 2000.
[91] *Life of Severos* 54; Chaniotis 2008: 244–245.
[92] Smith 2018: 272; Wilson 2019: 202.
[93] Jeffery 2019.
[94] Horsley and Luxford 2016.
[95] Pausanias 1.26.5; Jeffery 2019: 211–213.

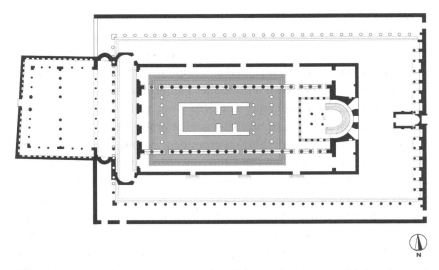

Figure 4.9 Aphrodisias. Composite plan showing the Temple of Aphrodite and the temple-church. Courtesy of NYU Excavations at Aphrodisias (Harry Mark).

access to it and could dole out its favors accordingly. A mixture of all three possible motivations for the temple's conversion (anti-pagan sentiment, practical reuse, and anxiety about heterodox uses of a sacred well) may have been at play.

Like at the Temple of Apollo at Sagalassos, the Temple of Aphrodite at Aphrodisias was turned inside out during the process of transformation: the cella walls were deconstructed and the marble blocks (along with those brought from elsewhere) were used to construct the outer walls of a three-aisled basilica far larger than the original temple. The north and south rows of columns from the peristasis were left in place and became the church colonnades separating the aisles from the nave. From the exterior, the building was a rectangle marble behemoth, built of blocks that were clearly spolia (some of them required plaster covering to hide old damage) but were fitted together in an orderly and classicizing arrangement.

The interior of the temple-church was rich with late antique texts, both inscriptions and graffiti, as Charlotte Roueché has demonstrated.[96] At least thirty-five Christian texts were found in the church or its environs. Prayers from the faithful congregated especially at liminal spaces, while fragmentary

[96] Roueché 2004: Plan 5.

Figure 4.10 Aphrodisias. *Tabulae ansatae* (marked) with inscriptions on the north colonnade of the temple-church (*I.Aphrodisias* 2007 1.4–1.8). Author, courtesy of NYU Excavations at Aphrodisias.

donor inscriptions named individuals such as Theodoretos and Kyriakos.[97] The texts span from late antiquity to the Middle Byzantine period, when the church was renovated. But these Christian texts were not alone: several pieces of Roman epigraphic spolia were visible in the church, sometimes in close proximity to the late antique texts.[98]

Remarkably, the goddess Aphrodite herself made an appearance within the church. Both the north and south colonnades were composed of columns from the temple, which were, technically speaking, not actually spolia: most had not been moved from their original temple foundations (Figure 4.10). Nonetheless they *appeared* as spolia, classical Ionic columns

---

[97] *I.Aphrodisias* 2007, 1.12 and 1.13.
[98] Sitz 2019b.

standing in a colorful late antique space. Dedications to Aphrodite from the first century CE (and later) appear on *tabulae ansatae* on a number of these columns above eye level, following a common Roman Anatolian practice in which donors paid a sum of money and gained the privilege of carving their dedication onto a column.[99] Two of the columns of the Aphrodisian temple were donated by an Attalos and Attalis, another two by a Eumachos Diogenes and Amias Olympias.[100] These donor inscriptions offer first and foremost the pedigree of the individuals ("Eumachos Diogenes, son of Athenagoras, son of Athenagoras, son of Eumachos, *philokaisar*, and Amias Olympias, [adopted] daughter of Dionysios, by nature daughter of Adrastos, son of Molon") followed by a curt dedication of the column "to the goddess Aphrodite and to the demos."[101] A third copy of the Eumachos and Amias dedication was added to another column sometime later, presumably when the funds donated were finally expended.[102] These dedications continued to be on view in the church, on the columns facing into the side aisle: there is no evidence for their covering or alteration, although they would have suffered from reduced visibility in this darker space. Graffiti added to the bases of the columns near these dedications indicate that the demos (people) to whom Eumachos and Amias had dedicated the temple finally took the opportunity to leave their own marks on the building; the columns were perceived as writing spaces, perhaps in part because they already bore the dedicatory texts higher up.[103]

One might have missed these ancient texts in the side aisles but could hardly miss dedications on the door lintels at the entrances to the nave from the narthex, which were well and truly spolia. The northernmost of the three entrances has on its lintel: "To the emperor, the god Augustus Caesar, *pater patridos*, Eusebes Philopatris, son of Menandros, and Eunikos, son of Menandros (gave it)" (Figure 4.11).[104] The origin of this block is not known. At some point after its original inscribing, an attachment hole was carved on the upper fascia, right on top of the terminal sigma of *patridos* (perhaps to

---

[99] Rumscheid 1999.
[100] Attalos and Attalis: *I.Aphrodisias* 2007 1.7 and 1.8; Eumachos and Amias: 1.4 and 1.5.
[101] *I.Aphrodisias* 2007 1.4: Εὔμαχος Ἀθηναγό|ρου τοῦ Ἀθηναγόρου | τοῦ Εὐμάχου Διογένη|ς Φιλόκαισαρ καὶ Ἀμιὰς ν. | Διονυσίου φύσι δὲ Ἀδρά<σ>του | τοῦ Μόλωνος Ὀλυνπιὰς | τὸν κίονα θεᾷ Ἀφροδίτῃ | καὶ τῷ Δήμῳ vacat.
[102] *I.Aphrodisias* 2007, 1.6. Pers. comm. Angelos Chaniotis.
[103] Graffiti: *I.Aphrodisias* 2007 1.29, 1.30, and 1.31.
[104] *I.Aphrodisias* 2007 1.102: [Αὐ]τοκράτορι θεῷ Σεβαστῷ Καίσαρι πατρὶ πατρίδος | [Εὐσ]εβὴς ν. Μενάνδρου φιλόπατρις καὶ Εὔνικος Μενάνδρου. The underlining indicates words seen by a previous editor but subsequently lost.

Figure 4.11 Aphrodisias. Door lintel of the northern entrance into nave with *I.Aphrodisias* 2007 1.102. Courtesy of NYU Excavations at Aphrodisias.

receive a metal hook for the occasional hanging of wreaths on festival days?) but most of the text was untouched and probably remained visible—never mind that Augustus is referred to as a god, as he was also on the temples at Ankara and Priene. Near this dedication to Augustus, the original doorframe from the Temple of Aphrodite was re-erected as the central door into the nave. The text on this lintel declared that a member of the local elite named Zoilos had built the temple for Aphrodite. This very visible and explicitly pagan text *did* require erasure—although as we will see in the next chapter, this was hardly a full obliteration of the text. Some of the letters on the lintel are completely untouched; it was unmistakably epigraphic spolia. This lintel too had an attachment hole added to it at an unknown point. The other doors entering into the nave and side aisles are not well preserved.

Churchgoers had already seen epigraphic spolia as they approached the narthex from the atrium at the west. Several blocks of an inscribed architrave originating from a gymnasium were found in the atrium, most as stray finds; one block was built into the base of a wall in the northwest atrium portico, inscribed face out. The other architrave stones were not reused as architraves, because the atrium was arcaded; they may have functioned as a base cornice or as foundations.[105] Two factors tip the weight against foundations: some of the blocks were recut for reuse (probably unnecessary if unseen), and part of the text was erased. This censuring of the text suggests that the inscription was visible (otherwise there would be no reason to erase it). Again, an emperor appears: Hadrian Augustus (Ἁδριανῷ Σεβαστῷ) is left untouched on one block.[106] But part of Hadrian's official titulature, as well as the name of the donor(s) and the deity to whom the gymnasium is dedicated, has been removed. Interestingly, these architrave blocks bear later letters on their sides to number them, but when put together according to these numbers, the text was in the wrong order: it was scrambled, as we have previously seen at Sagalassos.[107] Both erasure and scrambling served to negate this text.

Various other fragmentary Roman inscriptions (mainly non-architectural) were found in the area of the temple-church at Aphrodisias, but most were recorded without definite contexts and may have been brought in only in the Middle Byzantine renovation. The sanctuary barrier on view today in the ruins of the temple-church is built of statue bases dating from the Roman imperial period to the sixth century CE, each heavily inscribed. But it was probably installed in the tenth or eleventh century; these epigraphic spolia were plastered over and then painted.[108] Middle Byzantine construction projects frequently made use of ancient spolia, but we should not assume that the methods and meaning of this spoliation were identical over the course of these centuries. Still, in late antiquity as well, some inscribed texts were covered during the process of reuse: a badly damaged early imperial list of male names visible on the eastern wall of the temple-church at Aphrodisias was probably simply collateral damage in a late antique decorative program of revetting and plastering of this section of the temple-church exterior.[109] As at the Korykian Cave Clifftop temple-church, where the desire for a pristine exterior façade resulted in the careful erasure of a number of names, the aesthetic requirements of this decorative program at the temple-church at Aphrodisias trumped any impulse to preserve the list of names.

Throughout the Aphrodisias temple-church, therefore, epigraphic spolia including pagan dedications were built into the new Christian structure;

---

[105] Hebert 2000: 58.
[106] *I.Aphrodisias* 2007 1.174: [... αὐ]|[[τοκράτορι Καίσαρι Τρ[α]]]|[ἱα]νῷ Ἁδριανῷ Σεβαστ|[[ῷ ...]]. Here I use bars to indicate the original block breaks of the architrave, and I have added erasure marks.
[107] Doruk 1990: 74; Reynolds 1990: 40.
[108] Hebert 2000: 222.
[109] Sitz 2019b: 156–158.

much of this patrimony was left on display in its new context. Inscribed spolia was common throughout the cityscape of Aphrodisias, for example, in the ten-meter-high city wall, the outer face of which was built of dismantled tomb monuments and other marbles in the 350s–360s CE. The spolia was carefully arranged to create a regular surface, probably not under the duress of an invading force but as a planned project of the provincial governor. Figural imagery from grave reliefs and sarcophagi lids was reused decoratively or apotropaically in the walls, with paired images congregating around gateways. Epitaphs were not always so lucky as their figural counterparts: Peter De Staebler has demonstrated that the inscriptions built into this fortification wall were placed based on construction logic (some face out, others hidden) rather than a desire to display their texts.[110] The same principle of epigraphic reuse largely holds for the temple-church: the decision to use spolia in this construction project was probably more practical than quarrying and carving all new marbles or bringing in orphaned stones from other more distant buildings, and there is no indication that inscriptions were sought out for reuse. The stones at Aphrodisias were built into both the temple-church and city walls where they fit.

But even so, the use of spolia in the temple-church should not be compared too closely with that in the city walls. For one, the context (a religiously charged complex that had stood at the heart of the city from its distant past) was different, as was the architectural space: visitors to the temple-church probably came into much closer and more regular contact with the epigraphic spolia there than on the exterior of the city walls. The substantial amount of graffiti in the church is a sign of viewing and engagement.[111] Much of the graffiti congregates at the entrance to the atrium and at side entrances into the church, indicating that people loitered (and therefore looked) around doorways; it also communicated a specific message: despite the classicizing exterior of the building, the space was definitively Christian.[112] This focus on doorways suggests that the inscribed spolia entrances into the nave would have also prompted reading and reflection on the building's history. The lintels could have been completely smoothed and recarved with late antique texts (especially given Aphrodisias' robust marble workshop tradition), but instead, architectural conversion was showcased through the clearly

---

[110] De Staebler 2008a; De Staebler 2008b: 195–197. When given the option, the builders preferred to display the uninscribed faces.
[111] See Roueché 2004, Plan 5, for a drawing marking the locations of graffiti in the church.
[112] Sitz 2019b; see also Yasin 2015.

spoliated inscriptions. Each of these texts—both the reused ancient ones and the Christian additions—worked to define the space.

And what, exactly, was that definition? Here we return to the (hypothetical) cult of angels that has been proposed as the impetus for the Church's appropriation of the temple. As mentioned, angels such as Michael were venerated by pagans, Christians, and Jews alike in late antiquity, and by the late fifth century the persistence of these sorts of popular cults may have been perceived as a greater opponent to ecclesiastical orthodoxy than paganism itself. But the ancient texts left on display in the temple-church, specifically the dedications to Aphrodite on the aisle columns and the donor texts above entrances to the nave, proclaimed loud and clear that this was a *very normal* civic building that happened to be dedicated to Aphrodite (like so many other structures in Roman Aphrodisias), with the attendant political associations of civic temples. None of this funny business with the cult of angels. The inscriptions named prominent citizens and detailed their ancestry and in some cases titles, such as *philokaisar*. This title meaning "friend of the emperor" and the dedication to Augustus evoked Aphrodisias' much-celebrated close relationship with the first Roman emperor, also advertised on the Archive Wall of the city's theater. As we saw at Ankara, Augustus remained a well-known emperor in late antiquity. Hadrian too, who appeared on the architrave in the temple-church atrium, was remembered as a good emperor, even finding his way into the Forum of Theodosios in Constantinople in the form of a reused statue.[113] As throughout this book, the majority of the epigraphic "real estate" in these imperial-era inscriptions was devoted to the background, titles, and beneficence of the euergetes who paid for the monument, with few words left for the goddess.

The preservation of the name of Aphrodite on the columns of the nave may therefore have been in the interest of the ecclesiastical authorities: the goddess was an enemy they had already largely defeated, even if she remained popular with some of Aphrodisias' elites. She could be explained away as an allegorical or mythical figment and was therefore left untouched in various sculptural depictions around the city; only when she was present as an object of worship did she require removal (see Chapter 5). The city even kept the name "Aphrodisias" until the seventh century, not because paganism was alive and well, but because it had been defanged, if not taxidermied. The references to Aphrodite in the temple-church inscriptions therefore

---

[113] Bassett 2004: 211–212.

may have *helped* the Church in its fight against a more nebulous competitor, the popular cult of angels. According to the inscriptions, the building was emphatically *not* dedicated to angels, or to healing rites, or fertility rituals, or divination, or whatever else people were getting up to at the well: it had served a perfectly regular civic cult now safely relegated to the past. Only the lintel inscription explicitly dedicating the building to Aphrodite required editing, and only a partial one at that. Defining the old temple as a civic cult with the usual political associations was in the interests of both the Church and city officials: Aphrodisias' proud history of local benefactors and imperial connections remained on display alongside the neutralized Aphrodite. Other discourses were crowded out.

Uncertain Reuse at Baalbek

The church built over the steps and altar of the gargantuan Temple of Jupiter Heliopolitanus at Baalbek/Heliopolis (Lebanon) did not fare as well at the hands of modern archaeologists as did that at Aphrodisias. The church was completely dismantled in the 1930s to return the site to the appearance of its Roman glory days—and the Temple of Jupiter is certainly glorious.[114] Not everyone was a fan, however. Eusebius of Caesarea claims that at Heliopolis pagans "allowed their wives and daughters without restraint to act as prostitutes," prompting Constantine to outlaw this practice and write a letter urging all to accept the Christian faith.[115] He apparently also set up a church and bishop in the pagan city. Constantine's imperial proselytizing was unsuccessful, however: in the early fifth century, the monk Rabbula set out for the city in the hopes of smashing idols and winning martyrdom there, according to the Syriac *Life of Rabbula*. Heliopolis was "the most suitable destination for getting killed by pagans," but Rabbula was unsuccessful and had to become a bishop instead.[116] The idea that Baalbek was a locus of Christian-pagan conflict was still present in the sixth century, when Malalas stated that Theodosios I destroyed the "large and famous temple of Helioupolis, known as the Trilithon, and made it a church for the Christians."[117] "Trilithon" refers to the three massive stones, measuring nineteen meters each, used in the

---

[114] Ragette 1980.
[115] Eusebius *Vita Constantini* 3.58 (trans. Cameron and Hall).
[116] Minov 2010: 84.
[117] Malalas 344 (trans. Jeffreys, Jeffreys, and Scott).

wall of the Temple of Jupiter. But Malalas' seemingly precise knowledge of Baalbek is misleading: the archaeological record does not support his claims. Most of the Temple of Jupiter remained standing, and the architecture of the church suggests a date only in the later fifth or sixth century.[118]

Even with this chronological uncertainty, these stories of pagan-Christian conflict may tempt us to view the archaeological remains at Baalbek through this lens. Moralee notes that eight pagan inscriptions were reused in the walls of the basilica, "forming a virtual gallery of pagan relics leaving traces of the names of the old gods in old-fashioned scripts in Latin and Greek."[119] These texts offer further support to his interpretation of a polemical intertextual dialogue at Gerasa (about 250 kilometers south of Baalbek) between the older, pagan stones and the new, triumphalist Christian inscriptions built into the Church of St. Theodore. As we have already seen, the particular messages projected by the late antique inscriptions at that church and the methods of reuse validate this approach to the material at Gerasa. But at Baalbek/Heliopolis, it is not clear whether these inscriptions would have been visible in the church (as Moralee readily admits), or whether they might have had their inscribed faces turned inward or downward. The majority of the Roman inscriptions recovered from the church were actually in Latin (Heliopolis was a veteran colony in the Julio-Claudian period). One base reads *I(ovi) O(ptimo) M(aximo) H(eliopolitano)* | *T(itus) Pontius Cl(audius)* | *Bruttienus pro* | *salute sua et Ti|berinae filiae* | *et Iuventiae* | *uxoris v(otum) s(olvit)* (To Jove Optimus Maximus Heliopolitanus, Titus Pontius Claudius Bruttienus fulfilled his vow for the health of himself and his daughter Tiberina and his wife Iuventia).[120] There may have been a few Latin-speaking residents in late antique Baalbek, but they would have been in the minority: the late antique graffiti around the sanctuary are in Greek.[121] And how many people could solve the abbreviation IOMH? A Greek base extracted from the Christian basilica at Heliopolis had nothing especially pagan about it, being simply a dedication for the safety and victory of Caracalla, Geta, and their mother Julia Domna—no god is even named.[122] The particular inscriptions chosen for incorporation in the church do not suggest that anti-pagan sentiment was meant to be on display.

---

[118] Bayliss 2004: 116.
[119] Moralee 2006: 198.
[120] *IGLS* 6.2720.
[121] *IGLS* 6.2835 and 2836.
[122] *IGLS* 6.2744.

Finally, the Syriac *Chronicle of Pseudo-Zachariah Rhetor*, written around 560, associates the massive temple at Baalbek not with the pagan past, but with the biblical king Solomon. Sergey Minov argues that the Syriac word used to describe the structure should be translated as "palace" rather than "temple" (as it had been taken previously): "The palace of Solomon in Baalbek, the city of the house of the forest of Lebanon, as to which Scripture mentions that Solomon built it and stored arms in it, [was burnt]" by lightning.[123] The text goes on to describe the Trilithon (a sign of the Trinity, of course), leaving no doubt about which structure is meant. In at least some interpretive traditions, then, the Temple of Jupiter Heliopolitanus had lost its pagan associations, becoming instead a part of biblical history. The use of epigraphic spolia in the church is ambiguous: the reuse of these stones, along with the placement of the basilica on the steps of the Temple of Jupiter, *may* have signaled Christian triumph in the charged atmosphere of late antique Baalbek, or it may have been convenient and uncontroversial.

Klaros: Exporting Spolia

The oracular Temple of Apollo at Klaros experienced a different fate than did the temples at the Korykian Cave, Sagalassos, Aphrodisias, and Baalbek: it was abandoned rather than converted, but even so, its blocks did not escape spoliation. This extra-urban sanctuary initially belonged to the city of Kolophon on the coast of Ionia; it hosted an oracle of Apollo from the Archaic period onward. The oracle drew official delegations from cities all over the Greek world (especially Asia Minor); these delegates consulted Apollo's prophet on civic matters. In the Roman imperial period, brief records of these visits were recorded in stone. The formulaic inscriptions included the city name, the eponymous officials of the sanctuary, as well as the names of members of the delegation. For example, the group from the city of Hierapytna on Crete in 141/2 CE was commemorated as follows:

> (The delegation) of the Hierapytnians. In the 67th prytany of Apollo, when Gaius Julius Zotichos was priest, when Krito son of Artemidoros was the prophet for the third time . . . the *theopropoi* to the oracle were Epiktetos, son of Epiktetos, Eirinai(o)s, son of Philo for the third time, the young boys

---

[123] Minov 2010: 62.

were Dionysi(o)s, son of Epiktetos, [names follow], the young girls were Lakaina, daughter of Eirinaios [names follow].[124]

These records, more than four hundred of which are extant, were carved on stelai or on the blocks of the Temple of Apollo and its monumental altar from the mid-second century CE to the mid-third.[125] Small, dense letters covered the steps of the temple crepidoma and even the flutes of the columns, giving the temple an inscribed skin unparalleled at other sites. Nearly all potential writing surfaces at Klaros—bases, exedrae, the propylon—were filled with text: records of delegations, decrees, honorific texts, and dedications.

Despite the shrine's popularity in the imperial period, evidence for visits to Klaros declines in the third century and peters out by the mid-fourth. The site was largely abandoned after that date, and habitation at the nearby seaside polis of Notion, which had replaced Kolophon as the main city of this territory, was also much reduced (beginning already in the first century CE).[126] The cult statues of Apollo, Leto, and Artemis at Klaros were found within the cella of the Temple of Apollo at Klaros, where they had fallen from their bases—but missing their heads. This may indicate Christian defacement of the statues, but it is also possible that the final pagans of Klaros took the heads elsewhere for safekeeping.[127] In any case, Christian interference in the defunct sanctuary is confirmed by cross graffiti congregating in the subterranean room where the prophet of Apollo had offered divine advice. This room clearly maintained its fame, or infamy, even after the god fell silent.

The main motivation for late antique individuals to visit Klaros, however, seems to have been economic: the marble temple and other structures were an abundant source of spolia. The careful documentation of the blocks of the temple has allowed for a more precise understanding of the process of spoliation than what is possible at most sites.[128] First, a period of abandonment is apparent, during which the ground level increased about sixty centimeters due to alluvium. This rising ground protected marbles located below the new, late antique ground level. Then, the still-standing marble superstructure of the temple was dug into at various points in order to extract valuable metal clamps and lead. After this had taken place, deconstruction began in earnest,

---

[124] Trans. after Ferrary 2014: 311, no. 62.
[125] Ferrary 2014: 202.
[126] Ratté, Rojas, and Commito 2020: 333.
[127] Moretti et al. 2016: 304.
[128] Moretti et al. 2016: 301–308.

and the blocks of the temple were systematically taken down beginning with the cella and then proceeding to the columns of the peristasis and the front architrave of the temple, which bore a dedication from the emperor Hadrian in bold, large letters; pieces of this architrave were left intact at the site, while others have disappeared. The marbles were transported by the road linking Klaros to Notion, whose port was still viable in late antiquity. Many were recut into cubic shapes for this transport, and a few were abandoned along the way, leaving a bread-crumb trail marking the route. The blocks may have been reused in as yet undiscovered structures in Notion or, given the lack of late antique building projects at that city, they were more likely exported by sea to parts unknown.[129] This was the marbles' second sea voyage: they also arrived at Klaros by water. The Kızılburun shipwreck near Çeşme (Turkey), excavated from 2005 to 2011, contained the unfinished pieces of a column from Prokonnesian marble on its way to Klaros.[130]

But three orthostate blocks from the altar of Apollo did not take the sea journey in late antiquity. These blocks bearing inscribed records from delegations to the sanctuary were built into a well-outfitted church of approximately the sixth century, which stood between Klaros and Notion.[131] Unfortunately the findspots of the inscriptions within the church were not recorded, so we cannot say for certain that they were visible within the church. But visible or not, these three inscribed orthostates were selected as spolia and transported. Two other uninscribed orthostate blocks were found in their original context at the altar of Apollo at Klaros: they had not been chosen for export or reuse by the late antique builders.[132] This spoliation of the altar blocks raises unanswerable questions: was the inscribed nature of the stones a sought-after feature? Was it more desirable to use spolia from the august sanctuary of Apollo than from Notion itself? Had the altar of Apollo stood intact at Klaros until this act of spoliation?

At Klaros, there is no indication that the epigraphic spolia was read in late antiquity, and the small, dense letters of the records perhaps make this unlikely. Late antique individuals may have believed that old stones could carry oracular messages, sometimes even monotheistic musings delivered by Apollo himself, as explored in Chapter 2, but they would have been

---

[129] Moretti et al. 2016: 306. See also Russell 2013 for other instances of shipping spolia.
[130] Carlson and Aylward 2010.
[131] Macridy 1905; Macridy 1912: 37–42; Ferrary 2014: 9, 30 and no. 31, 34, 36, 37, 39, 40, 41, 43, 45, 59, 60; Moretti et al. 2016: 302. The church has now disappeared (pers. comm. Angela Commito, Chris Ratté, and Felipe Rojas, October 4, 2020).
[132] Ferrary 2014: 256.

sorely disappointed by the epigraphic harvest from the sanctuary at Klaros. Whereas the god had offered advice on both practical and theological matters, these oracular utterances were more likely to be recorded on perishable materials or inscribed at the city that received them, rather than at the sanctuary itself.[133] For example, a monotheistic oracle from Klaros was inscribed at Oinoanda in Lykia, discussed in Chapter 5. At Klaros itself, however, the texts inscribed on architecture recorded not esoteric wisdom, but rather lists of delegates who visited the sanctuary; as Jeanne and Louis Robert put it, it was "un peu monotone de trouver à chaque campagne des textes de cette catégorie," and the late antique literate may have felt likewise.[134] Nonetheless, the incorporation of the delegate inscriptions in the late antique church between Klaros and Notion may indicate that inscribed spolia was seen as desirable for this ecclesiastical building project. Whether the draw was aesthetic, archaeophiliac (in Rojas's sense), or a sign of Christian triumph over the old prophet is impossible to say.

Epigraphic Spolia Elsewhere

Not Only Christians: The Synagogue at Sardis

The display of ancient inscriptions in new religious spaces was not exclusive to late antique Christian contexts. The Jewish community at Sardis in the province of Lydia constructed a spectacular synagogue in probably the later part of the fourth century (or at the latest in the sixth century) next to the Roman Gymnasium and the "Byzantine shops."[135] The synagogue is an elongated hall nearly sixty meters long, terminating in a semi-circular apse; the structure was a spolia magnet, incorporating a wide range of older architectural and decorative material (Figure 4.12).[136] An acute case of "leontomania" can be diagnosed: reused Archaic lion sculptures were built into the synagogue's fabric and placed strategically near its entrance and next to the lectern where the Torah was read.[137] These sculptures probably evoked the distant Lydian past, when kings such as Kroisos put lions on their coins

---

[133] Henrichs 2003.
[134] Robert and Robert 1989: 3.
[135] Magness 2005: 454–460; Rautman 2011: 15–17; Rautman 2017: 233.
[136] Mitten and Scorziello 2008; Magness 2005: 458–460.
[137] Rojas 2019: 124–127.

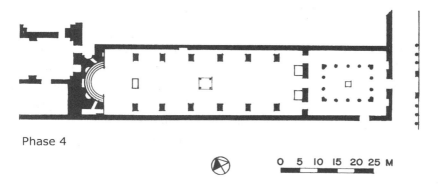

Figure 4.12 Sardis. Plan of the synagogue, fourth phase. © Archaeological Exploration of Sardis/President and Fellows of Harvard College.

and filled the city with carved representations of the same. Epigraphic spolia was on display as well: seven inscribed blocks originating from the antae of the city's Metroön (the sanctuary of the goddess Kybebe) and bearing Hellenistic letters and civic decrees were found built into rows of piers running along the synagogue's hall; other votive dedications from this sanctuary were incorporated into the synagogue's built fabric.[138] In the Hellenistic period, the temple's marble antae were used to record important documents, as we have seen also at Priene, Herakleia Latmia, and Lagina. Interestingly, two blocks from the Metroön built into the late antique piers bore letters of circa 213 BCE from Antiochos III the Great, the Seleukid king portrayed favorably by the Jewish historian Josephus.[139] Specifically, Josephus reproduces Antiochos' order that two thousand Jewish families should be granted land in Lydia and Phrygia—presumably the ancestors of the Jewish community in Sardis. Although the inscribed letters from Antiochos III built into the synagogue are rather less topical (they concern a new *synoikismos*, the incorporation of smaller communities into one, and are not related to the Jews), the king may have been remembered by the local Jewish community as a benefactor. The texts at the time of excavation showed no trace of plaster; they were on display within the worship space.[140] By contrast, a spolia relief depicting two goddesses was placed face down when it was reused. Ancient

---

[138] *I.Sardis* II 302, 307–312; Cahill 2019.
[139] Josephus *Jewish Antiquities* 12.147–153.
[140] Hanfmann 1964: 34; Mitten and Scorziello 2008: 138–145.

190 PAGAN INSCRIPTIONS, CHRISTIAN VIEWERS

words and images prompted different reactions, as we will see further in the following chapter.

Even more intriguing than the inclusion of the Hellenistic letters from the Metroön in the Sardis synagogue is the presence of an inscription whose contents were presumably as impenetrable for Sardis's late antique Jewish community as for us today. In one pier stood a stone inscribed in an epichoric script representing an unidentified ancient Anatolian language (Figure 4.13). It does not correspond with the Lydian language, which, as we saw in the

Figure 4.13 Sardis. Epichoric inscription in an unknown Anatolian language found in the synagogue. Sardis IN63.141. © Archaeological Exploration of Sardis/President and Fellows of Harvard College.

previous chapter, was present at Sardis's sanctuary of Artemis, although the text on this stone may have been mistaken in late antiquity for Lydian, given the visual similarities of the two writing systems. The stone in the synagogue, dated between the sixth and fourth century BCE, had been broken and repaired before it was reused. Although its position within the architectural space is not very prominent (it was hardly the main attraction), the incomprehensible text may have been endowed with imaginary content by the Jewish congregants, who perhaps saw it as uniquely their own, as suggested by Rojas.[141]

The interior of the Sardis synagogue was defined by multiple scripts: more than eighty texts in Greek, Hebrew, and the epichoric language, on mosaics and marbles. The majority were contemporaneous with the construction of the synagogue, recording donations made to the building, but some were far older. That there were pragmatic reasons to use spolia in the construction of the synagogue is clear—the piers also included uninscribed blocks from the Metroön's antae—but the particular means of displaying the inscriptions and Lydian lions within the highly decorative, even luxurious, space indicates at the very least an aesthetic of spoliation, and probably an awareness of, and appreciation for, the long history of both city and community. The Jews of Sardis, like the rest of the late Roman population, used the physical remains of the city and its surroundings to build their sense of the past.

The Temple of Zeus at Labraunda: Spolia *in medias res*

Not every attempted spoliation ultimately succeeded, however. At the rural site of Labraunda in the mountains of Karia, the Temple of Zeus Labraundos shows indications of both collapse and dismantling, most likely in late antiquity, but none of its carved marble elements was built into new construction projects. The fuller late antique context of this ancient Karian extra-urban sanctuary will be covered in the following chapter, but suffice it to say here that two churches were built at the southern border of the small settlement in the fifth century. The raison d'être of Labraunda shifted in late antiquity from pagan religious center to a convenient stopping and trading point on the road between Mylasa and Alinda farther up in the mountains, but its

---

[141] Rojas 2019: 122–123. Cf. a Christian chapel at Euromos in Karia, which incorporated an inscription written in ancient Karian: Ruggieri 2005: 90–91; Sitz 2019c: 220.

impressive, still-standing architecture and plentiful natural springs were surely also a draw (or at least a fringe benefit).[142] In this respect, its late antique situation paralleled that of Lagina, where a preexisting agricultural system and trade/festival network probably continued to encourage visits to the goddess's sanctuary.

The late Classical Temple of Zeus at Labraunda bore on its rear antae the first part of a dossier carved around 220 BCE or a little later, which detailed a dispute between the priest of Zeus Labraundos and the city of Mylasa over the right to revenue from the god's lands (Mylasa won).[143] The conflict was moderated by the local dynast Olympichos in the name of Seleukos II and, later, Philip V. Three anta blocks (two bearing an inscribed letter) were found next to the temple, but four additional blocks from the temple's southwestern rear anta had migrated into a nearby building called Andron A, a sizable late Classical feasting room located immediately behind the temple.[144] These marbles included two inscribed blocks, an ornate anta capital, and a plain, uninscribed anta block. The block with *I.Labraunda* 137 (a letter of Olympichos in which he states that he restored the land of Labraunda to Mylasa) came to light in the 2014 excavations (Figure 4.14).[145] The marbles were moved into the Andron probably in late antiquity: they were found lower than the level of a Middle Byzantine floor built of collapsed ashlars in approximately the tenth century. Prior to the laying of this floor, Andron A had been converted to a press for olive oil, evidenced by a counterweight stone and several pits (some with pithoi fragments). It is surprising that the weighty, bulky anta blocks (measuring approximately 0.69 × 0.70 × 0.30m) from the temple were transported to this space in one piece. There is no clear connection with the press installation; probably they were being stored here in anticipation of spoliation. The inscribed blocks are estimated to have come from approximately five meters high on the antae, so it is unlikely that they would have survived an accidental fall during an earthquake or collapse, suggesting that the temple was in part intentionally disassembled.

---

[142] See Blid 2016: 203 for the presence of African Red Slip and Phocaean Red Slip ceramics dating mainly from the fifth and first half of the sixth century, indicating trade.

[143] The dossier extended onto the antae of Andron A and the Andron of Maussollos: *I.Labraunda* 1–7 and 137.

[144] Found next to the temple: *I.Labraunda* 3; Hellström and Thieme 1982: 69–72. Found in Andron A: *I.Labraunda* 1 and 137.

[145] Henry et al. 2015: 350–352; Henry et al. 2016: 416–424; Henry and Aubriet 2015: 676–678; Unwin and Henry 2016: 37–39.

Figure 4.14 Labraunda. Interior of Andron A with *I.Labraunda* 137 marked. Courtesy of the Labraunda Excavations.

No flooring was found in the temple's cella: it may have been stripped after worship ended. The collapsed gneiss cella walls were found in a heap by the 1940s/50s excavators, but many of the temple's marble elements have never been recovered.[146] This is the result of two lime kilns, of uncertain date, located at the temple's east. Apparently the inhabitants of Labraunda preferred to burn temple elements rather than spoliate them, as no bits of the temple ended up in the two late antique churches, although other ancient spolia were incorporated in the Christian structures.

But the temple anta block bearing the text of *I.Labraunda* 137 may have only narrowly missed an afterlife as spolia: a deep cut (quarrying channel) is visible on the marble's top, right, and left sides, about thirty centimeters behind the inscribed face (Figure 4.15). The attempt was abandoned *in medias res*, but if completed, the cut would have resulted in two quadratic

---

[146] Hellström and Thieme 1982: 31, Pl. 28. The excavation notebooks describe late walls running across the cella and the pronaos pavement (Hellström and Thieme 1982: 7). It is unclear how these walls related stratigraphically with the collapsed cella.

Figure 4.15 Labraunda. Upper surface of the stone with *I.Labraunda* 137, showing original and later cutting marks. Courtesy of the Labraunda Excavations.

marble blocks of unequal size, one with the Olympichos inscription on its face. Either before or after this attempt, a single larger circular cavity was carved on its upper surface. In its final deposition in the Andron, the block was placed upside down in a rectangular pit. Through all of these misadventures, the inscription face remained in pristine condition. The attempt at cutting the stone seems to have aimed at removing this inscribed face from the rest of the block. The goal—displaying the inscription in a new context or simply freeing up the rest of the block to be used as spolia or burnt for lime—is unrecoverable, but regardless, the Hellenistic text appears to have been treated with care. None of these actions indicates that the dense, Hellenistic document was read per se, but the presence of "old text" itself may have engendered the desire to save the carved words (as we saw at the Korykian Cave Clifftop temple) or to display them as spolia.

Conclusion: Mixed Re-Views of Old Texts in New Buildings

At the beginning of this chapter, I used the ancient stelai laid as paving slabs in church floors to make the point that the majority of inscribed spolia was practically motivated, given the lack of explicit evidence for triumphalist narratives mapped onto physical structures. After the subsequent case studies, this point has become double-sided, like some of the stelai themselves: even if the use of spolia was mainly practical rather than polemical, we can still glean cultural attitudes from the manner of reuse. Nothing is "just" practical, nor are aesthetics neutral or universal. These spolia structures show what was acceptable, even desirable, within Christian and Jewish spaces in our period. Both ancient inscribed texts (often implicitly or explicitly pagan) and their categorization as spolia were welcomed in late antique built fabric. That is not to say that some individuals may not have perceived the act of stepping on older inscribed blocks or of embedding them in walls as a repudiation of the pre-Christian (or, in the case of the synagogue, the gentile) past. Late antique attitudes toward inscriptions must have varied. The scholarly differences of opinion on spolia may accurately reflect late antique beliefs.

To state that there is no single way of interpreting spolia in late antiquity is trite, but this chapter has brought greater precision to a number of individual cases. As we have seen, inscribed blocks deriving from sanctuaries were not treated as particularly problematic. Although the exact context of the architrave dedication to Apollo Klarios in the temple-church at Sagalassos is unclear, the text was most likely visible within the eastern portion of the nave, perhaps scrambled through disordering. At Aphrodisias, epigraphic spolia was highly visible at the entrances into the nave of the temple-church, and to a lesser degree elsewhere within the complex. Likewise, within the synagogue at Sardis, older inscriptions, both those from the city's Metroön and the enigmatic epichoric text, were on display. The large number of late antique donor inscriptions within the synagogue anticipates the act of reading; the ancient spolia may have occasionally been perused as well. At various sites, stelai and bases were laid inscribed face up in floors; although this may have aimed to conceal the unworked, rough reverses of these stones, the result was that the older texts were on view in ecclesiastical spaces. But other epigraphic spolia was hidden: at the Korykian Cave Clifftop temple-church the oldest (and most finely carved) section of the list of priests was concealed behind a transverse wall; so too was inscribed spolia hidden at sites like Paneas (Caesarea Philippi/Banias) and perhaps at Heliopolis/Baalbek. At the late antique basilica near Klaros, it is unclear whether the inscribed orthostate blocks from the altar of Apollo were on display. At Labraunda, we have no way of knowing the intended use for the partially cut inscribed block.

In every case, however, spolia was the product of a series of decisions, not simply the byproduct of economic or physical necessities. There was no one way to spoliate: at the Hexamilion wall spanning the Isthmus in Greece, different building teams on the same project made use of spolia in substantially different manners.[147] Likewise, at the sites we have considered, a range of possibilities was open. At the Korykian Cave, the builders might have chosen, perhaps more wisely, to bond the church's inscribed north wall with its east wall, or they might have expunged all traces of the names left on the interior wall of the church, as they did for those on the exterior. But instead many names were left in place. At Labraunda, both uninscribed and inscribed marbles from the defunct temple were moved into Andron A, and the stonecutter might have chosen any of these to partition—yet only an inscribed one was chosen. At Sagalassos, Aphrodisias, Klaros, and Sardis, the texts could have been erased but were, for the most part, not. The use of temple architectural spolia in the synagogue at Sardis is especially notable, given that all the other case studies presented here document spolia in Christian spaces—did cities divvy up their spolia on special request or on a "first-come, first-served" basis? Did the Jewish community of Sardis seek out these particular blocks, or were they simply what was available? Spolia from temples so often (although not always) ended up in churches, a phenomenon that continued into the Byzantine period. Did ecclesiastics exercise special rights over pagan sanctuary spolia, or is it simply the case that churches were one of the main *foci* of construction in late antiquity? To answer these questions requires more detailed publications on spolia, taking into account both what was reused and what was preserved.

The use of epigraphic spolia may even indicate an aesthetic of displayed text—it was perhaps in vogue to incorporate older inscriptions on floors, doors, and interiors of late antique religious spaces. Admittedly, this aesthetic is not especially prominent in the structures under consideration here (they all might have included more epigraphic spolia, had it been desirable), but late antique basilicas elsewhere made more extensive use of

---

[147] Frey 2015b: 128–174.

spoliated inscriptions. The Church of Christ-in-Jerusalem on the island of Kalymnos incorporated not only the "scrambled" architrave dedication to Apollo Delios discussed above, but also numerous other inscriptions from the god's sanctuary in its flooring and walls, especially at the opening of the apse.[148] There is evidence for plaster in the apse, but it stops short of the transverse wall. Meanwhile, in the rural area around Phoenix in the Karian Chersonese (Bozburun peninsula), the church at Kızlan Deresi incorporated blocks with dedications to Apollo and to Eleithya—in large letters (c. 3cm)— in the door jamb of an entrance into the nave (Figure 4.16).[149] They were upright and quite visible. Spolia in general was an element of late antique architectural aesthetics, and Niewöhner has recently argued that the taste for *varietas* identified in Rome's spolia churches was part of a wider visual trend of variegated forms, seen also in newly carved architectural elements of the eastern Mediterranean.[150] Ancient inscriptions in late antique structures contributed to this general aesthetic and added a certain *text*ure to these decorated spaces.

But are these examples of text for text's sake, or was the actual meaning of an inscription an essential component? Put another way, did the ancient inscriptions function like the sometimes random English phrases that appear on T-shirts produced for predominantly non-Anglophone markets? We have already seen in Chapter 2 that there was interest in the content of ancient texts—even if that content was often read to support preexisting beliefs or to bolster the Christian faith. The epigraphic spolia presented in this chapter gives a mixed impression: some texts may have been of interest to late antique readers, others perhaps were not. At Aphrodisias, the dedication to Augustus above a church door was short enough that people may have stopped and read it; the dedication to Aphrodite above another door was certainly read at least once, given that it suffered a selective erasure. I have suggested that the content of the inscriptions, which celebrated local connections with imperial rulers and civic euergetism in connection with a quite normal civic cult of Aphrodite, was a bonus to the ecclesiastical authorities, if not a motivating factor in the display of ancient texts in the temple-church. At Sardis, the Jewish community *may* have regarded Antiochos III as a benevolent figure in

---

[148] Deligiannakis 2016: 25, 172.
[149] *I.Rhodische Peraia* 105 and 106.
[150] Niewöhner 2018. See also Elsner 2004: 292 for the aesthetics of juxtaposed objects. In the west, Ostia boasted a number of funerary inscriptions displayed in domestic late antique opus sectile flooring (Murer 2019: 119), implying that the display of these inscriptions was à la mode.

Figure 4.16 Phoenix. Doorway into the nave of the Kızlan Deresi church with a dedication to Apollo (detail); the dedication to Eleithya is below it. Author, courtesy of the Phoenix Archaeological Project.

their own history, if they were able to recognize that monarch in the inscribed letter in the synagogue.

We may add to our discussion of content-based epigraphic spoliation another example from Athens: an architrave from the early Hellenistic choregic monument of Nikias was repurposed as spolia for the Beulé Gate, the new fortified entrance to the Acropolis after the Herulian attack in 267 CE. But the three blocks of the architrave were not reused in their original configuration: only the first inscribed block was placed front and center above the door leading into the Acropolis, while the second and third inscribed blocks were placed higher up, above the cornice. Here, the "scrambling" of the inscription served *not* to make it symbolically illegible, but instead to create an entirely new meaning: the opening words on the first block, prominently placed above the door, read Νι[κ]ίας Νικοδήμου (Nikias, son of Nikodemos).[151] As Tasos Tanoulas proposes, these names composed of the root words "victory" and "demos" may have served for the viewer as a memory-trigger of the victory of the demos over the Herulians.[152] Other, uninscribed architrave blocks were also available and might have been used here at this most attention-grabbing spot, if reading (and reinterpretation) was not wished.

But for many texts presented here, the content was probably uninspiring. The names on the Korykian Cave Clifftop temple were local micro-history, but it is questionable whether they would have been recognized as such, or even as priests' names. At Klaros, the records of visits to Apollo, taken as a whole, indicate the wide network of cities that engaged with this oracle; but on an individual scale, the texts provide little relevant information, and certainly nothing useful about the future. The dedication from Kollega at Sagalassos was probably too dense to be easily comprehensible, especially if it was, as I have proposed, scrambled. In any case, if any of this content had been deemed offensive to late antique Christian (or Jewish) eyes, it could have been removed; leaving the spoliated texts visible was a choice.

Ancient statues too had the potential to communicate about the past. We have seen in Chapter 3 how older statuary remained on display in public spaces of the eastern Mediterranean. Other sculpture migrated to entirely new cities or contexts.[153] These statues came the closest to fulfilling the ancient Roman understanding of spolia, that is, as the spoils of war, something taken by violence. Constantine's adornment of his new capital with imported statues may have been viewed by some as an act of retributive violence after the defeat of Licinius, or as an anti-pagan measure to lessen the draw of sanctuaries by removing their statuary. Constantine did not have the same interest in collecting historic inscriptions for his capital; inscriptions were neither the spoils of the (culture) war nor sought-after decorative elements

---

[151] *IG* II/III³ 4, 467.
[152] Tanoulas 2020: 89–92.
[153] Vassiliki and Nicolas 2019.

in their own right. Inscribed stones were more likely to become spolia, in our sense of the word, in their local contexts.

Occasionally statues too became actual building material: at Eleutherna (Crete), a basilica next to a temple of Hermes and Aphrodite repurposed two headless herms as door lintels.[154] In the west, broken statues were used to construct wall foundations (*Statuenmauern*) at sites in Italy; these were both public and private walls, defensive and domestic.[155] At Scythopolis/Beth Shean, the capital of Palaestina Secunda after the provincial reforms of the late fourth century, an over-life-size imperial torso became building material for the Silvanus Basilica in the sixth century.[156] For the most part, however, sculpture in the round was ill-suited as construction material, for the obvious reason that it was difficult to build stable walls with irregular pieces. When ancient statues were used in construction project, it was more often as lime mortar.[157] Figural reliefs, on the other hand, such as those marking graves or adorning ancient buildings, could quite easily be built into walls and were often used decoratively and apotropaically. The reliefs of Athena and Ares on the gate at Sagalassos are paralleled by lions and a Gorgon on a gate at Hierapolis and by Nike, satyrs, and Herakles on gates at Aphrodisias.[158] At this last city, the so-called Gaudin's Fountain was constructed entirely of spolia, including figural reliefs.

So sculpture in the round was rarely used as construction material, but figural reliefs (like inscriptions) frequently were. There is one key difference between figural reliefs and inscriptions, however: the contexts into which they were built. Epigraphic spolia was incorporated into churches, but relief sculpture usually was not. Each of the main sites under consideration here (except for the Korykian Cave) has also produced sculpture in the round or in relief. Yet this figural imagery was not found in churches. It is clear that sculpture in the round was not welcome in late antique churches, but even with various possibilities for concealing reused figural reliefs (laying them face down in floors; building them into walls; covering them with revetment), church builders did not frequently avail themselves of this type of spolia. Either figural reliefs were so valued for other projects that they would not be "wasted" on a church, where they would be covered, or those charged with

---

[154] Themelis 2004: 50; Saradi and Eliopoulos 2011: 297.
[155] Coates-Stephens 2007: 171–172; Witschel 2007: 125, Figs. 8–9.
[156] Kristensen 2013: 224; Tsafrir and Foerster 1997: 129, Fig. 39.
[157] Duckworth et al. 2020.
[158] Jacobs 2010: 277, fn. 70.

constructing churches were simply discomfited by the presence of sculpture, even when hidden. The fact that a figural relief *was* used face down in the synagogue at Sardis and that several Archaic Lydian lion sculptures decorated this Jewish space suggests the latter: ecclesiastical construction projects shied away from reliefs depicting figures, while Jewish builders were apparently more comfortable with sculpture. Of course, some churches installed directly into temple cellas kept their ancient reliefs (sometimes edited) and, in the case of the Parthenon, even the pedimental sculpture intact, but it would be centuries before churches, such as the Church of the Dormition at Merbaka, Greece, and the "Little Metropolis" in Athens, proudly showed off ancient reliefs on their walls. This differentiation of epigraphic and figural spolia can be traced to more fundamental beliefs about statues and texts, a point to which we will return in the next chapter.

5

Erasure

[[Damnatio Memoriae]] or Conscious Uncoupling?

Unnaming the Gods

In the sixth century, the emperor Justinian was hard at work constructing his revitalized Roman empire, both ideologically and physically. He built a palace in a suburban neighborhood near Constantinople, perhaps seeking refuge from the hustle and bustle of the capital and the disaffected masses. The name of this suburb? "Heraion, which they now call Hieron," according to Prokopios.[1] Heraion (Ἡραῖον), modern-day Fenerbahçe, was located across the Bosphoros from Constantinople and boasted a shrine to the goddess Hera. As Christianity shaped the cultural world of the late Romans, a clever shift of vowels and accent transformed the name to the more palatable Hieron (Ἱερόν), meaning simply "holy place" or "sanctuary." The manipulation or replacement of names is a widespread tool in the shaping of cultural memory, today as in yesteryear. Modern Greek villages, many of which had "foreign" names as a result of Ottoman rule, received new names in the twentieth century; the reverse process has been carried out in Turkey after the Turkish-Greek population exchange of 1923.[2] But in the case of Heraion/Hieron, there was no attempt to completely replace the pagan name with a new Christian one. Crucially, the presence of an ancient shrine was still acknowledged. It was simply made anonymous by removing the specific reference to Hera.

This chapter considers evidence for the late antique erasure of ancient inscriptions; in some instances, the result was to anonymize a pagan sacred space while still acknowledging its presence. I have argued in previous chapters that inscriptions preserved on temple walls and those spoliated for new building projects were *probably* read, given what we know of late

---

[1] *De Aedificiis* 1.11.16: ἔν τε τῷ Ἡραίῳ, ὃ νῦν Ἱερὸν ὀνομάζουσι. See also *De Aedificiis* 1.3.10.
[2] Davis 2007.

antique engagement with ancient inscriptions more generally. The epigraphic erasures in this chapter prove it: several cases show a clear process of reading and evaluating the older texts to erase only the most ostentatiously pagan parts. These erasures must be viewed within a broader range of responses to the past, including the anonymizing of pagan gods in written sources both Christian and pagan and the violence sometimes enacted against the figural instantiations of pagan deities, that is, their statues. The act of erasing inscriptions with pagan content was one facet of wider Roman habits of epigraphic erasures and iconoclasm against images, most famously seen in so-called damnatio memoriae. This chapter therefore requires more contextualization up front before moving to our main topic.

The "unnaming" of pagan gods, as in the shift from Heraion to Hieron, occurred widely in late antique thought. Rather than individual deities with characteristics unique to specific cults, the gods became generic *daimones* (demons) in many Christian texts and homilies.[3] Sometimes these demons kept their old pagan names (the Titans Kronos and Rhea experienced a curious revival in the imaginations of late antique polemicists and in magical spells alike), but very often they became an anonymous collective.[4] In Gregory of Nyssa's 383 CE eulogy for his predecessor Gregory Thaumaturgus (c. 210–275 CE), the earlier saint "entered some temple ... a notable one, where the temple custodians were visibly possessed by the attending demons."[5] The god associated with the temple is never named, although Gregory of Nyssa's fourth-century audience might well have had a residual cultural memory of such a "notable" cult in the region. Likewise, Theodoret of Cyrrhus (died circa 460) refers to "a sanctuary dedicated to daimones" rather than specifying the deities to whom it was dedicated.[6] Both these authors were well educated and surely could have named names if they had been so inclined. The trope appears in the Coptic literature as well: Shenoute of Atripe denigrated "a shrine of an unclean spirit," choosing not to give a specific pagan identity but suggesting that sacrifices to Satan had been made there.[7] Various other examples could be adduced.

The anonymizing of pagan gods was not exclusive to Christian invective. The idea was trendy among contemporary pagan intellectuals as well,

---

[3] Trombley 1993: 99–108; Caseau 2001: 82–86; Brakke 2008; Cameron 2010: 797.
[4] Faraone 2010.
[5] Gregory of Nyssa *Life of Gregory the Wonderworker* 5.35 (trans. Slusser).
[6] *Historia Religiosa* 1488A: τέμενος ἦν δαίμοσιν ἀνακείμενον.
[7] Shenoute, *Acephalous Work A6* (trans. Westerfeld 2019: 104).

with daimones understood as both good and bad spirits. Neoplatonist philosophers, such as Plotinos, Porphyry, and Iamblichos reinvented the traditional Greek and Roman gods as lesser iterations of The One; their individual identities became inconsequential. Iamblichos explored the unknowable divine names in theurgy (rituals aimed at mystically invoking deities).[8] This unnaming of the gods was supported by pagan oracles. A widely referenced oracle from Apollo at Klaros was inscribed at Oinoanda in Lykia in the late second or third century CE:

> Born of itself, untaught, without a mother, unshakeable, not contained in a name, known by many names, dwelling in fire, this is god. We, his angels (ἄγγελοι), are a small part of god. To you who ask this question about god, what his essential nature is, he has pronounced that aether is god who sees all. To him you should pray at dawn, gazing on him and looking towards the sunrise.[9]

Apollo declares himself naught but an angel, a speck of the all-encompassing divine. Angels were popular among pagans, Christians, and Jews in late antiquity (as discussed in reference to Didyma and Aphrodisias in previous chapters); the term "angel" was a catchall for a variety of local religious traditions.[10] This oracle and Neoplatonic writings indicate that the hyperlocal divinities of the ancient world were giving way to a new, monotheistic (or, in Chaniotis' terminology, "megatheistic") conception of the divine, due either to intellectual currents already running through pagan thought or to competition with the new Christian cult.[11]

The *Zeitgeist* among both pagans and Christians, then, favored anonymous pagan gods, generic agents of ineffable good or evil. This unnaming is apparent in figural imagery as well: the pagan-themed statuary visible in late antique cityscapes (Chapter 3) were mythologized (framed as fictional characters in myths) or anonymized (displayed as "classical" figures without specific attribution); in either case, their cultic significance was denied and names lost their (e)vocative power. The under-life-size mythological statuary used to decorate the north-south thoroughfare at Sagalassos in the sixth

---

[8] Addey 2011.
[9] *SEG* 27.933 (trans. Chaniotis 2010: 115). The oracle is also cited in Lactantius *Divine Institutes* 1.7 and the *Tübingen Theosophy* (on which see Chapter 2, p. 48); cf. Malalas *Chronographia* 3.13–14. For the wide diffusion of similar texts: Mitchell 1999; Jones 2005; Chaniotis 2010.
[10] Cline 2011a.
[11] Athanassiadi 1999; Mitchell and Nuffelen 2010; Chaniotis 2010.

century functioned as generic "adornment elements," in the words of Jacobs, rather than specific pagan figures.[12] It is only the modern archaeologist who seeks to classify them based on the staples of art history: attributes and figural types. These modern modes of identifying images, however, are not descriptive but normative: attributes and figural types can be deconstructed, and their efficaciousness depends on both the knowledge and willingness of viewers.[13] Later western examples of reused pagan objects indicate the inherent mutability of graven images: in the thirteenth century, a monk described a cameo used in child birthing as depicting a figure "holding in its right hand a spear on which a serpent creeps upward," either unwilling or unable to connect the iconography with the pagan healing god Asklepios.[14] In the ninth century, a cup with Dionysiac imagery was dedicated to the abbey of Saint-Denis. Subsequent descriptions of the vessel focused on the flora and fauna, conditioned by the ecclesiastical context not to see anything pagan. In other medieval appropriations, a new label could substitute the old identity: a cameo depicting the emperor Honorius and his wife Maria was later inscribed with the names "Sergius" and "Bacchus," thereby transforming the individuals (including a woman) into these saints. An Augustan Medusa cameo became the head of *David rex* in the thirteenth century.[15] Simply inscribing a name held the power to transmute the identity of the figure, from secular to religious, female to male, monstrosity to royalty.

The importance of inscribed text in stabilizing identity was recognized long before these medieval manipulations. A decree of 22 CE from the polis of Lindos on the island of Rhodes referred to uninscribed statues as "asemantic," meaningless or worthless.[16] The Lindians' neighbors in the city of Rhodes had a habit of erasing the honorific inscriptions on old statue bases and simply reinscribing them with the names of the most recently voted honorands, a practice lambasted by Dio Chrysostom in the later first century CE.[17] The reinscribing of statue bases took place elsewhere in the Greco-Roman world as well; it was simply practical and economical to replace the illustrious (but not too illustrious) figures of the past with more relevant,

---

[12] Jacobs 2016: 115.
[13] Dietrich 2018: 263–274.
[14] Kinney 2011: 111. Cf. the bronze Asklepios interpreted as a bishop in ninth-century Constantinople (Bassett 2004: 148).
[15] Zwierlein-Diehl 2007: 261.
[16] *I.Lindos* 419, l. 32: Ἄσαμοι. Zadorojnyi 2018: 62; Rous 2019: 149–153. See also Jacobs 2020: 804–808.
[17] *Oration* 31; Platt 2007: 252–262.

up-to-date benefactors.[18] Why go through the trouble of quarrying and carving new marble when ancient cities were chock-full of "ready-mades" just waiting for a new label?

The attribution of inscribed identity to statues is part of the more ubiquitous human practice of assigning names to individuals as a means of forming (and limiting) their identity.[19] Carved portraits became, in a sense, the represented individual her-/himself, regardless of how idealized or generic the image was. This is apparent in common Greek epigraphic formulae for statue dedications in the Hellenistic and Roman periods: the individual depicted in the statue (the recipient of the decreed honors) was named in the accusative or (in certain cases) the nominative, emphasizing that the depicted image *was* the individual.[20] As Paul Frosh has argued for today's habit of "tagging" photos on social media, "naming and figuration combine to construct and extend the self through objects which instantiate, replicate and disseminate the individual subject discursively, visually and materially."[21] Carving an onomastic on a statue base was the "tagging" of the ancient world, and although the opportunities to "tag" oneself or one's associates were more limited (and therefore carried more weight) than today, the identity-forming potential of such image dissemination was clearly understood by, for example, Roman emperors.

As with reinscribed bases on ancient Rhodes, images in late antiquity could be "un- and retagged," that is given a new, often Christian, meaning. Jacobs has recently pushed back against labeling this phenomenon as late antique "misunderstanding" of the images and instead focuses on the needs served by such renamings.[22] In Constantine's bid to decorate his new capital with statues snatched from other cities, most were moved without their inscribed bases, permanently alienating them from their original identities—and opening them to new interpretations and iconographic manipulation.[23] Constantine himself was the beneficiary of this epigraphic ambiguity in Rome, where the famous equestrian statue of Marcus Aurelius escaped destruction because of its reinterpretation as Constantine, at the latest by the tenth century, but quite probably earlier, given how exceptional the decision *not* to melt down this bronze monument for its material value was.

---

[18] Shear 2007.
[19] Bodenhorn and vom Bruck 2006.
[20] For the grammar of Greek statue base dedications: Kajava 2011; Ma 2013: 15–63.
[21] Frosh 2019: 118.
[22] Jacobs 2020: 803.
[23] Ma 2012.

The identity theft was probably due to the statue's original display location near the Lateran palace and basilica, built by Constantine; Marcus Aurelius presumably lost his identifying inscription at some point and conveniently became the first Christian emperor.[24] There is no evidence that the bronze monument received a new inscription, but it very well may have: in late antique Italy, the erasure and reinscription of statue bases was common, with an estimated 34 percent of statue bases showing evidence of reuse.[25] These appropriations were regulated official actions, with the urban prefect of Rome responsible for 40.9 percent of all reused bases in the city; even emperors and the Senate took advantage of available older bases.

Other instances of statue reidentification had more popular origins. At Paneas (Caesarea Philippi/Banias), Eusebius of Caesarea saw a bronze statue group of a woman kneeling next to a modestly garbed standing male. The locals identified these figures as Jesus and the woman with the issue of blood, standing in front of a house believed to belong to the woman.[26] Eusebius finds this identification plausible: he notes that the nations of old honored their deliverers by erecting statues. Eusebius is aware of the ancient honorific statue habit, as well as its decline in his own day. The biography of this statue of "Christ" at Paneas was not over, however. Philostorgios in the early fifth century claimed that its identity had been forgotten because the identifying inscription was covered by dirt; after cleaning, the statue was correctly identified and moved into a church.[27] The story may contained a kernel of truth: perhaps a real ancient inscription naming a *soter* (savior) and/or *euergete* (benefactor)—Hadrian?—was found on the base.[28] Remarkably, the narrative continues with Julian abusing the statue by having it dragged through the streets of Paneas and dismembered; only the head was available for Philostorgios to view. *Christus patiens*, indeed.

It was not always necessary to attribute a definite new identity to the depicted figure—merely the lack of a distinctively pagan one would do. We have already seen that medieval western viewers were unwilling or unable to connect clear pagan iconography with a definite pagan identity. This process began already in late antiquity. Zosimos, a pagan historian writing in the early

---

[24] Stewart 2012: 269–270.
[25] Machado 2017: 329–334.
[26] Eusebius *Historia Ecclesiastica* 7.18.3.
[27] Philostorgios *Historia Ecclesiastica (epit.)* 7.3; Stewart 2007: 32–33. Cf. Sozomen *Historia Ecclesiastica* 5.21.
[28] Wilson 2006: the figures originally may have been Hadrian with captured Judea. The statue group may be depicted on the fourth-century Lateran sarcophagus in Rome.

sixth century, describes a statue of Rhea (Kybele) brought to Constantinople from Kyzikos: Constantine "impaired this statue by taking away the lions that were on each side, and, changing the position of the hands... alter[ing them] into a supplicating posture."[29] With a new pose and the loss of her signature lions (as well as any inscription that had originally accompanied the statue), the old Anatolian goddess shed her pagan identity and became to Christian viewers an anonymous *orans*. Anonymity could protect.

Violence against Statues

From the point of view of remaining pagans, the above examples of reinterpreting or anonymizing the images of the old gods could be a form of semantic violence, of identity denial, of rewriting history. The same holds for statues of pagan gods left on display as allegorical or mythological figures denied a cultic role. But not all statues could have their identities manipulated, their names removed, or be relegated to the realm of mythology: their original pagan associations were inescapable, and physical violence or obliteration through burying took place. We have already seen in Chapter 1 the early Christian rhetoric of violence against cult buildings, as well as the frequent disconnect between these polemics and the archaeologically attestable damage. Yet violent desecration of both image and temple did sometimes happen.

Heads or Tails?

Gods sculpted from marble, bronze, wood, and ivory had little to protect them once their status as revered figures was called into question by Christians (following on a long history of Jewish concerns about idolatry). Graven images could be smashed completely, but more often, certain body parts were the focus of attack. Perhaps the most famous case of early Christian iconoclasm—both today and in late antiquity—was the destruction of the Serapeion in Alexandria around 391 CE, discussed in Chapter 2, where we saw that the "discovery" of a hieroglyphic ankh was taken as a prophesy of Christian triumph.[30] Rufinus, writing circa 401, described how a soldier

---

[29] Zosimos 2.31.3–5; see also Bassett 2004: 155.
[30] Chapter 2, —. See also Hahn 2008: 338–350.

armed with an axe attacked the wooden cult statue of Serapis, striking it first on the jaw; Theodoret of Cyrrhus a few decades later adds the colorful detail that mice ran out of the damaged figure.[31] The statue's head and extremities were broken off and paraded through the streets of Alexandria, proving the god's impotence. Troels Myrup Kristensen frames this dispersal of the Serapis' body parts as a reflection of the mob violence inflicted on real bodies in Alexandria—for example, the murder and dismemberment of the philosopher Hypatia in 415—in the framework of long-standing Egyptian beliefs about bodies and the afterlife.[32]

A marble statue of Serapis in Rome suffered similarly: it was found in twenty-three fragments, none from the head, surrounded by other smashed sculpture in a late antique shrine to Osiris on the Janiculum.[33] Was the head taken away, to be paraded through the streets, or was it utterly destroyed? The same question can be asked at Eretria (Greece), where imperial statues in a cult temple were found in fragments without heads; the excavators suggest that this destruction took place in the fifth century or later.[34] Farther east, the deposit of decapitated marble heads belonging to Athena and Aphrodite near Scythopolis/Beth Shean in the region of Galilee offers a clue to where numerous heads ended up: they were intentionally buried in a refuse pit outside the city in the fifth century.[35] At the same site, pieces of sculpture were thrown into the defunct hypocaust of a bath around the first quarter of the sixth century, including a decapitated Capitoline Venus sprawled like a murder victim.[36] As we saw in Chapter 4, the three cult statues at the oracular Temple of Apollo at Klaros were found without heads, while at the Mithraeum under the Terme del Mitra in Ostia, both Mithras and the bull lost their heads.[37] Decapitation was an especially effective means of neutralizing pagan cult images and shifting the sacred canopy.

Violence was not restricted to sacred figures nor to sculpture in the round. Philosophers and historical figures were defaced on a series of shield portraits at Aphrodisias and dumped in an alley behind the Atrium House, which they probably originally adorned. Even Alexander the Great was not immune: his neck shows a deep groove indicating an abortive decapitation,

---

[31] Rufinus *Historia Ecclesiastica* 2.23; Theodoret of Cyrrhus *Historia Ecclesiastica* 5.22.
[32] Kristensen 2013: 122–123; Pharaonic period iconoclasm: Nyord 2020: 70–76.
[33] Goddard 2008.
[34] Schmidt 2001: 140–141.
[35] Kristensen 2013: 230.
[36] Tsafrir and Foerster 1997: 129; Kristensen 2013: 222.
[37] Sauer 2003: 16–19, Figs. 2–4.

Figure 5.1 Aphrodisias. Bust of Alexander the Great with cut mark on the neck. Author, courtesy of NYU Excavations at Aphrodisias.

finally accomplished through a massive blow (Figure 5.1).[38] Metope and frieze reliefs could be chiseled away, as famously happened to some (but not all) of the reliefs on the Parthenon in Athens.[39] A mixture of destructive techniques could be applied in private as well as public contexts. The Omega House on the northern slope of the Areopagus in the same city produced classical reliefs with mutilated heads, as well as decapitated statues thrown into wells. The house was renovated in the first half of the sixth century, and it was probably at that time that the ancient figures were defaced.[40] It should be remembered, however, that ancient statues lost their heads for various reasons at various times (including in the mad dash to fill early modern

---

[38] Smith 1990: 136, Pl. 9, 1–3.
[39] Pollini 2013: 246; Anderson 2017.
[40] Anghel 2012: 110–111.

museums).⁴¹ Heads were frequently carved from a separate block and installed on busts, so ancient viewers also occasionally encountered headless specters lining their public spaces. The ease of removing these separate pieces facilitated the later habit of statue decapitation.

Even when heads were not removed, noses, eyes, ears, and mouths were wont to suffer damage, symbolically removing the statue's ability to breathe, speak, smell, taste, see, and hear.⁴² The over-life-size cult statue of Allat-Athena in Palmyra was found heavily fragmented and face down in her open-air shrine. She seems to have been attacked from behind, and the nose was missing.⁴³ Late fourth-century coins and lamps were found in this context: the destruction was perhaps carried out under Maternus Cyngeius, praetorian prefect of the Oriens from 384 to 388. An inscribed column from the sanctuary was reused in a nearby, undated *maison byzantine*.⁴⁴ The cult images at the sanctuaries of Bel and Baalshamin, on the other hand, seem to have been completely removed in late antiquity, leaving no traces for archaeologists (or ISIS, for that matter) to find, and we have already seen that many inscriptions in those sanctuaries were left in place. Was the difference in the treatment of these sanctuaries topographic (the sanctuary of Allat was located next to the Roman military camp, where Cyngeius presumably had his headquarters) or based on other, difficult-to-reconstruct factors?

The crosses added to the foreheads of a small number of ancient statues, as discussed in Chapter 3, occasionally appear in a more extreme iteration, completely disfiguring or obliterating the face. A Hera from Sparta, probably originally a cult statue, has crosses etched onto its forehead, eyes, and mouth; the nose was knocked off.⁴⁵ The result is ghoulish. An exquisite Praxitelean head of Athena, found in the Roman Agora in Athens, bears a roughly carved cross on its forehead; the nose is missing and the eyes show damage.⁴⁶ The face of a female head in the museum on Rhodes has been completely recarved in the form of a cross with the typical Christian triumphal formula Ἰ(ησοῦ)ς Χ(ριστὸ)ς νικᾷ (Jesus Christ triumphs).⁴⁷ A similar head recently published from Laodikeia lost its features and gained a staurogram with an alpha and omega.⁴⁸ The dates of these recarvings cannot be confirmed and

[41] Greenhalgh 2016.
[42] Kristensen 2013: 90–97. Similar ancient Near Eastern examples: May 2012.
[43] Kristensen 2013: 212–217; Gawlikowski 2017: 181; Intagliata 2018: 47.
[44] *IGLS* 17, 1.126.
[45] Kristensen 2012: 36; Kristensen 2013: 98, Fig. 1.20.
[46] Kristensen 2012: 55.
[47] Deligiannakis 2008: 156–157, Fig. 6.
[48] Şimşek 2018: 92–94, Fig. 14.

some may be Byzantine or later, but nothing about them is inconsistent with late antique practice.

Not only sculpted heads were problematic: body parts associated with sex were as well. Penises, testicles, pudenda, and female nipples all fell victim to chiseling at numerous sites, especially in Asia Minor; the editing applied to figures pagan, mythological, and historical—especially those displayed in baths, where late antique Christian anxiety about naked bodies was most pronounced.[49] Jacobs has argued that this censoring should be understood as "updating" statues in line with changing cultural attitudes, rather than as violence per se; Smith refers to this act as "tidying up."[50] In this view, genitalia were to statues like altars to temples: extraneous bits that were no longer appropriate in late antique cities and could simply be removed. Yet again, however, local contexts and the particularities of the physical act of editing must be taken into account. In some instances, the chiseling away of genitals was carefully done, so as to be minimally noticeable (as on the Sebasteion reliefs at Aphrodisias), but elsewhere the censorship left behind ugly gashes and a gaping cavity, as on a Grace from Perge (Figure 5.2).[51] Given the association of sculpted bodies with real ones, the removal of sex organs makes a statement: the raw power of a muscular Herakles also from Perge is undercut by his missing genitalia. If genital removal was intended merely to bring the statues in line with new Christian ideas about bodies, the chiseled-away areas might have been subsequently smoothed, rather than left as rough patches drawing attention to what is missing. Other methods of dealing with nudity might have been adopted: draping the statues with cloth or attaching sculpted fig leaves over the offending areas (the early-modern Vatican's preferred mode of censoring). In antiquity, nude statues were embodiments of beauty and proportionality: roughly hacking at them probably offended at least some viewers, of whatever religious persuasion. The mutilation of sculpted genitals created ugly spots on these idealized marble bodies, forcing viewers to reckon with new Christian beliefs about bodies and the omnipresent danger of sexual sin, perhaps even their own lustful thoughts.

---

[49] Hannestad 2001; Stirling 2016: 286–289.
[50] Jacobs 2010: 278; Smith 2012: 284.
[51] Jacobs 2010, no. 10.

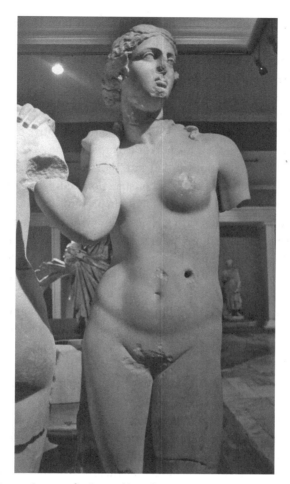

Figure 5.2 Perge. Statue of a Grace (Antalya Museum Inv. 2018/133) with damage to the pubic area and breast. Author, courtesy of the Antalya Museum.

Out of Sight, Out of Mind

Beyond physical violence, select statues in late antiquity were also subject to disappearing acts, erased from public spaces through their removal and deposition. This practice was distinct from the reuse of statues as spoliated building material, which had clear practical/economic motivations (discussed in Chapter 4). Statue deposits that can be dated to late antiquity (the deposition, not the statues) are primarily found at sanctuary sites.

Caches of statues may initially call to mind coin hoards, buried for safekeeping as enemy forces drew near, but Silviu Anghel has argued that pagan statues were often buried without evidence of haste (a pagan priest trying to hide the statues from a marauding horde of Christians) or hatred (Christians taking over a sanctuary and violently disposing of the old gods).[52] Rather, ritual needs motivated the careful interment of the statues. Already in the ancient period, the requirement to dispose of damaged votive offerings within the temenos resulted in their burial, for example on the Acropolis in Athens after the Persian destruction of 480 BCE. For the ancient Athenians, this deposition in preparation for new construction fulfilled a ritual-practical need; it also preserved the statues for their present-day museum afterlife. By late antiquity, the preservative effect of burying statues may have been recognized: several depositions seem to have been carried out by late pagans who aimed to save the images of gods from potential Christian defacement, or perhaps to save face themselves in predominantly Christian social circles.[53] Burying statues both bronze and marble may have been the final act by a retiring pagan priest fulfilling ritual duties, either compelled to close down her/his sanctuary or deciding to do so in the face of declining enthusiasm, resources, and official support.[54]

The most exciting find of deposited sculpture in recent years was made at Miletos: five Roman heads and busts (belonging to a male herm, two ideal males, and two caryatids, dated to the first or second century CE) were excavated in 2013 in a cave under the city's theater.[55] These damaged sculptures and late antique oil lamps were used to fill a sacred spring, probably an Asklepeian healing shrine, within the cave in the late fourth or fifth century CE, perhaps around the same time that the so-called *Erzengelinschrift* (an invocation of archangels to protect the city, discussed in Chapter 3) was carved on the west corner of the theater not far from the entry tunnel to the cave. At least two of the statues' faces (a caryatid and an ideal male) were intentionally bashed before burial; damage on the other pieces may have also been intentional. The sculpture likely came from the theater above: headless caryatid bodies were excavated at the stage building, where the editing of genitals on relief panels indicates late antique intervention. Although

---

[52] Anghel 2011: 3, 276–277. See also Caseau 2011; Leone 2013: 122–188.
[53] Jacobs 2010: 285. Note, however, that the ritual burial of statues of Artemis Ephesia in the Prytaneion at Ephesos (Jacobs's no. 37) can now be rejected based on a reappraisal of the stratigraphy: Steskal 2010: 197–202.
[54] Anghel 2011: 247–260.
[55] Niewöhner et al. 2017.

caryatids and ideal males were not controversial figures, the damage may have aimed to mar the beauty that classical cities worked so hard to show off, as I have also proposed for the rough removal of statue genitalia.[56] Philipp Niewöhner and his team attribute the statue violence to Christians but suggest that their orderly burial and the closing of the sacred spring was carried out by pagans to protect both sculptures and shrine from further damage. Given the presence of the *Erzengelinschrift* nearby, one wonders whether this shrine may have become associated with a syncretic angel cult in late antiquity (as has been argued for Aphrodite's well at Aphrodisias), provoking ecclesiastical discomfort. Regardless, these burials at Miletos served to get pagan-era statues "off the streets."

Sometimes, no physical traces of pagan statues remained, but their absence was implied by a disjuncture between an architectural setting and a new, late antique replacement. At Sagalassos, the city's Tyche was removed from her marble pavilion in 378 and a new statue dedicated to two subsequent empresses was set up.[57] But the distinctive canopy likely remained recognizable as a Tychaion for a time: the shrine had appeared on the city's Roman coins and had been celebrated just a few years earlier (365 or later) on a nearby honorific statue base. A more explicitly Christian replacement took place at Ephesos: an epigram set up in perhaps the second half of the fifth century declared, "Having destroyed the deceitful image of demonic Artemis, Demeas set up this sign of truth."[58] Regardless of whether Demeas' epigrammatic boasting corresponded with the actual destruction of a statue of Artemis or just its relocation, it reveals the rhetoric of religious change in Ephesos. The goddess's absence was noticeable: she was out of *site*, but not out of mind.

Ambiguous Afterlives

The difficulty of reading intention into statue damage allows for multiple possible interpretations. At Caesarea Maritima in Palaestina, the "Byzantine Esplanade," built between 545 and 606, featured two colossal, headless seated statues flanking the street at its termination.[59] One, probably originally

[56] Niewöhner et al. 2017: 132–135.
[57] Talloen 2019: 174–175.
[58] *I.Ephesos* 1351 (trans. Kristensen 2013: 9).
[59] Patrich 2011: 92–105. Kristensen 2013: 235–241.

Hadrian, was of porphyry; the other of white marble represented either a god/emperor or perhaps the personified demos. It is unclear how the statues lost their heads in the city inhabited by Christians, pagans, Jews, and Samaritans. The display of these two looming figures may indicate nostalgic and antiquarian tendencies, or it may have alerted the viewer to past iconoclasm and religious strife. Or perhaps the two monumental statues were displayed simply as wonders (*thaumata*) in their own right; the appreciation of wonders crossed religious affiliations. Individual viewers in Caesarea Maritima may have interpreted these headless statues according to their own attitudes. Both beauty and violence are in the eye of the beholder.

Scholars have noted that most of the instances of violence against statues (beyond genital editing) come from certain regions. Egypt and the Levant seem to have been more prone to deface or damage images. In Egypt this may in part have been due to the nature of the images themselves: many were carved in relief on temple walls, and therefore could not simply be taken down; some Egyptian gods were hybrid creatures, for example, the falcon-headed Horus, and therefore more likely to attract Christian derision than the anthropomorphic Greco-Roman deities.[60] At the massive Temple of Hathor in Dendara, Egypt, carved images of the gods were defaced systematically at ten meters above ground level, requiring ladders and significant dedication. Nonetheless, statue destruction in Asia Minor and Greece must have taken place more often than our archaeological evidence can confirm: preserved cult statues are few and far between, hinting that many statues were completely obliterated or very effectively hidden. Statues of imperial, rather than pagan, figures were also not immune to violence: statue monuments of emperors occupied contested spaces in late antiquity, as social relationships between populace and prince were negotiated—often through mob violence. The susceptibility of imperial statuary to violence contributed, according to Benjamin Anderson, to the decline of the statue habit overall: carved emperors could not be publicly scourged if there were no carved emperors available.[61] Some explicitly pagan statuary may have been taken down and burnt, broken up, or buried by civic authorities as a preventative measure *before* they became a magnet for the mob. Other significant instances of destruction are discussed in the following case studies.

---

[60] Sauer 2003: 89–113; Kristensen 2013: 107–176; Kristensen 2019: 272–279; Westerfeld 2019: 93.
[61] Anderson 2016.

Violence against Inscriptions

In the statue defacements outlined above, the corresponding inscribed bases are mostly missing. Perhaps the bases were spoliated for construction material elsewhere or simply left in place, empty; perhaps they were burnt for lime. But the violence enacted on the bodies of pagan statuary could occasionally extend to their epigraphic counterparts. In the preceding chapters, we have seen how inscriptions, even those with pagan content, were often tolerated on temple walls or were subject to spoliation in new architectural contexts. This chapter documents the most extreme—and rarest—reaction to inscriptions on temples: erasure and destruction.

The clever vowel shift at play in Prokopios' "Heraion, which they now call Hieron" was harder to carry out when the letters were literally set in stone. In Chapter 4, we saw how the epigraphic manipulation (including erasure) at Gerasa reveals the ideological lens through which inscriptions could be viewed. The intentional destruction of inscribed text is often conflated with the defacement of images, but the destruction of inscriptions could also take place independently, and violence against text did not function in the same way, or use the same methods, as that against statues. The problem of what to do with unwanted epigraphic memorialization was not novel in late antiquity—it was present already in ancient Mesopotamia and Egypt, where a number of texts show politically motivated erasures.[62] Ancient Greek city-states used epigraphic rasurae to break up with erstwhile benefactors or to give old statues new identities, as we have already seen at Rhodes and as also took place in Athens.[63] Here I use "erasure" or "*rasura*" to indicate carved texts that have been chiseled, hammered, hacked at, or elided through rubbing, whether this action resulted in the full annihilation of text (and potentially reinscribing) or merely light damage leaving the text still legible. Other types of text manipulation, such as the breaking up or burning of an inscribed stone through human agency, are described here as "destruction" (as distinct from natural processes such as damage wrought by weathering or through an accidental fire). Both the erasure and destruction of inscriptions show some degree of intentionality, even if the precise intentions cannot always be ascertained. We will return to this thorny methodological question at the end of the chapter.

---

[62] May 2012; Kühne-Wespi, Oschema, and Quack 2019.
[63] Shear 2007; Shear 2020; Byrne 2010; Moser 2017; Rhodes 2018; Low 2020.

Damnatio Memoriae

The erasure of ancient texts is most commonly associated with a particular Roman political habit termed "damnatio memoriae." "Damnatio" used in a narrow sense refers to memory sanctions enacted in the Roman Republic and Empire against condemned officeholders, emperors, and imperial family members. It is difficult to precisely define or delineate the practice of damnatio memoriae, but for the most part, "we know it when we see it." Or at least we think we do. As is the case with spolia, the term "damnatio memoriae" is modern (Harriet Flower prefers "memory sanctions"); the practice varied widely and encompassed everything from the recutting of imperial portraiture, countermarking coins, rasurae in inscriptions, and historiographic erasures, in which an individual, event, or even entire city is left out of an account.[64] The erasure of various statue bases in late antique Italy, discussed above in the context of "retagging" statues, was not damnatio because its motivations were practical rather than punitive and because it was not directed at specific individuals—even if the erasure may have felt like a condemnation, or at least an obsolescence, of memory to the honored individual's descendants.

In damnatio, it was the names of the disgraced, alongside their portraits, that were the most likely to undergo editing; like pagan gods in late antiquity, these individuals were unnamed (and unfaced). But despite pretensions at annihilating the memory of a disgraced figure, damnatio in practice served to perpetually shame and dishonor that individual in the public eye. Certainly no one has forgotten Nero or Domitian, two emperors who suffered censure and whose monuments were damaged or destroyed after their deaths (unevenly in the case of Nero and more systematically for Domitian).[65] In the Severan period, neither the gaping lacuna left on the famous imperial family portrait tondo nor the erased and clumsily reinscribed text on the Arch of Severus in the Forum Romanum allowed viewers to ignore the damned Geta after he had been killed by his brother Caracalla in 211/12 CE. Erasures and recarvings were only carried out on select monuments with a particular audience: the very elites who might threaten the political equilibrium or the imperial succession. They are therefore found primarily near the centers of power, for example, in the fora of Rome. At most, about 25 percent

---

[64] On Roman political damnatio memoriae: Hedrick 2000; Kelly 2003; Varner 2004; Benoist 2004; Flower 2006; Crespo Pérez 2014; Usherwood 2015 and 2022; Omissi 2016; Östenberg 2018.
[65] Flower 2006: 197–275.

of a disgraced emperor's inscriptions might undergo erasure.[66] Like book burnings in the modern period, there was no need to find and destroy every, or even most copies; it was the performative value of the act itself, or, in the case of Roman inscriptions, the perpetual performance of a visible lacuna or obvious reinscription that was desired.

Damnatio memoriae was always a fuzzy notion: there was no single prescription for condemning memory, nor a single agent initiating and carrying it out. Memory sanctions could be enacted by either the senate or emperors or by local initiative, as in the case of Julian, who occasionally suffered erasure despite never officially undergoing memory sanctions; he was even apotheosized after his death.[67] Whether one can even speak of "official" memory sanctions in late antiquity has now been called into question; the carrying out of such epigraphic or visual erasures was quite often probably a local interpretation of imperial propaganda, rather than the result of an explicit directive.[68] Moreover, damnation need not be eternal: individuals could be posthumously rehabilitated, as was the pagan senator Virius Nichomachus Flavianus (334–394), condemned in 394 and restored to good standing in an inscription of 431.[69] Even when there was no rehabilitation, punitive memory sanctions were rarely fully successful in their aim of perpetually dishonoring the individual, as Flower argues in the case of the late Republican reformer Gaius Gracchus, honored by the Roman populus even after his violent death.[70] Adrastos Omissi has recently argued that damnatio also includes the large number of generative practices it entailed—his so-called *creatio memoriae*—including panegyrical invective against the disgraced individual and monuments built to celebrate the victory of the "rightful" ruler.[71]

To sum up: damnatio memoriae was not about forgetting, but rather about controlling a political narrative (or political-personal narratives). Damnatio was carried out by a variety of actors (emperors, senators, local leaders) in response to immediate political situations. The particular physical spaces in which it was carried out (the fora of Rome) and the physical characteristics

---

[66] Usherwood 2015: 183.
[67] For example: *I.Magnesia* 201; *I.Pergamon* 633; *I.Aphrodisias* 2007 12.1001; *I.Aphrodisias* 2007 8.405; see also Delmaire 2003: 305.
[68] Usherwood 2015.
[69] Hedrick 2000.
[70] Flower 2006: 67–81.
[71] Omissi 2016.

of the material objects on which it was enacted (inscriptions with gaping lacunae, images missing central figures) were all essential to its aims.

Beyond Damnatio Memoriae

It is not surprising that the vicissitudes of Roman politics produced a large number of erasures in the ancient and late antique periods—and a concomitantly large number of scholarly studies of damnatio memoriae. Unofficial or (seemingly) nonpolitical rasurae are both rarer and rarely discussed, whatever the period of Greek or Roman history. As is the case with spolia, the scholarly invention of an appellation (damnatio memoriae) produced a large body of evidence available for study; other evidence that does not fit under this umbrella term has been left out in the rain. But violence against inscriptions afflicted both official and unofficial texts; it responded to immediate circumstances and to the distant past; it could be motivated by a deep-seated animus, by dispassionate orders, or by an anodyne desire for a text-free surface (and everything in between). Writing in public, in religious spaces, in domestic contexts, and on private memorials could be subject to such modifications: even a "good luck" text for a circus faction (the Greens) from Kyzikos underwent erasure, presumably by fans of a rival faction.[72] Epigraphic violence ranged from lightly chiseling a text to completely breaking apart an entire stone. This rich tapestry of the afterlives of inscriptions is just beginning to be woven.

Occasionally a non-damnatio erasure is so extraordinary that it has demanded study. The name of a mother of a deceased child was completely obliterated from a first-century CE funerary altar on the Via Flaminia in Rome; the father, M. Iunius Euphrosynus, added a second inscription on the back of the altar, essentially offering a postmortem (of the relationship).[73] Here we learn the mother's name: Acte. She had been Euphrosynus' slave before he freed and married her; in his telling, she attempted to poison him, was unfaithful, and ran off with the slaves. Euphrosynus curses her with a gruesome death: torture, hanging, and burning pitch to consume her heart. As in the case of official damnatio, the removal of Acte's name in the original inscription was clearly *not* about the annihilation of her memory,

---

[72] Liddel and Low 2019.
[73] *CIL* VI 20905; Carroll 2011: 75–76.

which Euphrosynus is only too eager to preserve and condemn. Few other modifications to grave epitaphs match the tone of almost palpable venom that Euphrosynus spits at Acte (they more commonly have to do with updating, as Ulrike Ehmig has demonstrated for Latin inscriptions: a widow becomes a wife again, a divorcee is removed from a family tomb, an official holds his office for an additional term, etc.), but the late antique erasures at various sanctuary sites in this chapter may initially appear as similar Christian spiteful epigraphic violence against the pagan past.[74] Alternatively, they may be taken as a clear metric of "Christianization," an almost inevitable response to the inscribed presence of a competing or vanquished religion.

But the actual process of erasure is not so straightforward: the devil is in the details. Elsewhere, I have presented a baptistery originally found at a small Turkish village called Uylupınar, which corresponds to an ancient site called by archaeologists "Alt Kibyra" in inland Anatolia, south of the region of Phrygia which we discussed in relation to hagiographies in Chapter 2.[75] The baptistery, now in the Burdur Museum, was built from Roman spolia in probably the fifth or sixth century CE. It made use of two older inscriptions, both dedications to pagan gods from a man named Eprios Agatheinos. But on one of those dedications (to the "great temple-sharing gods"), the name of Eprios Agatheinos is hardly legible: only the letters *v.* ΓΑ *v.* ΕΙ *v.* ΟΣ can be read with ease (Figure 5.3).[76] Prior publications understood this as accidental damage, but I argue it was an intentional, probably unprofessional erasure, perhaps carried out by rubbing the marble with another stone or tool: [[["Επ]ρ̣ι̣ος]] [[Ἀ]]γα[[θ]]εῖ[[γ]]ος.[77] The letters left behind on the stone in fact form a new name, Γάειος (Gaeios), a common Greek form of the Latin name Gaius—so common, in fact, that we have twelve preserved Roman attestations of the name on stones from within thirty kilometers of Uylupınar.[78] Why should someone have erased Agatheinos on this stone, replacing him with the made-up Gaeios? The key lies on the other, unerased stone. That one, pristinely preserved, is a dedication from Agatheinos to the "lord god above" (Κυρίῳ ἄνω θεῷ).[79] Although this was an epithet for a local

---

[74] Ehmig 2019.
[75] Sitz 2019a: 648–652.
[76] I.Mus. Burdur 184; I.Kibyra 94: Θεοῖς μεγάλοις συννάοις | [[["Επ]ρ̣ι̣ος]] [[Ἀ]]γα[[θ]]εῖ[[γ]]ος (updated reading from ed. Sitz 2019a: 650, fn. 49). Burdur Museum Inv. 236.93.94. Research permit: 51544244-155.02-E.158017; 64298988-155.02-E.156523.
[77] Stones were also frequently used to carve graffiti: Moretti et al. 2016: 309, Fig. 19.
[78] See Sitz 2019a: 650, fn. 50 for inscription numbers.
[79] I.Mus. Burdur 103; I.Kibyra 93: Κυρίῳ ἄνω θεῷ Ἔπριος | Ἀγαθεῖνος. Burdur Museum Inv. 237.93.94.

Figure 5.3 Burdur Museum. Inscribed spolia (*I.Mus. Burdur* 184) in a baptistery from Uylupınar (permit no. 51544244-155.02-E.158017; 64298988-155.02-E.156523). Author, courtesy of the Turkish Ministry of Culture and Tourism.

Roman deity, in late antiquity the text could be read as an early Christian dedication to *the* Lord God above. This Christian misreading of Κυρίῳ ἄνω θεῷ is paralleled at Ankara by the case of two saints, Basil and Basilissa: Busine has argued that the cult of these fictive holy figures was probably prompted by a number of pagan inscriptions around the city dedicated to two gods referred to as "king and queen" (Βασιλεῖ καὶ Βασιλίσσῃ).[80] A slight misreading instead produced two early Christian saints for Ankara. At Uylupınar, a clever erasure disguised Agatheinos' actual pagan identity by replacing him on the obviously polytheistic dedication (to the "great temple-sharing gods") with the made-up Gaeios.[81] The Agatheinos on the other marble could therefore be read as an early Christian convert. As we saw with the inscriptions incorporated into the *Life of Abercius* at Hier(o)polis in Phrygia, ancient inscribed stones could serve to create or enhance a proto-Christian past for a late antique community that found itself lacking in biblical attestations or famous martyrdoms. But at Uylupınar, the manipulation was physical, on the stone itself, rather than literary.

The following case studies of the erasure or destruction of epigraphic remains at sanctuaries drive home the point that there is profit in paying attention to the physical process of erasure and the precise letters removed versus

---

[80] Busine 2019b: 273; 284. See also below, page p. 239.
[81] Gaeios was still used as a name in late antiquity, but we need not assume an actual man named Gaeios was behind this creative erasure: Gaeios was simply a familiar name that could be made from the letters on the stone.

those left still legible or even untouched. The erasure of the names of pagan gods need not be read as an act of spite, nor are these rasurae a straightforward marker of "Christianization." Patterns emerge in these case studies, but they eschew easy labeling such as "official" erasures, "religious" violence, or "Christian damnatio memoriae." We begin at Aphrodisias, metropolis of Karia.

Selective Erasures

Identity Crisis at Aphrodisias

Late antique individuals were clearly aware of the power of names—and the possibility of un- or renaming orally, textually, and epigraphically. It is therefore remarkable that Aphrodisias, capital of the late antique province of Karia, managed to keep its explicitly pagan name derived from the goddess Aphrodite into the seventh century (and ἀφροδισιάζειν also had sexual connotations). It is only in 680 that we have definite evidence for the change of the city's name to Stauroupolis (Cross City), although the shift may have occurred in common parlance earlier.[82] This new identity was epigraphically instantiated in the partial erasure and replacement of an inscription on the city's Northeast Gate, on the side facing into the city (Figure 5.4). The first text carved on the gate's lintel commemorated the wall's construction circa 365 CE; a second on the lower fascia recorded a restoration project in the mid-/late fifth century. This latter text began, "+For the good fortune of the splendid metropolis of the Aphrodisians (Ἀφροδισιαίων)."[83] Select letters of the word "Aphrodisians" were erased and replaced with new ones, forming the name "Stauroupolitans" (<Σ>ταυρουπολίτων). Several old letters were left in place in the new name: [[Ἀφ]]ρο[[δισια]]ίων, saving the eraser and carver (probably the same person) a bit of effort.[84] Although the replacement letters are more irregular, they visually blend in well on the stone. Such manipulations of older inscriptions are rare: I know only of a Roman statue base at Ephesos where the last two letters of the name Antoneinos

---

[82] Roueché 2007: 186–187; Roueché 2004, vi. 48–52.
[83] *I.Aphrodisias* 2007 12.101.ii, *l*. 1: +ἐπὶ εὐτυχίᾳ τῆς λαμπρᾶς <Σ>ταυρουπολίτων μητροπ(όλεως) (trans. Roueché). Wilson 2018: 483; Sitz 2019b: 142, Fig. 2.
[84] Erasure brackets added. The unerased iota was altered to form a tau. The newly carved text in fact only reads ΤΑΥΡΟΥΠΟΛΙΤΩΝ, but the terminal sigma of the preceding word (λαμπρᾶς) was made to do double-duty, both ending that word and beginning Σταυρουπολίτων.

Figure 5.4 Aphrodisias. Northeast gate with erased and replaced inscription (*I. Aphrodisias* 2007 12.101ii). Courtesy NYU Excavations at Aphrodisias.

(Ἀντωνεῖνον) were modified from ΟΝ to ΘΧ, that is, Θ(εὸς) Χ(ριστός) (God Christ), perhaps at the time the base was rebuilt into a wall along the Stadium Street.[85] At Aphrodisias, a neat cross was inserted into the upper, earlier inscription on the Northeast Gate, accompanied by an alpha and omega. These new elements were carefully positioned to avoid damaging the text too much, and even reused the bars of the fourth-century letters when possible. The Christianizing alterations on this gate were cautious, even preservationist, in their approach to the preexisting inscriptions.

These modified texts marked the exit from the city; within the walls, residents encountered more censored inscriptions. On the exterior north wall of the theater's *skene* (stage building), a retrospective dossier of Roman documents carved in the third century CE, known as the Archive Wall, underwent a similar process of unnaming. "Aphrodisians" was carefully chiseled away at several places, especially in the lower registers; no replacement text was carved.[86] The documents of the Archive Wall, including friendly letters from Augustus himself, were intended as testimonies of the city's wide-ranging political-social connections; the date of the erasures is unclear, but it need not be at the same time as the Stauroupolis edit on the city gate. The

---

[85] *SEG* 34.1091; Roueché 2014: 139.
[86] Reynolds 1982; Hebert 2000: 136; Roueché 2007: 187–189. Roueché 2014: 138–139; Kousser 2017: 130.

theater continued to be used throughout late antiquity for spectacles, so the Archive Wall probably had higher viewership than the gate itself; an image of the Archangel Michael was painted in the fifth or sixth century in the northern room of the stage building—just behind the Archive Wall.[87] This painting indicates a shift away from Aphrodite as the preferred protector of the city. The location of the dossier across from the main entrance to the theater from the north and from the Tetrastoon to the east meant that these documents were easily viewed, though whether the dense, lengthy texts were ever read is another matter. The poor individual charged with removing the numerous instances of "Aphrodisians" obviously made an attempt but was not successful at catching every instance of the name. The impetus to carry out this editing was likely official: both daylight and a ladder were necessary, so it is unlikely these erasures could have been carried out clandestinely, as Roueché has pointed out.[88]

The erasures of the city gate and the Archive Wall were the exceptions rather than the rule, however: there was no citywide program of removing the name of the old goddess. Only a few other inscriptions around the city were erased, sometimes because of their pagan content, at others times because they had become obsolete; some may have been carried out by private initiative.[89] The inconsistent attitude toward the epigraphic remains of the pagan past is especially noticeable at the theater. Not far from the Archive Wall, the architrave of the *skene*'s portico continued to broadcast its first-century dedication from Zoilos (a freedman of Augustus) to Aphrodite, inscribed in far larger letters than the Archive Wall.[90] But a similar dedication to the goddess on the cornice blocks of the *frons pulpiti* (the edge of the stage, standing above the orchestra) was partially edited (Figure 5.5). This second-century text opened with "for the goddess Aphrodite and for the emperor Caesar Titus Ailius Hadrian Antoninus Augustus Pius" ([[Θεᾶι Ἀφροδείτηι]] καὶ Αὐτοκράτορι Καίσαρι Τ[[ίτῳ Αἰλίῳ Ἁδριανῷ]] Ἀ|ντωνείνῳ Σεβαστῷ Εὐσεβεῖ).[91] Both the dedication to Aphrodite and, unusually, parts of the name of Antoninus Pius were erased, perhaps in the fourth century,

---

[87] For the late antique use of the theater: Cormack 1991: 119–121; Roueché 1991; Bowes 2014: 107–108; de Chaisemartin and Theodorescu 2017: 46–47.
[88] Roueché 2014: 138–139.
[89] Jones 1981: 126; Roueché 1993: 206; Roueché 2004, vi.48–54; Roueché 2014: 138–139.
[90] *I.Aphrodisias* 2007 8.1.i.
[91] *I.Aphrodisias* 2007 8.85.i. The bar here indicates a block break. Aphrodite's name is erased a second time later in the inscription.

Figure 5.5 Aphrodisias. Theater with *skene* architrave and *frons pulpiti* marked. Author, courtesy of NYU Excavations at Aphrodisias.

when a secondary dedicatory text was added to this cornice, or later.[92] In comparison with the higher architrave of the *skene*'s portico, this text was easier to access while standing in the orchestra, if an upside-down erasure by leaning over the edge of the stage was not performed. The name of the goddess was also removed from a block commemorating donations to the theater by Aristokles Molossos: [[τῇ Ἀφροδείτῃ]] καὶ τοῖς Σεβασ|τοῖς.[93] Meanwhile the name of the goddess was removed from some (but not all) of inscriptions at the Hadrianic Baths, which continued to be used and renovated in late antiquity.[94]

This lackadaisical attitude toward the inscribed name of Aphrodite contrasts with the more strongly iconoclastic reaction toward her figural images, which stood a much higher chance of being removed.[95] A votive

---

[92] Jones 1981: 126, n. 68: "I cannot understand, however, the motive for erasing part of Pius' name"; nor can I.

[93] *I.Aphrodisias* 2007 8.108, *ll.* 1–2, erasure brackets added. See Reynolds 1991: 23 for a photo. Aphrodite is also erased on *I.Aphrodisias* 2007 8.115 (a dedication on orthostats of the theater's orchestra).

[94] E.g., *I.Aphrodisias* 2007 5.109 has the name of the goddess and her epithet erased; 5.108 (the twin of this text) is unerased. For the baths: McDavid 2016; Wilson 2018: 481–483.

[95] Kousser 2017.

relief plaque from the theater depicting the goddess was chiseled away, leaving only her outline.[96] Two over-life-size marble figures of Aphrodite in her cultic persona (wearing a long, stiff, decorated robe and a headdress) were found in a sorry state near the Bouleuterion. One had a damaged face and was reused in the foundations of a Middle Byzantine wall; the other was broken into small fragments, probably intentionally, and found in the Bouleuterion and in the nearby Triconch House.[97] Neither of these statues is likely to be the actual cult statue from the sanctuary (which has never been found), but the presence of fragments in the Triconch House *may* suggest that the statue was moved into a private residence during the period of rising Christian dominance.[98] At the Sebasteion, which became a marketplace from the mid-fourth century onward, pagan gods were intensively chiseled away in the extensive relief panels decorating the space; in one instance, a cross was added (Figure 5.6).[99] But scenes that were largely mythological in nature (as opposed to cultic) kept their protagonists: Aphrodite was permitted to remain with her mythological lover, Anchises, and their lovechild, Aeneas, in two relief panels. The same distinction held at "Gaudin's Fountain," a late antique structure reusing a Roman façade, perhaps originally the propylon of a pagan sanctuary.[100] Here a bust of Aphrodite was totally removed, but the relief depicting a gigantomachy remained. There was no concerted effort to expunge the pagan past at Aphrodisias, but it was edited when needed. This need was felt to be the greatest when Aphrodite herself in cultic guise was involved.

The tension between preservation and destruction at Aphrodisias is also apparent in the temple-church. As we saw in the previous chapter, the church was constructed of spoliated blocks, including inscribed ones from the Temple of Aphrodite and elsewhere, around 500 CE or a little earlier. The reused architrave in the atrium kept most of the name of Hadrian in clear, sharp letters below a luxurious (and eye-catching) vine frieze. The dedications on columns in the side aisles referred to local euergetes, while the north entrance into the nave was dedicated to the god Augustus. These texts are an indication of the tolerance expressed by church builders and

---

[96] Brody 2007: 24; Kousser 2017: 128–129.
[97] Brody 2007: 8–15, Figs. 3 and 4.
[98] Berenfeld 2009: 221–222.
[99] Smith 2012; Smith 2013: 44–49; Ogus 2018: 174–177.
[100] Öğüş 2015: 318–319.

228　PAGAN INSCRIPTIONS, CHRISTIAN VIEWERS

Figure 5.6 Aphrodisias. Chiseled relief of Aphrodite from the Sebasteion, with cross added at lower left. Author, courtesy of NYU Excavations at Aphrodisias.

congregants at Aphrodisias toward inscribed reminders of the pagan past and may have played a role in the church's appropriation of an angel cult perhaps centered on the old well of Aphrodite: the inscriptions built into the temple-church insisted that this had been a quite normal, civic temple, with all its attendant political associations. The texts were not so much about what the temple was, as much about what it was *not*: it was not devoted to angels, to healings, to fertility rites, or to any other suspect activities.

But there were limits to what was appropriate for display within the church. The same Hadrian architrave reused in the atrium was also chiseled to remove the name of a god. Likewise, the central entrance from the narthex into the nave required a significant intervention. This monumental doorframe had originally graced the Temple of Aphrodite with a dedication: "Gaios Julios Zoilos, priest of the god Aphrodite, savior and benefactor

Figure 5.7 Aphrodisias. Door lintel from the Temple of Aphrodite (*I. Aphrodisias* 2007 1.2), reused at the main entrance into the nave of the temple-church. Author, courtesy of NYU Excavations at Aphrodisias.

of the fatherland, (built) the sanctuary for Aphrodite" (Figure 5.7).[101] At the entrance to the church nave and in large, clear lettering, this text had a far greater "impact factor" than the dedications on the columns of the side aisles. It was, to co-opt Rudolf Haensch's terminology, a *Hauptbauinschrift*: a text

---

[101] *I.Aphrodisias* 2007 1.2, as published there: Γάϊος Ἰούλιος Ζώ[ι]λος ὁ ἱερεὺς θεοῦ Ἀφροδείτη[ς] | ν. σωτὴρ καὶ εὐεργέτης τῆς πατρίδος τὸ ἱερὸν Ἀφροδείτῃ.

recording the construction of an entire building, placed either at its entrance or in a prominent location.[102] Although Haensch uses the term specifically to refer to late antique church donor inscriptions, typically on floor mosaics, it works well in this context because the Zoilos inscription *appeared* to be the *Hauptbauinschrift* of the temple-church due to its placement above the main entrance and its dedicatory nature. This text was uniquely in need of careful censoring because of the combined factors of its pagan content, its prominent large letters, and its location. And edited it was: "deliberately but not quite efficiently erased," in the words of Joyce Reynolds.[103]

An examination of the stone (now broken into three pieces) allows for more precision: some letters are untouched by the chiseling, some received only light blows following the outline of the letters, and others are completely removed through a "block erasure" (a long rectangular band of chisel marks). The word *hieron* (sanctuary) was so thoroughly annihilated that the original published edition read *naon* (temple) there instead, while the name Gaios is still fairly legible, even if some of its letters have been lightly defaced.[104] I have here added double brackets to indicate that a letter has been touched by a chisel and used bolding to indicate which letters remained fairly legible on the stone (to an average viewer standing on the ground, not to a trained epigrapher at close range), whether lightly chiseled or entirely untouched:

Γ[[άϊος Ἰούλιος Ζώ[ι]λ]]ος ὁ ἱερ[[εὺς θεοῦ Ἀφροδείτη[ς]]]
σ[[ωτὴρ καὶ εὐεργέτη]]ς τῆς πατ[[ρίδος τὸ ἱερὸν Ἀφροδείτη]].

The bolding offers a closer approximation of what the viewer of the edited stone actually saw, and could potentially read, as they entered the church.

The degrees of deletion are content-based: the portion declaring Zoilos a priest "of the god Aphrodite," as well as the object of the dedication, "the sanctuary for Aphrodite," disappeared almost completely through the block erasure; the name of Zoilos and his honorific titles (savior and benefactor) received chisel marks following the strokes of the letters, which in fact ensured that they remained visible, if distorted. A few discrete letters received no visible chisel marks at all. The correlation of erasure thoroughness and content is not exact: the ends of ὁ ἱερ[[εὺς]] (the priest) and τῆς πατ[[ρίδος]] (of the fatherland) were subject to the block erasure, perhaps indicating that

---

[102] Haensch 2017: 539–540.
[103] Reynolds 1990: 37.
[104] Reynolds 1982, no. 37.

the editing was directed by a literate person but carried out by an illiterate one, who removed more letters than were strictly necessary. But the text that remained legible on the stone (even if some letters were lightly chiseled) was, at the least, inoffensive to Christian readers, and parts (*soter*, savior) would have even had Christian connotations.

The visible erasure marks and fragmentary letters left on the stone transformed this inscription into a metatextual commentary *on itself*: the value of the older text was acknowledged and at the same time subverted by damaging the names of goddess and euergete. Particularly at Aphrodisias, a thriving city with a local marble workshop and the resources to undertake a major urban renewal program after an earthquake of the late fifth century, leaving traces of these letters on the stone was surely intentional, rather than a product of privation or an inattention to the details of the marble. By following a program of epigraphic tolerance combined with selective edits, the ecclesiastical authorities got to have their cake and eat it too: a visible reminder that the stones of the church had come from a pagan building, over which they now exerted control, but also an advertisement that the building had a significant civic history and a repertoire of dedications from past euergetes. Aphrodisians of late antiquity likely saw themselves as the stewards of this classical patrimony embarking on yet another major construction program, rather than fanatics forging an entirely new identity on the ruins of a disgraced past.

The inscriptions of the temple-church at Aphrodisias therefore serve as an index of tolerance at the provincial capital of Karia, and its limits. Rather than straightforward markers of a generic "Christianization," the erased texts from Aphrodisias shed light on the late antique population's epigraphic comprehension, intentional manipulation, and largely tolerant attitude. Three general observations can be made. First, liminal spaces (entrances/exits) were particularly important for (re)defining a city or building. The city's Northeast gate, the Archive Wall at an entrance to the theater, and the main door into the temple-church all required the editing or removal of Aphrodite/Aphrodisians. The entrance into the temple-church atrium (which preserves no ancient text) was also heavily graffitied with Christian prayers and crosses, so both visible Christian symbols and partially erased ancient texts were active agents in characterizing space and limiting its present religious affiliation. Second, texts that were easier to access were more likely to undergo erasure. The theater's *frons pulpiti* text was partially erased, while the harder-to-access architrave of the *skene* was not; instances of "Aphrodisians" lower on the Archive Wall were more likely to be erased than those higher up. Ease of access was also facilitated through construction. The door lintel of the temple, repurposed for the church, was chiseled, probably during the construction process, as was the architrave from a gymnasium built into the atrium; at the same time, the texts on the temple peristasis columns/church colonnade (which were not moved during the conversion) were left in place. This leads to the third observation: prominence played a role in the decision to erase or not erase. The name of Aphrodite in small letters set within a longer dedication on the columns of the temple-church was left alone; that on the entry door lintel was not only erased, it warranted a more thorough expunging than other parts of Zoilos' building dedication. Not all erasures at Aphrodisias or elsewhere follow this playbook, but these three variables—placement at an entrance, ease of access, and prominence—correlate with several erasures in our subsequent case studies.

Labraunda: A Rasura Out of Place

A similar concern for defining entrances can be seen at Labraunda. Like Aphrodisias, Labraunda lay within the province of Karia, but the two settlements could hardly be more different. Whereas Aphrodisias was an urbanized provincial capital, Labraunda was a small mountainous settlement centered on the former sanctuary of Zeus Labraundos. As was the case at Lagina, the rural population living around Labraunda in the Roman period and some temple personnel probably remained at the site after pagan worship ceased; they benefited from rich agricultural land, natural springs, and a favorable location on a road between two sizable poleis, Mylasa and Alinda.[105] Agricultural activity slowly encroached into the formerly monumental spaces of the site, including the olive press installed in Andron A and another in front of the Built Tomb.[106] Whereas Aphrodisias' educated citizens produced inscriptions through the course of late antiquity, Labraunda offers curiously little epigraphic evidence from the new era: a handful of Christian graffiti but not a single inscription, a stark departure from the robust Hellenistic and Roman epigraphic habit at the site. But the late antique population left its mark in other ways. Epigraphic spolia was occasionally

---

[105] Blid 2016: 203–205; Frejman 2020.
[106] Andron A: Henry et al. 2015: 334–355; Henry et al. 2016: 416–424; Built Tomb: Henry et al. 2018: 297–301.

used in the two fifth-century churches built near the road. A Hadrianic octagonal base found in a late wall near the fifth-century East Church had its first three lines erased: [[. . . Εὐ]]|τύχου ἀνέθη|κεν, "[[to (a god) so-and-so son of Eu]]tychos dedicated it."[107] Although difficult to see in photographs, the damage on the surface of the first three lines is distinct from accidental damage elsewhere on the stone; they have been abraded, perhaps with a blunt object. Yet again, the selective nature of the erasure, with the final, innocuous word (ἀνέθηκεν, "he dedicated it") untouched, indicates that a literate person was present to direct the editing. What was left clearly signaled the original nature of the object (a pagan dedication) while making it anonymous: not only the god, but also the donor, were unnamed. This erasure most likely took place in late antiquity, when the base may have been used in the fifth-century church.

In contrast, most inscriptions at Labraunda were not erased. As discussed in Chapter 4, marble antae blocks from the Temple of Zeus Labraundos, including two inscribed ones, were moved into Andron A; one of these (bearing a Hellenistic letter) shows marks of an attempt to cut the inscription face off, but the text itself was not damaged. The Temple of Zeus probably closed in the fourth century CE; the latest datable pagan dedication was in the third.[108] Many marble elements of the temple ended up in lime kilns. Only portions of the temple architrave dedication from the Hekatomnid ruler Idrieus (r. 351–344 BCE) to Zeus Labraundos ("Idrieus son of Hekatomnos, a Mylasan, dedicated the temple to Zeus Labraundos"), inscribed in bold and legible letters, were uncovered where they fell, but these stones show no indication of erasure.[109] Several other dedications to Zeus at the site, including prominent architraves from both Idrieus and his more famous brother, Maussollos, remained on display even at buildings with clear late antique use phases, such as the Andron of Maussollos (a domestic complex by the fifth/sixth century) and the Oikoi (renovated with a fine dome into a building of uncertain function in probably the sixth century).[110]

The preservation of monumental dedications was the norm at Labraunda—except for a single architrave at the South Propylaea, the entrance to the site (Figure 5.8). This text, inscribed on three blocks, reads: Ἰδριεὺς Ἑκατό|[[μνω Μυλασεὺς ἀνέθ|[ηκε τὸν πυλῶνα Διὶ Λαμβραύ]γδωι]] (Idrieus son of

---

[107] I.Labraunda 35, ll. 3–6; Blid 2016: 163.
[108] I.Labraunda 39.
[109] I.Labraunda 16: Ἰδριεὺς Ἑκα[τόμνω Μυλασεὺς ἀνέθηκε τὸν ναὸν Διὶ λαμβραύ]νδωι.
[110] Hellström and Blid 2019: 223–227; Blid 2016: 197–202.

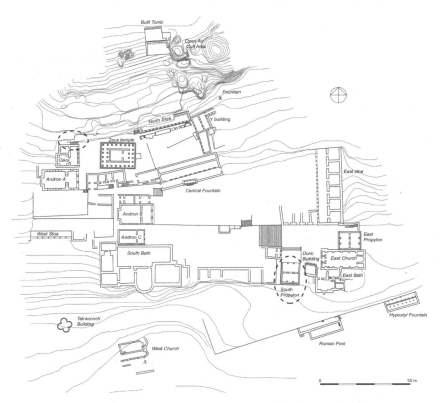

Figure 5.8 Labraunda. Site plan with the South Propylaea and find area of the architrave blocks marked in dashed lines. Courtesy of the Labraunda Excavations.

Hekato[[mnos, a Mylasan, dedic[ated the gate to Zeus Labrau]ndos]]).[111] But only the first block (part of the name of the Hekatomnid dynast, Ἰδριεὺς Ἑκατό) was found unerased and next to the Propylaea. The other two blocks came to light approximately a hundred meters up the slope, behind the Temple of Zeus and near the Oikoi. The text-bearing upper fascia of one stone and both fasciae of the other have been "re-worked with a cruder chisel," amounting to an effective rasura that nearly completely obscured the text (Figure 5.9).[112] It is unclear what brought down the South Propylaea: an

[111] *I.Labraunda* 18, block breaks indicated by a single vertical line; erasure brackets added.
[112] Crampa 1972: 15–16.

ERASURE 235

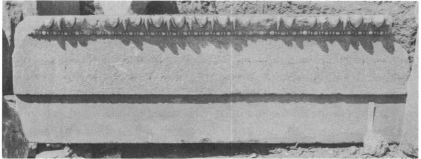

Figure 5.9 Labraunda. Architrave of the South Propylaea (*I.Labraunda* 18), unerased and erased blocks. Photos: Arthur Nilsson, Labraunda Excavation 1949, courtesy of the Labraunda Archives, Uppsala University Library (LabArP:1949:399 and LabArP:1949:328).

earthquake, gradual collapse, or planned disassembly? Presumably the erasure took place after the blocks were on the ground and at hand. The date of their transport up the slope was most likely late antiquity, when coordinated construction and disassembly activity took place in the area of the Temple of Zeus and the Oikoi. The Middle Byzantine occupation at the site was at a more modest scale, indicated by the size of chapels built into the late antique church ruins and the relative austerity of the graves recently excavated in a necropolis dated to circa 1000 CE.[113] A Middle Byzantine military establishment installed within the old acropolis fortification at the peak of the mountain did not make use of marble.[114] In any case, the collapse of the South Propylaea presumably took place after the construction of the East Church

[113] Blid 2016: 96–99; Sitz and Delibaş 2022.
[114] Karlsson 2010: 67–74; Karlsson 2011: 233–247.

236 PAGAN INSCRIPTIONS, CHRISTIAN VIEWERS

in the fifth century, since no spolia from the gateway was reused in that structure.

The key to understanding the obliteration of text on the South Propylaea architrave lies in its original display location: the entrance to the site. While the late antique Labraundians tolerated sundry pagan dedications around their settlement, they wished to project a more up-to-date identity at its gateway, as Aphrodisias had also done. The architrave at Labraunda functioned as a *Hauptbauinschrift* defining not just a building. With the South Propylaea demonumentalized through collapse or disassembly, the East Church located immediately behind it became the most monumental structure greeting visitors to the site. The gateway was further "updated" through the addition of (undatable) cross graffiti to its blocks, including on an overturned column drum.[115] The effect of the erasure, removal of the blocks, and this graffiti was to de-paganize the entrance of the site. Although the circumstances behind the limited epigraphic violence at Labraunda are unclear, the erasure on the South Propylaea can be understood only in relation to the many texts that were *not* erased. Even if the entrance to Labraunda appeared to visitors as a Christianized ruin, once within the site, epigraphic reminders of the pre-Christian past were everywhere.

A Tale of Two Temples at Aizanoi: Artemis in Absentia

The city of Aizanoi in Phrygia shows a similar wish to remove the prominent name and cultic associations of a goddess through a targeted erasure. The site had two temples available for reuse in late antiquity. As discussed in Chapter 3, the Temple of Zeus was preserved largely intact and was transformed into a church, quite plausibly in late antiquity. The imperial texts on its walls from officials and from Hadrian (recording a dispute over sacred lands), Antoninus Pius (praising a leading citizen), and Septimius Severus (praising the city as a whole) remained in place, now located within the extended bema of the church and on its outer wall. No part of these texts were erased, despite occasional mentions of Zeus; crosses and Middle Byzantine inscriptions were added to the walls.

The Temple of Artemis' fate was rather different. The façade was taken apart and the pieces used around 400 CE to build a new porticoed street, the

---
[115] Blid 2016: 179.

Säulenstraße. A section of this street near the round macellum was excavated and re-erected from 1991 to 1995.[116] Parts of the temple tympanum, including a carved relief of a deer (sacred to Artemis), were built into the paving of this street, while the inscribed temple architrave dating from the period of Claudius was built into the northeast colonnade. Its uppermost fascia bore an inscription:

[[For Artemis the most sacred and for the emperors and for the demos, Asklipiades Charax, son of Asklipiades, son of Artemon, priest for life,]] had the temple built from his own funds.

[[[Ἀρ]|τέμιδι ἁγιωτάτηι καὶ τοῖς Σεβαστοῖς καὶ τῶι δήμ|ι Ἀσκληπιάδης Ἀσκληπιάδου τοῦ | [Ἀρτέμωνος Χάραξ ἱερεὺς διὰ βίο]|υ]] τὸν ναὸν ἐκ τῶν ἰδίων ὑπαρχόν|των κατεσκεύα[σεν.][117]

The entire first part of the inscription—the name of the goddess, her epithet, and references to the emperors, the city, and the euergete who funded the project—was carefully chiseled away, up to the mention of τὸν ναὸν (the temple) (Figure 5.10). The street's porticoes collapsed in the sixth century and were never cleared; there can be no doubt that the erasure took place in late antiquity. The eraser's modus operandi was to roughen the entire fascia where the inscription was located (as at Labraunda), leaving behind traces of letters but obscuring them to the point of functional illegibility. The name of the goddess and her epithet "most sacred" are thoroughly expunged, while letters forming the name of her priest, Asklipiades, along with his patronymics and designation as "priest for life," are just barely visible.

The later portion of the inscription in contrast is untouched: perfectly preserved and legible. We might think that the eraser simply ran out of steam and ended his work at a block break, except for a single letter: the terminal upsilon of βίου, which is located on the block with the phrase τὸν ναὸν (the temple). The decision was made to remove the name and descriptors of goddess and priest, but nothing more. As at Aphrodisias, a literate individual evaluated the text and determined which parts, exactly, required editing.

---

[116] Rheidt 1995; Rheidt 2003.

[117] *SEG* 45.1708 = Wörrle 1995a, no. 2, block breaks indicated by a single vertical line. The block bearing the "priest for life" phrase was not recovered (it was probably scavenged post antiquity), but the chiseling of the terminal upsilon of [[[βίο]|υ]] on the preserved block confirms the erasure. For the restoration of the missing text, see Wörrle 1995b: 63–68.

Figure 5.10 Aizanoi. *Säulenstraße*, erased and unerased sections of the Artemis architrave (*SEG* 45.1708). Photos: D. Johannes, courtesy of the Deutsches Archäologisches Institut Istanbul (D-DAI-IST-Ai-93-454 and D-DAI-IST-Ai-93-342).

And why was the final part of the text, mentioning "the temple" (as well as a standard donation formula), left in place? The structure to which the architrave now belonged was clearly *not* a temple, but a street colonnade. It was quite all right to acknowledge the blocks' origin in a pagan sanctuary—so long as the sanctuary was made anonymous by removing Artemis' name.

This "unnaming" is all the more striking in light of the other texts left intact along the same street. The portico opposite also reused an older architrave of uncertain origin, carrying a dedication to Zeus of Aizanoi and to Nero in crisp, large letters (Figure 5.11).[118] The name of Zeus was not erased—but that of Nero was, centuries earlier. This damnatio shows a different erasure technique: only the bars of the letters (rather than the entire fascia) were chiseled. As on the

---

[118] *SEG* 45.1711 = Wörrle 1995a, no. 1: Διὶ Αἰζανῶν καὶ [[Νέρωνι]] Κλαυδίω|[ι...]. Vertical lines indicate the block breaks.

Figure 5.11 Aizanoi. *Säulenstraße*, partially erased dedication to Zeus and Nero (*SEG* 45.1711). Photo: D. Johannes, courtesy of the Deutsches Archäologisches Institut Istanbul (D-DAI-IST-Ai-94-1).

temple door lintel at Aphrodisias, this method left behind letter-shaped scars still legible as the name of the disgraced emperor. In addition, at the moment of collapse in the sixth century, the street also held at least two inscribed statue bases. One (Severan period) honored a citizen named Aurelios Demetrios, designated as the *neokoros* (temple warden) of Zeus: [νεω]κόρον τοῦ Διός.[119] The name of Zeus is unerased and clearly visible on the stone. *Neokoriai* (the official designation of a city as the caretaker of an important sanctuary, bestowed by the emperor and Senate) were usually associated with imperial cult temples; indeed, Aizanoi is the only city known to have received a neocorate for Zeus.[120] It must have been a source of local pride during the Roman period. Why this base in particular was chosen for display on the *Säulenstraße* in late antiquity, and whether the phrase "neokoros of Zeus" still had any social cachet, is impossible to say, but at the least, the name of the god provoked no erasure.

Why would the name of Zeus be left untouched, while that of Artemis was erased on the colonnaded street of Aizanoi? Perhaps the origin of the spolia determined its disagreeableness: this Artemis dedication had graced a temple, while the Zeus architrave comes from an unknown location, but in any case not the Temple of Zeus (which had a bronze architrave dedication). Or, one could note that the Zeus dedication is preserved only on

---

[119] *SEG* 45.1713 = Wörrle 1995a, no. 4.
[120] Burrell 2004: 116.

one architrave block: the following block was apparently not reused in this section of the *Säulenstraße*. Like at the Sagalassian Basilica E, the scrambling of the Zeus text through splitting up the architrave blocks may have been enough to symbolically de-semanticize or disavow its pagan content. Another possibility is that the name of Zeus could more easily be "misread" as an inoffensive name. Busine has argued that the cult for saints named Dios and Gordios in Caesarea (Kayseri) in Cappadocia was the result of Christian misunderstandings of dedications to Διὶ Γορδίῳ ἐπηκόῳ (Zeus Gordios, swift to listen).[121] Dios/Deios was also the name of a month in the calendar used in parts of the Roman East.[122] The root of the name of Zeus was connected with δῖος, the word for "heavenly," "noble"; Dios could also be a name in the ancient period, as attested twice at Priene.[123] Though none of these options corresponds grammatically to the dedication to Διὶ, perhaps "folk" etymology explained away this prominent references to the pagan god—not to mention the possibility that *Dii* may have been reinterpreted in the Latin sense, as unnamed gods in the plural. Or perhaps Zeus, father of gods and men, was simply reinterpreted as the Christian God, father of all. The theophoric name Diogenes (Zeus-born) continued to be used by Christians, while the city of Dios Hieron in Lydia (also called Diosopolis) kept its pagan name until the seventh century, just as Aphrodisias had done.

Leaving aside the possible "creative" readings of Zeus at the *Säulenstraße* of Aizanoi, the god's name met a different fate on the Temple of Zeus, where it featured far less prominently on the temple walls. There the name is embedded within longer documents; it does not stand out visually, as the name of Artemis did on the reused architrave. It may be this prominence and the direct reference to her temple that necessitated Artemis' unnaming even as *ton naon* remained. Removed of the associations of her name and the specific local festivals and traditions attached to it, the anonymized temple had been neutralized, as in the accounts of Gregory of Nyssa and Theodoret of Cyrrhus. This disassociation of a pagan element from a specific pagan referent may be seen at another spot along the *Säulenstraße*. A base originally dedicated to a local *matron*, Markia Tateis, around 150 CE (and probably originally bearing her statue) was reused to decorate this street, paired with a new statue, a satyr.[124] The satyr crashed to the ground in the earthquake that

---

[121] Busine 2019a: 112–113.
[122] Samuel 1972: 175.
[123] *I.Priene B—M* 330; 354.289.
[124] *SEG* 45.1712 = Wörrle 1995a, no. 3.

brought down the whole street in the sixth century; it was displayed without its head at the time of this natural disaster. But the statue perhaps was incognito in late antiquity: nothing actually identifies it as a satyr, except for its distinguishing attribute of a panther skin. As we saw earlier in this chapter, iconography and attributes could be deconstructed. In its local context, the panther skin may have been a reference to the son of Markia also recorded on her base, named Pardalas (Παρδαλᾶς): the Greek word for panther was πάρδαλις.[125] The display of this statue on this particular base was therefore quite clever, showing an intentional pairing of older monuments and a willingness to play with a technically pagan figure (even if satyrs were not objects of veneration). Nameless and headless, the statue could simply be a youth with a panther skin.[126] The *Säulenstraße* at Aizanoi indicates the high degree of variability in the decision to erase or not to erase.

Roll of the Dice at Antioch ad Cragum

An erasure at Antioch ad Cragum in western Rough Kilikia (Isauria) challenges one of the variables contributing to erasure so far identified: prominence. Here an inscription of an entirely different sort, a lengthy dice oracle, underwent partial erasure. This text was inscribed in more than one hundred ninety lines on the cella wall blocks of the Northeast Temple, constructed in the late second century CE or early third century.[127] Dice or astragal oracles were "played" in antiquity using knuckle bones to obtain a series of numbers one through five. The numbers were then matched with the corresponding entry inscribed on the wall. Each entry was headed by the name of a god or deified personification (Time, Toil, etc.) and accompanied by a short, generic prediction, "fortune cookie" style. For example, if one rolled the numbers 11113, the heading was "Apollo Pythios" and the advice given was: "Phoebos

---

[125] Rheidt 1997: 490, Figs. 24 and 25.
[126] Cf. the satyrs in the nymphaeum of C. Laecanius Bassus at Ephesos, who had both their genitals and telltale tails chiseled away (Jacobs 2010: 280). At Aizanoi the satyr, who lacked a tail from the outset, does not seem to have suffered intentional editing of his genitals (the testicles are intact), reminding us yet again of the highly localized nature of late antique responses to statuary and inscriptions.
[127] *I.Westkilikien Rep.* Antiocheia epi Krago 19. Bean and Mitford 1965: 37–41, no. 43. Nollé 2007: 192–211. For dice (astragal) oracles in general: Nollé 2007: 7–17; Talloen 2018: 122–127.

Figure 5.12 Antioch ad Cragum. Northeast Temple block with dice oracle inscription (*I. Westkilikien Rep.* Antiocheia epi Krago 19). Bean and Mitford 1965, no. 43.

tells you everything clearly in advance: you have Nike as a helper, together with the gods. Hurry up, finish, do not stop!"[128]

There is no evidence for the conversion of the temple into a church, but a wine press was installed abutting it in late antiquity; Christian burials took place in the cella, probably in the Middle Byzantine period.[129] Despite the centering of the late antique settlement on the site's acropolis to the south, the temple was not left untouched: a pedimental bust of Apollo appears to be intentionally damaged.[130] More to our interest, selected names were erased in the oracle text, in the headings of six out of thirty-eight entries. These are Apollo Pythios (the heading for the numbers 11113 above), Hermes, Himeros (Desire), Chara (Joy), Glaukopis (Bright-Eyed, usually an epithet of Athena), and Herakles (Figure 5.12). Other names were left untouched. That several personifications remained in place is not surprising; more unexpected are the intact names of Zeus, Athena, the Dioskouroi, and Isis, all well-known polytheistic deities.

---

[128] *I.Westkilikien Rep.* Antiocheia epi Krago 19, Column 1, Entry 2: Ἅπανθ' ὁ Φοῖβός σοι σαφῆ προμηνύει· | Νείκην ἀρωγὸν σὺν θεοῖς ἕξεις ἅμα· | σπεῦδε, καταπράσσου, μηδὲ ἐπίσχεσιν ποιοῦ (trans. after Nollé 2007: 199). I follow Nollé's edition as well as his column and entry numbers.

[129] For the press: Dodd 2020; burials: Hoff et al. 2015.

[130] Hoff et al. 2015: 209–210.

What can we make of these sporadic erasures? An examination of the stones, which were refound in the excavations conducted since 2009, is helpful.[131] The inscribed text follows the pattern of being "at hand" at the time of erasure: although the blocks were found in the ruins of the temple and cannot be precisely placed on its north wall, the nature of the lengthy text, written in small letters measuring one centimeter or less in height, required it to be near eye-level for a viewer to find her/his fortune. But the erasures do *not* follow the paradigm in which only particularly prominent pagan names are erased. The names were written in the same small letters as the rest of the text, although set apart through a *vacat*. The layout of the erasures is instructive: the name of Zeus Lamotos in the first entry is not erased, but that of Apollo Pythios in the second is. Hermes is snuffed out near the bottom of the first column of text, while the second column shows the greatest concentration of rasurae, with Desire, Joy, Bright-Eyed, and Heracles removed. All the erasures take place on the first block. The second block, where the names of Zeus, Athena, the Dioskouroi, and Isis occur, shows not a single erasure. Was this block somehow inaccessible at the time the modifications were carried out? Perhaps. More likely, whoever decided to do the editing began reading from the beginning of the text, and lost interest halfway through: the script is dense and crowded.

And what about the name of Zeus in first entry? Why was it not erased, when that of Apollo immediately below it was? Was Apollo a greater target because the temple bore his image on its pediment? Another possibility is that Zeus was a victim of mistaken identity: the name may not have been immediately recognizable because it was written without a word break between "Zeus" (in the genitive) and his local epithet, Lamotos: ΔΙΟΣΛΑΜΩΤΟΥ. At a glance it may have been taken as a single name, Dioslamotos (roughly on the pattern of Diodotos, Diogenes, etc.). Alternatively, Zeus may have provoked less violent erasure than his Olympian peers in general, as we have seen at Aizanoi. Zeus disappeared from another inscription at Antioch ad Cragum, a statue base from the demos honoring a man for his service as a priest of the imperial cult and of Zeus (ἱερασάμενον τῶν Σεβαστῶν | καὶ [[τοῦ Δι]]ός).[132] The name of Zeus is marked as partially erased in line 3—so too, however, are completely innocuous words in the middle of the subsequent lines (e.g.,

---

[131] Hoff et al. 2015: 207–210.
[132] Bean and Mitford 1965: 34–35, no. 37, *ll.* 2–3 ("in places capriciously defaced, seemingly in antiquity"); Nollé 2007: 194, n. 1037 ("Auch in dieser Inschrift wurde—anscheinend in christlicher Zeit—der Name des Gottes ausgemeißelt").

line 6, ε[[ὐν[ο]ία]]ς; line 7, [[εἰς αὐ]]τόν). Although this damage has been attributed to Christians, the seemingly random removal of the middle of the text across several lines makes me suspect that the damage was rather indiscriminate vandalism—but *non vidi*, and no photograph has been published. While the misbehaving Olympian Zeus of the poets invoked Christian censure in apologetic or polemical works, on the ground he may have been less problematic than some of his peers.

The selective erasures in the dice oracle on the Northeast Temple at Antioch ad Cragum are difficult to assess. The combination of damage to the temple's pedimental depiction of Apollo and the erasures of names (including Apollo's) in the text could indicate a concerted anti-pagan program. But the modifications of texts and images may have taken place at different times, possibly even later than the seventh century. It is tempting to draw a link between this astragal oracle and the late antique habit of reading prophecy into stones, discussed in Chapter 2. As we saw, the discovery of an ancient text on a wall block could presage a barbarian invasion or offer a justification for converting a temple into a church, or even precipitate conversion and save a multitude (we are told). Was the astragal oracle at Antioch ad Cragum put to God's work in late antiquity in order to save soul and city, never mind the imperial prohibitions on divination? The erasures on the stone offer a tantalizing hint of *some* kind of interaction, but provide no further details. In any case, a few salient points emerge: the emphasis of the erasures in the dice oracle remained on the *names* of divine figures; the erasure was not indiscriminate or violent; it was carried out on a text that was close at hand. Whether this removal was the spontaneous act of an individual, or was a deliberate venture by an authority (the city? the local ecclesiastical leaders?) is impossible to reconstruct.

Indiscriminate Erasure and Destruction

Reverse Graffiti at the Korykian Cave Clifftop Temple

Not every ancient text on formerly pagan temples was so carefully assessed, nor was every erasure carried out with such circumspection as those at Aphrodisias, Labraunda, Aizanoi, and Antioch ad Cragum. More indiscriminate removals happened as well. In the previous chapter, we saw how the presence of inscribed text on the Clifftop Temple at the Korykian Cave in Kilikia guided the construction principles of the fifth-century church builders: the temple's anta with its list of priests' names was fully rebuilt as a wall of the church, with some names hidden behind a transverse wall—even if it made more sense structurally to dejoin the inscribed limestone blocks in order to bond with this wall.[133] Some of the later names added to this list continued onto the anta's flank wall, now the interior wall of the side aisle of the church. And some underwent a haphazard erasure—those on the lowest three blocks, which were easily accessible.[134] Names high up on the anta wall were left in place. As described in the previous chapter, those from the middle blocks (the fourth and fifth from the bottom) are completely missing because these blocks were turned upside down and carefully, thoroughly erased at the time of construction in order to create a pristine outer wall for the church. This reworking of the stones is, to my eyes, indistinguishable from the original surface of the temple blocks; the rough limestone construction material is more forgiving to the mason than marble.

The erasures visible on the interior of the church, however, were clearly carried out with different methods and probably by different actors. Here on the anta wall (the side aisle of the church), the lower names from the list of priests have been visibly damaged but not completely removed (Figure 5.13). Names on the third course from the ground show elongated, horizontal gouge marks stretching nearly across the full line (comprising name and patronymic), for example: Κλ[[— ca. 11 — -]]νου | [[τοῦ καὶ Π[α]πίου]] (Kl. . .[son of] -nos also called Papios).[135] Line 2 is almost completely obliterated, and line 3 shows a gouge mark through the center of the letters. Interestingly, the use of elongated, horizontal gouge marks imitates "official" erasures, such as those on the Archive Wall at Aphrodisias. Other names on the lowest two courses of the anta wall appear to be hacked at (with a tool or sharp object?) in a manner that obscures parts, but not all, of the texts. The final entry on the wall reads: Μ. Αὐρ. [[— ca. 10 — -]]ιος Ἀθηνόδωρος υἱος [[.]]αυ[[..]] γ' τοῦ κὲ Λε[ο]ν[τι]ανοῦ (M. Aurelios..ios Athenodoros son of . . . also called Leontianos, thrice).[136] The central part of the text is lost to deep pockmarks. Snippets of text remain on all three courses, indicating that the erasures were not meant to be a total obfuscation of the building's epigraphic history. As mentioned in the previous chapter, the interior walls

---

[133] Chapter 4, C4S2.
[134] Heberdey and Wilhelm 1896 text sections designated B6, C6, B7, C7, B8, C8.
[135] *I.Westkilikien Rep.* Korykion Antron 1, section B6, *ll.* 2–3, erasure brackets added.
[136] *I.Westkilikien Rep.* Korykion Antron 1, section C8, *ll.* 6–8, erasure brackets added.

Figure 5.13 Korykian Cave (Kilikia). Clifftop temple-church, *I. Westkilikien Rep.* Korykion Antron 1, partially erased. Author, courtesy of Hamdi Şahin.

of this church may have been covered with plaster, but there is no evidence for it on this part of the wall, and the erasures themselves suggest that the walls were, at some point, visible; the imitation of an "official" erasure form (elongated gouge mark) suggests that the act took place in late antiquity. The names were targeted probably not because of their technically pagan content (which would require the "outside" information that they belonged to priests of the sanctuary; few of the names are theophoric), but rather simply because of their presence on the wall, where they were easily accessible. Writing attracts more writing, but it can also attract erasure.

These erasures on the anta flank wall appear to be unplanned and without clear aims, probably carried out by individuals rather than church or civic authorities, at some point after the construction of the church (perhaps much later). The extent of the rasurae suggests a fairly dedicated eraser; someone casually defacing the wall out of boredom likely would have given up his or her game before damaging each name on these lowest three block courses. This individual may have been illiterate—there is no evidence for evaluating the text based on content. The damage at the Korykian Cave Clifftop temple-church can be understood as the flip side of graffiti—spontaneous, haphazard, on easily accessible wall space, and without official sanction.

Breaking the Past at Pisidian Antioch?

At Aphrodisias, Labraunda, Aizanoi, and Antioch ad Cragum, the targeted erasure of inscriptions at former sanctuary sites marked new Christian city- and religioscapes. The erasure at the Korykian Cave temple-church was less targeted but still left behind substantial portions of text and clear evidence that a rasura had taken place. Rarely was a text removed entirely through reworking, although the "erasure habit" varied from site to site. For example, at Leptis Magna (Tripolitana) in North Africa, inscriptions were routinely chiseled away before the blocks were spoliated in late antique construction projects. Creating "phantom" inscriptions was so common there that more texts were erased than produced in the third and fourth century: "il tasso di mortalità era più alto di quello di natalità," in the words of Ignazio Tantillo.[137]

But there is more than one way to crack an egg. Inscriptions could undergo epigraphic violence not just with chisels, but through more destructive means: breaking up a block by hammering; using gravity to shatter it; burning it for lime. These activities could be related, as marble pieces selected for burning in a lime kiln needed to be of a manageable size; large blocks could be intentionally broken up to facilitate transfer to the kiln and burning therein.[138] Obviously, burnt or otherwise obliterated inscriptions leave behind no traces, and we cannot guess the prevalence of this destructive activity. Obtaining lime for mortar had practical motivations (even if the stones chosen for burning were subject to a selection process). It is hard to determine when an inscribed stone has been deliberately shattered versus broken up through an accidental fall or weathering. The methodological difficulty of distinguishing human-made blows from accidental damage is well known to those who study the fate of statuary and has not, in my opinion, been satisfactorily resolved in that sphere, but in any case, a broken-off nose calls for a close look to determine whether the marks of hammer or chisel are apparent. Inscriptions lacked such an obvious, single target for destruction; the

---

[137] Tantillo 2017: 237.
[138] For the breaking up of marbles in preparation for burning: Munro 2016: 59–65.

epigrapher has to consider the stone holistically in her evaluation of whether it has undergone deliberate defacement.

Pisidian Antioch (Yalvaç; not to be confused with Antioch on the Orontes) may offer rare evidence for the intentional destruction of sanctuary inscriptions—though the agents and reasons for these actions are far from certain. Located in central Anatolia at the border of Pisidia and Phrygia, the city was refounded as a Roman colony in the province of Galatia by Augustus. Antioch by Pisidia, as it was called, was the familial home of a proconsul of Cyprus named Sergios Paullos, converted by the fiery Christian proselytizer, St. Paul (formerly known as Saul), during his first missionary journey (*Acts* 13).[139] The apostle then embarked on a visit to Pisidian Antioch, perhaps on the recommendation of his new brother, and taught in a synagogue there. In the early fourth century CE, Pisidian Antioch became the capital of the newly created province of Pisidia; recent investigations have revealed an impressive Tetrarchic *quadriburgia* military fort to the south of the city, probably related to its new administrative role.[140] The Christian population thrived already in the fourth century: a sizable basilica called by archaeologists the "Church of St. Paul" (although this attribution is uncertain) was built within the walls in probably the late fourth century, based on the dating of a mosaic with an inscription mentioning the bishop Optimus, in attendance at the council of Constantinople in 381 (assuming a homonymous bishop was not meant).[141] The basilica was rebuilt in the fifth or sixth century, and at least three additional churches sprung up within the city walls.[142] In the sixth century or later, Pisidian Antioch fell on hard times: recent excavations in the city center chanced upon skeletons unceremoniously dumped in subterranean storage pits or wells in former Roman villas.[143]

About three and a half kilometers outside of Pisidian Antioch and connected to it by a sacred way, the sanctuary of the local Anatolian god Men Askaenos disappeared from view in the same period that Christianity visibly inserted itself into the built fabric of the city. The sanctuary comprised a main temple within a porticoed temenos, a smaller temple, and various other buildings (*oikoi*) for feasting, similar to the extra-urban sanctuaries at Lagina and Labraunda; the pagan faithful included both wealthier and more humble

---

[139] Breytenbach 1996.
[140] Balkaya et al. 2018: 298.
[141] Taşlıalan 2002; Herring-Harrington 2011: 117–122.
[142] Özhanlı 2016; Özhanlı et al. 2020: 94.
[143] Özhanlı 2014: 15; Özhanlı 2015: 2–3.

members of society, many of whom left behind a freestanding votive stele or relief aedicula carved on the temenos walls.[144] The cult was active from the mid-second century to at least the mid-fourth: recent excavations have uncovered coins of the Constantinian dynasty (305–363 CE) in the temenos' porticoes and fourth-century coins and lamps at the smaller temple, probably dedicated to Hekate.[145] Eclectic assemblages of pagan-era objects, including statuettes of Kybele, Apollo, Athena, Men, and Hekate, were found within some of the collapsed *oikoi*, in one case in conjunction with a domestic altar surrounded by lamps and small votive vessels; the excavators attribute these finds to the revival of pagan cult under Julian.[146]

But pagan worship did eventually end. Cella wall blocks from the temple of Men Askaenos, some inscribed with agonistic victories, were used in the construction of a church outside of the temenos in perhaps the fifth century; the temple's columns, capitals, and entablature completely disappeared, buried, burnt, or carted away.[147] No traces of the cult statue or main altar were found. The early twentieth-century excavators found inscribed votive stelai damaged and dispersed around the sanctuary; this was presumably carried out by Christians engaged in the appropriation of the site. One piece of a broken stele was found within the temenos, another piece of the same stele without. The sanctuary is located on a hilltop at a distance from both the late antique city and the later village of Yalvaç, so it was an inconvenient place to harvest spolia. Did Christians partially destroy the former sanctuary and its inscriptions *because* it was a pagan site?

Finally, near the end of this book, the physical manifestation of the Christian triumphalist violence promoted in various hagiographical and polemical sources seems to have materialized at the sanctuary of Men Askaenos near Antioch in Pisidia—how cathartic. But yet again, deeply unsatisfying qualifications are needed. Many, many inscribed votive aediculae with their crescent moons emblematic of Men remained in place on the temenos walls.[148] There are no erasures or Christian graffiti, so far as I know.[149] Several inscriptions use the verb *tekmoreuein* (τεκμορεύειν), the precise meaning of

---

[144] Khatchadourian 2011; Raff 2011.
[145] For the end of the cult: Mitchell and Waelkens 1998: 12–13; Blanco-Perez 2016: 122–129; Özhanlı et al. 2020: 181–184.
[146] Özhanlı 2018: 92–93. Cf. the deposit of heterogeneous pagan objects found in the so-called House of Proklos in Athens: Karivieri 1994.
[147] Mitchell and Waelkens 1998: 50, 85–86; Herring-Harrington 2011: 129. Bayliss 2004: 59 argues for a controlled deconstruction of the temple based on the disappearance of the super structure.
[148] See the drawings in Hardie 1912 and the photographs in Levick 1970.
[149] For the lack of crosses: Özhanlı et al. 2020: 187–188.

which is disputed (probably the sharing of sacred meals), but which certainly had pagan cultic connotations; it is also attested in inscriptions belonging to the Tekmoreian Guest-Friends (*Xenoi Tekmoreioi*), a local pagan group active in the second and third centuries CE.[150] Yet *tekmoreuein* remained in full view on numerous votive inscriptions. Christians did not need to make a special outing from the polis just to wreak havoc on the old sanctuary. Some of the *oikoi* around the temenos of Men Askaenos went over to domestic use at some point: further publication of the recent excavations should reveal more.[151] If the sanctuary was the victim of Christian epigraphic violence in some form, as on the whole seems likely, it was hardly a systematic obliteration of the pagan past; the church was built nearby, not directly on top of the sanctuary, and numerous inscriptions naming Men remained on view.

Another broken-up inscription from Pisidian Antioch has been labeled a victim of Christian destruction, but in this case, the interpretation is more suspect. The centerpiece of the Roman refounding of the city circa 25 BCE was a sanctuary of the imperial cult at the center of a massive hemicycle cut directly into the bedrock. The sanctuary was entered through a propylon in the form of a triumphal arch, which bore an inscription in bronze Latin letters from the year 2/1 BCE dedicating the space to Augustus, *divi f(ilius)* and *pater patriae*; only the attachment holes for the bronze letters remain.[152] This arch opened onto a broad street referred to in an inscription as the *Tiberia Platea*, which functioned as a market through late antiquity, into the eighth century.[153] Two or three crosses were carved onto the pavement of this square.

It was scattered along this *platea* that fragments of an inscription of great importance were found—a Latin copy of the *Res Gestae divi Augusti*, carved sometime after 14 CE on ten slabs approximately 0.32 meter thick and currently on display in the museum at Yalvaç—or what is left of it.[154] In Chapter 3, the remarkable preservation history of the *Res Gestae* (in Latin and Greek) on the walls of the imperial cult temple in Ankara was highlighted; the text and temple protected each other. The contrast with the fate of the text at Pisidian Antioch could not be more extreme. Here the inscription was broken up into more than two hundred irregular fragments, approximately fist-sized, and widely scattered (although precise findspots

---

[150] Ramsay 1912: 154–156; Blanco-Perez 2016: 141.
[151] Özhanlı et al. 2020: 187–188.
[152] Mitchell and Waelkens 1998: 147.
[153] Rubin 2011: 41, n. 29. *AE* 1925 0126.
[154] *SEG* 6.586. Robinson 1926; Ramsay and von Premerstein 1927: 8–13; Drew-Bear and Scheid 2005.

ERASURE 251

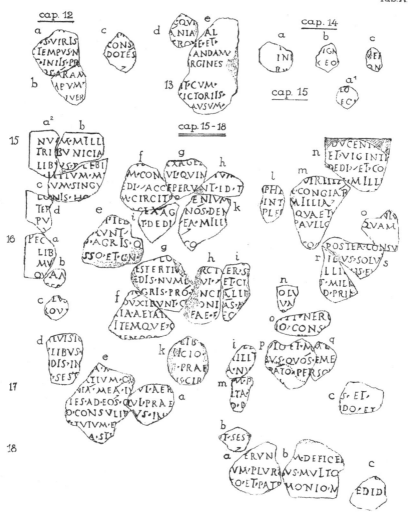

Figure 5.14 Pisidian Antioch. Fragments of the *Res Gestae divi Augusti*. Ramsay and von Premerstein 1927, Pl. 11.

were not always published) (Figure 5.14).[155] The majority of the inscribed text is simply missing. Early reconstructions of the arch assumed that this

---

[155] Although Robinson 1926: 2–3 claims that some of the fragments show evidence of an iconoclastic hammer and chisel, Ramsay and von Premerstein 1927: 9 dispute this. I have not spotted any hammer or chisel marks.

text was inscribed on its frontal piers or within the passageways passing through it. Recent reappraisal has shown that the inscribed blocks would not fit these spaces; the *Monumentum Antiochenum*, as the inscription is called, must have been displayed on a nearby feature, such as an equestrian or dynastic statue base, or perhaps even on the temple itself, as at Ankara.[156] Only the foundations of the temple remain in place; elements of the superstructure were found collapsed around it, and no architrave inscription defining the building has come to light. Undated pithoi representing agricultural or industrial activity were excavated behind the building.[157] The original display location of the *Res Gestae* at Antioch in Pisidia remains uncertain, as does the date of the temple's disuse and collapse.

This thorough breaking-up of the *Res Gestae* of Augustus and its distribution in the public space of the *platea* has sometimes been attributed to iconoclastic Christians: the act of shattering the inscription—essentially the foundation document of the Roman empire—on the steps of the imperial arch would certainly be a memorable performance of a new, higher allegiance. A church was built in approximately the fifth century at the western termination of the *Tiberia Platea*, on axis with the temple and perhaps creating an alternative urban focal point.[158] A hint of religious conflict in the city may be found in the (apocryphal) *Acts of Paul and Thekla*, partially set in Pisidian Antioch (although this may be a mix-up with Antioch on the Orontes).[159] When the devout Thekla was accosted by an Alexandros, a prominent man and priest (probably of the imperial cult), "she tore his cloak and pulled off his (priestly) crown and made him a laughing-stock."[160] The saint was sentenced by the proconsul to death by beasts in the arena (she survives and even manages to baptize herself amid the spectacle in a pool of seals). Did later devotees of Thekla, lacking an Alexandros to publicly shame, carry out a new act of civil disobedience by breaking up the *Res Gestae*? But

---

[156] Ossi 2016: 441–443. The third surviving copy of the *Res Gestae divi Augusti*, found at Apollonia (also in the province of Galatia in the Augustan age) was in Greek and inscribed on a base honoring the Julio-Claudian dynasty. The fate of the text is unclear: some fragments of the stones are quadrilinear and appear to have been recut. They were reportedly found on the site's acropolis. Rose 1997: 169–170; Cooley 2012b: 172–178; Botteri 2018b: 24–29; McKechnie 2019: 188–191. Thonemann 2012c's identification of a small fragment of text at Sardis as yet another Greek copy of the *Res Gestae* should be rejected because of the layout of his purported text (in lengthy lines as opposed to columns: Nollé 2012: 143–145).
[157] Mitchell and Waelkens 1998: 145.
[158] Taşlıalan 2013: 129.
[159] Eyice 2002: 113; McKechnie 2019: 89–90.
[160] *The Acts of Paul and Thekla* 26 (trans. Elliott).

the text barely mentions the old gods; it focuses on military and financial matters. Why should it have been the target of Christian animus? Such a repudiation of *Romanitas* and imperial power in late antiquity is unparalleled, excluding perhaps a few fringe ascetics. An alternative culprit for the breaking up of the *Res Gestae* may be the invading Arabs, who destroyed the city in the early eighth century.[161] Could they have known the symbolic importance of this inscription for the empire they were presently attacking, or at least recognized the ideological importance of whatever monument the text was attached to? A more mundane explanation is that the stone was broken up, not as an act of violence, but in order to be burnt in a lime kiln; some of the fragments are said to show signs of fire.[162] But where was this kiln, and why was the text so thoroughly broken up, only for many of the fragments to escape destruction? Perhaps the slabs had been displayed somewhere high above ground level and were destroyed in a fall—although such a display location would have rendered the small, dense text illegible in the first place. After the attack by the Arabs, occupation continued into the eleventh century; the entire ancient city became an occasional stone quarry for the later village of Yalvaç, so some remains may have been disturbed. A final verdict on the destruction of the *Res Gestae* at Antioch in Pisidia will probably never be possible.

Inscribed texts from two sanctuaries at Pisidian Antioch *may* show intentional late antique Christian destruction of the epigraphic remains of the past, although in the case of the *Res Gestae* displayed at the imperial cult sanctuary, I find this unlikely. The sanctuary of Men Askaenos is a better candidate for late antique violence against inscribed stelai and the appropriation of a pagan cult place as a quarry for a Christian church. Perhaps the early monumental presence of Christianity in the city, indicated by the so-called Church of St. Paul, bolstered a more forceful reaction to pagan sanctuaries in its territory than is typical in Asia Minor. The location of the Men Askaenos shrine outside the city (and therefore out of the view of local civic or bureaucratic

---

[161] Rubin 2011: 44, n. 46.

[162] Ossi 2016: 442. Cf. the *tropaeum* of Augustus at Nikopolis, constructed after his victory at Actium in 31 BCE: "numerous smashed marble fragments . . . were found in piles, which suggests deliberate dismantlement" in a layer associated with burning (Zachos 2003: 83). The *tropaeum* was perhaps repaired under Constantine (who transported a statue from the victory monument to Constantinople: Bassett 2004: 213) or Julian; the city of Nikopolis was plundered by the Vandals in the late fifth century and fell to the Goths in the sixth. Were these two quintessential early imperial monuments, the *Res Gestae* inscription at Pisidian Antioch and the *tropaeum* at Nikopolis, the object of anti-imperial sentiment from invading forces, or were they dismantled and broken up because they had become obsolete?

authorities) may have made it more vulnerable to rough handling by individual groups of Christians. But even here, the particular circumstances in which the sanctuary and a number of its texts were destroyed are not clear.

Conclusion: Epigraphic Unnamings and a Fresh Start

This chapter charted the patterns that emerge from a close consideration of erased or destroyed inscriptions, their physical characteristics, and surrounding topography. Given the uncertainties of the dating and motivations lying behind these epigraphic modifications, caution is needed. While a number of the erasures can be ascribed with great confidence or certainty to late antiquity, others may have taken place only later, although I argue that these actions fit best within late antique contexts. The only probable exception is the destruction of the *Res Gestae* at Pisidian Antioch, which may have taken place quite late.

A rasura is not always what it first appears. In 2013 a Roman votive column in the Turkish village of Belenören, south of Prousa (Bursa), was published.[163] The text was a dedication to Zeus Kersoullos; all eight lines were erased, not very thoroughly. We may initially assume a late antique censoring of a pagan dedication. But the villagers reported that the text was erased only around 1920, in the midst of the Greco-Turkish War. With Greek troops advancing, the Turkish villagers wished to negate any possible territorial claims that Greeks might have to this village based on the presence of Greek script. Whether or not this account is accurate, it was taken for granted that a writing system could encode ethnicity and make claims of ownership on its setting; other erasures too may be the result of more recent historical circumstances. The ninth-century BCE Mesha Stele discovered at Dibon (Dhiban) in Jordan is of enormous importance because it confirms the existence of a biblical figure, Omri, king of Israel. This basalt stone is currently in numerous fragments in the Louvre. But it was intact until 1868: a dispute among western researchers, Ottoman authorities, and a local Bedouin tribe resulted in a dramatic act of epigraphic violence: the Bedouins tossed the basalt stele in a hot fire and then poured cold water over it, causing the stone to shatter.[164] This story calls to mind yet again the fragmentary *Res Gestae* at

---

[163] *SEG* 63.1028 = Battistoni and Rothenhöfer 2013: 123–125, no. 18.
[164] Cline 2009: 16–19.

Pisidian Antioch. When the archaeological team under David Robinson in 1924 excitedly began to find fist-sized fragments of Augustus' autobiography in the waste dirt from William Ramsay's previous excavations, they offered a cash reward to any of the locals who produced pieces of the inscription. Not surprisingly, the archaeologists were presented with ever smaller and smaller fragments of the text, as fist-sized pieces were broken up in order to maximize the reward money.[165] The economics of archaeological research at Pisidian Antioch further damaged the already smashed inscription.

We must exercise caution: the act of erasing or destroying leaves behind no palaeographic or prosopographic dating clues, and it is therefore difficult to link to a specific time period or to specific motivations. A stone from the Latin west is instructive: a dedication to Sol Invictus from a Roman military group in Corstopitum (Corbridge, UK) dates to the period of Marcus Aurelius (r. 161–180) and reads in its first part *[[Soli Invicto]] vexillatio leg(ionis) VI Vic(tricis) P(iae) F(idelis) f(ecit)* (To Sol Invictus, a detachment of the Sixth Legion Victrix Pia Fidelis made it).[166] The name of the god has been damaged, most thoroughly over *Soli*, less intensively over *Invicto*. This has been attributed variously to the condemnation of Commodus (epithet *Invictus*, d. 193), or to the censure of Elagabalus (priest of Sol Invictus, d. 222).[167] But a later Christian erasure of the pagan dedication is also possible: how many pagans would risk angering a god in order to express disapproval of an emperor? Religious and political motivations are difficult to untangle. Meanwhile, at Iasos, a Classical inscription outlining the privileges and responsibilities of the priest of Zeus Megistos, which was found built into a "Byzantine house," has been violently damaged in its entire central section by a pointed instrument such as a pick or pointed chisel, leaving behind a pockmarked surface with only a few traces of letters.[168] The portions of the inscriptions to the left and right are untouched and were presumably hidden behind other wall stones. It is clear that the exposed text motivated the chiseling: the marks from the pick start with the top line of text and peter out around its lowest line, as has been noted by Roberta Fabiani.[169] But is it a coincidence that this central, damaged portion of the inscription had in its

---

[165] Robinson 1926: 3.
[166] *RIB* 1137.
[167] Lefebvre 2004: 200–202. For similar Latin examples of the Christian erasure of texts, see Cooley 2012a: 319–320; Ehmig 2019: 113–114.
[168] *I.Iasos* 220.
[169] Fabiani 2016: 162.

top line the name of Zeus Megistos (as painstakingly read by epigraphers)? And even more of a coincidence that the inscription ended precisely with a prohibition on destroying the text?[170] Or was the erasure aimed against the presence of inscribed writing, perhaps carried out by an illiterate person?

A return to the very first case study from Chapter 3 adds to these methodological difficulties. We saw how the "Temple of Hadrian" on the Embolos at Ephesos maintained most of its inscribed architrave dedication (to Artemis and Hadrian from local benefactors), even when the building was repaired at some point in the fourth century and a statue base to Theodosios I's father was set up between 379 and 387. But the name of the goddess is missing: it was not technically erased but was never reinscribed on the fourth-century replacement architrave block.[171] Donor inscriptions were protected by Roman law; the full text (including Artemis' name) may perhaps have been painted on this *ersatz* marble in order to save money or time.[172] But the extremely careful carving of the egg and dart molding, which is almost indistinguishable from the second-century original, shows that this was no quick-and-dirty replacement. A decision may have been made not to reinscribe the new architrave block precisely *because* the name of Artemis was no longer desirable. The structural necessity of repairing the building accomplished what zealous Christians in the city perhaps dreamed of and did in fact carry out on other inscriptions, where the name of the goddess is physically erased. An architrave originating somewhere along the Embolos has Artemis' name removed on a dedication to the goddess and Trajan; a similar erasure took place in the Greek text of a bilingual statue base found at the *Hafengymnasium*.[173] Here the rasura of the goddess left behind a grammatically correct dedication only to Trajan: it presumed the continued reading of the Greek text. The erasure of an honorary inscription dating from the second or third century CE likewise left behind an intelligible text: the man named Timotheos was "the pious and voluntary *neopoios* of our lady [[Artemis]]."[174] With the name of Artemis removed, the "our lady" instead evoked the Theotokos, elevated to

---

[170] *I.Iasos* 220, ll. 7–8, ed. Fabiani 2016: . . . ἢν δέ τι[[σ τὴν στήλην ἀφαν[ίσηι ἢ τὰ] γ[ρ]άμ[ματτα] πα]]σχέτω | ὡς ἱερόσυλος (But if anyone [[should obliterate this stele or the writing (on it),]] let him be punished as a temple-robber.) Only the visible section, not covered by other wall blocks (and therefore subject to the violent erasure) could be read by the eraser. See also Fabiani 2016: 179.

[171] *I.Ephesos* 429. Given the number of letters missing (thirty-three), any replacement text would have begun at the far left of the architrave block, which is preserved and shows no traces of inscribing (the right portion of the block is a modern replacement).

[172] Quatember 2017: 83.

[173] *I.Ephesos* 422; Miltner 1959: 346–347. *I.Ephesos* 509; Betz 1970: 29; Sitz 2019a: 647.

[174] *I.Ephesos* 3263, ll. 6–8: τὸν εὐσεβῆ καὶ αὐθαίρετον | νεοποιὸν τῆς κυρίας ἡμῶν [[Ἀρ|τέμιδος]] (trans. Horsley 1992: 108–109).

new prominence in Christian theology through the council that took place at Ephesos in 431. The erasure was not trying to fool readers by hiding Artemis; it provocatively made the point that the city had a new divine protector. These examples indicate that erasure can both prove and presume reading. Other erasures at Ephesos were more haphazard: erased inscriptions from the so-called sanctuary of Domitian were reused in the fifth century to build an opulent late antique structure, while the spoliated grave stones in the atrium of the Church of Mary were chiseled to varying degrees (Chapter 4).[175] Despite these other instances of erasure by chiseling, classifying the absence of Artemis' name on the "Temple of Hadrian" as an act of epigraphic violence is fraught with too many uncertainties.

By primarily focusing on epigraphic erasures, by which I mean the removal of inscribed letters through chiseling, hammering, or rubbing, we are on firmer ground, as there is definite evidence that *something* happened to these stones. It is clear that these were, for the most part, not random or instinctive reactions to the presence of writing itself (after all, thousands and thousands of ancient inscribed texts have come down to us unscathed), but were rather dependent on the specific content and context of the texts under consideration. As already argued in Chapter 2, erasures are the exceptions that prove the rule: people in late antiquity could, and did, read older inscriptions, and only occasionally felt the need to edit them.

There is a clear divergence between the fates of ancient statuary and ancient inscriptions in late antiquity. As a substantial body of literature has indicated, numerous ancient statues suffered intentional damage to their heads; others had crosses carved onto them, as a means of either "updating" these old-fashioned figures or exorcizing the demon within the stone. This relates to long-standing ancient and late antique beliefs about statues, who had wills and could act independently (and often idiosyncratically) for either good or ill.[176] If some late antique Christian intellectuals and churchmen protested against this animistic attitude and argued that statues were merely stone and wood, then all the better to smash, bash, and trash them in order to prove that they really were incapable of defending themselves.

Inscriptions were different. They might contain esoteric messages from another world, but were not themselves animized; they did not require the same violence that statues did. Nor were they collector items, as

---

[175] Ladstätter 2019: 31.
[176] Mango 1963; James 1996.

statues were among the elite of Constantinople. Whereas statue caches have been excavated around the Mediterranean, I know of no such caches of inscriptions from our period. For the most part, ancient inscriptions do not bear marks meant merely to deface and delegitimize them. It is rare to see Christian graffiti or crosses cutting across older texts; at Aphrodisias, the insertion of a cross into the inscription on the Northeast city gate was carried out with minimal damage to the preexisting words. The Çavdar graffiti carved directly on top of the Roman inscriptions on the Temple of Zeus at Aizanoi (Chapter 3) throws into sharp relief the *lack* of such Christian encroachments onto similar texts. The situation is the same if we look at the literary sources: the destruction of "idols" is broadcast in several texts, while the erasure of inscriptions is rarely narrated. Abercius of Hier(o)polis, whose tombstone we (probably) encountered in Chapter 2, is said in his *Life* to have entered a temple and beat up statues of gods with a wooden club, but even here, the hagiographer, so willing to use inscriptions to build his narrative, did not include any acts of epigraphic violence committed by the saint.[177] Literary attestations of erasures in late antiquity are few: the *Historia Augusta* describes a couple acts of imperial memory sanctions, and Prokopios in his *Secret History* claims that Domitian's name was removed from every inscription in Rome.[178] The Arrian bishop at the shrine of St. Thekla in Kilikia tried (and failed) to have an orthodox mosaic inscription removed.[179]

This tendency toward iconoclasm, rather than what we might call "grammatoclasm," extends beyond late antiquity. Statues from the distant past up to today have been lightning rods for dissatisfaction and performative protest, as well as the nexus of deep-seated religious anxieties and superstitions.[180] Political, religious, and cultural uprisings around the globe have been sparked or commemorated by the destruction of figural imagery—but usually not publicly inscribed texts. Religious extremists have selected sculpture for publicized destruction; although books get burnt as well, public inscriptions usually are not worth the dynamite expenditure. The recent popular protests in the United States and the United Kingdom against racism have coalesced around statues as the embodiments of political and cultural systems; statue defenders too have imbued these sometimes

---

[177] *Life of Abercius* 4.
[178] *Historia Augusta: Life of Elagabalus* 13.6; *The Three Gordians* 34.5; Prokopios *Anecdota* 8.14.
[179] Chapter 2, —.
[180] Boldrick, Brubaker, and Clay 2013.

flimsy memorials with profound significance for identity and "history."[181] Historical plaques are rarely either censured or lauded on social media or on the news. James F. Osborne has termed violent interventions against memorials "counter-monumentality" and noted how these statues in fact reveal the vulnerability of cultural memory through the violence inflicted on them; "counter-epigraphicality" is rarer.[182] The close assimilation of figural imagery with the figures themselves, as well as the mirroring of corporeal punishments onto stone bodies, makes statues a more popular choice for violence or removal than inscriptions.

Despite the distinct afterlives of statues and inscriptions, one particular point of confluence does emerge: pagan gods in their cultic guises were the most susceptible to both figural and epigraphic violence. Cult statues are rare finds, indicating that most were destroyed or buried; depictions of pagan gods as figures that might receive worship were more likely to undergo iconoclasm than those same gods embedded within mythological narratives, where they could be fictionalized away, as we saw at Aphrodisias. It was also the *names* of these gods that were most likely to be erased. At Aphrodisias, Labraunda, Aizanoi, and Antioch ad Cragum, the monikers of a smattering of deities were removed. At Antioch ad Cragum, *only* the divine names, not the associated oracular advice, underwent rasura. In some cases, pagan priests also suffered from this onomastic violence, as was the case for Zoilos at Aphrodisias, Asklipiades at Aizanoi, and the long list of names at the Korykian Cave Clifftop Temple. As I have argued at Aizanoi, it may have been the specific source of the spoliated architrave bearing the name of Asklipiades and Artemis that necessitated its erasure, while the name of Zeus appeared prominently just across the street. Other erasures responded more to the variable of being located at an entrance or at hand, but in any case, names were usually the target of removal.

At the outset of this chapter, I presented a common rhetorical strategy used by late antique Christians to mitigate the continuing power of pagan gods: unnaming. The distinctive deities of old, with their foibles and follies, became nameless demons in many early Christian hagiographies and homilies. The epigraphic evidence matches this discursive habit. On the *Säulenstraße* at Aizanoi, the rasura stopped short of the word "naos," temple—the source of the architrave was acknowledged, but the temple from

---

[181] Frank and Ristic 2020.
[182] Osborne 2017.

which it came was made anonymous. The stone lost its association with a specific place and a specific goddess. Likewise at Aphrodisias, the traces of letters left on the Zoilos door lintel made it crystal clear that the stone was spoliated; the viewer could guess from where, even if the word *hieron* was quite thoroughly removed. This is also the case on a door lintel from the sanctuary of Apollo Hylates at Kourion on Cyprus, dated to the period of Nero: the name of Apollo and most of the following text was roughly chiseled away.[183] A few letters were left, making it clear that the stone had once held an inscription, and, given the stone's location at the Temple of Apollo, late antique viewers, like modern epigraphers, could get the gist. The first name to be removed from the dice oracle at Antioch ad Cragum was the name of Pythian Apollo; the temple was probably dedicated to him. Apollo stood behind the majority of oracular enterprises in the ancient world. Eradicating his name here at Antioch ad Cragum, near the beginning of the astragal oracle, perhaps removed, or at least repudiated, its specific association with Apollo.

What's in a name, anyways? Quite a lot, according to both late antique authors and popular practitioners of piety/magic. The fourth-century Latin poet Ausonius drew the connection between name loss and death: "Are we to wonder that man perishes? His monuments decay, and death comes even to his marbles and his names."[184] At the same time that the names of pagan gods were excised from the inscriptions presented in this chapter, new Christian *nomina sacra* were popping up everywhere. The Chi-Rho (representing the first two letters of Christ's name in Greek) appeared on coins and in decorative sculpture in the fourth century. Painting and mosaic programs bore labels identifying saints, who also appeared in magical spells and on amulets. Origen in the third century proclaimed: "In fact the name of Jesus is so powerful against the daemons that sometimes it is effective even when pronounced by bad men."[185] We have already seen how Aphrodisias changed its name to Stauroupolis and projected that change epigraphically. Antioch on the Orontes too underwent a name change: after a devastating earthquake, Justinian rechristened it as Theoupolis (God's City). According to Malalas, Justinian's order was confirmed by a minor miracle: "a written [inscribed?]

---

[183] *I.Kourion* 105. The reasons for this erasure have been debated (a Neronic damnatio?), but given the comparanda given here, a late antique erasure of the name and associates of a pagan god seems likely.

[184] Ausonius *Epitaphs* 6.32 (trans. Evelyn-White).

[185] *Contra Celsum* I.6 (trans. Chadwick).

oracle was discovered at Antioch, which read as follows, 'And you, unhappy city, shall not be called the city of Antiochos.'"[186] The city hoped to improve its fortunes through this new appellation. Names were believed to hold very real power, even the power of life and death. We have also seen the close connection between names and the self; the destruction of names as a way of harming an individual is one of the oldest forms of memory sanctions. Removing the names of gods from public writing was a profound act, one that denied allegiance to the old divinities and, given the close connection between names and identity, perhaps denied their very person- or godhood.

This chapter has brought to the fore many points of contact between the official Roman practice of damnatio memoriae and our erasures. Damnatio also fixated on names (and faces), and they were in most cases directed or carried out by a literate individual. The resulting texts cannot simply be labeled as erased: method and degree vary. The incomplete erasure of text created a reflexive metatext, in which the remaining chiseled letters give a commentary on the (now lost) complete version of the text. Finally, as in damnatio, it was not necessary to search out and erase every name of the *persona non grata* (or *dea non grata*); a few prominent and visible examples would do.

The proximal causes lying behind these erasures, however, may initially seem to differ. Damnatio memoriae is an explicitly political act; the late antique erasures of the names of gods reads as an explicitly religious one. And no doubt these erasures were ultimately the products of the changing sacred canopy in the late Roman world. But such a mono-causal motivation does not stand up to closer inspection. Our erasures show no obvious religious animus: they were not replaced by new Christian inscriptions (except for "Stauroupolis" at Aphrodisias). Crosses were not added over the gaps, nor, for that matter, were texts defaced through the addition of crosses on top of the earlier writing. Any discussion of motivations obviously requires a discussion of actors, and for the most part we cannot identify the movers and shakers behind late antique erasures. But in some cases, it was likely civic, not ecclesiastical, agents who removed the names of pagan gods: at Aphrodisias, both the editing of the Archive Wall and the Northeast city gate were probably official actions; at Aizanoi, the erasure of the spoliated Artemis architrave on a city street bears all the hallmarks of a decision made by the officially sanctioned building team. In other instances, ecclesiastical authorities likely

---

[186] Malalas *Chronographia* 443 (trans. Jeffreys, Jeffreys, and Scott); Roueché 2004, vi.52.

took the lead on directing erasures for stones reused in churches. Individuals or communities could carry out "unofficial" erasures or destructions, as was probably the case at rural sites. At the Korykian Cave, we can perhaps see the tension between an ecclesiastical policy of preservation and unofficial defacement: the clergy in charge of the construction may have wished for the list of male names on the anta to be preserved (resulting in that face of the anta being hidden behind a wall), while the "average Joe" who encountered names in the side aisle of the church felt they should be removed. Or have I got it backward? Maybe the construction team arranged for the preservation of the anta text, but a priest later scratched out the names in the side aisle. At other sites, pagans themselves may even have taken the initiative on removing explicitly pagan content as a means of avoiding controversy and showing their good faith toward the new imperial religion. When the Capitoline Museum in Rome voluntarily covered up all their nude statues before the 2016 visit of Iranian president Hassan Rouhani, this did not portend a change in attitude toward the ancient nude by the Italian populus. It was simply going along to get along.

Regardless of the actors behind the late antique erasures, in many cases, the removal of pagan-associated text can be ascribed to political motivations. At Aphrodisias, the erasure of the city's name on the Archive Wall carried the same political-social connotations as the original carving of the dossier. As members of the imperial court increasingly projected Christian identity, so too did those eager to maintain or cultivate relationships with them. Both the inscribing of the dossier of the Archive Wall and its selective erasure were part and parcel of political maneuvering in (late) antiquity. This catering to Constantinople could lie behind a number of other erasures.

Even if we attribute both damnatio memoriae and a number of our sanctuary erasures to political motivations, that does not mean that their intended *effects* were the same. Here a closer look at the particular physical characteristics of the erased stones is important. As discussed, damnatio memoriae often aimed not at forgetting the condemned individual but at perpetually shaming her/him and presenting an example to other would-be dissidents. This was achieved by leaving parts of the name or titulature of the condemned individual on display, by performing public denigration of the individual in panegyric speeches, or by erecting new memorials highlighting his/her fall from grace. But the late antique erasures of pagan gods show little evidence of this tendency. The names of the gods were usually the most carefully erased section. The *Säulenstraße* at Aizanoi is particularly instructive.

The names of Artemis and her priest are thoroughly erased on one side of the street; across from it, the damnatio-ed name of Nero is still quite legible because the chisel marks follow the letters of his name, leaving behind a blurred text that can still be read as NEPΩNI and allowing the disgraced emperor to be perpetually recognized and condemned.[187] A public shaming of the old gods would also equate to a public shaming of the old inhabitants of a city: the illustrious ancestors and famous individuals whose epigraphic *Nachlass* was still on display on various monuments, including the preserved or spoliated temples discussed in Chapters 3 and 4. Rather than a perpetual shaming, the late antique erasures presented in this chapter strike me as more of a "conscious uncoupling": a desire to amicably part ways with the pagan past through a public announcement (the act of erasure) and, in some cases, a name change.[188]

But unnaming the pagan gods was not always successful. The passage from Prokopios with which this chapter opened refers to the suburb near Constantinople as "Heraion, which they now call Hieron." Despite efforts, perhaps by the ecclesiastical leaders, the local community, or even Justinian himself to "rebrand" the neighborhood, Prokopios still knew and recorded the old pagan name.[189] The transformation from Aphrodisias to Stauroupolis likewise did not stick: in the medieval period the city was known simply as "Karia," the name of the province it led and was metonymically associated with. The name "Karia" is apparently preserved in the modern Turkish village "Geyre."[190] The replacement of Antioch on the Orontes with Theoupolis did not catch on either: the modern city is still called Antakya. Older toponyms continued to be used in the papyri records of Christianizing Egypt; the Caesareum of Alexandria kept its name even after the building was converted to a church.[191] Similarly, a temple of Artemis in Constantinople, which, according to Malalas, was given by Theodosios to dice players, was referred to as "the Temple."[192] Constantine's stripping of the lions from a statue of Rhea/Kybele in his new capital did not fool Zosimos: he still recognized the statue as a goddess rather than Christian *orans*.

---

[187] *SEG* 45.1711 = Wörrle 1995a, no. 1.
[188] To borrow a trendy twenty-first-century relationship term referring to an amicable divorce.
[189] Cf. Agathias' (*Histories* 3.5.7) explicit statement that he prefers to use the old name (Onogouris) for a city in Colchis even though in his time "most people do not use it," instead calling the town after the Protomartyr Stephen.
[190] Roueché 2004 vi.54.
[191] Westerfeld 2012.
[192] ὁ ναός: Malalas *Chronographia* Book 13.39.

But often the strategy of unnaming was not meant to be successful. Late antique cities did not need to pretend that the classical era never happened. Erasure was, on the one hand, a semantic annihilation, an obliteration of specific content originating (in these cases) in the distant past. But the process of erasing itself left behind persistent evidence that a rasura had taken place. All the erased stones in this chapter maintained at least some traces of letters, or a hollowed-out gap advertising that text had once been there. This was certainly an intentional decision: other modes of epigraphic violence, such as shattering the stone or a more careful reworking of the surface, could have been enacted. Partially erased inscriptions were therefore a feature of late antique city- and sanctuary-scapes, just as defunct or reused temples were. These stones attest the ever-evolving relationship of the late antique (largely) Christian present with the pagan past.

6

Conclusion

Unepigraphic Readings

Reading at the Temple of Augustus at Ankara Once More

In August 1949, Giorgos Seferis, Greek poet and diplomat, was in Ankara, the capital of the Turkish Republic. While there, he visited the Temple of Augustus and Roma and read the ninth- or tenth-century grave text of the *tourmarches* Eustathios, whom we met in Chapter 3. Eustathios was one of several Byzantines whose mortal remains were interred at the ancient Temple of Augustus, and as we saw, his funerary epigram in the cella seems to have drawn its inspiration for its majuscule letter forms from the Greek copy of the *Res Gestae divi Augusti*, inscribed on the cella's outer wall nearly a millennium earlier.[1] Seferis too wrote his own verses about his visit to the temple, comparing Eustathios (whom he calls by the modern Greek informal version of his name, Stathis), to Augustus and to King Asitawandas, thereby collapsing Anatolia's Iron Age, Roman, and Christian history into a single continuum. His poem continues:

> But Stathis the monk who exhausted himself roaming and was once a swordbearer, swordbearer and hangman, sits at the fountain, the blindness bringing water, stares into the sunset, speaks, and relates: "Unto the world below you sent me, my Lord and Christ, and bodily I departed and bodily I went; now I seek your grace, guardian of sin; seed of Charon I sowed, for others to reap, yet make me sprout for you from my grave a carnation of my lament and come to your side.[2]

---

[1] *I.Ancyra* 501.
[2] Seferis 1974: 117 (trans. Anagnostopoulos).

Seferis perfectly captures the gist of the funerary lament of Eustathios' epitaph, in which the deceased rued his sinfulness and asked Christ for mercy while being sure to mention his high military rank—all quite appropriate for a Byzantine grave text. But Seferis has made one tiny "mistake": nowhere does Eustathios state in his epitaph that he became a monk. The modern poet seems to have assumed this based on his reading of *another* Byzantine text also inscribed on the Temple of Augustus, the epitaph of Hyphatios (ninth/tenth century), which states that he was a hegoumenos, the leader of a monastery. Or perhaps Seferis got his information from either oral or written reports that the Temple of Augustus had first become a church in late antiquity (indicated by the so-called square apse) and subsequently a Byzantine monastery, as published by Krencker and Schede in 1936. In Chapter 3, we saw that the square apse is unlikely to relate to a church, but the overall sequence of events (temple to late antique church to Byzantine monastery) is plausible, if unverifiable. Like his ancient and late antique predecessors, Seferis read Eustathios' grave text not in scientific isolation, but in its surrounding architectural and (perhaps mistaken) local historical context. The Byzantine *tourmarches* Eustathios became the monk Stathis through his proximity to the epitaph of the hegoumenos Hyphatios, through his burial within the supposed monastic space of the former temple, and through Seferis' own perceived familiarity with this fellow Greek, whose lament sounded distinctively monastic to twentieth-century ears.

An Archaeology of Reading

In this manner of reading, Seferis was not alone. We have seen in Chapter 2 that late antique authors read the ancient inscriptions surrounding them through the prism of their own time and place. In this they followed many ancient Greek and Roman readers, and preceded later medieval and modern ones. It is, actually, present-day professional epigraphers who are the strange ones, outsiders to this tradition, in their critical mode of reading and dismissal of unfounded assumptions and folk histories of inscriptions and places. The late antique textual sources gathered in Chapter 2 indicate that late antique Christians, such as Kosmas Indikopleustes and Sokrates Scholastikos, interpreted ancient inscriptions through a biblical worldview even as they show genuine interest in, and knowledge of, historical epigraphic material. Kosmas Indikopleustes in particular grasped the importance of the materiality of texts and physical writing-bearers. History writers, such as Agathias of Myrina and Ammianus Marcellinus, used older inscribed texts to support their historiographic aims in the service of the late Roman empire. While Agathias' understanding of an Augustan-era base was colored by local, probably oral, history, Prokopios used inscriptions critically to challenge stories he had heard even as he acknowledged the impossibility of knowing the distant past. The anonymous authors of the *Life of Abercius* and the *Martyrdom of Ariadne of Prymnessos* were happy to copy directly from Roman inscriptions, using them to legitimize their hagiographies by replicating correct, old-fashioned official language or, in the case of the *Life of Abercius*, building an entire narrative around the tombstone of Abercius. As we saw, the text of the Abercius epitaph, as transmitted in the *Life of Abercius*, has recently been called into question—with serious consequences for our understanding of the early Christianization of Asia Minor, of the development of the Eucharist, and even of the primacy of the church at Rome. I have argued that we need not throw the *Life*'s text of the Abercius epitaph out just yet: the preserved fragment of inscribed stone now in the Vatican shows every indication of being an early Christian text, while the grave prohibition, which prescribes an astronomical fine for disturbing the tomb, makes sense as an original element of Abercius' tombstone in the context of early Christianity in Phrygia. These and other literary sources indicate the ability to read, comprehend, and copy even much older inscribed texts—and in fact to do quite a bit more with them.

By viewing textual sources through the theoretical framework of transtextuality, it became apparent in Chapter 2 that late antique authors did not simply reflect "what people thought" about inscriptions but cited, quoted, and appropriated ancient Greek, Roman, and Egyptian inscriptions in their projects of world-building, whether that world was explicitly Christian or traditional Roman. Late antique textual sources used inscriptions in two primary ways: to legitimate and transform the past, and to make claims about divine providence's control of the future. In particular, I have identified an expansion of the prophetic role of inscriptions in late antique historiography (classicizing or ecclesiastical) and religious sources such as the *Tübingen Theosophy*. The increasing oracular role of inscriptions in these texts is paralleled by a decrease in actual opportunities to consult traditional oracles or soothsayers. Epigraphic omens in literature became "safe," de-personalized sources of information about the future, without running afoul of late Roman legal condemnation of traditional divination. Even so, prophetic inscriptions, like ancient oracles and omens, remained otherworldly, double-edged swords: they could give "trick" advice or portend unavertable disasters.

So much, then, for the uses of ancient inscriptions in late antique textual sources. Chapters 3–5 next considered the fates of actual, physical ancient inscribed stones standing at ground zero of the "culture wars" of late antiquity: pagan sanctuaries. These archaeological chapters allowed us to chart three main fates that befell these stones: preservation in place, spoliation as building material, and erasure (whether spoliated or left in place). Chapter 3 documented the presence of inscribed ancient inscriptions on still-standing monuments in late antique cities and sanctuaries at sites such as Priene, Athens, Ankara, Palmyra, Lagina, and Medinet Habu. These texts in late antique contexts have largely been ignored by archaeologists and epigraphers alike, who have instead focused on the original period of construction/inscribing: what we might call an "originalist" interpretation (that the primary meaning of an inscribed text—like the US Constitution—is its meaning at the time of its composition). We may assume that the late antique population likewise ignored these leftover texts, but in several of the case studies in Chapter 3, graffiti in the area around or below inscribed texts, or the construction of new Christian buildings at temple sites, suggests an engagement with the epigraphic material. Indeed, rather than an "originalist" interpretation, I propose a "living text" approach: the meaning of inscribed words changed with the times, with the evolving surrounding contexts, and even with individuals of different worldviews. In Chapter 3, we saw that several of the preserved inscriptions mentioned popular rulers such as Alexander, Hadrian, or Augustus. In particular, I argued that the decision to keep the *Res Gestae divi Augusti* on display in late antique Ankara was both the result of, and contributor to, the continuing imperial importance of the city even as it Christianized. I proposed that the Temple of Augustus in Ankara may very well have become a church in late antiquity, at the same time that Augustus became increasingly linked with the rise of Christendom. At other sites, inscribed texts, even those mentioning pagan gods, or those in unintelligible writing systems (such as Egyptian hieroglyphs) were also kept in place. At the very least, these inscriptions are a testament to the tolerance shown by late antique individuals to older epigraphic material: even at sites where churches were constructed in or next to temples, many ancient texts remained on display. When taken in conjunction with the findings of Chapter 2, these inscriptions had the potential to corroborate local stories of connections with important rulers, visually demonstrating the continuity between the glorious Hellenic/Roman past and the late Roman present—and perhaps foretelling future glories.

Chapter 4 took on the subject of epigraphic spolia, that is, inscriptions reused as building material. It is clear that the antagonistic attitude toward the spoliated remains of pagan sanctuaries apparent in some hagiographies, such as the *Life of Porphyry of Gaza*, cannot be unthinkingly mapped onto archaeological remains. While previous research has concluded that spoliated inscriptions were primarily used for practical reasons, I argue that building teams *did* pay attention to the inscribed texts at sites such as the Korykian Cave, Sagalassos, Aphrodisias, Sardis, and Labraunda. While in some cases, the original, pagan content was "scrambled" by breaking up the texts during reuse, in others, the euergetic and honorific content of older texts may have actually been *desirable* in Christian holy spaces, as I have argued for Aphrodisias. At that site, I suggested that the epigraphic remains of the neutralized pagan past were used to crowd out other, more difficult to suppress, heterodox discourses while also advertising past relationships with Roman emperors. The Korykian Cave Clifftop temple in particular shows the continued interest in ancient inscribed texts: the builders carefully re-erected the anta bearing a long list of names when the complex was converted into a church, preserving part of the list behind a wall. As we saw at the synagogue at Sardis, even illegible inscriptions, such as an epichoric Anatolian text, potentially worked to define a community's identity. In line with other recent work on spolia, Chapter 4 distinguished the process of spoliation (the decisions made during construction) from the product of spolia and also argued for a middle way between pragmatism and polemics: reuse can be practical and at the same time reveal cultural attitudes toward the past.

Chapter 5 turned toward the physical confirmation of late antique reading and reimagining of older inscriptions: the selective erasure of several pagan texts. At sites such as Aphrodisias, Aizanoi, Antioch ad Cragum, and Ephesos, erasure focused especially on the names of pagan gods and their priests. While this phenomenon naturally recalls the Roman political habit of damnatio memoriae, I connect it instead with a wider habit of "unnaming" pagan gods in late antiquity: making them anonymous and removing specific associations, festivals, and places connected with their names. Based on the physical properties of erasure—careful, not fanatical, thorough, not contemptuous—I propose that the goal was not to shame the old gods and (by association) previous inhabitants of Greco-Roman cities, but rather to put some distance between the late antique present and the pagan past, without disavowing positive affiliations with good Roman emperors or proud euergetes. Very few of the thousands of ancient inscriptions that have come down to us show erasure marks; when erasures did take place, it was only under very specific circumstances. For example, at Aphrodisias, many ancient inscriptions were built into the temple-church; but one of the only erasures was carried out on a prominent dedication to the goddess at the entrance to the nave. Some letters from the inscription (though not the name of Aphrodite) were left visible, even untouched by the eraser's chisel, drawing attention to the stone's status as epigraphic spolia. As we saw at the baptistery in the Burdur Museum, the process of erasure can just as effectively create new content as remove the old. The name of the (pagan, Roman) Eprios Agatheinos was partially erased on a spoliated dedication to create the fictitious "Gaeios," thereby allowing another dedication from Eprios Agatheinos, to the "lord god above," to be read as an early Christian text suitable for a baptistery. An early Christian is created through the *fiat* of a few erased letters. The destructive and creative act was simultaneous on this inscription, indicating a sophisticated interaction with the ancient marbles and an awareness of their power to shape the present. Chapter 5 therefore brought together this group of erased pagan inscriptions for the first time, arguing that they do not represent a simple adoption of damnatio practice in Christian contexts, but rather a different phenomenon altogether.

Spolia: Breaking the Monolith

One of the main goals of this book is to demonstrate that we cannot study these fates in isolation: each mode of dealing with ancient inscribed stones was one choice among many and can only be understood in relation to others. In particular, I want to make the point that the perennially popular concept of spolia, while fruitful in its own right, has done the field of late antique archaeology something of a disservice by deflecting attention away from non-spoliated ancient material that was still on display. *Spolienforschung* has so far been a monolith that must be broken apart: documenting *only* inscriptions (or other marbles) that were reused misses the many, many stones that were left visible, even in spolia-hungry cities. There is no indication that late ancient viewers flocked to spolia-laden walls while ignoring preserved Hellenic or Roman façades in the same way late antique researchers have done. Imagine, for a moment, that the temple blocks bearing the *Res Gestae divi Augusti* at Ankara had been taken apart and rebuilt, inscription face out, in a late antique church. There would be no end to the publications discussing this spolia and its implications for memory studies. Yet because this document was left in place on a standing temple, scholars have taken its preservation for granted and focused their attentions on the original meaning of the text. Only by paying attention to what might have been reused, but was not, and the particular building logic at play in the process of spoliation, can we understand the full range of possibilities available to people in late antiquity and their priorities.

This book likewise draws attention to the problem of periodization, that is, categorizing material in the archaeological record based on its period of origin ("Classical inscription"; "Roman temple"; "late antique wall") without considering its diachronic nature: its full lifespan. This has resulted in Hellenistic inscriptions being studied (sensibly) by Hellenistic epigraphers—but largely ignored by archaeologists who found them in late antique buildings. In spaces such as the Aphrodisias temple-church, however, the older Roman inscriptions appeared side-by-side with late antique donor texts and Christian graffiti, creating a synchronic, cumulative epigraphic landscape. We can go one (provocative) step further: what does "late antique material culture" even mean, if a significant portion of the art, objects, and buildings encountered daily in late antiquity were, in fact, much older? I do not mean to imply that there is no value in studying newly built late antique monuments or newly made objects as categories of material, only that it is possible to expand our field of vision significantly and ask new questions of the archaeological remains. Can "late antique material culture" be fully appreciated without consideration of the juxtaposition of old and new permeating late antique spaces?

Word and Image: Inscriptions and Statues

The diachronic lives of statues have spent much more time in the scholarly limelight, and the presence of these ancient, often explicitly pagan, sometimes nude, figures in late antique city centers has drawn attention. This previous work on statuary has both served as fertile ground from which to extrapolate to inscriptions—particularly Smith's research on synchronic statue-scapes—and has allowed me to compare the fates of ancient statues with those of ancient inscriptions.[3] While we can fit statues into the three main categories I have also used to organize epigraphic material (preserved, spoliated, and destroyed/erased), figural imagery had, for the most part, a very different afterlife from that of inscriptions. Here, the metaphors of "object biographies" and "afterlives" are, actually, more apt: figural imagery was either believed to have some sort of a spirit, an animating principle, to be, in some sense, "alive"—or it was tacitly treated that way. Meanwhile, inscribed text was treated primarily as document, as memento of the past, as potentially desirable or potentially offensive content, perhaps prophetic but, for the most part, not really animated itself.

We saw how these differing ontologies of statues and inscriptions resulted in diverging treatment of these two types of objects in late antiquity: statues not infrequently underwent some sort of violence, editing, neutralization, or burial, while inscriptions were only rarely erased and even more seldom still intentionally destroyed. The animating principles of statues meant that they could also be imbued with a kind of beauty that could easily result in slippage between humans and stones, as in the myth of Pygmalion and Galatea. Desirable statues were moved around and displayed in late antique cities, or taken to new places, as in the great statue migration to Constantinople. Inscriptions were not valued in the same way: they were neither collected nor moved around, except as building material. In literature, too, inscriptions are more rarely commented upon than statues: late antique hagiographies are rife with descriptions of statue destruction, but not epigraphic erasure. Inscriptions were, in fact, more often subject to erasure precisely at the point where they blur the boundary between word and image: when the name of a pagan god was prominently displayed in large letters at a noticeable spot. The name of the god was so immediately recognizable—like an image—that it required editing, even as "embedded" mentions of gods in smaller, denser, texts were left in place. In short, the physical characteristics of inscriptions, including their size, placement, and layout, contributed to the decision of whether to preserve, spoliate, or erase.

---

[3] Smith 2007.

Land, Men, and Gods

I have argued that these three potential afterlives, or we might say continued lives, of inscriptions were not random but were dependent on the actual content of the inscriptions themselves, which usually had to do with (to paraphrase the title of Stephen Mitchell's tomes) land, men, and gods—in approximately that order. As we have seen, most ancient inscriptions say very little about the gods, but a lot about land ownership, city territorial rights, taxation privileges, and the men and women who put up monuments for those gods. Stripped of their surrounding pagan ritual activity, these stones could be read in late antiquity as overwhelmingly civic, not sacred, messages memorializing great citizens, rulers, and civic undertakings from ages past. There were, of course, exceptions, and we saw in Chapters 4 and 5 strategies for dealing with unwanted pagan epigraphic material, including scrambling the stones to visually desemanticize the inscribed text and the unnaming of the gods through erasure or (probably very rarely) destroying the stone.

The recognition of this tendency to present polis and economic, rather than cult, matters at sanctuaries adds a new facet to the study of "Christianization" in the eastern Mediterranean. It was not only an additive process, of building temples and erecting crosses, but also a preservative one: keeping around older monuments that could be put to work in this new world. In many cases it was the inscriptions themselves, I propose, that facilitated the use of pagan patrimony as building blocks of the new world. As Saradi writes, "the *Lives* of saints are marked by an anti-pagan and anti-urban message"; temples are frequently portrayed as demon-haunted and dangerous.[4] Recent scholarship has often remarked upon the disconnect between these depictions and the archaeological remains, which indicate that most temples were actively preserved, peacefully abandoned, reused as churches, or taken apart for their building material. The hagiographical texts were, of course, written by biased authors and fulfilled certain expectations of the genre, including dramatic showdowns between the saint and pagans. Even so, it may seem strange that such extremes—hagiographies encouraging destruction versus frequent preservation/reuse—existed in the same cultural setting.

I propose that the texts inscribed at sanctuaries provided a counterweight to the hagiographical polemics, emphasizing instead the positive, civic, and economic history of temples and shaping cultural memory around these

---

[4] Saradi 2008: 113.

poles, rather than around religious rituals or the attributes of individual gods. When temples were allowed to "speak for themselves," they proclaimed primarily civic messages. This finding lends additional weight to other recent research on the "fate of temples," which emphasizes their nonreligious roles, including as aesthetic markers and guarantors of economic and social hierarchies. Alongside traditions passed orally from generation to generation, these inscribed texts ensured that temples continued as repositories of important historical documents and records of illustrious citizens and kings of the past. These inscriptions offered late antique populations the option to continue to view temples positively, fitting them into a local, polis-centered narrative, rather than as focal points of religious conflict.

Epigraphy: A New Direction

Perhaps one of the most surprising findings of this book is the incredibly conservationist—one might even say respectful—attitude shown toward ancient inscriptions in most parts of the late antique eastern Mediterranean. Wanton violence enacted on inscriptions is rare at the cities and sanctuaries considered here. The majority of inscriptions reused as spolia in our case studies do not show particular damage to the texts, and some building projects seem to have aimed at preserving texts, even if hidden or scrambled. Most ancient inscriptions come to us without the addition of crosses or new Christian graffiti. The occasional erasure of texts was usually directed by a literate individual, with only select parts of the inscription removed. But we need not give all the credit for the general preservation of epigraphic material only to literate late antique viewers. Both literate and illiterate individuals may have played a role in preserving ancient texts. After all, for a late antique illiterate viewer, each and every inscribed stone might have contained important historical, patriographical, hagiographical, or oracular information. Any stone might have been the epitaph of Abercius. Reading is only one way of approaching inscribed text.

We now return to Ankara one final time. As detailed in Chapter 3, the preservation of the *Res Gestae* on the walls of the Temple of Augustus and Roma should not be viewed as a happy accident, but as the result of a series of receptions and decisions, beginning in late antiquity (when the temple was first at risk of disassembly or defacement). Not only the late antique stakeholders decided in favor of the preservation of the temple and its texts.

Figure 6.1 Ankara. Temple of Augustus within the Hacı Bayram complex in 1881 or 1882. Photo: John Henry Haynes (HayAr.239 AKP160). Courtesy of Special Collections, Fine Arts Library, Harvard University.

Later residents of Ankara did too. In the early fifteenth century, when Ankara was a mercantile center in the burgeoning Ottoman empire, a Turkish holy man called Hacı (Hajj) Bayram Veli built a mosque—and he chose to build it right next to the Temple of Augustus. Hacı Bayram himself was buried in a tomb beside the mosque, as the temple was used as a medrese (religious school). The tomb of the Muslim saint and the minaret are located directly in front of the temple, and a corner of the mosque touches the temple's pronaos wall.[5] Ottoman houses were built abutting the exterior wall of the temple, obscuring but not obliterating the Greek copy of the *Res Gestae*, and Muslim graves were dug in the temple pronaos, under the Latin text. The circuit wall of the Hacı Bayram complex enclosed the temple as well as the mosque and attendant buildings, creating a single, synchronic monument of Roman, Byzantine, and Islamic heritage (Figure 6.1). Indeed, the area has even been referred to as the "Hacı Augustus" complex because of the interweaving of the site's elements.[6] The temple has more recently been declared a protected archaeological site and cleared of its Ottoman surroundings, experiencing a

---

[5] Hayden et al. 2019: 52.
[6] Hayden et al. 2019: 56.

new phase of "museumification" and—from some perspectives—an alienation from the surrounding religious context of the Hacı Bayram mosque.[7] The text of the *Res Gestae* is yet again under threat in twenty-first century Ankara, this time by pollution and the corresponding deterioration of the building's fabric. The next set of decisions about the preservation of the *Res Gestae divi Augusti* and the temple itself must soon be made.

For much of its disciplinary history, the field of Greek and Latin epigraphy has focused on getting back to the original *text* and its meaning. Only recently has a sustained interested in the "materiality of inscribed texts" appeared: the text's meaning was in many ways shaped by its physical writing-bearing, location, and contextualization with other monuments. As I hope to have demonstrated by taking an archaeological approach to epigraphy in this book, we can do even more with inscriptions. Careful attention to (and for ongoing field research, careful documentation of) findspots, evidence for later manipulation, preservation in place, and erasures can teach us much about the reception of these inscriptions and their continuing agency in shaping the world around them centuries or millennia after their original carving. The sum total of the decisions at various sites—to spoliate or not, to preserve inscriptions in place or not, to erase texts and break them up or not—is what has resulted in the field of epigraphy, and it is high time we started paying attention to it.

---

[7] Hayden et al. 2019: 152–155.

Bibliography

Journal abbreviations follow those of the Oxford Classical Dictionary

Addey, C. 2011. "Assuming the Mantle of the Gods: 'Unknowable Names' and Invocations in Late Antique Theurgic Ritual," in *Sacred Words: Orality, Literacy and Religion*, ed. A. P. M. H. Lardinois, Leiden, 279–294.

Agosti, G. 2010. "Saxa loquuntur? Epigrammi epigrafici e diffusione della *paideia* nell'oriente tardoantico," *Antiquité Tardive* 18, 163–180.

Agusta-Boularot, S. 2006. "Malalas épigraphiste? Nature et fonction des citations épigraphiques dans la *Chronique*," in *Recherches sur la Chronique de Jean Malalas* Vol. 2, ed. S. Agusta-Boularot, J. Beaucamp, A.-M. Bernardi, and E. Caire, Paris, 97–135.

Ahmad, T. 2018. *Il complesso monumentale di Baitokaike (Hoson Sulaiman—Siria)*, Oxford.

Aliquot, J. 2008. "Sanctuaries and Villages on Mt Hermon during the Roman Period," in *The Variety of Local Religious Life in the Near East in the Hellenistic and Roman Periods*, ed. T. Kaizer, Leiden, 73–96.

Allgaier, B. 2022. *Embedded Inscriptions in Herodotus and Thucydides*, Wiesbaden.

Altekamp, S. 2017. "Reuse and Redistribution of Latin Inscriptions on Stone in Post-Roman North-Africa," in *Perspektiven der Spolienforschung* Vol. 2, *Zentren und Konjunkturen der Spoliierung*, ed. S. Altekamp, C. Marcks-Jacobs, and P. Seiler, Berlin, 43–65.

Amandry, P. 1981. "Chronique delphique (1970–1981)," *BCH* 105.2, 673–769.

Anderson, B. 2011. "Classified Knowledge: The Epistemology of Statuary in the *Parastaseis Syntomoi Chronikai*," *Byzantine and Modern Greek Studies* 35, 1–19.

Anderson, B. 2016. "The Disappearing Imperial Statue: Toward a Social Approach," in *The Afterlife of Greek and Roman Sculpture: Late Antique Responses and Practices*, ed. T. M. Kristensen and L. M. Stirling, Ann Arbor, MI, 290–309.

Anderson, B. 2017. "The Defacement of the Parthenon Metopes," *GRBS* 57.1, 248–260.

Anderson, J. C. 2013. "Description of the Miniatures and Commentary," in *The Christian Topography of Kosmas Indikopleustes. Firenze, Biblioteca Medicea Laurenziana, Plut. 9.28: The Map of the Universe Redrawn in the Sixth Century*, ed. J. C. Anderson, Rome, 33–63.

Anghel, S. 2011. "Burying the Gods: Depositing Statues in Late Antiquity" (diss. Columbia University).

Anghel, S. 2012. "Living with the Past: The City and Its Philosophers in Late Antique Athens," *Zeitschrift für Religionswissenschaft* 20.1, 93–118.

Athanassiadi, P. 1991. "The Fate of Oracles in Late Antiquity: Didyma and Delphi," Δελτίον της Χριστιανικής Αρχαιολογικής Εταιρείας 15, 271–278.

Athanassiadi, P. 1992. "Philosophers and Oracles: Shifts of Authority in Late Paganism," *Byzantion* 62, 45–62.

Athanassiadi, P., ed. 1999. *Pagan Monotheism in Late Antiquity*, Oxford.

Aydaş, M. 2009. "New Inscriptions from Stratonikeia and Its Territory," *Gephyra* 6, 113–130.
Aydın, M., and C. Zoroğlu. 2016. "Ankara'da Erken Bizans Dönem Mezar Alanı Kazısı," *SEFAD* 35, 295–328.
Bagnall, R. S. 2011. *Everyday Writing in the Graeco-Roman East*, Berkeley.
Baldini, I., and E. Bazzechi. 2016. "About the Meaning of Fortifications in Late Antique Cities: The Case of Athens in Context," in *Focus on Fortifications: New Research on Fortifications in the Ancient Mediterranean and the Near East*, ed. R. Frederiksen, S. Müth, P. I. Schneider, and M. Schnelle, Oxford, 696–710.
Balkaya, Ç., Ü. Y. Kalyoncuoğlu, M. Özhanlı, G. Merter, O. Çakmak, and G. Talih. 2018. "Ground-penetrating Radar and Electrical Resistivity Tomography Studies in the Biblical Pisidian Antioch City, Southwest Anatolia," *Archaeological Prospection* 25.4, 285–300.
Barker, S. J. 2018. "The Demolition, Salvage, and Recycling Industry in Imperial Rome," *Ædificare: Revue internationale d'histoire de la construction* 4, 37–88.
Barrett, J. C. 1993. "Chronologies of Remembrance: The Interpretation of Some Roman Inscriptions," *World Archaeology* 25.2, 236–247.
Baslez, M.-F. 2020. "L'épitaphe de l'éveque Aberkios: les Écritures de foi dissimulées sous l'écriture civique," *Journal of Epigraphic Studies* 3, 149–166.
Bassett, S. 2004. *The Urban Image of Late Antique Constantinople*, Cambridge.
Battistoni, F., and P. Rothenhöfer. 2013. "Inschriften aus dem Raum Keles und Orhaneli (Provinz Bursa, Türkei)," *EA* 46, 101–165.
Bauer, F. A. 1996. *Stadt, Platz und Denkmal in der Spätantike: Untersuchungen zur Ausstattung des öffentlichen Raums in den spätantiken Städten Rom, Konstantinopel und Ephesos*, Mainz.
Bauer, F. A. 2001. "Urban Space and Ritual: Constantinople in Late Antiquity," *Acta ad archaeologiam et artium historiam pertinentia* 15, 27–61.
Bauer, F. A. 2004. *Das Bild der Stadt Rom im Frühmittelalter: Papststiftungen im Spiegel des "Liber Pontificalis" von Gregor dem Dritten bis zu Leo dem Dritten*, Wiesbaden.
Bauer, F. A., and C. Witschel, eds. 2007. *Statuen in der Spätantike*, Wiesbaden.
Baumeister, P. 2007. *Der Fries des Hekateions von Lagina. Neue Untersuchungen zu Monument und Kontext*, Istanbul.
Bayliss, R. 2004. *Provincial Cilicia and the Archaeology of Temple Conversion*, Oxford.
Bazzechi, E. 2016. "Das Stadtzentrum Athens in der Spätantike," *MDAI(A)* 129/130, 217–256.
Bean, G. E. 1966. *Aegean Turkey: An Archaeological Guide*, London.
Bean, G. E., and T. B. Mitford. 1965. *Journeys in Rough Cilicia in 1962 and 1963*, Vienna.
Beatrice, P. F. 1995. "Pagan Wisdom and Christian Theology according to the *Tübingen Theosophy*," *Journal of Early Christian Studies* 3.4, 403–418.
Beatrice, P. F. 1997. "Monophysite Christology in an Oracle of Apollo," *IJCT* 4.1, 3–22.
Belke, K. 2017. "Transport and Communication," in *The Archaeology of Byzantine Anatolia: From the End of Late Antiquity until the Coming of the Turks*, ed. P. Niewöhner, New York, 28–38.
Bell, H. W. 1916. *Sardis XI. Coins. Part I: 1910–1914*, Leiden.
Ben-Dov, J., and F. Rojas, eds. 2021. *Afterlives of Ancient Rock-Cut Monuments in the Near East: Carvings in and out of Time*, Leiden.
Benoist, S. 2004. "Titulatures impériales et damnatio memoriae: l'enseignement des inscriptions martelées," *Cahiers du Centre Gustave Glotz* 15, 175–189.

Bent, J. T. 1890. "Explorations in Cilicia Tracheia," *Proceedings of the Royal Geographical Society* 12.8, 445–463.
Berenfeld, M. L. 2009. "The Triconch House and the Predecessors of the Bishop's Palace at Aphrodisias," *AJArch.* 113.2, 203–229.
Bersani, S. G. 2003. "*Quoad stare poterunt monumenta*: Epigrafi e scrittura epigrafica in Ammiano Marcellino," in *L'uso dei documenti nella storiografia antica*, ed. A. M. Biraschi, P. Desideri, S. Roda, and G. Zecchini, Naples, 625–643.
Berti, I., K. Bolle, F. Opdenhoff, and F. Stroth, eds. 2017. *Writing Matters: Presenting and Perceiving Monumental Inscriptions in Antiquity and the Middle Ages*, Berlin.
Betz, A. 1970. "Ephesia," *Klio* 52, 27–32.
Beyazıt, M. 2016. "Aizanoi Zeus Tapınağı Duvar Yüzeylerindeki Okçu Süvari Tasvirleri," in *Aizanoi II*, ed. E. Özer, Ankara, 273–304.
Beyazıt, M. 2018. *Aizanoi III: Aizanoi Zeus Tapınağı'ndaki Türk İzleri*, Ankara.
Biraschi, A. M., P. Desideri, S. Roda, and G. Zecchini, eds. 2003. *L'uso dei documenti nella storiografia antica*, Naples.
Blanco-Perez, A. 2016. "Mên Askaenos and the Native Cults of Antioch by Pisidia," in *Between Tarhuntas and Zeus Polieus: Cultural Crossroads in the Temples and Cults of Graeco-Roman Anatolia*, ed. M. P. de Hoz, J. P. Sanchez Hernandez, and C. Molina Valero, Leuven, 117–150.
Blid, J. 2016. *Labraunda 4: Remains of Late Antiquity*, Stockholm.
Blümel, W. 1999. "Epigraphische Forschungen im westen Kariens 1997," *Araştırma Sonuçları Toplantısı* 16.1, 403–407.
Bodel, J. 2001. "Epigraphy and the Ancient Historian," in *Epigraphic Evidence: Ancient History from Inscriptions*, ed. J. Bodel, London, 1–56.
Bodel, J. 2015. "Inscriptions and Literacy," in *The Oxford Handbook of Roman Epigraphy*, ed. C. Bruun and J. Edmondson, Oxford, 745–763.
Bodenhorn, B., and G. vom Bruck. 2006. "'Entangled in Histories:' An Introduction," in *An Anthropology of Names and Naming*, ed. G. vom Bruck and B. Bodenhorn, Cambridge, 1–30.
Boeft, J. den, J. W. Drijvers, D. den Hengst, and H. Teitler. 1998. *Philological and Historical Commentary on Ammianus Marcellinus XXIII*, Leiden.
Boeye, K., and N. B. Pandey. 2018. "Augustus as Visionary: The Legend of the Augustan Altar in S. Maria in Aracoeli, Rome," in *Afterlives of Augustus, AD 14–2014*, ed. P. J. Goodman, Cambridge, 152–177.
Boldrick, S., L. Brubaker, and R. Clay. 2013. *Striking Images, Iconoclasms Past and Present*, Abingdon.
Bolle, K., C. Machado, and C. Witschel, eds. 2017. *The Epigraphic Cultures of Late Antiquity*, Stuttgart.
Botteri, P. 2018a. "L'iscrizione greca del tempio: testo, traduzione, esegesi," in *Progetto Ancyra: il tempio di Augusto e Roma ad Ankara*, ed. P. Botteri, Trieste, 41–114.
Botteri, P. 2018b. "Progetto Ancyra: presentazione," in *Progetto Ancyra: il tempio di Augusto e Roma ad Ankara*, ed. P. Botteri, Trieste, 3–39.
Bowersock, G. W. 2013. *The Throne of Adulis: Red Sea Wars on the Eve of Islam*, Oxford.
Bowes, K. 2014. "Christians in the Amphitheater? The 'Christianization' of Spectacle Buildings and Martyrial Memory," *Mélanges de l'École française de Rome—Moyen Âge* 126.1, 93–114.
Brakke, D. 2008. "From Temple to Cell, from Gods to Demons: Pagan Temples in the Monastic Topography of Fourth-Century Egypt," in *From Temple to Church: Destruction*

and Renewal of Local Cultic Topography in Late Antiquity, ed. J. Hahn, S. Emmel, and U. Gotter, Leiden, 92-113.

Bravi, L. 2006. *Gli epigrammi di Simonide e le vie della tradizione*, Rome.

Brent, A. 2019. "Has the *Vita Abercii* Misled Epigraphists in the Reconstruction of the Inscription?," in *The First Urban Churches 5: Colossae, Hierapolis, and Laodicea*, ed. J. R. Harrison and L. L. Welborn, Atlanta, 325-361.

Breytenbach, C. 1996. *Paulus und Barnabas in der Provinz Galatien. Studien zu Apostelgeschichte 13f.; 16,6; 18,23 und den Adressaten des Galaterbriefes*, Leiden.

Breytenbach, C., and C. Zimmermann. 2017. *Early Christianity in Lycaonia and Adjacent Areas: From Paul to Amphilochius of Iconium*, Leiden.

Brock, S. P. 2013. *Two Early Lives of Severos, Patriarch of Antioch*, Liverpool.

Brody, L. R. 2007. *The Aphrodite of Aphrodisias*, Mainz.

Brown, H. 2020. "Altar to Greek God Found in Wall of Byzantine Church Raises Questions," *The Jerusalem Post* Dec. 1, 2020.

Brown, P. 1978. *The Making of Late Antiquity*, Cambridge, MA.

Browning, R. 1978. "Literacy in the Byzantine World," *Byzantine and Modern Greek Studies* 4, 39-54.

Bruns Özgan, C. 2013. *Knidos. Ergebnisse der Ausgrabungen von 1996-2006*, Istanbul.

Buchwald, H. 2015. *Churches EA and E at Sardis*, Cambridge, MA.

Bumke, H. 2009. "Didyma in der Spätantike," in *ZeitRäume. Milet in Kaiserzeit und Spätantike*, ed. O. Dally, M. Maischberger, A. Schneider, and A. Scholl, Regensburg, 68-82.

Burkhardt, N. 2016. "The Reuse of Ancient Sculpture in the Urban Spaces of Late Antique Athens," in *The Afterlife of Greek and Roman Sculpture: Late Antique Responses and Practices*, ed. T. M. Kristensen and L. M. Stirling, Ann Arbor, MI, 118-149.

Burkhardt, N., and M. Wilson. 2013. "The Late Antique Synagogue in Priene: Its History, Architecture, and Context," *Gephyra* 10, 166-196.

Burrell, B. 2004. *Neokoroi: Greek Cities and Roman Emperors*, Boston.

Busine, A. 2005. *Paroles d'Apollon: pratiques et traditions oraculaires dans l'Antiquité tardive, IIe-VIe siècle*, Leiden.

Busine, A. 2012. "The Discovery of Inscriptions and the Legitimation of New Cults," in *Historical and Religious Memory in the Ancient World*, ed. B. Dignas and R. R. R. Smith, Oxford, 241-256.

Busine, A. 2013. "From Stones to Myth: Temple Destruction and Civic Identity in the Late Antique Roman East," *Journal of Late Antiquity* 6.2, 325-346.

Busine, A. 2014. "Bishop Markellos and the Destruction of the Temple of Zeus at Apamea," *Studia Patristica* 72, 219-232.

Busine, A. 2019a. "Basil and Basilissa at Ancyra: Local Legends, Hagiography, and Cult," *GRBS* 59.2, 262-286.

Busine, A. 2019b. "The Origin and Development of the Cults of Saint Gordius and Saint Mamas in Cappadocia," in *Early Christianity in Asia Minor and Cyprus: From the Margins to the Mainstream*, ed. S. Mitchell and P. Pilhofer, Leiden, 109-125.

Butterworth, G. W. 1919. *Clement of Alexandria*. Cambridge, MA.

Büyükkolancı, M. 1996. "1994 Yılı Notion Kazıları," in *VI. Müze Kurtarma Kazıları Semineri: 24—26 Nisan 1995, Didim*, ed. İ. Eroğlu, Ankara, 371-381.

Büyükkolancı, M. 2018. "Efes ve Magnesia Bizans Surlarının Yeniden Değerlendirilmesi / Dating of the Byzantine City Walls of Ephesus and Magnesia on the Maeander

Reconsidered," in *Geç Antik Çağ'da Lykos Vadisi ve Çevresi*, ed. C. Şimşek and T. Kaçar, Istanbul, 401–427.

Büyüközer, A. 2018. "The Sanctuary of Hekate at Lagina in the 4th Century BC," *Arkhaia Anatolika: The Journal of Anatolian Archaeological Studies* 1, 15–30.

Byrne, S. G. 2010. "The Athenian *Damnatio Memoriae* of the Antigonids in 200 B.C.," in *Philathenaios: Studies in Honour of Michael J. Osborne*, ed. A. Tamis, C. J. Mackie, and S. G. Byrne, Athens, 157–177.

Cahill, N. 2019. "Spotlight: The Metroön at Sardis," in *Spear-Won Land: Sardis from the King's Peace to the Peace of Apamea*, ed. A. Berlin and P. J. Kosmin, Madison, WI, 91–96.

Cahill, N., and C. H. Greenewalt Jr. 2016. "The Sanctuary of Artemis at Sardis: Preliminary Report, 2002–2012," *AJArch* 120.3, 473–509.

Cameron, A. D. E. 1993. *The Greek Anthology: From Meleager to Planudes*, Oxford.

Cameron, A. D. E. 2010. *The Last Pagans of Rome*, Oxford.

Cameron, A. M., and A. D. E. Cameron. 1966. "The Cycle of Agathias," *JHS* 86, 6–25.

Cameron, A. M., and S. G. Hall. 1999. *Eusebius. Life of Constantine*, Oxford.

Cameron, A. M., and J. Herrin. 1984. *Constantinople in the Early Eighth Century: The "Parastaseis Syntomoi Chronikai." Introduction, Translation and Commentary*, Leiden.

Canepa, M. 2015. "Inscriptions, Royal Spaces and Iranian Identity: Epigraphic Practices in Persia and the Ancient Iranian World," in *Viewing Inscriptions in the Late Antique and Medieval World*, ed. A. Eastmond, Cambridge, 10–35.

Carbon, J. M., and V. Pirenne-Delforge. 2012. "Beyond Greek 'Sacred Laws,'" *Kernos* 25, 163–182.

Carile, M. C. 2018. "Imperial Bodies and Sacred Space? Imperial Family Images between Monumental Decoration and Space Definition in Late Antiquity and Byzantium," in *Perceptions of the Body and Sacred Space in Late Antiquity and Byzantium*, ed. J. Bogdanović, London, 59–86.

Carlson, D. N., and W. Aylward. 2010. "The Kızılburun Shipwreck and the Temple of Apollo at Claros," *AJArch*. 114.1, 145–159.

Carrara, L., and I. Männlein-Robert. 2018. *Die Tübinger Theosophie. Eingeleitet, übersetzt und kommentiert*, Stuttgart.

Carroll, M. 2011. "*Memoria* and *Damnatio Memoriae*: Preserving and Erasing Identities in Roman Funerary Commemoration," in *Living through the Dead: Burial and Commemoration in the Classical World*, ed. J. E. Rempel and J. F. Drinkwater, Oxford, 65–90.

Carter, J. C. 1983. *The Sculpture of the Sanctuary of Athena Polias at Priene*, London.

Caseau, B. 2001. "ΠΟΛΕΜΕΙΝ ΛΙΘΟΙΣ: La désacralisation des espaces et des objets religieux païens durant l'antiquité tardive," in *Le sacré et son inscription dans l'espace à Byzance et en Occident: Études comparées*, ed. M. Kaplan, Paris, 61–123.

Caseau, B. 2011. "Religious Intolerance and Pagan Statuary," in *The Archaeology of Late Antique "Paganism*," ed. L. Lavan and M. Mulryan, Leiden, 479–502.

Cassibry, K. 2017. "The Tyranny of the *Dying Gaul*: Confronting an Ethnic Stereotype in Ancient Art," *The Art Bulletin* 99.2, 6–40.

Chadwick, H. 1980. *Origen. Contra Celsum*, Cambridge.

Chaisemartin, N. de, and D. Theodorescu. 2017. *Aphrodisias VIII. Le Théâtre d'Aphrodisias: Les structures scéniques*, Wiesbaden.

Chambers, A. C. 2009. "Re-Centering the Temple: The Origin and Expansion of the Decapolis Churches, 4th to 7th C. CE" (diss. Miami University).

Chaniotis, A. 1995. "Illness and Cures in the Greek Propitiatory Inscriptions and Dedications of Lydia and Phrygia," in *Ancient Medicine in Its Socio-Cultural Context*, ed. H. F. J. Horstmanshoff, P. J. van der Eijk, and P. H. Schrijvers, Leiden, 323–344.

Chaniotis, A. 2002a. "The Jews of Aphrodisias: New Evidence and Old Problems," *SCI* 21, 209–242.

Chaniotis, A. 2002b. "Zwischen Konfrontation und Interaktion: Christen, Juden, und Heiden im spätantiken Aphrodisias," in *Patchwork: Dimensionen multikultureller Gesellschaften. Geschichte, Problematik und Chancen*, ed. A. Ackermann and K. E. Müller, Bielefeld, 83–128.

Chaniotis, A. 2004. "Under the Watchful Eyes of the Gods: Divine Justice in Hellenistic and Roman Asia Minor," in *The Greco-Roman East: Politics, Culture, Society*, ed. S. Colvin, Cambridge, 1–43.

Chaniotis, A. 2005. "Ritual Dynamics in the Eastern Mediterranean: Case Studies in Ancient Greece and Asia Minor," in *Rethinking the Mediterranean.*, ed. W. V. Harris, Oxford, 141–166.

Chaniotis, A. 2008. "The Conversion of the Temple of Aphrodite at Aphrodisias in Context," in *From Temple to Church: Destruction and Renewal of Local Cultic Topography in Late Antiquity*, ed. J. Hahn, S. Emmel, and U. Gotter, Leiden, 243–273.

Chaniotis, A. 2010. "Megatheism: The Search for the Almighty God and the Competition of Cults," in *One God: Pagan Monotheism in the Roman Empire*, ed. S. Mitchell and P. Van Nuffelen, Cambridge, 112–140.

Chaniotis, A. 2011. "Graffiti in Aphrodisias: Images—Texts—Contexts," in *Ancient Graffiti in Context*, ed. J. Baird and C. Taylor, London, 191–207.

Chiabà, M. 2018. "Roma, i Galati e l'istituzione della Provincia Galatia," in *Progetto Ancyra: il tempio di Augusto e Roma ad Ankara*, ed. P. Botteri, Trieste, 115–126.

Chiricat, É. 2013. "The 'Crypto-Christian' Inscriptions of Phrygia," in *Roman Phrygia*, ed. P. Thonemann, Cambridge, 198–214.

Clark, V. A., and J. M. C. Bowsher. 1986. "The Church of Bishop Isaiah at Jerash. The Inscriptions," in *Jerash Archaeological Project 1981–1983*, ed. F. Zayadine, Amman, 303–341.

Cline, E. H. 2009. *Biblical Archaeology: A Very Short Introduction*, New York.

Cline, R. 2011a. *Ancient Angels: Conceptualising "Angeloi" in the Roman Empire*, Leiden.

Cline, R. 2011b. "Archangels, Magical Amulets, and the Defense of Late Antique Miletus," *Journal of Late Antiquity* 4.1, 55–78.

Coates-Stephens, R. 2002. "Epigraphy as Spolia: The Reuse of Inscriptions in Early Medieval Buildings," *PBSR* 70, 275–296.

Coates-Stephens, R. 2007. "The Reuse of Ancient Statuary in Late Antique Rome and the End of the Statue Habit," in *Statuen in der Spätantike*, ed. F. A. Bauer and C. Witschel, Wiesbaden, 171–187.

Connors, C. L. 1999. "The Epigram in the Church of Hagios Polyeuktos in Constantinople and Its Byzantine Response," *Byzantion* 69, 479–527.

Cooley, A., ed. 2000. *The Afterlife of Inscriptions: Reusing, Rediscovering, Reinventing & Revitalizing Ancient Inscriptions*, London.

Cooley, A. 2009. *Res Gestae Divi Augusti. Text, Translation, and Commentary*, Cambridge.

Cooley, A. 2012a. *The Cambridge Manual of Latin Epigraphy*, Cambridge.

Cooley, A. 2012b. "From Document to Monument: Inscribing Roman Official Documents in the Greek East," in *Epigraphy and the Historical Sciences*, ed. J. Davies, Oxford, 159–184.

Cormack, R. 1991. "The Wall-Painting of St. Michael in the Theater," in *Aphrodisias Papers 2. The Theater, A Sculptor's Workshop, Philosophers and Coin-Types*, ed. R. R. R. Smith and K. T. Erim, Ann Arbor, MI, 109–122.

Coşkun, A. 2014. "Neue Forschungen zum Kaiserkult in Galatien. Edition der Priester-Inschriften des Ankyraner Sebasteions (*OGIS* 533 = Bosch 51) und Revision der frühen Provinzialgeschichte," in *Der Beitrag Kleinasiens zur Kultur- und Geistesgeschichte der griechisch-römischen Antike*, ed. J. Fischer, Vienna, 35–73.

Crampa, J. 1972. *Labraunda 3.2: The Greek Inscriptions*, Lund.

Crespo Pérez, C. 2014. *La condenación al olvido (damnatio memoriae). La deshonra pública tras la muerte en la política romana (siglos I–IV d.C.)*, Madrid-Salamanca.

Dalgıç, Ö., and A. Sokolicek. 2017. "Aphrodisias," in *The Archaeology of Byzantine Anatolia: From the End of Late Antiquity until the Coming of the Turks*, ed. P. Niewöhner, New York, 269–280.

Davis, J. 2007. "Memory Groups and the State: Erasing the Past and Inscribing the Present in the Landscapes of the Mediterranean," in *Negotiating the Past in the Past*, ed. N. Yoffee, Tucson, 227–256.

De Staebler, P. D. 2008a. "The City Wall and the Making of a Late-Antique Provincial Capital," in *Aphrodisias Papers 4: New Research on the City and Its Monuments*, ed. C. Ratté and R. R. R. Smith, Portsmouth, RI, 284–318.

De Staebler, P. D. 2008b. "Re-Use of Carved Marble in the City Wall," in *Aphrodisias'tan Roma Portreleri. Roman Portraits from Aphrodisias*, ed. R. R. R. Smith, Istanbul, 184–198.

Deichmann, F. W. 1939. "Frühchristliche Kirchen in antiken Heiligtümern," *JDAI* 54, 105–229.

Deligiannakis, G. 2008. "Christian Attitudes towards Pagan Statuary: The Case of Anastasios of Rhodes," *Byzantion* 78, 142–158.

Deligiannakis, G. 2011. "Late Paganism on the Aegean Islands and Processes of Christianisation," in *The Archaeology of Late Antique "Paganism,"* ed. L. Lavan and M. Mulryan, Leiden, 311–345.

Deligiannakis, G. 2015. "Pagans, Christians and Jews in the Aegean Islands: The Christianization of an Island Landscape," in *Religious Practices and Christianization of the Late Antique City (4th–7th cent.)*, ed. A. Busine, Leiden, 188–205.

Deligiannakis, G. 2016. *The Dodecanese and East Aegean Islands in Late Antiquity, AD 300–700*, Oxford.

Deligiannakis, G. 2017. "Heresy and Late Antique Epigraphy in an Island Landscape: Exploring the Limits of the Evidence," in *The Epigraphic Cultures of Late Antiquity*, ed. K. Bolle, C. Machado, and C. Witschel, Stuttgart, 514–533.

Deligiannakis, G. 2021. "'Live Your Myth' in Athens. The Last Rebranding of Greece in the Time of the Emperor Constantine and His Successors," in *Proceedings of a Conference: Byzantine Athens, May 21–23, 2016, Byzantine and Christian Museum Athens*, ed. H. Saradi, Athens, 21–36.

Delmaire, R. 2003. "La *damnatio memoriae* au Bas-Empire à travers les textes, la législation et les inscriptions," *Cahiers du Centre Gustave Glotz* 14, 299–310.

Déroche, V. 1989. "Delphes: la christianisation d'un sanctuaire païen," *Publications de l'École française de Rome* 123.1, 2713–2723.

Destephen, S. 2010. "La christianisation de l'Asie Mineure jusqu'à Constantin: le témoignage de l'épigraphie," in *Le problème de la christianisation du monde antique*, ed. H. Inglebert, S. Destephen, and B. Dumézil, Paris, 159–194.

Destephen, S. 2019. "The Time Travelling Emperor: Hadrian's Mobility as Mirrored in Ancient and Medieval Historiography," *SCI* 38, 59–82.
Dewing, H. B. 1928. *Procopius: History of the Wars* Vol. 5, *Books 7.36–8*, Cambridge, MA.
Dey, H. W. 2015. *The Afterlife of the Roman City: Architecture and Ceremony in Late Antiquity and the Early Middle Ages*, Cambridge.
Dietrich, N. 2018. *Das Attribut als Problem. Eine bildwissenschaftliche Untersuchung zur griechischen Kunst*, Berlin.
Dietrich, N., J. Fouquet, and C. Reinhardt. 2020. *Schreiben auf statuarischen Monumenten: Aspekte materialer Textkultur in archaischer und frühklassischer Zeit*, Berlin.
Dijkstra, J. 2008. *Philae and the End of Ancient Egyptian Religion: A Regional Study of Religious Transformation (298–642 CE)*, Leuven.
Dinç, R. 1998. "Tralleis Kazısı (1996)," *Kazı Sonuçları Toplantısı* 19.2, 205–236.
Dinç, R. 2003. *Tralleis: Rehber/Guide*, Istanbul.
Dinter, M. 2013. "Inscriptional Intermediality in Latin Literature," in *Inscriptions and Their Uses in Greek and Latin Literature*, ed. P. Liddel and P. Low, Oxford, 303–316.
Djurslev, C. T. 2019. *Alexander the Great in the Early Christian Tradition*, London.
Dmitriev, S. 2018. "John Lydus' Knowledge of Latin and Language Politics in Sixth-Century Constantinople," *Byz. Zeitschr.* 111.1, 55–70.
Dodd, E. 2020. "Late Roman Viticulture in Rough Cilicia: An Unusual Wine Press at Antiochia Ad Cragum," *JRA* 33, 467–482.
Doruk, S. 1990. "The Architecture of the Temenos," in *Aphrodisias Papers: Recent Work on Architecture and Sculpture*, ed. C. Roueché and K. T. Erim, Ann Arbor, MI, 66–74.
Dow, S. 1969. *Conventions in Editing: A Suggested Reformulation of the Leiden System*, Durham, NC.
Downey, R. E. G. 1935. "References to Inscriptions in the Chronicle of Malalas," *TAPA* 66, 55–72.
Drew-Bear, T., and J. Scheid. 2005. "La copie des 'Res Gestae' d'Antioche de Pisidie," *ZPE* 154, 217–260.
Duckworth, C. N., and A. Wilson, eds. 2020. *Recycling and Reuse in the Roman Economy*, Oxford.
Duckworth, C. N., A. Wilson, A. V. Oyen, C. Alexander, J. Evans, C. Green, and D. J. Mattingly. 2020. "When the Statue Is both Marble and Lime," in *Recycling and Reuse in the Roman Economy*, ed. C. N. Duckworth and A. Wilson, Oxford, 449–459.
Duggan, T. M. P. 2019. "On Early Antiquarians in Asia Minor to the Start of the 19th Century," *Gephyra* 17, 115–167.
Dumser, E. A. 2018. "Visual Literacy and Reuse in the Architecture of Late Imperial Rome," in *Reuse and Renovation in Roman Material Culture: Functions, Aesthetics, Interpretations*, ed. D. Y. Ng and M. Swetnam-Burland, Cambridge, 140–159.
Eastmond, A., ed. 2015. *Viewing Inscriptions in the Late Antique and Medieval World*, Cambridge.
Eck, W. 2016. "Die römische Armee und der Ausbau der heißen Bäder von Hammat Gader," in *When West Met East. The Encounter of Greece and Rome with the Jews, Egyptians, and Others. Studies Presented to Ranon Katzoff in Honor of His 75th Birthday*, ed. D. M. Schaps, U. Yiftach, and D. Dueck, Trieste, 117–130.
Edgerton, W. F., ed. 1937. *Medinet Habu Graffiti: Facsimiles*, Chicago.
Ehmig, U. 2019. "Rasuren in lateinischen Inschriften. Beobachtungen zu ihrer Verbreitung und ihrem nicht-öffentlichen Gebrauch," in *Zerstörung von Geschriebenem. Historische*

und transkulturelle Perspektiven, ed. C. Kühne-Wespi, K. Oschema, and J. F. Quack, Berlin, 103–120.
Eich, A., P. Eich, and W. Eck. 2018. *Die Inschriften von Sagalassos* Part 1, Bonn.
Eichner, I. 2011. *Frühbyzantinische Wohnhäuser in Kilikien. Baugeschichtliche Untersuchung zu den Wohnformen in der Region um Seleukeia am Kalykadnos*, Tübingen.
El Daly, O. 2005. *Egyptology: The Missing Millennium. Ancient Egypt in Medieval Arabic Writing*, London.
Elliott, J. K. 1993. *The Apocryphal New Testament: A Collection of Apocryphal Christian Literature in an English Translation*, Oxford.
Elsner, J. 2004. "Late Antique Art: The Problem of the Concept and the Cumulative Aesthetic," in *Approaching Late Antiquity: The Transformation from Early to Late Empire*, ed. S. Swain and M. Edwards, Oxford, 271–309.
Elton, H., E. Equini Schneider, and D. Wannagat. 2007. *Temple to Church: The Transformation of Religious Sites from Paganism to Christianity in Cilicia*, Istanbul.
Evelyn-White, H. G. 1919. *Ausonius* Vol. 1, *Books 1–17*, Cambridge, MA.
Everett, N. 2009. "Literacy from Late Antiquity to the Early Middle Ages, c. 300–800 AD," in *The Cambridge Handbook of Literacy*, ed. D. R. Olson and N. Torrance, Cambridge, 362–385.
Eyice, S. 2002. "Thekla at Antioch," in *Actes du Ier Congres International sur Antioche de Piside*, ed. T. Drew-Bear, M. Taşlıalan, and C. M. Thomas, Lyon, 111–122.
Fabiani, R. 2016. "*I.Iasos* 220 and the Regulations about the Priest of Zeus Megistos: A New Edition," *Kernos* 29, 159–184.
Faraone, C. 2010. "Kronos and the Titans as Powerful Ancestors: A Case Study of the Greek Gods in Later Magical Spells," in *The Gods of Ancient Greece: Identities and Transformations*, ed. J. N. Bremmer and A. Erskine, Edinburgh, 388–405.
Feissel, D. 1994. "L'ordonnance du préfet Dionysios inscrite à Mylasa en Carie (1er août 480)," *Travaux et mémoires du Centre de Recherche d'Histoire et Civilisation de Byzance* 12, 263–297.
Feissel, D. 1999. "Épigraphie administrative et topographie urbaine: l'emplacement des actes inscrits dans l'Éphèse protobyzantine (IVe–VIe s.)," in *Efeso paleocristiana e bizantina / Frühchristliches und byzantinisches Ephesos*, ed. R. Pillinger, O. Kresten, F. Krinzinger, and E. Russo, Vienna, 121–132.
Feissel, D. 2004. "Un rescrit de Justinien découvert à Didymes (1er avril 533)," *Chiron* 34, 251–324.
Feissel, D. 2009. "Les actes de l'Etat impérial dans l'épigraphie tardive (324–610): prolégomènes à un inventaire 2009," in *Selbstdarstellung und Kommunikation. Die Veröffentlichung staatlicher Urkunden auf Stein und Bronze in der römischen Welt*, ed. R. Haensch, Munich, 97–128.
Feissel, D. 2010. *Documents, droit, diplomatique de l'Empire romain tardif*, Paris.
Feissel, D. 2012. "Inscriptions of Early Byzantium and the Continuity of Ancient Onomastics," in *Epigraphy and the Historical Sciences*, ed. J. Davies and J. Wilkes, Oxford, 1–14.
Feissel, D. 2016. "Les breviatica de Kasai en Pamphylie: un jugement du maître des offices sous le règne de Zénon," in *Recht haben und Recht bekommen im Imperium Romanum: das Gerichtswesen der römischen Kaiserzeit und seine dokumentarische Evidenz*, ed. R. Haensch, Warsaw, 659–737.

Feld, O., and H. Weber. 1967. "Tempel und Kirche über der Korykischen Grotte (Cennet Cehennem) in Kilikien," *Ist. Mitt.* 17, 254–278.
Ferrary, J. L. 2014. *Les mémoriaux de délégations du sanctuaire oraculaire de Claros, d'après la documentation conservée dans le fonds Louis Robert*, Paris.
Fildhuth, J. 2017. *Das byzantinische Priene. Stadt und Umland*, Wiesbaden.
Fishwick, D. 1990. "Prudentius and the Cult of Augustus," *Hist.* 39.4, 475–486.
Flower, H. I. 2006. *The Art of Forgetting: Disgrace and Oblivion in Roman Political Culture*, Chapel Hill, NC.
Focken, F. E., and M. R. Ott. 2016. "Metatexte und schrifttragende Artefakte," in *Metatexte. Erzählungen von schrifttragenden Artefakten in der alttestamentlichen und mittelalterlichen Literatur*, ed. F. E. Focken and M. R. Ott, Berlin, 1–9.
Foschia, L. 2005. "Les mythes de la fin du paganisme dans le monde grec (IIIe–VIe siècles)," in *Mythes et sociétés en Méditerranée orientale. Entre le sacré et le profane*, ed. C. Bobas, A. Muller, and D. Mulliez, Lille, 89–104.
Foss, C. 1976. *Byzantine and Turkish Sardis*, Cambridge, MA.
Foss, C. 1977. "Late Antique and Byzantine Ankara," *DOP* 31, 27–87.
Fournet, J. L. 2020. "Temples in Late Antique Egypt: Cultic Heritage between Ideology, Pragmatism, and Artistic Recycling," in *Coptic Literature in Context (4th–13th Cent.): Cultural Landscape, Literary Production and Manuscript Archaeology*, ed. P. Buzi, Rome, 29–50.
Fowden, G. 1978. "Bishops and Temples in the Eastern Roman Empire A.D. 320–435," *JTS* 29.1, 53–78.
Frank, S., and M. Ristic. 2020. "Urban Fallism: Monuments, Iconoclasm, and Activism," *City* 24, 552–564.
Fränkel, M. 1890. *Altertümer von Pergamon VIII.1: Die Inschriften von Pergamon*, Berlin.
Frantz, A. 1965. "From Paganism to Christianity in the Temples of Athens," *DOP* 19, 185–205.
Freeman, P. 2001. *The Galatian Language: A Comprehensive Survey of the Language of the Ancient Celts in Greco-Roman Asia Minor*, Lewiston, NY.
Frejman, A. 2020. "With Gods as Neighbours: Extra-Temenal Activity at Greek Rural Sanctuaries, 700–200 BCE" (diss. Uppsala University).
French, D. 2016. *Roman Roads and Milestones of Asia Minor* Vol. 4, *The Roads. Fasc. 4.1: Notes on the Itineraria*, Ankara.
Frendo, A. J. 2007. "Back to the Bare Essentials, 'Procopius' Phoenician Inscriptions: Never Lost, Not Found'—a Response," *Palestine Exploration Quarterly* 139.2, 105–107.
Frendo, J. D. C. 1975. *Agathias. The Histories*, Berlin.
Freund, S. 2006. "Christian Use and Valuation of Theological Oracles: The Case of Lactantius' Divine Institutes," *Vig. Chr.* 60.3, 269–284.
Frey, J. M. 2015a. *Spolia in Fortifications and the Common Builder in Late Antiquity*, Leiden.
Frey, J. M. 2015b. "The Archaic Colonnade at Ancient Corinth: A Case of Early Roman Spolia," *AJArch.* 119.2, 147–175.
Frey, J. M. 2019. "Spolia and the 'Victory of Christianity,'" in *The Oxford Handbook of Early Christian Archaeology*, ed. W. R. Caraher, T. W. Davis, and D. K. Pettegrew, Oxford, 257–274.
Frosh, P. 2019. "You Have Been Tagged: Magical Incantations, Digital Incarnations and Extended Selves," in *Digital Existence: Ontology, Ethics and Transcendence in Digital Culture*, ed. A. Lagerkvist, London, 117–136.

Gawlikowski, M. 2017. *Le sanctuarie d'Allat à Palmyre*, Warsaw.
Gawlinski, L. 2021. "Greek Religion and Epigraphic Corpora: What's *Sacrae* about *Leges Sacrae?*," in *Greek Epigraphy and Religion: Papers in Memory of Sara B. Aleshire from the Second North American Congress of Greek and Latin Epigraphy*, ed. E. Mackil and N. Papazarkadas, Leiden, 11–26.
Gell, A. 1998. *Art and Agency: An Anthropological Theory*, Oxford.
Genette, G. 1982. *Palimpsestes: la littérature au second degré*, Paris.
Gero, S. 1992. "The Alexander Legend in Byzantium: Some Literary Gleanings," *DOP* 46, 83–87.
Gider, Z. 2005. "Lagina'daki Dor Mimarisi" (diss. Pamukkale Üniversitesi).
Gider, Z. 2012. "Lagina Kuzey Stoanın Ön Cephe Düzenlemesi," in *Stratonikeia'dan Lagina'ya. Ahmet Adil Tırpan Armağanı*, ed. B. Söğüt, İstanbul, 263–280.
Głogowski, P. 2020. "The Epigraphic Curve in the Levant: The Case Study of Phoenicia," in *Epigraphic Culture in the Eastern Mediterranean in Antiquity*, ed. K. Nawotka, London, 166–183.
Goddard, C. 2008. "Nuovo osservazioni sul santuario cosidetto 'Siriaco' al Gianicolo," in *Culti orientali: tra scavo e collezionismo*, ed. B. Palma Venetucci, Rome, 165–174.
Görkay, K. 2012. "The Temple of Augustus and Roma in Ancyra: A Reassessment," in *Dipteros und Pseudodipteros: bauhistorische und archäologische Forschungen*, ed. T. Schulz-Brize, Istanbul, 203–218.
Graf, F. 2015. *Roman Festivals in the Greek East: From the Early Empire to the Middle Byzantine Era*, Cambridge.
Greenhalgh, M. 2016. "Travelers' Accounts of Roman Statuary in the Near East and North Africa: From Limbo and Destruction to Museum Heaven," in *The Afterlife of Greek and Roman Sculpture: Late Antique Responses and Practices*, ed. T. M. Kristensen and L. M. Stirling, Ann Arbor, MI, 330–348.
Gregg, R. C., and D. Ûrman. 1996. *Jews, Pagans, and Christians in the Golan Heights: Greek and Other Inscriptions of the Roman and Byzantine Eras*, Atlanta.
Grethlein, J. 2014. "The Value of the Past Challenged: Myth and Ancient History in the Attic Orators," in *Valuing the Past in the Greco-Roman World*, ed. C. Pieper and J. Ker, Leiden, 326–354.
Grossmann, P. 2002. *Christliche Architektur in Ägypten*, Leiden.
Gusmani, R. 1964. *Lydisches Wörterbuch. Mit Grammatischer Skizze und Inschriftensammlung*, Heidelberg.
Güven, S. 1998. "Displaying the *Res Gestae* of Augustus: A Monument of Imperial Image for All," *Journal of the Society of Architectural Historians* 57.1, 30–45.
Haake, M. 2013. "Illustrating, Documenting, Making-Believe: The Use of *Psephismata* in Hellenistic Biographies of Philosophers," in *Inscriptions and Their Uses in Greek and Latin Literature*, ed. P. Liddel and P. Low, Oxford, 79–124.
Haensch, R. 2017. "Zwei unterschiedliche epigraphische Praktiken. Kirchenbauinschriften in Italien und im Nahen Osten," in *The Epigraphic Cultures of Late Antiquity*, ed. C. Witschel, C. Machado, and K. Bolle, Stuttgart, 535–554.
Hahn, H. P. 2015. "Dinge sind Fragmente und Assemblagen: Kritische Anmerkungen zur Metapher der 'Objektbiografie,'" in *Biography of Objects: Aspekte eines kulturhistorischen Konzept*, ed. D. Boschung, P.-A. Kreuz, and T. Kienlin, Paderborn, 11–33.
Hahn, J. 2008. "The Conversion of the Cult Statues: The Destruction of the Serapeum 392 A.D. and the Transformation of Alexandria into the 'Christ-Loving' City," in

From Temple to Church: Destruction and Renewal in Local Cultic Topography in Late Antiquity, ed. J. Hahn, S. Emmel, and U. Gotter, Leiden, 335–366.

Hahn, J. 2011a. "Gesetze als Waffe? Die kaiserliche Religionspolitik und die Zerstörung der Tempel," in *Spätantiker Staat und Religiöser Konflikt. Imperiale und Lokale Verwaltung und die Gewalt gegen Heiligtümer*, ed. J. Hahn, Berlin, 201–220.

Hahn, J., ed. 2011b. *Spätantiker Staat und religiöser Konflikt. Imperiale und lokale Verwaltung und die Gewalt gegen Heiligtümer*, Berlin.

Haines-Eitzen, K. 2000. *Guardians of Letters: Literacy, Power, and the Transmitters of Early Christian Literature*, Oxford.

Hallett, C. H. 2018. "Three Bouleuteria from Roman and Late Antique Aphrodisias," in *Sculpture in Roman Asia Minor: Proceedings of the International Conference at Selcuk, 1st–3rd October 2013*, ed. M. Aurenhammer, Vienna, 353–364.

Handley, M. 2000. "Epitaphs, Models, and Texts: A Carolingian Collection of Late Antique Inscriptions from Burgundy," in *The Afterlife of Inscriptions: Reusing, Rediscovering, Reinventing & Revitalizing Ancient Inscriptions*, ed. A. Cooley, London, 47–56.

Hanfmann, G. M. A. 1964. "The Sixth Campaign at Sardis (1963)," *Bulletin of the American Schools of Oriental Research* 174, 3–58.

Hanfmann, G. M. A., and N. H. Ramage. 1978. *Sculpture from Sardis: The Finds through 1975*, Cambridge, MA.

Hannestad, N. 2001. "Castration in the Baths," in *Macellum: Culinaria Archaeologica. Robert Fleischer zum 60. Geburtstag von Kollegen, Freunden und Schülern*, ed. N. Birkle and S. Fähnrich, Mainz, 67–77.

Hardie, M. M. 1912. "The Shrine of Men Askaenos at Pisidian Antioch," *JHS* 32, 111–150.

Harmanşah, Ö. 2015. "Isis, Heritage, and the Spectacles of Destruction in the Global Media," *Near Eastern Archaeology* 78.3, 170–177.

Harper, K. 2008. "The Greek Census Inscriptions of Late Antiquity," *JRS* 98, 83–119.

Harris, E. 2015. "Toward a Typology of Greek Regulations about Religious Matters: A Legal Approach," *Kernos* 28, 53–83.

Harris, W. V. 1991. *Ancient Literacy*, Cambridge, MA.

Hayden, R., A. Erdemir, T. Tanyeri-Erdemir, T. Walker, D. Rangachari, M. Aguilar-Moreno, E. Lopez-Hurtado, and M. Bakic-Hayden. 2019. *Antagonistic Tolerance: Competitive Sharing of Religious Sites and Spaces*, London.

Heather, P. J., and D. Moncur. 2001. *Politics, Philosophy, and Empire in the Fourth Century: Select Orations of Themistius*, Liverpool.

Heberdey, R., and A. Wilhelm. 1896. *Reisen in Kilikien. Ausgeführt 1891 und 1892 im Auftrag der Kaiserlichen Akademie der Wissenschaften*, Vienna.

Hebert, L. 2000. "The Temple-Church at Aphrodisias" (diss. New York University).

Hedrick, C. W. 2000. *History and Silence: Purge and Rehabilitation*, Austin.

Heimann, F. U. M., and U. Schädler. 2014. "The Loop within Circular Three Mens Morris," *Board Game Studies* 8, 51–61.

Heineman, K. M. 2018. *The Decadence of Delphi: The Oracle in the Second Century AD and Beyond*, Abingdon.

Hellström, P., and J. Blid. 2019. *Labraunda 5: The Andrones*, Stockholm.

Hellström, P., and T. Thieme. 1982. *Labraunda 1.3: The Temple of Zeus*, Stockholm.

Hennemeyer, A. 2013. *Das Athenaheiligtum von Priene. Die Nebenbauten—Altar, Halle und Propylon—und die bauliche Entwicklung des Heiligtums*, Wiesbaden.

Henrichs, A. 2003. "'Hieroi Logoi' and 'Hierai Bibloi:' The (Un)Written Margins of the Sacred in Ancient Greece," *Harv. Stud.* 101, 207–266.

Henry, O. 2017. "Hyssaldomos'un Oğlu Hekatomnos: Pers Tarihinde Benzersiz Bir Kişilik / Hecatomnus, Son of Hyssaldomus: A Unicum in Persian History," in *Persler: Anadolu'da Kudret ve Görkem / The Persians: Power and Glory in Anatolia*, ed. K. İren, Ç. Karaöz, and Ö. Kasar, Istanbul, 350–365.

Henry, O., E. Anderson, C. Bost, Ö. Çakmaklı, F. Cederling, A. Commito, M. Cormier-Huguet, A. Coutelas, A. Dolea, D. Ergenc, A. Freccero, A. Frejman, P. Lebouteiller, F. Lesguer, D. Löwenborg, V. Lungu, F. Marchand-Baulieu, A. Sitz, P. de Staebler, and B. Vergnaud. 2016. "Labraunda 2015," *Anatolia Antiqua* 24, 339–457.

Henry, O., E. Andersson, J. Blid, C. Bost, Ö. D. Çakmaklı, N. Carless-Unwin, G. Cimen, A. Eyigör, A. Freccero, A. Frejman, C. Georgescu, E. Goussard, A.-M. Gummier-Sorbets, M. Hauchart, R. Hedlund, N. Lamare, V. Lungu, and F. Marchand-Beaulieu. 2018. "Labraunda 2017," *Anatolia Antiqua* 26, 309–320.

Henry, O., E. Andersson, C. Bost, Ö. D. Çakmaklı, A. Commito, M. Cormier-Huguet, P. de Staebler, P. Dupont, D. Ergenc, A. Frejman, B. Kepenek, P. Lebouteiller, H. Nilsson, F. Rojas, and B. Vergnaud. 2015. "Labraunda 2014," *Anatolia Antiqua* 23, 301–394.

Henry, O., and D. Aubriet. 2015. "Le territoire de Mylasa et le serment d'Olympichos: Autour d'une nouvelle inscription découverte au sanctuaire de Zeus Labraundos en Carie," in *CR Acad. Inscr.* 159.2, Paris, 673–702.

Herring-Harrington, L. 2011. "The 'Church of St. Paul' and Religious Identities in 4th-Century Pisidian Antioch," in *Building a New Rome: The Imperial Colony of Pisidian Antioch (25 BC–AD 700)*, ed. E. K. Gazda, Ann Arbor, MI, 109–130.

Hesberg, H. von. 2009. "Archäologische Charakteristika der Inschriftenträger staatlicher Urkunden—einige Beispiele," in *Selbstdarstellung und Kommunikation. Die Veröffentlichung staatlicher Urkunden auf Stein und Bronze in der römischen Welt*, ed. R. Haensch, München, 19–56.

Hild, F. 2014. *Meilensteine, Strassen und das Verkehrsnetz der Provinz Karia*, Vienna.

Hild, F., and H. Hellenkemper. 1990. *Kilikien und Isaurien*, Vienna.

Hjort, Ø. 1993. "Augustus Christianus—Livia Christiana: Sphragis and Roman Portrait Sculpture," in *Aspects of Late Antiquity and Early Byzantium*, ed. L. Rydén and J. O. Rosenqvist, Istanbul, 99–112.

Hoff, M., R. Townsend, E. Erdoğmuş, and T. Howe. 2015. "Antioch ad Cragum in Western Rough Cilicia," in *The Archaeology of Anatolia. Recent Discoveries (2011–2014)*, ed. S. R. Steadman and G. McMahon, Newcastle upon Tyne, 201–226.

Hoff, R. von den. 2011. "New Research in Aizanoi 2007–2009," in *Archaeological Research in Western Central Anatolia*, ed. A. N. Bilgen, Kütahya, 122–139.

Hölscher, U. 1954. *The Excavation of Medinet Habu* Vol. 5, *Post-Ramessid Remains*, Chicago.

Horsley, G. H. R. 1992. "The Inscriptions of Ephesos and the New Testament," *Novum Testamentum* 34.2, 105–168.

Horsley, G. H. R., and J. M. Luxford. 2016. "Pagan Angels in Roman Asia Minor: Revisiting the Epigraphic Evidence," *Anat. St.* 66, 141–183.

Horster, M. 2001. *Bauinschriften römischer Kaiser. Untersuchungen zu Inschriftenpraxis und Bautätigkeit in Städten des westlichen Imperium Romanum in der Zeit des Prinzipats*, Stuttgart.

Humann, C. 1904. *Magnesia am Maeander. Bericht über die Ergbnisse der Ausgrabungen der Jahre 1891–1893*, Berlin.

Huttner, U. 2013. *Early Christianity in the Lycus Valley*, Leiden.

Huttner, U. 2018. "Pagane Relikte in der Spätantike. Griechische Katasterinschriften als religionsgeschichtliche Quellen," in *Authority and Identity in Emerging Christianities in Asia Minor and Greece*, ed. C. Breytenbach and J. M. Ogereau, Leiden, 3–32.

Iluk, J. 2013. *Amendes sépulcrales dans les épitaphes de l'époque de l'Empire romain*, Gdańsk.

Intagliata, E. E. 2018. *Palmyra after Zenobia AD 273–750*, Oxford.

Işık, C. 2019. *Die Wandmalereien in der Grabkammer des Hekatomneions. Beobachtungen zu Figurentypen, zur Komposition, Ikonographie und zum Stil*, Bonn.

Jackson, B. 1892. *A Select Library of Nicene and Post-Nicene Fathers of the Christian Church, Second Series* Vol. 3, *The Ecclesiastical History, Dialogue, and Letters of Theodoret*, Grand Rapids, MI.

Jacobs, I. 2010. "Production to Destruction? Pagan and Mythological Statuary in Asia Minor," *AJArch*. 114.2, 267–303.

Jacobs, I. 2013. *Aesthetic Maintenance of Civic Space: The "Classical" City from the 4th to the 7th C. AD*, Leuven.

Jacobs, I. 2016. "Old Habits Die Hard: A Group of Mythological Statuettes from Sagalassos and the Afterlife of Sculpture in Asia Minor," in *The Afterlife of Greek and Roman Sculpture: Late Antique Responses and Practices*, ed. T. M. Kristensen and L. M. Stirling, Ann Arbor, MI, 93–117.

Jacobs, I. 2017. "Cross Graffiti as Physical Means to Christianize the Classical City: An Exploration of Their Function, Meaning, Topographical, and Socio-Historical Contexts," in *Graphic Signs of Power and Faith in Late Antiquity and the Early Middle Ages*, ed. I. Garipzanov, C. Goodson, and H. Maguire, Turnhout, 175–222.

Jacobs, I. 2020. "Old Statues, New Meanings. Literary, Epigraphic and Archaeological Evidence for Christian Reidentification of Statuary," *Byz. Zeitschr.* 113.3, 789–836.

Jacobs, I., and J. Richard. 2012. "'We Surpass the Beautiful Waters of Other Cities by the Abundance of Ours': Reconciling Function and Decoration in Late Antique Fountains," *Journal of Late Antiquity* 5, 3–71.

Jacobs, I., and L. Stirling. 2017. "Re-using the Gods. A 6th-c. Statuary Display at Sagalassos and a Re-evaluation of Pagan-Mythological Statuary in Early Byzantine Civic Space," *JRA* 30, 196–226.

Jacobs, I., and M. Waelkens. 2014. "Sagalassos in the Theodosian Period," in *Production and Prosperity in the Theodosian Period*, ed. I. Jacobs, Leuven, 91–126.

Jacobs, I., and M. Waelkens. 2017. "'Christians Do Not Differ from Other People': The Down-to-Earth Religious Stance of Late Antique Sagalassos," in *Die Christianisierung Kleinasiens in der Spätantike*, ed. W. Ameling, Bonn, 175–198.

James, L. 1996. "'Pray Not to Fall into Temptation and Be on Your Guard': Pagan Statues in Christian Constantinople," *Gesta* 35.1, 12–20.

Jeffery, H. 2019. "Eight Hundred Years of the Cult of the Archangels at Aphrodisias/Stauropolis: Modern and Ancient Narratives," in *Trends and Turning Points: Constructing the Late Antique and Byzantine world*, ed. M. Kinloch and A. MacFarlane, Leiden, 205–228.

Jeffreys, E., M. Jeffreys, and R. Scott. 1986. *The Chronicle of John Malalas*, Melbourne.

Jes, K., R. Posamentir, and M. Wörrle. 2010. "Der Tempel des Zeus in Aizanoi und seine Datierung," in *Aizanoi und Anatolien. Neue Entdeckungen zur Geschichte und Archäologie im Hochland des westlichen Kleinasien*, ed. K. Rheidt, Mainz, 58–87.

Jones, A. M., and N. Boivin. 2010. "The Malice of Inanimate Objects: Material Agency," in *The Oxford Handbook of Material Culture Studies*, ed. D. Hicks and M. C. Beaudry, Oxford, 333–351.
Jones, C. P. 1981. "Two Inscriptions from Aphrodisias," *Harv. Stud.* 85, 107–129.
Jones, C. P. 2005. "Ten Dedications 'To the Gods and Goddesses' and the Antonine Plague," *JRA* 18, 293–301.
Jones, C. P. 2011. "An Inscription Seen by Agathias," *ZPE* 179, 107–115.
Jones, C. P. 2012. "The Fuzziness of 'Paganism,'" *Common Knowledge* 18.2, 249–254.
Jones, C. P. 2018. "A Letter of Antoninus Pius and an Antonine Rescript Concerning Christians," *GRBS* 58.1, 67–76.
Jones, W. H. S. 1935. *Pausanias. Description of Greece* Vol. 4, Books 8.22–10, Cambridge, MA.
Jördens, A. 2018. "Festbetrieb als Wirtschaftsfaktor," *Marburger Beiträge zur antitken Handels-, Wirtschafts- und Sozialgeschichte* 36, 217–248.
Kadıoğlu, M., K. Görkay, and S. Mitchell. 2011. *Roman Ancyra*, Istanbul.
Kahlos, M. 2012. "The Shadow of the Shadow: Examining Christian Fourth and Fifth Century Depictions of Pagans," in *The Faces of the Other: Religious Rivalry and Ethnic Encounters in the Later Roman World*, ed. M. Kahlos, Turnhout, 165–195.
Kahlos, M. 2019. *Religious Dissent in Late Antiquity, 350–450*, Oxford.
Kajava, M. 2011. "Honorific and Other Dedications to Emperors in the Greek East," in *More than Men, Less than Gods: Studies in Royal Cult and Imperial Worship*, ed. P. P. Lossif, A. D. Chankowski, and C. C. Lorber, Leuven, 553–592.
Kalas, G. 2015. *The Restoration of the Roman Forum in Late Antiquity: Transforming Public Space*, Austin.
Kaldellis, A. 2008. *Hellenism in Byzantium: The Transformations of Greek Identity and the Reception of the Classical Tradition*, Cambridge.
Kaldellis, A. 2009. *The Christian Parthenon: Classicism and Pilgrimage in Byzantine Athens*, Cambridge.
Kaldellis, A. 2016. "The Forum of Constantine in Constantinople: What Do We Know about Its Original Architecture and Adornment?," *GRBS* 56.4, 714–739.
Karivieri, A. 1994. "The 'House of Proclus' on the Southern Slope of the Acropolis: A Contribution," in *Post-Herulian Athens: Aspects of Life and Culture in Athens A.D. 267–529*, ed. P. Castrén, Helsinki, 115–139.
Karlsson, L. 2010. "Labraunda 2009. A Preliminary Report on the Swedish Excavations with Contributions by Jesper Blid and Olivier Henry," *Opuscula. Annual of the Swedish Institutes at Athens and Rome* 3, 61–104.
Karlsson, L. 2011. "The Forts and Fortifications of Labraunda," in *Labraunda and Karia*, ed. L. Karlsson and S. Carlsson, Uppsala, 217–252.
Karydis, N. 2019. "The Development of the Church of St. Mary from Late Antiquity to the Dark Ages," *Anat. St.* 69, 175–194.
Kelly, G. 2003. "The New Rome and the Old: Ammianus Marcellinus' Silences on Constantinople," *CQ* 53.2, 588–607.
Khatchadourian, L. 2011. "The Cult of Mên at Pisidian Antioch," in *Building a New Rome: the Imperial Colony of Pisidian Antioch (25 BC–AD 700)*, ed. E. K. Gazda, Ann Arbor, MI, 153–172.
Kiilerich, B. 2005. "Making Sense of the Spolia in the Little Metropolis in Athens," *Arte Medievale New Series* 4, 95–114.

Kinney, D. 2011. "Ancient Gems in the Middle Ages: Riches and Ready-Mades," in *Reuse Value: Spolia and Appropriation in Art and Architecture from Constantine to Sherrie Levine*, ed. R. Brilliant and D. Kinney, Farnham, 97–120.

Klotz, D. 2010. "Triphis in the White Monastery: Reused Temple Blocks from Sohag," *Anc. Soc.* 40, 197–213.

Knoll, F., E. Reisch, and J. Keil. 1932. *Die Marienkirche in Ephesos*, Vienna.

Koenigs, W. 2015. *Der Athenatempel von Priene*, Wiesbaden.

Kolb, A., ed. 2018. *Literacy in Ancient Everyday Life*, Berlin.

Kominko, M. 2013. *The World of Kosmas: Illustrated Byzantine Codices of the Christian Topography*, Cambridge.

Köroğlu, G. 2016. "Aizanoi Kazısı'nda Gün Işığına Çıkarılan Kutsal Ekmek Mührü," in *Aizanoi II*, ed. E. Özer, Ankara, 227–245.

Köroğlu, G., İ. Filiz, K. Ferray, and E. G. Alper. 2019. "Sinop Balatlar Yapı Topluluğu Kazılarında 2010–2015 Yılları Arası Sürdürülen Çalışmalarının Genel Sonuçları," in *Uluslararası XIX. Ortaçağ ve Türk Dönemi Kazıları ve Sanat Tarihi Araştırmaları Sempozyumu II. 21–24 Ekim 2015*, ed. C. Ünal and C. Gürbıyık, Ankara, 21–38.

Köroğlu, G., F. İnanan, and E. G. Alper. 2014. "Sinop Balatlar Kilisesi Kazısı 2012 ve 2013 Yılı Çalışmaları," *Kazı Sonuçları Toplantısı* 36.1, Ankara, 511–534.

Kouremenos, A. 2022. "'The City of Hadrian and Not of Theseus:' A Cultural History of Hadrian's Arch," in *The Province of Achaea in the Second Century CE*, ed. A. Kouremenos, London, 345–374.

Kousser, R. 2017. "Mutilating Goddesses: Aphrodite in Late Antique Aphrodisias," in *Prähistorische und antike Göttinnen. Befunde—Interpretationen—Rezeption*, ed. J. K. Koch, C. Jacob, and J. Leskovar, Münster, 119–134.

Krencker, D., and M. Schede. 1936. *Der Tempel in Ankara*, Berlin.

Kristensen, T. M. 2012. "Miraculous Bodies: Christian Viewers and the Transformation of 'Pagan' Sculpture in Late Antiquity," in *Patrons and Viewers in Late Antiquity*, ed. S. Birk and B. Poulsen, Aarhus, 31–66.

Kristensen, T. M. 2013. *Making and Breaking the Gods: Christian Responses to Pagan Sculpture in Late Antiquity*, Aarhus.

Kristensen, T. M. 2019. "Statues in Late Antique Egypt: From Production and Display to Archaeological Record," in *Statues in Context: Production, Meaning and (Re)uses*, ed. A. Masson-Berghoff, Leuven, 269–280.

Kristensen, T. M., and L. M. Stirling, eds. 2016. *The Afterlife of Greek and Roman Sculpture: Late Antique Responses and Practices*, Ann Arbor, MI.

Kühne-Wespi, C., K. Oschema, and J. F. Quack, eds. 2019. *Zerstörung von Geschriebenem. Historische und transkulturelle Perspektiven*, Berlin.

Laborde, L. de. 1838. *Voyage de l'Asie mineure*, Paris.

Ladstätter, S. 2019. "The So-Called Imperial Cult Temple for Domitian in Ephesos," in *Religion in Ephesos Reconsidered*, ed. D. Schowalter, S. Ladstätter, S. J. Friesen, and C. Thomas, Leiden, 11–40.

Ladstätter, S., and J. Auinger, eds. 2009. *Neue Forschungen zur Kuretenstraße von Ephesos*, Vienna.

Laffi, U. 1971. "I terreni del tempio di Zeus ad Aizanoi," *Athenaeum* 49, 3–53.

Lambrinou, L. 2015. "Η υστερορρωμαϊκή επισκευή του Παρθενώνα και τα χρησιμοποιηθέντα σε αυτήν ελληνιστικά στωϊκά κτήρια" (diss. University of Athens).

Lanckoroński, K. 1892. *Städte Pamphyliens und Pisidiens* Vol. 2, *Pisidien*, Vienna.

Larsen, L. I., and S. Rubenson, eds. 2018. *Monastic Education in Late Antiquity: The Transformation of Classical Paideia*, Cambridge.
Latour, B. 2005. *Reassembling the Social: An Introduction to Actor-Network-Theory*, Oxford.
Laurent, J. 1899. "Delphes chrétien," *BCH* 23, 206–279.
Lauxtermann, M. 2003. *Byzantine Poetry from Pisides to Geometres: Text and Contexts* Vol. 1, Vienna.
Lavan, L. 2011a. "Introduction. The End of the Temples: Towards a New Narrative?," in *The Archaeology of Late Antique "Paganism,"* ed. L. Lavan and M. Mulryan, Leiden, xv–lxv.
Lavan, L. 2011b. "Political Talismans? Residual 'Pagan' Statues in Late Antique Public Spaces," in *The Archaeology of Late Antique "Paganism,"* ed. L. Lavan and M. Mulryan, Leiden, 439–478.
Lavan, L. 2015. "The *Agorai* of Sagalassos in Late Antiquity: An Interpretive Study," *Field Methods and Post-Excavation Techniques in Late Antique Archaeology*, ed. L. Lavan and M. Mulryan, Leiden, 289–353.
Leatherbury, S. V. 2020. *Inscribing Faith in Late Antiquity: Between Reading and Seeing*, London.
Lefebvre, S. 2004. "Les cités face à la *damnatio memoriae*: Les martelages dans l'espace urbain," *Cahiers du Centre Gustave Glotz* 15, 191–217.
Lehmann, S., and A. Gutsfeld. 2013. "Spolien und Spolisation im spätantiken Olympia," in *Sanktuar und Ritual. Heilige Plätze im archäologischen Befund*, ed. I. Gerlach and D. Raue, Berlin, 91–104.
Leone, A. 2013. *The End of the Pagan City: Religion, Economy, and Urbanism in Late Antique North Africa*, Oxford.
Lepelley, C. 2020. "Témoignages épigraphiques sur le maintien des temples et des statues des divinités dans le patrimoine et l'espace public des cités sous l'empire chrétien," *Antiquité Tardive* 28, 247–260.
Levick, B. 1970. "Dedications to Mên Askaenos," *Anat. St.* 1970, 37–50.
Liddel, P., and P. Low. 2019. "Four Unpublished Inscriptions (and One Neglected Collector) from the World Museum, Liverpool," in *From Document to History: Epigraphic Insights into the Greco-Roman World*, ed. C. F. Noreña and N. Papazarkadas, Leiden, 408–430.
Liddel, P., and P. Low, eds. 2013. *Inscriptions and Their Uses in Greek and Latin Literature*, Oxford.
LiDonnici, L. R. 1995. *The Epidaurian Miracle Inscriptions: Text, Translation and Commentary*, Atlanta.
Liuzzo, P. M. 2019. "*RIÉ* 277: An Inscription of the Time of Ptolemy II?," *Aethiopica* 22, 227–235.
Low, P. 2016. "Lives from Stone: Epigraphy and Biography in Classical and Hellenistic Greece," in *Creative Lives in Classical Antiquity: Poets, Artists and Biography*, ed. R. Fletcher and J. Hanink, Cambridge, 147–174.
Low, P. 2020. "Remembering, Forgetting, and Rewriting the Past: Athenian Inscriptions and Collective Memory," *Histos Supplement* 11, 235–268.
Lupu, E. 2005. *Greek Sacred Law. A Collection of New Documents*, Leiden.
Ma, J. 2012. "Traveling Statues, Travelling Bases? Ancient Statues in Constantinople," *ZPE* 180, 243–249.
Ma, J. 2013. *Statues and Cities: Honorific Portraits and Civic Identity in the Hellenistic World*, Oxford.

Machado, C. 2017. "Dedicated to Eternity? The Reuse of Statue Bases in Late Antique Italy," in *Epigraphic Cultures of Late Antiquity*, ed. K. Bolle, C. Machado, and C. Witschel, Stuttgart, 323–357.

MacKay, T. 1990. "Major Sanctuaries of Pamphylia and Cilicia," in *ANRW: Geschichte und Kultur Roms im Spiegel der neueren Forschung*, ed. H. Temporini and H. Wolfgang, Berlin, 2045–2124.

Macridy, T. 1905. "Altertümer von Notion," *JÖAI* 8, 155–173.

Macridy, T. 1912. "Antiquités de Notion II," *JÖAI* 16, 36–67.

Mägele, S. 2017. "Das Nachleben von Kaiserbildnissen in der Spätantike. Die kolossalen Statuen aus Sagalassos," in *Urbanitas—urbane Qualitäten. Die antike Stadt als kulturelle Selbstverwirklichung*, ed. A. W. Busch, J. Griesbach, and J. Lipps, Mainz, 433–457.

Magness, J. 2005. "The Date of the Sardis Synagogue in Light of the Numismatic Evidence," *AJArch.* 109.3, 443–475.

Mango, C. 1963. "Antique Statuary and the Byzantine Beholder," *DOP* 17, 53–75.

Mango, C. 1995. "The Conversion of the Parthenon into a Church: The Tübingen Theosophy," Δελτίον της Χριστιανικής Αρχαιολογικής Εταιρείας 18, 201–203.

Mango, C. 2015. "Some Lessons of Byzantine Epigraphy," in *Inscriptions in Byzantium and Beyond. Methods—Projects—Case Studies*, ed. A. Rhoby, Vienna, 33–38.

Maranci, C. 2015. *Vigilant Powers: Three Churches of Early Medieval Armenia*, Turnhout.

Marek, C., and E. Zingg. 2018. *Die Versinschrift des Hyssaldomos und die Inschriften von Uzunyuva (Milas/Mylasa)*, Bonn.

Marginesu, G. 2014. "Use, Re-Use and Erasure of Archaic and Classical Gortynian Inscriptions. An Archaeological Perspective," in *Cultural Practices and Material Culture in Archaic and Classical Crete*, ed. O. Pilz and G. Seelentag, Berlin, 207–218.

Mathews, T. F. 1972. *The Early Churches of Constantinople: Architecture and Liturgy*, University Park, PA.

May, N. N., ed. 2012. *Iconoclasm and Text Destruction in the Ancient Near East and Beyond*, Chicago.

Mazzoleni, D. 2015. "The Rise of Christianity," in *The Oxford Handbook of Roman Epigraphy*, ed. C. Bruun and J. Edmondson, Oxford, 445–468.

McCabe, A. 2020. "Byzantine Funerary Inscriptions on the Hephaisteion (Church of St George) in the Athenian Agora," in *Inscribing Texts in Byzantium: Continuities and Transformations.*, ed. M. D. Lauxtermann and I. Toth, London, 234–263.

McCrindle, J. W. 1897. *The Christian Topography of Cosmas, an Egyptian Monk*, London.

McDavid, A. 2016. "Renovation in the Hadrianic Baths in Late Antiquity," in *Aphrodisias Papers 5: Excavation and Research at Aphrodisias, 2006-2012*, ed. R. R. R. Smith and A. Chaniotis, Portsmouth, RI, 209–225.

McInerney, J. 2006. "On the Border: Sacred Land and the Margins of Community," in *City, Countryside, and the Spatial Organization of Value in Classical Antiquity*, ed. R. Rosen and I. Sluiter, Leiden, 33–59.

McKechnie, P. 2019. *Christianizing Asia Minor: Conversion, Communities, and Social Change in the Pre-Constantinian Era*, Cambridge.

McKenzie, J. S., S. Gibson, and A. T. Reyes. 2004. "Reconstructing the Serapeum in Alexandria from the Archaeological Evidence," *JRS* 94, 73–121.

Mendel, G. 1914. *Musées impériaux ottomans. Catalogue des sculptures grecques, romaines et byzantines*, Istanbul.

Menninga, C. 2004. "The Unique Church at Abila of the Decapolis," *Near Eastern Archaeology* 67.1, 40–49.

Mergen, Y. 2016. "Aizanoi Tapınak Kilisesi Hıristiyanlık Dönemi Grafitileri," in *Aizanoi II*, ed. E. Özer, Ankara, 247–271.
Miltner, F. 1959. "Vorläufiger Bericht über die Ausgrabungen in Ephesos," *JÖAI* 44, 315–380.
Minov, S. 2010. "The Story of Solomon's Palace at Heliopolis," *Le muséon* 123, 61–89.
Mitchell, M. M. 2008. "Looking for Abercius: Reimagining Contexts of Interpretation of the 'Earliest Christian Inscription,'" in *Commemorating the Dead: Texts and Artefacts in Context. Studies of Roman, Jewish, and Christian Burials*, ed. L. Brink and D. Green, Berlin, 303–336.
Mitchell, M. M. 2011. "The Poetics and Politics of Christian Baptism in the Abercius Monument," in *Ablution, Initiation, and Baptism: Late Antiquity, Early Judaism, and Early Christianity*, ed. D. Hellholm, T. Vegge, Ø. Norderval, and C. Hellholm, Berlin, 1743–1782.
Mitchell, M. M. 2017. *Paul and the Emergence of Christian Textuality: Early Christian Literary Culture in Context*, Tübingen.
Mitchell, S. 1977. "R.E.C.A.M. Notes and Studies No. 1: Inscriptions of Ancyra," *Anat. St.* 27, 63–103.
Mitchell, S. 1993. *Anatolia: Land, Men, and Gods in Asia Minor* Vol. 2, *The Rise of the Church*, Oxford.
Mitchell, S. 1999. "The Cult of Theos Hypsistos between Pagans, Jews, and Christians," in *Pagan Monotheism in Late Antiquity*, ed. P. Athanassiadi and M. Frede, Oxford, 81–148.
Mitchell, S. 2005. "An Apostle to Ankara from the New Jerusalem: Montanists and Jews in Late Roman Asia Minor," *SCI* 24, 1–17.
Mitchell, S. 2008. *The Imperial Temple at Ankara and the Res Gestae of the Emperor Augustus / Ankara'daki Roma İmparatorluğu Tapınağı ve İmparator Augustus'un Başarılarının Yazıtı*, Ankara.
Mitchell, S. 2017a. "Die Ausbreitung und Einbettung des Christentums in Galatien ab 325 n. Chr.," in *Die Christianisierung Kleinasiens in der Spätantike*, ed. W. Ameling, Bonn, 125–141.
Mitchell, S. 2017b. "The Christian Epigraphy of Asia Minor in Late Antiquity," in *The Epigraphic Cultures of Late Antiquity*, ed. K. Bolle, C. Machado, and C. Witschel, Stuttgart, 271–286.
Mitchell, S. 2017c. "Epigraphic Display and the Emergence of Christian Identity in the Epigraphy of Rural Asia Minor," in *Öffentlichkeit—Monument—Text. XIV Congressus Internationalis Epigraphiae Graecae et Latinae 27.-31. Augusti MMXII: Akten*, ed. W. Eck and P. Funke, Berlin, 275–297.
Mitchell, S. 2022. "Das *Monumentum Ancyranum*: Text, Gebäude, Geschichte," in *Inschriften edieren und kommentieren. Beiträge zur Editionspraxis, -methodik und -theorie*, ed. A. Eich, Berlin, 51–74.
Mitchell, S., and D. French, eds. 2012. *The Greek and Latin Inscriptions of Ankara (Ancyra)* Vol. 1, Munich.
Mitchell, S., and D. French, eds. 2019. *The Greek and Latin Inscriptions of Ankara (Ancyra)* Vol. 2, Munich.
Mitchell, S., and P. V. Nuffelen, eds. 2010. *One God: Pagan Monotheism in the Roman Empire*, Cambridge.
Mitchell, S., and M. Waelkens. 1998. *Pisidian Antioch: The Site and Its Monuments*, London.

Mitten, D. G., and A. F. Scorziello. 2008. "Reappropriating Antiquity: Some Spolia from the Synagogue at Sardis," in *In Love for Lydia: A Sardis Anniversary Volume Presented to Crawford H. Greenewalt, Jr.*, ed. N. D. Cahill, Cambridge, MA, 135–146.

Momigliano, A. 2012. *Essays in Ancient and Modern Historiography*, Chicago.

Mommsen, T. 1883. *Res Gestae divi Augusti: Ex monumentis ancyrano et apolloniensi iterum*, Berlin.

Montecalvo, M. S. 2007. "L'iscrizione di Orrippo da Megara ad Avignone e al Cabinet des médailles: storia ed interpretazioni di IG VII 52," in *Acta XII Congressus Internationalis Epigraphiae Graecae et Latinae, Provinciae Imperii Romani Inscriptionibus Descriptae (Barcelona, 3-8 Septembris 2002)*, ed. M. M. Olivé, G. Baratta, and A. G. Almagro, Barcelona, 973–982.

Moore, S. V. 2013. "A Relational Approach to Mortuary Practices within Medieval Byzantine Anatolia" (diss. Newcastle University).

Moore, W., H. A. Wilson, and H. C. Ogle. 1893. *A Select Library of Nicene and Post-Nicene Fathers of the Christian Church, Second Series* Vol. 5, *Gregory of Nyssa. Dogmatic Treatises, Etc.* New York.

Moralee, J. 2006. "The Stones of St. Theodore: Disfiguring the Pagan Past in Christian Gerasa," *Journal of Early Christian Studies* 14.2, 183–215.

Moralee, J. 2018. *Rome's Holy Mountain: The Capitoline Hill in Late Antiquity*, New York.

Moretti, J.-C., N. Bresch, I. Bonora, M. Jean-Jacques, and R. Olivier. 2016. "Claros, le temple d'Apollon: travaux réalisés en 2015," *Anatolia Antiqua* 14, 299–310.

Moser, M. 2017. "Reused Statues for Roman Friends: The Past as a Political Resource in Roman Athens," in *Strategies of Remembering in Greece under Rome (100 BC–100 AD)*, ed. T. M. Dijkstra, I. N. I. Kuin, M. Moser, and D. Weidgenannt, Leiden, 169–181.

Munro, B. 2016. "Sculptural Deposition and Lime Kilns at Roman Villas in Italy and the Western Provinces in Late Antiquity," in *The Afterlife of Greek and Roman Sculpture: Late Antique Responses and Practices*, ed. T. M. Kristensen and L. Stirling, Ann Arbor, MI, 47–67.

Murer, C. 2016. "The Reuse of Funerary Statues in Late Antique Prestige Buildings at Ostia," in *The Afterlife of Greek and Roman Sculpture: Late Antique Responses and Practices*, ed. T. M. Kristensen and L. M. Stirling, Ann Arbor, MI, 177–196.

Murer, C. 2019. "From the Tombs into the City: Grave Robbing and the Reuse of Funerary Spolia in Late Antique Italy," *Acta ad archaeologiam et artium historiam pertinentia* 30.16, 115–137.

Mylonopoulos, I. 2011. "Divine Images 'Behind Bars': The Semantics of Barriers in Greek Temples," in *Current Approaches to Religion in Ancient Greece*, ed. M. Haysom and J. Wallensten, Stockholm, 269–291.

Nasrallah, L. S. 2018. "The Formation of a Pauline Letter Collection in Light of Roman Epigraphic Evidence," in *Authority and Identity in Emerging Christianities in Asia Minor and Greece*, ed. C. Breytenbach and J. M. Ogereau, Leiden, 281–302.

Naumann, R., ed. 1979. *Der Zeustempel zu Aizanoi. Nach den Ausgrabungen von Daniel Krencker und Martin Schede*, Berlin.

Naumann, R. 1980. "Aizanoi. Bericht über die Ausgrabungen und Untersuchungen 1978," *Arch. Anz.* 1980, 123–136.

Naumann, R. 1982. "Aizanoi. Bericht über die Ausgrabungen und Untersuchungen 1979 und 1980," *Arch. Anz.* 1982, 345–382.

Nawotka, K. 2020. *Epigraphic Culture in the Eastern Mediterranean in Antiquity*, London.

Newton, C. T. 1862. *A History of Discoveries at Halicarnassus, Cnidus and Branchidae*, London.
Ng, D. Y., and M. Swetnam-Burland, eds. 2018. *Reuse and Renovation in Roman Material Culture: Functions, Aesthetics, Interpretations*, Cambridge.
Niewöhner, P. 2007. *Aizanoi, Dokimion und Anatolien. Stadt und Land, Siedlungs- und Steinmetzwesen vom späteren 4. bis ins 6. Jahrhundert n. Chr.*, Wiesbaden.
Niewöhner, P. 2010. "Aizanoi, Anatolien und der Nahe Osten. Siedlungsentwicklung, Demographie und Klima in frühbyzantinischer Zeit," in *Aizanoi und Anatolien. Neue Entdeckungen zur Geschichte und Archäologie im Hochland des westlichen Kleinasien*, ed. K. Rheidt, Mainz, 146–153.
Niewöhner, P. 2016. *Bauwerke in Milet. Die byzantinischen Basiliken von Milet*, Berlin.
Niewöhner, P. 2018. "Varietas, Spolia, and the End of Antiquity in East and West," in *Spolia Reincarnated: Afterlives of Objects, Materials, and Spaces in Anatolia from Antiquity to the Ottoman Era*, ed. I. Jevtić and S. Yalman, Istanbul, 237–257.
Niewöhner, P. 2019. "Byzantine Preservation of Ancient Monuments at Miletus in Caria: Christian Antiquarianism in Western Asia Minor," in *Die Weltchronik des Johannes Malalas im Kontext spätantiker Memorialkultur*, ed. J. Borsch, O. Gengler, and M. Meier, Stuttgart, 191–216.
Niewöhner, P., L. Audley-Miller, E. Erkul, S. Giese, S. Huy, and H. Stümpel. 2017. "An Ancient Cave Sanctuary Underneath the Theatre of Miletus: Beauty, Mutilation, and Burial of Ancient Sculpture in Late Antiquity, and the History of the Seaward Defences," *Arch. Anz.* 2016.1, 67–156.
Nollé, J. 2007. *Kleinasiatische Losorakel. Astragal- und Alphabetchresmologien der hochkaiserzeitlichen Orakelrenaissance*, Munich.
Nollé, J. 2012. "Anmerkungen zu Inschriften 1–2," *Gephyra* 7, 127–148.
Norman, A. F. 1977. *Libanius. Selected Orations Vol. 2, Orations 2, 19–23, 30, 33, 45, 47–50*, Cambridge, MA.
Nörr, D. 2012. "Der Kaiser und sein Interpret. MAMA IX p. XXXVI Sq.: Dossier über den Ager Aezanensis Iovi Dicatus," *ZSS* 129, 315–363.
Nyord, R. 2020. *Seeing Perfection: Ancient Egyptian Images beyond Representation*, Cambridge.
Öğüş, E. 2015. "A Late-Antique Fountain at Aphrodisias and Its Implications for Spoliation Practices," *JRA* 28, 302–324.
Ogus, E. 2018. "Urban Transformations at Aphrodisias in Late Antiquity: Destruction or Intentional Preservation?," in *Reuse and Renovation in Roman Material Culture: Functions, Aesthetics, Interpretations*, ed. D. Y. Ng and M. Swetnam-Burland, Cambridge, 160–185.
Oliver, J. H. 1989. *Greek Constitutions of Early Roman Emperors from Inscriptions and Papyri*, Philadelphia.
Omissi, A. 2016. "*Damnatio Memoriae* or *Creatio Memoriae*? Memory Sanctions as Creative Processes in the Fourth Century AD," *Cambridge Classical Journal* 62, 170–199.
Onur, F. 2017. "The Anastasian Military Decree from Perge in Pamphylia: Revised 2nd Edition," *Gephyra* 14, 133–212.
Osborne, J. 2017. "Counter-Monumentality and the Vulnerability of Memory," *Journal of Social Archaeology* 17.2, 163–187.
Ossi, A. J. 2016. "The Arch of Augustus at Pisidian Antioch: Reconstructing Archaeological Context through Digital Analysis of an Excavation Archive," *AJArch.* 120.3, 411–446.

Östenberg, I. 2018. "*Damnatio Memoriae* Inscribed: The Materiality of Cultural Repression," in *The Materiality of Text: Placement, Perception, and Presence of Inscribed Texts in Classical Antiquity*, ed. A. Petrovic, I. Petrovic, and E. Thomas, Leiden, 324–347.

Otten, T. 2010. "Research in Byzantine Pergamon," in *Byzanz. Das Römerreich im Mittelalter*, ed. F. Daim and J. Drauschke, Mainz, 809–830.

Ousterhout, R. G. 2019. *Eastern Medieval Architecture: The Building Traditions of Byzantium and Neighboring Lands*, New York.

Özgümüş, F. 1992. "Knidos'taki Bizans Eserleri," *Sanat Tarihi Araştırmaları Dergisi* 11, 2–17.

Özhanlı, M. 2014. "Pisidia Antiokheiası Kazısı 2013. Excavations at Pisidian Antioch in 2013," *ANMED* 12, 14–19.

Özhanlı, M. 2015. "Pisidia Antiokheia Kazısı 2014. Excavations at Pisidian Antioch in 2014," *ANMED* 13, 1–7.

Özhanlı, M. 2016. "Pisidia Antiokheia Kazısı 2015. Excavations at Pisidian Antioch in 2015," *ANMED* 14, 9–15.

Özhanlı, M. 2018. "Excavations at Pisidian Antioch in 2017. Pisidia Antiokheia Kazısı 2017," *ANMED* 16, 90–94.

Özhanlı, M., H. Alpaslan, Z. T. Güngör, E. Özen, and A. Gündoğan. 2020. "Pisidia Antiokheia 2018 Yılı Kazı ve Düzenleme Çalışmaları," *Kazı Sonuçları Toplantısı* 41.3, 181–195.

Pallis, G. 2019. "The Second Life of Inscriptions in Late Antique and Byzantine Asia Minor: Some Remarks on the Reuse of the Inscribed Material," *Gephyra* 18, 59–76.

Papalexandrou, A. 2007. "Echoes of Orality in the Monumental Inscriptions of Byzantium," in *Art and Text in Byzantine Culture*, ed. L. James, Cambridge, 161–187.

Papalexandrou, N. 2008. "Boiotian Tripods: The Tenacity of a Panhellenic Symbol in a Regional Context," *Hesp.* 77, 251–282.

Parker, R. 1983. *Miasma: Pollution and Purification in Early Greek Religion*, Oxford.

Paschoud, F. 1986. *Zosime. Histoire nouvelle* Vol. 3.1, *Livre V*, Paris.

Patrich, J. 2011. *Studies in the Archaeology and History of Caesarea Maritima: Caput Judaeae, Metropolis Palaestinae*, Leiden.

Perlman, P. J. 2004. "Writing on the Walls. The Architectural Context of Archaic Cretan Laws," in *Crete beyond the Palaces*, ed. L. P. Day, M. S. Mook, and J. D. Muhly, Philadelphia, 181–197.

Peschlow, U. 2015. *Ankara. Die bauarchäologischen Hinterlassenschaften aus römischer und byzantinischer Zeit*, Vienna.

Petrovic, A. 2007. *Kommentar zu den simonideischen Versinschriften*, Leiden.

Petrovic, A., and I. Petrovic. 2016. *Inner Purity and Pollution in Greek Religion* Vol. 1, *Early Greek Religion*, Oxford.

Petrovic, A., I. Petrovic, and E. Thomas, eds. 2019. *The Materiality of Text: Placement, Perception, and Presence of Inscribed Texts in Classical Antiquity*, Leiden.

Petzl, G. 2018. "Im Artemis-Tempel zu Sardeis. Bitte um Schatten von Säulen?," *ZPE* 208, 138–143.

Pfaff, C. A. 2018. "Late Antique Symbols and Numerals on Altars in the Asklepieion at Epidauros," *Hesp.* 87, 387–428.

Pharr, C. 1952. *The Theodosian Code and Novels and the Sirmondian Constitutions*, Princeton.

Pilhofer, P. 2018. *Das frühe Christentum im kilikisch-isaurischen Bergland. Die Christen der Kalykadnos-Region in den ersten fünf Jahrhunderten*, Berlin.

Platt, V. 2007. "'Honour Takes Wing': Unstable Images and Anxious Orators in the Greek Tradition," in *Art and Inscriptions in the Ancient World*, ed. Z. Newby and R. E. Leader-Newby, Cambridge, 247-271.

Pococke, R. 1745. *A Description of the East, and Some Other Countries* Vol. 2.2, *Observations on the Islands of the Archipelago, Asia Minor, Thrace, Greece, and Some Other Parts of Europe*, London.

Pollini, J. 2013. "The Archaeology of Destruction: Christians, Images of Classical Antiquity, and Some Problems of Interpretation," *Chaos E Kosmos* 14, 1-29.

Posamentir, R. 2020. "Latmos Herakleiası. Heracleia under Latmus," in *Karialılar, Denizcilerden Kent Kuruculara. The Carians, From Seafarers to City Builders*, ed. O. C. Henry and A. Belgin-Henry, Istanbul, 446-465.

Poulou-Papadimitriou, N., E. Tsavelli, and J. Ott. 2012. "Burial Practices in Byzantine Greece: Archaeological Evidence and Methodological Problems for Its Interpretation," in *Rome, Constantinople and Newly-Converted Europe. Archaeological and Historical Evidence*, ed. M. Salamon, M. Wołoszyn, A. Musin, and P. Špehar, Leipzig, 377-428.

Proietti, G. 2019. "La Stele dei Megaresi caduti durante la seconda guerra persiana," *Axon* 3, 31-48.

Pucci Ben Zeev, M. 1995. "Josephus, Bronze Tablets and Greek Inscriptions," *Ant. Class.* 64, 211-215.

Pullan, R. 1881. "Mr. Pullan's Report on the Excavations at Priene," in *Antiquities of Ionia* Part 4, ed. Society of the Dilettanti, London, 28-30.

Quatember, U. 2017. *Der Sogenannte Hadrianstempel an der Kuretenstrasse*, Vienna.

Quatember, U. 2019. "The Bouleuterion Court of Aphrodisias in Caria: A Case Study of the Adaptation of Urban Space in Asia Minor from the Roman Imperial Period to Late Antiquity and Beyond," *Ist. Mitt.* 69, 59-102.

Raeck, W., A. Filges, and I. H. Mert. 2020. *Priene von der Spätklassik bis zum Mittelalter: Ergebnisse und Perspektiven der Forschungen seit 1998*, Bonn.

Raff, K. A. 2011. "Architecture of the Sanctuary of Mên Askaênos: Exploration, Reconstruction, and Use," in *Building a New Rome: The Imperial Colony of Pisidian Antioch (25 BC-AD 700)*, ed. E. K. Gazda, Ann Arbor, MI, 131-152.

Ragette, F. 1980. *Baalbek*, London.

Ramsay, W. M. 1882. "Les trois villes phrygiennes Brouzos, Hiéropolis et Otrous," *BCH* 6, 503-520.

Ramsay, W. M. 1883. "The Cities and Bishoprics of Phrygia," *JHS* 4, 370-436.

Ramsay, W. M. 1897. *The Cities and Bishoprics of Phrygia: Being an Essay of the Local History of Phrygia from the Earliest Time to the Turkish Conquest* Vol. 1.2, *West and West-Central Phrygia*, Oxford.

Ramsay, W. M. 1912. "The Tekmoreian Guest-Friends," *JHS* 32, 151-170.

Ramsay, W. M., and A. von Premerstein. 1927. *"Monumentum antiochenum," die neugefundene Aufzeichnung der "Res gestae Divi Augusti" im pisidischen Antiochia*, Leipzig.

Rapp, C. 2000. "Mark the Deacon: *Life of St. Porphyry of Gaza*," in *Medieval Hagiography: An Anthology*, ed. T. Head, London, 53-75.

Rapp, C. 2011. "Hagiography and the Cult of Saints in the Light of Epigraphy and Acclamations," in *Byzantine Religious Culture: Studies in Honor of Alice-Mary Talbot*, ed. D. Sullivan, E. A. Fisher, and S. Papaioannou, Leiden, 291-311.

Ratté, C., F. Rojas, and A. Commito. 2020. "Notion Archaeological Survey 2017-2018," *Araştırma Sonuçları Toplantısı* 37.1, Ankara, 333-353.

Rautman, M. 2011. "Sardis in Late Antiquity," in *Archaeology and the Cities of Asia Minor in Late Antiquity*, ed. D. Ortwin and C. Ratté, Ann Arbor, MI, 1–25.

Rautman, M. 2017. "Sardis," in *The Archaeology of Byzantine Anatolia: From the End of Late Antiquity until the Coming of the Turks*, ed. P. Niewöhner, Oxford, 231–237.

Remijsen, S. 2015. *The End of Greek Athletics in Late Antiquity*, Cambridge.

Reynolds, J. M. 1982. *Aphrodisias and Rome: Documents from the Excavation of the Theatre at Aphrodisias Conducted by Kenan T. Erim; Together with Some Related Texts*, London.

Reynolds, J. M. 1990. "Inscriptions and the Building of the Temple of Aphrodite," in *Aphrodisias Papers: Recent Work on Architecture and Sculpture*, ed. C. Roueché and K. T. Erim, Ann Arbor, MI, 37–40.

Reynolds, J. M. 1991. "Epigraphic Evidence for the Construction of the Theatre: 1st C. B.C. to the Mid 3rd C. A.D," in *Aphrodisias Papers 2: The Theatre, a Sculptor's Workshop, Philosophers and Coin-Types*, ed. R. R. R. Smith and K. T. Erim, Ann Arbor, MI, 15–28.

Rheidt, K. 1995. "Aizanoi: Bericht über die Ausgrabungen und Untersuchungen 1992 und 1993," in *Arch. Anz.* 1995, 696–715.

Rheidt, K. 1997. "Römischer Luxus—Anatolisches Erbe," *Antike Welt* 28, 479–499.

Rheidt, K. 2001. "Die Ausgrabungen und Forschungen 1997 bis 2000," *Arch. Anz.* 2001, 241–267.

Rheidt, K. 2003. "Archäologie und Spätantike in Anatolien. Methoden, Ergebnisse und Probleme der Ausgrabungen in Aizanoi," in *Die spätantike Stadt und ihre Christianisierung*, ed. G. Brands and H. G. Severin, Wiesbaden, 239–247.

Rhoby, A. 2014. *Byzantinische Epigramme auf Stein: Nebst Addenda zu den Bänden 1 und 2*, Vienna.

Rhodes, P. J. 2007. "Documents and the Greek Historians," in *A Companion to Greek and Roman Historiography*, ed. J. Marincola, Hoboken, NJ, 43–52.

Rhodes, P. J. 2018. "Erasures in Greek Public Documents," in *The Materiality of Text: Placement, Perception, and Presence of Inscribed Texts in Classical Antiquity*, ed. A. Petrovic, I. Petrovic, and E. Thomas, Leiden, 145–166.

Rives, J. 1995. "Human Sacrifice among Pagans and Christians," *JRS* 85, 65–85.

Robert, L. 1969. "Les inscriptions," in *Laodicée du Lycos: le nymphée. Campagnes 1961–1963*, ed. J. Des Gagniers, P. Devambez, L. Kahil, and R. Ginouvès, Paris, 247–364.

Robert, L. 1980. *A travers l'Asie Mineure. Poètes et prosateurs, monnaies grecques, voyageurs et géographie*, Paris.

Robert, L., and J. Robert. 1989. *Claros I: décrets hellénistiques*, Paris.

Roberto, U. 2015. "La memoria inquietante del tiranno: la mancanza di castità/Sophrosyne di Ottaviano Augusto nel dibattito politico tardoantico," in *Il bimillenario augusteo*, ed. G. Cuscito, Trieste, 123–140.

Robertson Brown, A. 2016. "Hellenic Heritage and Christian Challenge: Conflict over Panhellenic Sanctuaries in Late Antiquity," in *Violence in Late Antiquity: Perceptions and Practices*, ed. H. A. Drake, Burlington, VT, 309–319.

Robertson, N. 2013. "The Concept of Purity in Greek Sacred Laws," in *Purity and the Forming of Religious Traditions in the Ancient Mediterranean World and Ancient Judaism*, ed. C. Frevel and C. Nihan, Leiden, 195–243.

Robinson, D. M. 1926. "The Deeds of Augustus as Recorded on the *Monumentum Antiochenum*," *AJPhil.* 47, 1–54.

Robu, A. 2020. "Le cult des héros dans l'antiquité tardive autour des épigrammes de Mégare *IG* VII 52–53," in *Théories et pratiques de la prière à la fin de l'antiquité*, ed. P. Hoffmann and A. Timotin, Turnhout, 39–60.

Roels, E. J. J. 2018. "The Queen of Inscriptions Contextualized: The Presence of Civic Inscriptions in the *Pronaos* of Ancient Temples in Hellenistic and Roman Asia Minor (Fourth Century BCE–Second Century CE)," in *Sacred Thresholds: The Door to the Sanctuary in Late Antiquity*, ed. E. M. van Opstall, Leiden, 221–253.

Rojas, F. 2017. "Archaeophilia: A Diagnosis and Ancient Case Studies," in *Antiquarianisms: Contact, Conflict, Comparison*, ed. B. Anderson and F. Rojas, Oxford, 8–30.

Rojas, F. 2019. *The Pasts of Roman Anatolia: Interpreters, Traces, Horizons*, Cambridge.

Rojas, F. In progress. "Urartian Inscriptions and Local Identities in Late Antique and Early Medieval Armenia."

Rojas, F., and J. Ben-Dov. 2021. "Introduction," in *Afterlives of Ancient Rock-Cut Monuments in the Near East: Carvings in and out of Time*, ed. J. Ben-Dov and F. Rojas, Leiden, 1–38.

Rolfe, J. C. 1939. *Ammianus Marcellinus: History* Vol. 3, Books 27–31, Cambridge, MA.

Romer, F. E. 1998. *Pomponius Mela's Description of the World*, Ann Arbor, MI.

Rose, C. B. 1997. *Dynastic Commemoration and Imperial Portraiture in the Julio-Claudian Period*, Cambridge.

Roueché, C. M. 1989. *Aphrodisias in Late Antiquity: The Late Roman and Byzantine Inscriptions Including Texts from the Excavations at Aphrodisias Conducted by Kenan T. Erim*, London.

Roueché, C. M. 1991. "Inscriptions and the Later History of the Theater," in *Aphrodisias Papers 2: The Theatre, a Sculptor's Workshop, Philosophers and Coin-Types*, ed. R. R. R. Smith and K. T. Erim, Ann Arbor, MI, 99–108.

Roueché, C. M. 1993. *Performers and Partisans at Aphrodisias in the Roman and Late Roman Periods: A Study Based on Inscriptions from the Current Excavations at Aphrodisias in Caria*, London.

Roueché, C. M. 2002. "The Image of Victory: New Evidence from Ephesus," in *Mélanges Gilbert Dagron*, ed. V. Déroche, Paris, 527–546.

Roueché, C. M. 2004. "Aphrodisias in Late Antiquity: The Late Roman and Byzantine Inscriptions, Revised Second Edition," http://insaph.kcl.ac.uk/ala2004/.

Roueché, C. M. 2007. "From Aphrodisias to Stauropolis," in *Wolf Liebeschuetz Reflected: Essays Presented by Colleagues, Friends, & Pupils*, ed. J. F. Drinkwater and R. W. B. Salway, London, 183–192.

Roueché, C. M. 2009. "The *Kuretenstrasse*: The Imperial Presence in Late Antiquity," in *Neue Forschungen zur Kuretenstrasse von Ephesos*, ed. S. Ladstätter, J. Auinger, and I. Kowalleck, Vienna, 155–169.

Roueché, C. M. 2014. "Using Civic Space: Identifying the Evidence," in *Öffentlichkeit—Monument—Text. XIV Congressus Internationalis Epigraphiae Graecae et Latinae 27.-31. Augusti MMXII: Akten*, ed. W. Eck and P. Funke, Berlin, 135–158.

Rous, S. 2019. *Reset in Stone: Memory and Reuse in Ancient Athens*, Madison, WI.

Rubin, B. 2011. "Ruler Cult and Colonial Identity: The Imperial Sanctuary at Pisidian Antioch," in *Building a New Rome: The Imperial Colony of Pisidian Antioch (25 BC–AD 700)*, ed. E. K. Gazda, Ann Arbor, MI, 33–60.

Ruggieri, V. 2005. *La Caria Bizantina: topografia, archeologia ed arte (Mylasa, Stratonikeia, Bargylia, Myndus, Halicarnassus)*, Soveria Mannelli.

Ruggieri, V. 2008. "Annotazioni in margine alla trasformazione del tempio in chiesa in ambito rurale: il caso di Lagina in Caria," *Bizantinistica: Rivista di Studi Bizantini e Slavi* 2007, 73–99.

Ruggieri, V. 2011. "In margine a Mylasa (Milas) bizantina: disjecta membra," *Orientalia christiana periodica* 77, 503–531.
Rumscheid, F. 1999. "Vom Wachsen antiker Säulenwälder. Zu Projektierung und Finanzierung antiker Bauten in Westkleinasien und Anderswo," *JDAI* 114, 19–63.
Rumscheid, F. 2004. "Der Tempel des Augustus und der Roma in Mylasa. Eine kreative Mischung östlicher und westlicher Architektur," *JDAI* 119, 131–178.
Rumscheid, F. 2010. "Maussolos and the Uzunyuva in Mylasa: An Unfinished Proto-Maussolleion at the Heart of a New Urban Center?," in *Hellenistic Karia*, ed. R. Van Bremen and J.-M. Carbon, Talence, 69–102.
Rüpke, J. 2018. *Pantheon: A New History of Roman Religion*, tran. D. M. B. Richardson, Princeton.
Russell, B. 2013. "Roman and Late-Antique Shipwrecks with Stone Cargoes: A New Inventory," *JRA* 26, 331–361.
Sage, M. 2000. "Roman Visitors to Ilium in the Roman Imperial and Late Antique Period: The Symbolic Functions of a Landscape," *Studia Troica* 10, 211–231.
Şahin, H. 2012. "Korykion Antron'daki Tapınak Zeus Tapınağı Mıdır?," *Adalya* 15, 65–79.
Şahin, H., F. A. Yüksel, and Z. Görücü. 2010. "Korykion Antron ve Göztepesi: Eski Problemler, Yeni Bulgular, Yeni Çözüm Önerileri," *Adalya* 13, 65–89.
Şahın, M. Ç. 2010. *Die Inschriften von Stratonikeia* Vol. 3, Bonn.
Saliou, C. 2017. "Toposinschriften. Écriture et usages de l'espace urbain," *ZPE* 202, 125–154.
Saliou, C. 2019. "Espace urbain et mémoire des empereurs en Orient dans l'Antiquité Tardive," in *Sprachen—Schriftkulturen—Identitäten der Antike. Beiträge des XV. Internationalen Kongresses für Griechische und Lateinische Epigraphik, Wien, 28. August bis 1. September 2017*, ed. F. Beutler and T. Pantzer, Vienna. DOI: https://doi.org/10.25365/wbagon-2019-1-19
Samuel, A. E. 1972. *Greek and Roman Chronology: Calendars and Years in Classical Antiquity*, Munich.
Saradi, H. 1997. "The Use of Ancient Spolia in Byzantine Monuments: The Archaeological and Literary Evidence," *IJCT* 3, 395–423.
Saradi, H. 2006. *The Byzantine City in the Sixth Century: Literary Images and Historical Reality*, Athens.
Saradi, H. 2008. "The Christianization of Pagan Temples in the Greek Hagiographical Texts," in *From Temple to Church: Destruction and Renewal of Local Cultic Topography in Late Antiquity*, ed. J. Hahn, S. Emmel, and U. Gotter, Leiden, 113–134.
Saradi, H., and D. Eliopoulos. 2011. "Late Paganism and Christianisation in Greece," in *The Archaeology of Late Antique "Paganism,"* ed. L. Lavan and M. Mulryan, Leiden, 261–310.
Saradi-Mendelovici, H. 1990. "Christian Attitudes toward Pagan Monuments in Late Antiquity and Their Legacy in Later Byzantine Centuries," *DOP* 44, 47–61.
Sauer, E. W. 2003. *The Archaeology of Religious Hatred in the Roman and Early Medieval World*, Stroud.
Scheid, J. 2007. *Res gestae divi Augusti. Hauts faits du divin Auguste*, Paris.
Schmidt, S. G. 2001. "Worshipping the Emperor(s): A New Temple of the Imperial Cult at Eretria and the Ancient Destruction of Its Statues," *JRA* 14, 113–142.
Schmitz, P. C. 2007. "Procopius' Phoenician Inscriptions: Never Lost, Not Found," *Palestine Exploration Quarterly* 139.2, 99–104.

Schörner, H. 2014. "Revival of Intraurban Burial in Greek *Poleis* during the Roman Imperium as a Creation of Identity," in *Attitudes towards the Past in Antiquity: Creating Identities*, ed. B. Alroth and C. Scheffer, Stockholm, 151–162.

Schott, J. M. 2019. *Eusebius of Caesarea. The History of the Church: A New Translation*, Oakland.

Schulz, T. 2010. "Die Gebälk- und Dachkonstruktion des Zeustempels," in *Aizanoi und Anatolien. Neue Entdeckungen zur Geschichte und Archäologie im Hochland des westlichen Kleinasien*, ed. K. Rheidt, Mainz, 88–97.

Schuster, R. 2017. "Major Early Christian Church Found in Israeli Town of Beit Shemesh," *Haaretz* Dec. 20, 2017. https://www.haaretz.com/archaeology/MAGAZINE-major-early-christian-church-found-in-israeli-town-of-beit-shemesh-1.5629204.

Seeliger, H. R., and W. Wischmeyer. 2015. *Märtyrerliteratur. Herausgegeben, übersetzt, kommentiert und eingeleitet*, Berlin.

Seferis, G. 1974. *Days of 1945–1951: A Poet's Journal*, tran. A. Anagnostopoulos, Cambridge, MA.

Sergueenkova, V., and F. Rojas. 2017. "Asianics in Relief: Making Sense of Bronze and Iron Age Monuments in Classical Anatolia," *CJ* 112.2, 140–178.

Serin, U. 2011. "Late Antique and Byzantine Ankara: Topography and Architecture," in *Marmoribus vestita: miscellanea in onore di Federico Guidobaldi*, ed. F. Guidobaldi, O. Brandt, and P. Pergola, Vatican City, 1257–1280.

Serin, U. 2014. "Bizans Ankarası ve Kaybolan Bir Kültür Mirası: 'St. Clement' Kilisesi," *METU Journal of the Faculty of Architecture* 2, 65–92.

Serin, U. 2018. "Ankara and the Temple of Rome and Augustus in the Late Antique, Byzantine and Turkish Periods," in *Progetto Ancyra: il Tempio di Augusto e Roma ad Ankara*, ed. P. Botteri, Trieste, 335–378.

Shear, J. 2007. "Reusing Statues, Rewriting Inscriptions and Bestowing Honours in Roman Athens," in *Art and Inscriptions in the Ancient World*, ed. Z. Newby and R. Leader-Newby, Cambridge, 221–246.

Shear, J. 2020. "An Inconvenient Past in Hellenistic Athens: The Case of Phaidros of Sphettos," *Histos Supplement* 11, 269–301.

Shepardson, C. 2019. *Controlling Contested Places: Late Antique Antioch and the Spatial Politics of Religious Controversy*, Oakland, CA.

Sherwin-White, S. M. 1985. "Ancient Archives: The Edict of Alexander to Priene, a Reappraisal," *JHS* 105, 69–89.

Simić, K. 2018. "The Byzantine Augustus: The Reception of the First Roman Emperor in the Byzantine Tradition," in *Afterlives of Augustus, AD 14–2014*, ed. P. J. Goodman, Cambridge, 122–137.

Şimşek, C. 2018. "Geç Antik Çağ'da Laodikeia. Laodikeia in the Late Antiquity," in *Geç Antik Çağ'da Lykos Vadisi ve Çevresi. The Lykos Valley and Neighbourhood in Late Antiquity*, ed. C. Şimşek and T. Kaçar, Istanbul, 81–116.

Sitz, A. M. 2019a. "Beyond Spolia: A New Approach to Old Inscriptions in Late Antique Anatolia," *AJArch*. 123.4, 643–674.

Sitz, A. M. 2019b. "Hiding in Plain Sight: Epigraphic Reuse in the Temple-Church at Aphrodisias," *Journal of Late Antiquity* 12.1, 136–168.

Sitz, A. M. 2019c. "Inscribing Caria: The Perseverance of Epigraphic Traditions in Late Antiquity," in *Early Christianity in Asia Minor and Cyprus: From the Margins to the Mainstream*, ed. S. Mitchell and P. Pilhofer, Leiden, 202–225.

Sitz, A. M., and D. Delibaş. 2022. "La zone du bâtiment tétraconque et le cimetière byzantin," Section in O. Henry et al. "Labraunda 2019." *Anatolia Antiqua* 30: 83–120.

Slater, N. 2009. "Reading Inscriptions in the Ancient Novel," in *Readers and Writers in the Ancient Novel*, ed. M. Paschalis, S. Panayotakis, and G. Schmeling, Groningen, 64–78.

Sloan, M. C. 2018. "Augustus, the Harbinger of Peace: Orosius' Reception of Augustus in *Historiae Adversus Paganos*," in *Afterlives of Augustus, AD 14–2014*, ed. P. J. Goodman, Cambridge, 103–121.

Slusser, M. 1998. *St. Gregory Thaumaturgus: Life and Works*, Washington, DC.

Smith, R. R. R. 1990. "Late Roman Philosopher Portraits from Aphrodisias," *JRS* 80, 127–155.

Smith, R. R. R. 2002. "The Statue Monument of Oecumenius: A New Portrait of a Late Antique Governor from Aphrodisias," *JRS* 92, 134–156.

Smith, R. R. R. 2007. "Statue Life in the Hadrianic Baths at Aphrodisias, AD 100–600: Local Context and Historical Meaning," in *Statuen in der Spätantike*, ed. F. A. Bauer and C. Witschel, Wiesbaden, 203–235.

Smith, R. R. R. 2012. "Defacing the Gods at Aphrodisias," in *Historical and Religious Memory in the Ancient World*, ed. B. Dignas and R. R. R. Smith, Oxford, 283–326.

Smith, R. R. R. 2013. *The Marble Reliefs from the Julio-Claudian Sebasteion*, Mainz.

Smith, R. R. R. 2018. "Aphrodisias 2016," *Kazı Sonuçları Toplantısı* 39.2 Ankara, 263–283.

Smith, R. R. R., and C. Ratté. 1995. "Archaeological Research at Aphrodisias in Caria, 1993," *AJArch.* 99.1, 33–58.

Smith, R. R. R., and B. Ward-Perkins, eds. 2016. *Last Statues of Antiquity*, Oxford.

Söğüt, B. 2008. "*Naiskoi* from the Sacred Precinct of Lagina Hekate: Augustus and Sarapis," in *Cult and Sanctuary through the Ages (From the Bronze Age to the Late Antiquity)*, ed. M. Novotná, Trnava, 421–431.

Söğüt, B. 2011. "The Sarapis Relief from Lagina," in *Roman Sculpture in Asia Minor*, ed. F. D'Andria and I. Romeo, Ann Arbor, MI, 294–301.

Söğüt, B. 2018. "Geç Antik Çağ'da Stratonıkeia (Stratonikeia in Late Antiquity)," in *Geç Antik Çağ'da Lykos Vadisi ve Çevresi (The Lykos Valley and Neighbourhood in Late Antiquity)*, ed. C. Şimşek and T. Kaçar, Istanbul, 429–458.

Söğüt, B. 2019. *Stratonikeia (Eskihisar) ve Kutsal Alanları*, Istanbul.

Sokolowski, F. 1969. *Lois sacrées des cités grecques*, Paris.

Speiser, J. M. 1976. "La christianisation des sanctuaires païens en Grèce," in *Neue Forschungen in griechischen Heiligtümern*, ed. U. Jantzen, Tübingen, 309–320.

Spielberg, L. 2019. "Monumental Absences in Ancient Historiography," *Trends in Classics* 11.1, 51–73.

Stein, A. 1931. *Römische Inschriften in der antiken Literatur*, Prague.

Steskal, M. 2010. *Das Prytaneion in Ephesos*, Vienna.

Stevenson, T. 2007. "What Happened to the Zeus of Olympia?," *Ancient History Bulletin* 21.1-4, 65–88.

Stewart, P. 2007. "Continuity and Tradition in Late Antique Perception of Portrait Statuary," in *Statuen in der Spätantike*, ed. F. A. Bauer, Wiesbaden, 27–43.

Stewart, P. 2012. "The Equestrian Statue of Marcus Aurelius," in *A Companion to Marcus Aurelius*, ed. M. Van Ackeren, Malden, MA, 264–277.

Stirling, L. M. 2016. "Shifting Use of a Genre: A Comparison of Statuary Décor in Homes and Baths of the Late Roman West," in *The Afterlife of Greek and Roman Sculpture: Late Antique Responses and Practices*, ed. T. M. Kristensen and L. M. Stirling, Ann Arbor, MI, 265–289.

Stoneman, R. 2008. *Alexander the Great: A Life in Legend*, New Haven.
Sturm, J. P. 2016. "The Afterlife of the Hephaisteion: The *Interpretatio Christiana* of an Ancient Athenian Monument," *Hesp.* 85.4, 795–825.
Sundermeyer, A. 2020. "Interpretations and Reuse of Ancient Egyptian Hieroglyphs in the Arabic Period (Tenth–Sixteenth Centuries CE)," in *The Oxford Handbook of Egyptian Epigraphy and Paleography*, ed. V. Davies and D. Laboury, Oxford, 176–192.
Sweetman, R. J. 2010. "The Christianization of the Peloponnese: The Topography and Function of Late Antique Churches," *Journal of Late Antiquity* 3, 203–261.
Sweetman, R. J. 2015. "Memory, Tradition, and Christianization of the Peloponnese," *AJArch.* 119, 501–531.
Takács, S. A. 2007. "Divine and Human Feet: Records of Pilgrims Honouring Isis," in *Pilgrimage in Graeco-Roman and Early Christian Antiquity: Seeing the Gods*, ed. J. Elsner and I. Rutherford, Oxford, 353–370.
Talbot, A. M., and S. F. Johnson. 2012. *Miracle Tales from Byzantium*, Cambridge, MA.
Talloen, P. 2007. "Test Soundings in the Sanctuary of Apollo Klarios," *Kazı Sonuçları Toplantısı* 28.2, Ankara, 327–330.
Talloen, P. 2015. *Cult in Pisidia: Religious Practice in Southwestern Asia Minor from Alexander the Great to the Rise of Christianity*. Turnhout.
Talloen, P. 2018. "Rolling the Dice: Public Game Boards from Sagalassos," *Herom* 7.1–2, 97–132.
Talloen, P. 2019. "The Rise of Christianity at Sagalassus," in *Early Christianity in Asia Minor and Cyprus*, ed. S. Mitchell and P. Pilhofer, Leiden, 164–201.
Talloen, P., and J. Poblome. 2016. "The 2014 and 2015 Control Excavations on and around the Upper Agora of Saglassos: The Structural Remains and General Phasing," *Anatolica* 42, 111–150.
Talloen, P., and L. Vercauteren. 2011. "The Fate of Temples in Late Antique Anatolia," in *The Archaeology of Late Antique "Paganism,"* ed. L. Lavan and M. Mulryan, Leiden, 347–388.
Tanaseanu-Döbler, I., and L. von Alvensleben, eds. 2020. *Athens II: Athens in Late Antiquity*, Tübingen.
Tanoulas, T. 2020. "The Acropolis in Late Antiquity," in *Athens II: Athens in Late Antiquity*, ed. I. Tanaseanu-Döbler and L. von Alvensleben, Tübingen, 83–121.
Tantillo, I. 2017. "La trasformazione del paesaggio epigrafico nelle città dell'Africa romana, con particolare riferimento al caso di Leptis Magna (Tripolitana)," in *The Epigraphic Cultures of Late Antiquity*, ed. K. Bolle, C. Machado, and C. Witschel, Stuttgart, 213–270.
Taşlıalan, M. 2002. "Excavations at the Church of St. Paul," in *Actes du Ier Congrès international sur Antioche de Pisidie*, ed. T. Drew-Bear, M. Taşlıalan, and C. M. Thomas, Lyon, 9–32.
Taşlıalan, M. 2013. "1981–2001 Yılları Arasında Pisidia Antiocheia'asında Yapılan Çalışmalar," in *Pisidia Araştırmaları I. Sempozyum Bildiri Kitabı (05–06.11.2012)*, ed. B. Hürmüzlü,. M. Fırat, and A. Gerçek, Isparta, 108–141.
Tentori Montalto, M. 2017. *Essere primi per il valore. Gli epigrammi funerari greci su pietra per i caduti in guerra (VII–V sec. a.C.)*, Rome.
Themelis, P. 2004. "Η Πρωτοβυζαντινή Βασιλική," in *Πρωτοβυζαντινή Ελεύθερνα*, ed. P. Themelis, Athens, 46–63.
Thonemann, P. 2007. "Estates and the Land in Late Roman Asia Minor," *Chiron* 37, 435–478.

Thonemann, P. 2012a. "Abercius of Hierapolis: Christianization and Social Memory in Late Antique Asia Minor," in *Historical and Religious Memory in the Ancient World*, ed. B. Dignas and R. R. R. Smith, Oxford, 257–282.

Thonemann, P. 2012b. "Alexander, Priene, and Naulochon," in *Epigraphical Approaches to the Post-Classical Polis*, ed. P. Martzavou and N. Papazarkadas, Oxford, 23–36.

Thonemann, P. 2012c. "A Copy of Augustus' *Res Gestae* at Sardis," *Hist.* 61, 282–288.

Thonemann, P. 2015. "The Martyrdom of Ariadne of Prymnessos and an Inscription from Perge," *Chiron* 45, 151–170.

Thür, H. 1999. "Die spätantike Bauphase der Kuretenstraße," in *Efeso paleocristiana e bizantina / Frühchristliches und byzantinisches Ephesos*, ed. R. Pillinger, O. Kresten, F. Krinzinger, and E. Russo, Vienna, 104–120.

Tırpan, A. A., Z. Gider, and A. Büyüközer. 2012. "The Temple of Hekate at Lagina," in *Dipteros und Pseudodipteros: bauhistorische und archäologische Forschungen*, ed. T. Schulz-Brize, Istanbul, 181–202.

Tırpan, A. A., and B. Söğüt. 2005. *Lagina*, Yatagan, Mugla.

Tırpan, A. A., and B. Söğüt. 2010. "Lagina, Börkükçü, Belentepe ve Mengefe 2008 Yılı Çalışmaları," in *Kazı Sonuçları Toplantısı* 31.3, Ankara, 505–527.

Toth, I., and E. Rizos. 2016. "Abstract. Consecrated to God, Written for the Salvation of His People: The Agency of Normative Epigraphy Across Space and Time," in *Proceedings of the 23rd International Congress of Byzantine Studies: Round Tables, Belgrade, 22–27 August 2016*, ed. B. Krsmanović, L. Milanović, and B. Pavlović, Belgrade, 911–914.

Tougher, S. 2018. "Julian Augustus on Augustus: Octavian in the Caesars," in *Afterlives of Augustus, AD 14–2014*, ed. P. J. Goodman, Cambridge, 87–102.

Trombley, F. R. 1993. *Hellenic Religion and Christianization c. 370–529*, 2 vols., Leiden.

Tsafrir, Y., and G. Foerster. 1997. "Urbanism at Scythopolis-Bet Shean in the Fourth to Seventh Centuries," *DOP* 51, 85–146.

Tül, Ş., and M. Aydaş. 2011. "Mesogis Üstündeki Larisa-Derira-Siderus," *Ege Defterleri* 2, 3–17.

Tyrell, E. 2020. *Strategies of Persuasion in Herodotus' "Histories" and Genesis-Kings: Evoking Reality in Ancient Narratives of a Past*, Leiden.

Tzavella, E. 2012. "Urban and Rural Landscape in Early and Middle Byzantine Attica (4th–12th c. AD)" (diss. University of Birmingham).

Tzifopoulos, Y. 2013. "Inscriptions as Literature in Pausanias' Exegesis of Hellas," in *Inscriptions and Their Uses in Greek and Latin Literature*, ed. P. Liddel and P. Low, Oxford, 149–165.

Unwin, N. C., and O. Henry. 2016. "A New Olympichos Inscription from Labraunda: I.Labraunda 137," *EA* 49, 27–45.

Usherwood, R. 2015. "Merited Oblivion: 'Damnatio Memoriae' and the Constantinian Dynasty" (diss. University of Nottingham).

Usherwood, R. 2022. *Political Memory and the Constantinian Dynasty: Fashioning Disgrace*, London.

Usta, E. N. 2018. "Revealing and Restrengthening the Relation of Memory Places and Heritage Places: The Case of the Hisarbaşı Neighborhood in Milas" (diss. Middle East Technical University).

Vaes, J. 1986. "Christliche Wiederverwendung antiker Bauten. Ein Forschungsbericht," *Anc. Soc.* 17, 305–443.

Van Bremen, R. 2010. "The Inscribed Documents on the Temple of Hekate at Lagina and the Date and Meaning of the Temple Frieze," in *Hellenistic Karia*, ed. R. Van Bremen and J.-M. Carbon, Talence, 483–503.
Van Dam, R. 2018. "Inscriptions," in *A Companion to Late Antique Literature*, ed. S. McGill and E. J. Watts, Hoboken, NJ, 505–521.
Varner, E. R. 2004. *Mutilation and Transformation: Damnatio Memoriae and Roman Imperial Portraiture*, Leiden.
Vassiliev, A. 1893. *Anecdota graeco-byzantina: Pars prior*, Moscow.
Vassiliki, G.-R., and de L. Nicolas, eds. 2019. *La sculpture et ses remplois*, Bordeaux.
Venturi, R., D. Scott Brown, and S. Izenour. 1972. *Learning from Las Vegas*, Boston.
Verlinde, A. 2015. *The Roman Sanctuary Site at Pessinus: From Phrygian to Byzantine Times*, Leuven.
Vinzent, M. 2019. *Writing the History of Early Christianity: From Reception to Retrospection*, Cambridge.
Waelkens, M. 1997. "The 1994 and 1995 Excavation Seasons at Sagalassos," in *Sagalassos IV: Report on the Survey and Excavation Campaigns of 1994 and 1995*, ed. M. Waelkens and J. Poblome, Leuven, 103–216.
Waldner, A. 2020. *Die Chronologie der Kuretenstrasse. Archäologische Evidenzen zur Baugeschichte des unteren Embolos von Ephesos von der lysimachischen Neugründung bis in die byzantinische Zeit*, Vienna.
Walser, G., ed. 1987. *Die Einsiedler Inschriftensammlung und der Pilgerführer durch Rom "Codex Einsidlensis 326": Facsimile, Umschrift, Übersetzung und Kommentar*, Stuttgart.
Ward-Perkins, B. 2011. "The End of Temples: An Archaeological Problem," in *Spätantiker Staat und Religiöser Konflikt. Imperiale und locale Verwaltung und die Gewalt gegen Heiligtümer*, ed. J. Hahn, Berlin, 187–200.
Watt, J. W., and F. R. Trombley. 2000. *The Chronicle of Pseudo-Joshua the Stylite*, Liverpool.
Watts, E. 2005. "Winning the Intracommunal Dialogues: Zacharias Scholasticus' *Life of Severus*," *Journal of Early Christian Studies* 13.4, 437–464.
Welch, K. 1998. "The Stadium at Aphrodisias," *AJArch.* 102.3, 547–569.
Westerfeld, J. T. 2012. "Saints in the Caesareum: Remembering Temple-Conversion in Late Antique Hermopolis," in *Memory and Urban Religion in the Ancient World*, ed. M. Bommas, J. Harrisson, and P. Roy, London, 59–86.
Westerfeld, J. T. 2019. *Egyptian Hieroglyphs in the Late Antique Imagination*, Philadelphia.
Westphalen, S. 1998. "Die Basilika von Priene. Architektur und liturgische Ausstattung," *Ist. Mitt.* 48, 279–340.
Westphalen, S. 2000. "The Byzantine Basilica at Priene," *DOP* 54, 275–280.
Westphalen, S. 2006. "Studien zur frühbyzantinischen Bauornamentik im Rauhen Kilikien: Diokaisareia/Uzuncaburç," *Ist. Mitt.* 56, 391–405.
Wharton, A. J. 1995. *Refiguring the Post Classical City: Dura Europos, Jerash, Jerusalem, and Ravenna*, Cambridge.
Whitby, M. 2006. "The St. Polyeuktos Epigram (*AP* 1.10): A Literary Perspective," in *Greek Literature in Late Antiquity: Dynamism, Didacticism, Classicism*, ed. S. F. Johnson, Aldershot, 159–187.
Wiedergut, K. 2018. "Wider die Inflationshypothese: Zur Höhe der Bußgelder in Grabinschriften aus dem ostlykischen Olympos," *EA* 51, 147–163.
Wiegand, T. 1924. *Achter vorläufiger Bericht über die von den Staatlichen Museen in Milet und Didyma unternommenen Ausgrabungen*, Berlin.

Wiemer, H.-U., and D. Kah. 2011. "Die Phrygische Mutter im hellenistischen Priene: Eine neue Diagraphe und Verwandte Texte," *EA* 44, 1–54.
Wilfong, T. 2002. *Women of Jeme: Lives in a Coptic Town in Late Antique Egypt*, Ann Arbor, MI.
Wilhelm, A. 1899. "Simonideische Gedichte," *JÖAI* 2, 221–244.
Williamson, C. G. 2013. "Civic Producers at Stratonikeia: The Priesthoods of Hekate at Lagina and Zeus at Panamara," in *Cities and Priests: Cult Personnel in Asia Minor and the Aegean Islands from the Hellenistic to the Imperial Period*, ed. M. Horster and A. Klöckner, Berlin, 209–246.
Wilson, A. 2018. "Earthquakes at Aphrodisias," in *Visual Histories of the Classical World*, ed. C. M. Draycott, R. Raja, K. E. Welch, and W. T. Wootton, Turnhout, 469–488.
Wilson, A. 2019. "Aphrodisias in the Long Sixth Century," in *Asia Minor in the Long Sixth Century: Current Research and Future Directions*, ed. I. Jacobs and H. Elton, Oxford, 197–223.
Wilson, J. F. 2006. "The 'Statue of Christ' at Banias: A Saga of Pagan-Christian Confrontation in 4th Century Syro-Palestine," *ARAM* 18, 1–11.
Winand, J. 2020. "When Classical Authors Encountered Egyptian Epigraphy," in *The Oxford Handbook of Egyptian Epigraphy and Paleography*, ed. V. Davies and D. Laboury, Oxford, 163–175.
Wirbelauer, E. 2002. "Aberkios, der Schüler des reinen Hirten, im Römischen Reich des 2. Jahrhunderts," *Hist.* 51, 359–382.
Wischmeyer, W. 1980. "Die Aberkiosinschrift als Grabepigramm," *Jahrbuch für Antike und Christentum* 23, 22–47.
Wiśniewski, R. 2016. "Pagan Temples, Christians and Demons in the Late Antique East and West," *Sacris Erudiri* 54, 111–128.
Wiśniewski, R. 2020. *Christian Divination in Late Antiquity*, Amsterdam.
Witschel, C. 2007. "Statuen auf Spätantiken Platzanlagen in Italien und Africa," in *Statuen in der Spätantike*, ed. F. A. Bauer and C. Witschel, Wiesbaden, 113–169.
Wood, J. 2014. "Suetonius and the *De Vita Caesarum* in the Carolingian Empire," in *Suetonius the Biographer: Studies in Roman Lives*, ed. T. Power and R. K. Gibson, Oxford, 273–291.
Wörrle, M. 1995a. "Inschriftenfunden von Der Hallenstraßengrabung in Aizanoi 1992," *Arch. Anz.* 1995, 719–727.
Wörrle, M. 1995b. "Neue Inschriftenfunde aus Aizanoi II: Das Problem der Ära von Aizanoi," *Chiron* 25, 63–82.
Xagorari-Gleißner, M. 2008. *Die Göttermutter bei den Griechen*, Mainz.
Xenaki, M. 2016. "Les inscriptions byzantines datées du Parthénon (VIIe–XIIe siècles)," in *Inscriptions in the Byzantine and Post-Byzantine History and History of Art*, ed. C. Stavrakos, Wiesbaden, 233–252.
Xenaki, M. 2020. "The (In)Formality of the Inscribed Word at the Parthenon: Legibility, Script, Content," in *Inscribing Texts in Byzantium: Continuities and Transformations*, ed. M. D. Lauxtermann and I. Toth, London, 211–233.
Yasin, A. M. 2000. "Displaying the Sacred Past: Ancient Christian Inscriptions in Early Modern Rome," *IJCT* 7, 39–57.
Yasin, A. M. 2015. "Prayers on Site: The Materiality of Devotional Graffiti and the Production of Early Christian Sacred Space," in *Viewing Inscriptions in the Late Antique and Medieval Worlds*, ed. A. Eastmond, Cambridge, 36–60.

Yegül, F. 2014. "A Victor's Message: The Talking Column of the Temple of Artemis at Sardis," *Journal of the Society of Architectural Historians* 73.2, 204–225.

Yegül, F. 2020. *The Temple of Artemis at Sardis*, Cambridge, MA.

Zachos, K. 2003. "The Tropaeum of the Sea-Battle of Actium at Nikopolis: Interim Report," *JRA* 16, 64–92.

Zadorojnyi, A. 2013. "Shuffling Surfaces: Epigraphy, Power, and Integrity in the Graeco-Roman Narratives," in *Inscriptions and Their Uses in Greek and Latin Literature*, ed. P. Liddel and P. Low, Oxford, 365–386.

Zadorojnyi, A. 2018. "The Aesthetics and Politics of Inscriptions in Imperial Greek Literature," in *The Materiality of Text: Placement, Perception, and Presence of Inscribed Texts in Classical Antiquity*, ed. A. Petrovic, I. Petrovic, and E. Thomas, Leiden, 48–68.

Zavagno, L. 2017. *Cyprus between Late Antiquity and the Early Middle Ages (ca. 600–800): An Island in Transition*, London.

Zenos, A. C. 1890. *A Select Library of Nicene and Post-Nicene Fathers of the Christian Church*, Second Series Vol. 2, *The Ecclesiastical History of Socrates Scholasticus*, New York.

Zwierlein-Diehl, E. 2007. *Antike Gemmen und ihr Nachleben*, Berlin.

Index

For the benefit of digital users, indexed terms that span two pages (e.g., 52–53) may, on occasion, appear on only one of those pages.

Figures are indicated by *f* following the page number

Abdul Hamid (Ottoman sultan), 53–55
Abercius. See *Life of Abercius (Vita Abercii)*
Aberkios. See *Life of Abercius (Vita Abercii)*
Abila (Qweilbeh, Jordan), 152–53
Account of the Logia about the Lord. See Papias, bishop of Hierapolis
Achaemenids, 4–6
Acts, 42, 47, 50–51, 52–53, 135, 248
Acts of Paul and Thekla, 252–53
Adulis (Zula, Eritrea), 38–40, 41–43, 105
Aegina, island of, 148–49, 164n.56
Aelia Flaccilla, 74–75
Aeneas, 44n.60, 226–27
Agamemnon, 43–44
Agathias of Myrina, 34–38, 43–45, 66–67, 144
  epigrams, 32–33, 35
  Histories, 35, 37–38, 58
  reading/copying inscriptions, 20, 37–39, 58, 70, 266–67
Aizanoi (Çavdarhisar), Phrygia, 62–63, 115–17, 119–20, 144
  Byzantine burials, 112n.164
  erasure of inscriptions, 22–23, 236, 237–247 *passim*, 259–60, 261–63, 269–70
  Säulenstraße, 117, 236–37, 238–41, 259–60, 262–63
  Temple of Artemis, 236–37, 238*f*, 261–62
  Temple of Zeus, 113–16, 119–20, 144–45, 236, 257–58
    conversion, 102, 117, 119–20, 121–22, 236
    excavation, 95

Aksumite kingdom, 38–39
Alexander the Great, 64–65, 77–79, 144, 210*f*, 268–69
  Alexander Romance, 28–29, 83–84
  Arch of Alexander (fictional inscription), 28–30
  invasion of Asia Minor, 51–52
  in late antiquity, 83–84, 92–93
  "Temple of Alexander," 47–48
  violence against statue of, 209–11, 210*f*
Alexandria, 9, 48–49
  Asklepiodotos, 173–74
  Caesareum, 263
  Kosmas Indikopleustes, 38–39
  Serapeion, 11–12, 47–48, 79–81, 134–35, 208–9
Alexandros, son of Antonios, 56, 57*f*, 58–59, 60–62
Allat-Athena statue, Palmyra, 79–81, 121, 211
alpha and omega, 71–72, 81–82, 211–12, 223–24
Altar of the Chians, Delphi, 94–95, 94*f*
Altar of Victory, Curia in Rome, 69–70, 143
Ambrose, bishop of Milan, 69–70
Ammianus Marcellinus (historian), 20, 31–32, 34–35, 106–7, 134–35, 266–67
  prophetic inscriptions, 45–46, 153–54
amulets, 141–42, 260–61
Anatolia, 26–27, 96–98, 265
  "Asianic" ancestors, 66–67
  erasure of inscriptions, 221–22
  inscribing texts onto architecture, 86–87, 125–26, 177–78
  Kybele (goddess), 51, 207–8

312 INDEX

Anatolia (cont.)
  lack of crypts underneath church apses, 98–100
  languages, 6–7, 19, 125–26, 190–91
  Latin texts, 111
  literacy, 17–18
  Marcus Aurelius names, 160–63
  reuse of buildings, 102
  tombstones, 59n.106, 60–62
Ancyra/Ankyra. See Ankara
Andron A. See Labraunda
angels, cult of, 175–76, 182–83, 204, 214–15, 227–28
Ankara (Ancyra/Ankyra), 95–113 passim, 144–45, 268–69, 270–71, 274–76. See Res Gestae divi Augusti; Temple of Augustus and Roma
  Christian misreading, 221–22
  "direct transformation," 121–22
  Giorgos Seferis' visit, 265
anonymizing spaces and gods, 202–5, 207–8, 240–41. See also unnaming gods
Anthologia Palatina, 32–33
Antioch ad Cragum, 22–23, 112n.164, 241–42, 242f, 243–45, 247, 259–60, 269–70
Antioch in Pisidia. See Pisidian Antioch
Antioch on the Orontes, 9–10, 46, 113n.165, 260–61, 263
Antiochos III, Seleukid king, 90–92, 188–90, 197–98
Antoninus Pius (emperor), 33–34, 119–20, 122–24, 225–26
  letters from, 31n.18, 62–63, 115–16, 144, 236
  Temple of, 104–5, 166
Apamea (Syria). See Temple of Zeus
Aphrodisias, 22–23, 85–86, 180–82, 185
  Archive Wall, 245–46, 261–62
  change of name, 182–83, 260–61, 262, 263
  cult of angels, 204, 214–15
  erasure, 222–30, 228f, 247, 259–60
    circumspective, 236, 237–38, 244–45, 257–58, 259, 269
    desirability of older texts, 196, 231, 269
    as official sanction, 245–46, 261–62
  pagan gods and priests, 22–23, 261–62, 269–70
  philosophers and historical figures, 209–11, 210f
  tolerance, 226–30, 231–33, 238–40
  inscriptions/graffiti, 17–18, 71–72, 144, 172–74, 180
  mixed population of Christians, Jews, and pagans, 173–74, 175–76
  relief of Herakles, 200
  Sebasteion, 104–5, 172, 212
  temple maintenance and reuse, 72n.9
  Temple of Aphrodite, 172–84 passim, 195–96, 197–98, 227–30, 271
Apollo Delios, 170–71, 196–97
apotropaic habits, 141–42, 180–81, 200
appropriating, 13–14, 70, 165–66, 204–5
  architectural elements, 24–25, 81–82, 147–48, 151–52
  inscriptions, 56–58, 62, 64–66, 95, 267–68
  for triumphalist Christian narrative, 4–6, 10
  statues/statue bases, 79–81, 204–5
  temples, 173–76, 182, 227–28, 249, 253–54
    courtyard, 138
    imperial cult, 104–5
Arabia, 38–39, 41–42
Aramaic inscriptions, 24–25, 120, 121, 143
Arcadius (emperor), 12–13, 103–4
Arch of Alexander. See Alexander the Great
Arch of Constantine, 20–21
Arch of Hadrian, 92–93
Arch of Septimius Severus. See Septimius Severus
archaeophilia, 34, 122–28, 187–88
Archelaos I, king of Kappadokia, 158–60
architectural violence. See violence
Archive Wall at Aphrodisias, 182, 224–26, 231–32, 245–46, 261–62
Areopagus, 209–11
  council of the, 115–16
Ares (god of war), 41–42, 171–72, 200
"Asianic" ancestors, 66–67
Artemis Leukophryene, festival of, 88–89

INDEX 313

Artemis Orthosia, altar of, 150–51
Artemision. *See* Temple of Artemis
Asklepiodotos of Alexandria, 173–74
Asklepios, 16–17, 70–71, 165–66, 204–5
Athena Promachos, 92–93
Aurelius, bishop of Carthage, 48

Baalbek/Heliopolis, Lebanon, 9, 22, 183–85, 196
  Temple of Jupiter Heliopolitanus, 183–84, 185
Bactria, 41
Baitokaike (Hosn Soleiman, Syria), 90–93, 144–45
Balatlar Kilesesi in Sinope, 102
baths, 11, 33–34, 100n.103, 102, 165–66, 212, 225–26
Battle of Plataia, 67–68
Bêt Djaluk temple, Phoenice (Syria), 117
Beth Shemesh, Israel, 110–11
bilingual texts, 24–25, 120, 121, 126–27, 256–57
Bosphoros, 14, 31–32, 202
Bostra (Syria), 154–55
boustrophedon inscriptions, 18–19
Burdur Museum, 221–22, 222*f*, 269–70

Caesarea (Kayseri), Cappadocia, 239–40
Caesarea Maritima, Palaestina, 104–5, 215–16
Caligula (emperor), 170–71
Capitoline Museum, Rome, 261–62
Caracalla (emperor), 33–34, 48, 160–63, 184, 218–19
Carthage, 45–48, 60–62
caryatids, 214–15
Çavdar graffiti, 116–17, 257–58
Celtic names, 109–10
ceramics, 72–73, 133–34, 192n.142
Chalcedon, 28, 45–46, 66–67, 70, 153–54
  Council of, 58–60
Chi-Rho, 15–16, 71–72, 81–82, 94–95, 260–61
"Christianization," 26–27, 145, 220–21, 266–67, 273
  Alexandria, 47–48, 134–35
  Aphrodisias, 172–74
  markers of, 222–23, 231–32
  period of, 72–73, 95

  resistance to, 2–3, 126–27
  Sardis, 122–24
Christian Topography, 38–39, 40*f*
Christian triumphalism, 13–14, 22, 147–48, 152–53, 184, 195, 211–12, 249–50
  Gerasa, 4–6, 22, 149–51
  Priene, 150–51
Chronicle of Pseudo-Zachariah Rhetor, 185
Chronicon. *See* Eusebius of Caesarea
Chronographia. *See* John Malalas
Chrysanthios (philosopher), 126–28
Church of Bishop Isaiah, Gerasa, 152–53
Church of Christ-in-Jerusalem, Kalymnos, 196–97
Church of Mary, Ephesos, 151–52, 170–71, 256–57
Church of St. Clement, Ankara, 101–2
Church of St. Theodore, Gerasa, 149–50, 152–53, 184
Church of the Dormition, Merbaka, 200–1
Circus Maximus, Rome, 31–32, 34–35
Clement of Alexandria, 9
Clifftop Temple. *See* Korykian Cave Clifftop Temple
Codex Theodosianus, 12–14, 82–83, 93–94, 145
coins, 60–62, 122–24, 213–14
  as basis for dating, 100n.103, 122–24, 128–30, 175, 211, 248–49
  countermarking, 218
  image on, 188–90, 215, 260–61
Commodus (emperor), 33–34, 48, 122–24, 255–56
Constantine (emperor), 10, 12–13, 18–19, 96–98, 183–84
  appropriating statues, 14, 31–32, 67, 79–81, 199–200, 206–8, 263
  conversion of, 23–24, 128
  dedications to, 94–95, 111
Constantinople, 23–24, 25–26, 45, 96–100, 104–5, 202
  Council of, 248
  erasures and unnaming, 262, 263
  Goths, 43n.57, 153–54
  Hagios Polyeuktos in, 32–33, 98–100
  literacy, 17–18
  reading ancient inscriptions, 32, 67
  statues, 67–68, 73, 79–81, 182, 207–8, 253n.162, 257–58, 272

Constantius II (emperor), 12–13, 69–70, 106–7, 143
Constantius Chlorus (emperor), 76
Coptic
    monks, 139
    writings, 9, 19, 24–25, 135–37, 138–39, 203
Corstopitum (Corbridge, UK), 255–56
Council of Chalcedon. *See* Chalcedon
Council of Constantinople, 248
Council of Ephesos, 151–52, 256–57
"counter-monumentality," 258–59
Crete, 90–92, 185, 200
cross graffiti. *See* graffiti
cultural memory, 202, 203, 258–59, 273–74
Cyprus, 41, 160–63, 248, 259–60
Cyriacus of Ancona, 85–86

damnatio memoriae, 22–23, 76, 87–88, 202–3, 218–23, 260–63, 269–70. *See also* erasures
    Domitian, 44n.60, 113, 218–19, 257–58
    Nero, 218–19, 238–39, 260n.183, 262–63
Daniel, 42–43, 105
Darius I, stelai of, 150–51
De Genio Socratis, 51–52
decapitation of sculptures, 145–46, 209–11
Decapolis, 152–53
defacement, 246–47, 274–76
    of figural images, 122–24, 138–39, 173–74, 186, 209–11, 213–14, 216–17
    of inscriptions, 109, 116–17, 149–50, 230, 243n.132, 247–48, 261–62
    through addition of crosses, 86n.62, 257–58, 261–62
Delphi, 3–4, 21–22, 24–25, 51–52, 93–95, 145
    statues removed from, 67–68, 93–94
demons, 9–10, 56–58, 109–10, 173–74, 203, 259–60, 273
    exorcising, 8–9, 10, 63–64, 76, 257
Dendara, Egypt, 216
desacralization, 12–13, 17, 89–90, 94–95, 166
desemanticization, 239–40, 273
dice oracles. *See* oracles

Didyma, 48–49, 51–52, 93–94, 140–42, 143–44, 151–52
digamma (F), 19, 32, 67–68
Diocese of the Oriens, 11
Dio Chrysostom, 205–6
Diocletian (emperor), 76, 79–81, 88–89, 151–52
Diokaisareia-Olba (Uzuncaburç), 22, 85–86, 121–22, 144–45
Dionysos, 31–32, 139–40, 151–52, 165–66
    Dionysiac imagery, 166, 204–5
"direct transformations," 11, 121–22
Domitian (emperor), 44n.60, 113, 218–19, 256–58
donor inscriptions, 14, 16–17, 176–77, 256–57, 271
    on columns, 125–26, 177–78, 182
    on floor mosaic, 152–53, 228–30
    in synanogue, 191, 195–96
    unnaming of, 22–23, 179–80, 225–26, 232–33
Doric dialect, 3–4

Edessa (Şanlıurfa), 12–13, 82–83
Egeria, 31–32
Egyptian obelisks at Rome, 31–32, 34–35
Elagabalus (emperor), 255–56
Eleithya, dedication to, 196–97, 198*f*
Eleutherna (Crete), 200
Ephesos, 151–52, 170–71, 215, 223–24, 269–70
    Council of, 151–52, 256–57
    the Embolos, 74–75, 76–77, 93–94, 144, 256–57
    genital editing, 241n.126
    "Temple of Hadrian," 76–77, 82–83, 256–57
Epidauros, 16–17, 70–71
epigraphic violence. *See* violence
Eretria (Greece), 209
Ethiopia, 38–39, 66–67, 138
Eudokia (empress), 33–34
Eunapios (historian and sophist), 9–10, 127–28
Eusebius of Caesarea, 9, 31–32, 79–81, 96–98, 183–84, 207
    Chronicon, 3–4
Eutropios, 105

excavations, 154–55, 257–58
  Aizanoi, 95, 113–15, 115f, 117–19, 236–37
  Ankara, 98–101, 103–4
  Antioch ad Cragum, 243
  Aphrodisias, 172, 173f–76f
  Beth Shemesh, Israel, 110–11
  Çeşme (Turkey), 186–87
  Didyma, 140
  Eretria (Greece), 209
  Jeme (Medinet Habu), 136–37
  Labraunda, 192–93, 193f–94f, 233–36, 234f
  Lagina, 128–31
  Magnesia on the Maeander, 89n.71
  Miletos, 214–15
  Mylasa, 84–85, 87–88
  Paneas, 152–53
  Pisidian Antioch, 248–52, 254–55
  Priene, 79, 82–83, 150
  Sagalassos, 168–70, 171–72
  Sardis, 188–90
exorcism, 56–58, 63–64, 76, 257

Faustina the Elder (empress), 122–24
Faustina the Younger (empress), 56–59
fertility rites, 182–83, 227–28
flat earth, belief in, 38–39, 41–42
Flavius Eudoxius, 86–87
Flavius Illus Pusaeus Dionysius, 86–87
"forest inscriptions" of Lebanon. See Hadrian

Galatia, province of, 96–98, 104–5, 109–10, 248, 252n.156
Galerius (emperor), 76
gameboards, 172
Gaza. See *Life of Porphyry of Gaza*
Genette, Gérard, 29–30
genital editing of statues. See violence
Gerasa (Jerash), Jordan, 150–53, 170–71, 184, 217
  Christian triumphalism, 4–6, 22, 149–51
Golan Heights, 90–92, 152–53
Gospel of Luke, 105
Goths, 160–63, 253n.162
  attack on Constantinople, 45–46, 153–54
Göztepesi, 157

graffiti, 42–43, 72–73, 107–9, 249–50, 257–58, 268–69, 274
  Aizanoi, 116–17, 116f, 257–58
  Ankara, 108f, 112–13
  Aphrodisias, 17–18, 172, 176–78, 181–82, 231–32, 257–58, 271
  Athens, 92–93
  Baalbek, 184
  Delphi, 90–95
  Egypt, 24–25, 134–35, 138–39
  Kilikia, 157, 244–47
  Klaros, 186
  Labraunda, 232–33, 236
  Lagina, 131–34, 131f
  Magnesia on the Maeander, 89–90
  Miletos, 140
  Mylasa, 84–85, 86–87
  Palmyra, 121
  Priene, 81–82
  Sagalassos, 71–72
  Sardis, 124f, 125
Gratian (emperor), 69–70, 82–83
Great Persecution. See persecution of Christians
Greco-Turkish War, 254–55
Gregory of Nyssa, 135–36, 203, 240–41
Gregory the Great, pope, 9

Hacı Bayram mosque, 112–13, 274–76
Hadrian (emperor), 120, 179–80, 186–87, 207, 215–16, 227–30
  Aizanoi's connection with, 115–16, 119–20, 144, 236
  "forest inscriptions," 24–25
  Hadrianic Baths, 225–26
  remembrance of, 76–77, 92–93, 182, 268–69
  "Temple of Hadrian," Ephesos, 75, 75f, 76–77, 82–83, 256–57
Hagia Sophia, 104–5
Hammat Gadar (Emmantha/Umm Qais), 33–34
Hebrew inscriptions, 19, 42–43, 191
Hebrew Bible, 31n.18, 34
Hekate, 16n.57, 128–34, 144–45, 248–49
Hekatomnids, 26–27, 79–81, 82–85, 233–36
Heliopolis. See Baalbek/Heliopolis

Helladios (priest), 1, 2–3, 4, 16–18
Hellenic and Roman past, 14, 24–25, 26–27, 29–30, 66–67, 268–69
Hephaisteion, Athens, 117–18, 121–22
Hera (goddess), 30–31, 202, 211–12
  Samian, 73
Heraion/Hieron (Fenerbahçe), 202, 203, 217, 263
Herakleia Latmia, Karia, 150–51, 188–90
Herakles, 42–43, 200, 212, 242–43
Hercules, 41. *See* Herakles
Hermes, 42–43, 156–58, 200, 242–43
Herodotos, xvii–xviii, 30–31, 34, 65–66, 150–51
Herulians, 92–93, 198–99
Hierapolis (Pamukkale), 52–55, 60–62, 200
Hier(o)polis (Koçhisar), 53–64 *passim*, 221–22, 258–59
hieroglyphic writing/text, 19, 134–35, 138–39
  late antique attitudes, 4–6, 134–37
    Coptic-speaking Christians, 135–37, 139
    prophesy of Christian triumph, 47–48, 208–9
  left untouched, 136–37, 139
  translation, 34–35, 134–35
  unintelligible, 6, 24–25, 134–35, 268–69
Hieroglyphica, 134–35
Historia Augusta, 64–65, 257–58
Historia Ecclesiastica
  of Eusebius, 31n.18, 59–60
  of Theodoret of Cyrrhus, 8–9
Historia Nova. See Zosimos
Histories. See Agathias of Myrina
Hittites, 19, 156–57
Homer, xvii–xviii, 26–27, 43–44
honorific texts, 6–7, 24–25, 90–92, 121, 154–55, 186
  decrees, 16n.57, 64–65, 150, 151–52
Honorius (emperor), 12–13, 103–4, 204–5
Horapollo, 134–35
human sacrifices. *See* sacrifices
Hypatia (philosopher), 208–9

Iamblichos (philosopher), 203–4
Iasos, 255–56

iconoclasm, 93–94, 202–3, 226–27, 251n.155, 252–53, 258–59
  decapitation of statues, 79n.36, 216
  destruction of Serapeion in Alexandria, 208–9
  untouched hieroglyphic writing, 136–37
Ikaria, island of, 50–51
Iliad, xvii–xviii
Ilion/Troy, 12, 43–44
illegible inscriptions, 111, 143–44, 170–71, 198–99, 252–53
  Anatolian, 269–70
  Egyptian, 6, 139
Institutiones Grammaticae. See Priscian
intermediality, 29–30, 62–63, 64
Ionia, 46, 81–82, 117, 185
Isauria, 11, 85–86, 121–22, 155, 241–42
ISIS (Islamic State), 7–9, 211
Isis (goddess), 9, 173–74, 242–43
Islam, 8, 29–30, 154–55, 274–76
  Islamic State (*see* ISIS)
Israel, 24–25, 34, 110–11. *See* Beth Shemesh
  Omri, king of, 254–55

Jason and the Argonauts, 51
Jeme (Medinet Habu), 21–22, 134–39, 268–69
Jerash. *See* Gerasa
Jerome, 14, 109–10
Jews, 14, 42–43, 90–92, 188–90
  Aphrodisias, 173–74
  Caesarea Maritima, 215–16
  island of Ikaria, 50–51 (*see also* Sardis)
  veneration of angels, 175–76, 182, 204
John Malalas, 33–34, 183–84, 260–61, 263
  Chronographia, 34, 51
Josephus (historian), 188–90
Julian (emperor), 12, 89–90, 106–7, 111, 207, 219
  Column of "Julian," 101–2, 112–13
  pagan sympathies, 12–13, 69–70, 89–90, 140, 248–49
  period of, 79–81, 126–27, 140
    death, 46, 89–90, 126–27
Julius Caesar (emperor), 32–33, 79
Julius Pollux (writer), 19–20

Justinian (emperor), 92–93, 110–11, 202, 260–61, 263
  (re)dedication of Column of "Julian," 101–2, 112–13
  period of, 35, 103–4, 106
Justinianopolis, 140

Kaleb Ella Asbeha of Aksum, King, 38–39, 41–42
Karia, 84, 86–87, 128, 141–42, 150–52, 196–97
  Aphrodisias, 85–86, 172–74, 222–24, 231–32
  earthquake, 35
  Karians, 19, 66–67
  Labraunda, 26–27, 191–92, 232–33
  name of, 263
Kerkyra/Corfu, island of, 43–44
Kilikia, 121–22, 158–63, 241–42, 257–58
  Korykian Cave, 22, 155, 157*f*, 160*f*, 161*f*, 244–45, 246*f*
Kızılburun shipwreck, 187
Kızlan Deresi Church, 196–97, 198*f*
Klaros
  Apollo, 79–81, 185, 186–88
    oracles, 48–49, 93–94, 132–33, 199, 203–4, 209
  spoliation, 22, 185, 186–88, 195–96, 209
Knidian Aphrodite, 73
Korykian Cave Clifftop Temple, 155–65, 185, 199, 246*f*
  erasure of inscriptions, 22–23, 180, 245–47, 259, 261–62
  spoliation, 22, 158, 166–67, 195–96, 200–1, 244–45, 269
Korykos (city), 157, 160–63
  Temple of Zeus Korykos, 157
Kosmas Indikopleustes, 20, 38–45, 66–67, 83–84, 105, 144, 266–67
Kroisos, king, 188–90
Kybebe. *See* Kybele
Kybele (Anatolian mother goddess), 51, 188–90, 207–8, 248–49, 263.
  See also Rhea
Kyzikos, 49–50, 51, 207–8, 220

de Laborde, Léon, 113–15
Labraunda, 26–27, 112n.164, 248–49
  erasure of inscriptions, 22–23, 196–247, 259, 269
  spoliation, 22, 191–94, 195–96, 232–33
Lactantius (author), 76, 140
Lagina, 128–34, 170–71, 188–90, 191–92, 232–33, 248–49
  inscriptions remaining on display, 21–22, 109, 134, 144–45, 268–69
Lanckoroński, Karl, 168–72
Laodikeia on the Lykos, 71–72, 87–88, 211–12
"late wall," 154–55, 193n.146, 232–33
Law Code of Gortyn, 90–92
Learning from Las Vegas, 15
Leo I (emperor), 49, 175
Leptis Magna (Tripolitana), 247
Leto, statue of, 79–81, 186
Levant, the, 25–26, 152–53, 216
  inscriptions, 4–6, 19, 24–25, 90–92
Libanios of Antioch, 9–10, 11, 87–88, 103–4
Licinius (emperor), 128, 199–200
Life of Abercius (Vita Abercii), 53–65, 144, 221–22, 266–67, 274
Life of Eusebia, 84–85
Life of Porphyry of Gaza, 62, 147–48, 149–50, 152–54, 269
Life of Rabbula, 183–84
Life of Severos, Patriarch of Antioch, 9, 173–75
Life of St. Makarios of Rome. See St. Makarios
ligatured monograms, 141–42
lime, 25–26, 90–92, 101–2, 154, 193–94, 217
  kilns, 145–46, 192–93, 233
  mortar, 145–46, 154, 200, 247–48
limestone, 158, 164–65, 244–45
Lindian Athena, 73
Lindos. *See* Rhodes
literacy, 14–15, 17–18, 246–47, 274
  editing directed by literate person, 230–31, 232–33, 237–38, 261, 274
  editing performed by illiterate person, 163–64, 230–31, 246–47, 255–56
"living text" approach, 268–69
Lucian of Samosata, 30–31, 34
Lucilla, princess, 56–58, 63–64

318   INDEX

Lydia, province of, 122–24, 126–27, 188–90, 239–40
Lydian language, 125–27, 190–91
Lydians, 19, 66–67, 125–26, 190–91, 200–1
Lykia, 48–49, 51–52, 187–88, 203–4

magic, 141–42, 175–76, 260–61
  spells, 173–74, 203, 260–61
Magnesia on the Maeander, 21–22, 79–81, 88–90
manufactured violence. *See* violence
Marcus Aurelius (emperor), 55, 122–24, 206–7, 255–56
  letter from, 62–64
Markellos, Bishop, 8–9, 11–12
Martyrdom of Ariadne of Prymnessos, 64–65, 266–67
Maternus Cyngeius (praetorian prefect), 211
Maximian (emperor), 76, 151–52
Maximinus Daia (emperor), 128
Medinet Habu (Jeme), 21–22, 134–39, 268–69
Megara, 1, 2–4, 6, 7, 16–18, 71–72
Melito of Sardis, 105
memory sanctions. *See* damnatio memoriae
Men Askaenos (Anatolian god), 248–50, 253–54
metal clamps, 96, 186–87
metatext, 29–30, 231, 261
Michael III (emperor), 96–98, 101–2
Miletos (city), 104–5, 139–42, 214–15
Miracles of St. Thekla. See St. Thekla
Montanism, treatise against, 59–60
monumental inscriptions, 17–18, 233–36
  Egyptian, 24–25
  Persian, 4–6
mosaic, 73, 119–20, 150, 168–70, 191, 260–61
  floor, 110–11, 152–53, 228–30
  inscription, 46, 152–53, 248, 257–58
Mosul Museum, Iraq, 7–8
Mt. Tmolos, 127–28
"museumification," 77–84, 274–76
Mylasa (Milas), 84–89, 144–45, 191–93, 232–33

Neoplatonist writings, 203–4
Nero (emperor), 218–19, 238–39, 239*f*, 259–60, 262–63
Nike (Victory), 74–75, 79, 200, 241–42
Nikomedia, 33–34, 79–81
nomina sacra, 138–39, 152–53, 260–61
Notion, polis of, 117, 186–88

object agency, 6–7, 276
Odysseus, 43–44
Odyssey, 43–44
Oinoanda (Lykia), 48–49, 187–88, 203–4
Olympia, 82–83, 154
Olympic games, 3–4
omens, epigraphic, 45–48, 51–52, 267–68. *See also* oracles
onomastic violence. *See* violence: against inscriptions
oracles, 51–52, 65–67, 105, 175, 187–88, 260–61. *See also* omens
  dice, 241–42, 244
  fake, 45–46, 49, 51, 121–22
  Oinoanda in Lykia, 48–49, 187–88, 203–4
  Tübingen Theosophy, 48–51, 267–68
Origen, 105, 260–61
Ostia, 73, 197n.150, 209
ostraca, 136–37

Palmyra, Syria, 7–8, 12, 22, 120–22, 145–46, 211, 268–69
  Zenobia (queen), 24–25, 121, 160–63
Pamphylia, 64, 110–11
Pan (god), 152–53, 156–58
Paneas (Caesarea Philippi/Banias), 152–53, 195–96, 207
Papias, bishop of Hierapolis (Pamukkale), 52–55
  Account of the Logia about the Lord, 52–53
papyri, 51, 136–38, 141–42, 263
Parastaseis Syntomoi Chronikai, 67–68
Parthenon, 50–51, 92–93, 121–22, 200–1, 209–11
Paul (apostle). *See* St. Paul
Pausanias (traveler), 3–4, 30–32, 34, 133–34, 175–76
Pergamon, 71–72, 154–55

Perge, Pamphylia, 64, 212
periodization, problems of, 4, 271
persecution of Christians, 31n.18, 76, 79–81, 140
Persians, 66–67, 96–98, 101–2, 172, 213–14
 Persian War, 32–33, 51–52, 67–68
Pheidias, 73, 154
Philostorgios, 207
Phoenicians, 18–19, 24–25, 34, 42–43
Phrygia, 64, 113, 188–90, 236, 248
 Abercius, 53–56, 58–62, 221–22, 266–67
 tombstones, 25–26, 59–62, 221–22, 266–67
pilgrims, 31–33, 96–98, 132–34
Pisidia, province of, 165–66, 248
 Pisidian Antioch (Yalvaç), 111–12, 248–55
plaster, 137–38, 176, 196–97, 245–46
 covering inscriptions, 74, 150–51, 180
 lack of, 74, 138–39, 164–65, 168, 170–71, 188–90
Plotinos (philosopher), 203–4
Plutarch, 51–52
Pococke, Robert, 84, 85–86, 88n.67
polemical use of ancient inscriptions, 7, 150–51, 152–53, 195, 269, 273–74
Pomponius Mela, geographer, 156–57
Porphyry. See *Life of Porphyry of Gaza*
Priene, 21–22, 77–84, 86–87, 144–45, 150–51, 178–79, 187–88, 268–69
Priscian, Latin grammarian, 32–33, 67–68
 Institutiones Grammaticae, 32
Prokopios, 20, 34, 43–45, 202, 217, 257–58, 263, 266–67
Pro Templis, 9–10
Prudentius (poet), 32–33
Prymnessos, Phrygia, 59–60, 64
Pseudo-Cyril (author), 47–48
Ptolemy III Euergetes, 39–43, 66–67

Quodvultdeus, bishop of Carthage, 48
quoting, xvii–xviii, 53–55, 59–60, 62–63
 Apollo, 15–17
 epigraphic material, 30–32, 41, 62, 64–65, 267–68
 transtextuality, 29–30

Ramesses II, 34–35
Ramesses III, mortuary sanctuary of, 136–37, 138
Ramsay, William, 53–55, 56–58, 254–55
Red Sea, 38–39, 41–42
religioscape, 155–56, 157–58, 165, 247
Res Gestae divi Augusti
 Ankara, 96, 265, 270–71, 274–76
  Christian engagement with, 100–1, 105–10, 111–13, 144, 268–69, 274–76
 Apollonia, 111–12, 252n.156
 Pisidian Antioch, 111–12, 250–55
resurrection, 60–62, 81–82, 105
Rhea (goddess), 51, 203, 207–8, 263. *See also* Kybele
Rhodes, 206–7, 211–12, 217
 Lindos, 73, 205–6
Roma (goddess), 84, 87–88, 109–10, 144–45. *See also* Temple of Augustus and Roma
Roman Republic, 218
Rough Kilikia (Isauria), 155, 241–42
Rufinus, 208–9

sacrifices, 15–17, 32–33, 70–71, 76, 173–74, 203
 animal, 1–3, 15
 human, 9, 147
 prohibition of, 2–3, 12–13, 133–34
Sagalassos, 22, 74–75, 185, 200, 204–5, 215, 269
 Basilica E, 166–68, 170–72, 239–40
 Basilica E1, 166
 Temple of Antoninus Pius, 104–5, 166
 Temple of Apollo Klarios, 166–72, 176, 179–80, 195–96, 199
 Upper Agora, 71–72, 165–66, 171–72
Sardis, 122–28, 143–44, 196
 Jewish community at, 22, 188–91, 195–96, 197–98, 200–1, 269
Sassanians, 4–6, 25–26, 106–7, 160–63
satyrs, 166, 200, 240–41
scriptio continua, 170–71
Scythopolis/Beth Shean, 200, 209
Sebasteion, Aphrodisias, 104–5, 172, 212, 226–27, 228*f*
Seferis, Giorgos (poet), 265, 266–67

semantic violence. *See* anonymizing spaces and gods; unnaming gods
Septimius Severus (emperor), 115–16, 144, 236
  Arch of Septimius Severus, Palmyra, 8
  Arch of Septimius Severus, Rome, 218–19
Serapeion at Alexandria, 139–40
  destruction of, 11–12, 47–48, 79–81, 134–35, 208–9
Serapis (god), 47, 79–81, 128–30, 139–40, 208–9
sex organs, removal of. *See* violence
Shapur, Sassanian king, 160–63
Shenoute of Atripe, abbot, 135–38, 139, 203
Simonides of Keos, 1–4, 32–33
Sinai, 42–43
Sohag, Upper Egypt, 135–38
Sokrates (philosopher), 64–65
Sokrates Scholastikos, 20, 45, 47–48, 66–67, 153–54, 266–67
Solomon (biblical king), 185
St. Clement. *See* Church of St. Clement
St. Makarios, 28–30
  Life of St. Makarios of Rome, 28–30, 64–65
St. Paul, 33–34, 47, 248
  Church of, 248, 253–54
St. Thekla
  shrine in Kilikia, 257–58
  Miracles of St. Thekla, 46
St. Theodore. *See* Church of St. Theodore
staurogram, 211–12
Stauroupolis (Cross City). *See* Aphrodisias: change of name
Stephanos of Byzantium, 133–34, 157–58
Stilicho (general), 46
Stratonikeia (city), Karia, 71–72, 128, 130–31, 132–34
Suetonius, 51–52, 106–7
Symmachus, senator, 69–70, 143
synagogue, 155, 248
  at Sardis, 22, 125–26, 188–91, 195–96, 197–98, 200–1, 269
Syriac language, 46, 183–84, 185

"tagging" of statues, 206–7, 218
taxation, 9–10, 86–89, 273
temple destruction. *See* violence
Temple of Antoninus Pius. *See* Antoninus Pius
Temple of Aphrodite at Aphrodisias, 172–83 *passim*, 195–96, 227–28
Temple of Apollo
  Bulla Regia (Tunisia), 82–83
  Delphi, 93–95
  Didyma, 140–42
  Klaros, 185, 186, 209
Temple of Apollo Klarios at Sagalassos, 166–72, 176, 195–96
Temple of Artemis
  Aizanoi, 113, 117, 236–37
  Constantinople, 263
  Gerasa, 150–51
  Sardis, 122–24, 124f, 125–28
Temple of Athena Polias at Priene, 77–79, 80f, 81f, 150
Temple of Augustus and Roma. *See also* Roma
  Ankara (Ancyra/Ankyra), 95––96, 98–100, 111–12, 265, 274–76
  Caesarea Maritima, Palestina, 104–5
  Mylasa (Milas), 84, 85–86, 87–88
Temple of Baalshamin, Palmyra, 7–8, 120, 121, 144–45, 211
Temple of Bel, Palmyra, 7–8, 120, 211
Temple of Dionysos, 139–40, 151–52, 166
"Temple of Hadrian," Ephesos. *See* Hadrian
Temple of Hathor in Dendara, Egypt, 216
Temple of Hekate at Lagina, 128–32, 133–34
Temple of Jupiter Heliopolitanus. *See* Baalbek/Heliopolis
Temple of Zeus
  Aizanoi, 102, 113–19 *passim*, 144, 236, 239–41, 257–58
  Apamea (Syria), 8–9, 11–12
  Labraunda, 191–93, 233–36
  Olympia, 82–83
Temple of Zeus Korykos, 157

INDEX 321

Temple of Zeus Labraundos. *See* Labraunda
Temple of Zeus Marnas at Gaza, 147
Temple of Zeus Olbios, 121–22
Temple of Zeus Sosipolis at Magnesia on the Maeander, 88–90, 91*f*
Tertullian of Carthage, 60–62
Thebes (Luxor), Upper Egypt, 112n.164, 134–35, 136–37, 138
Themistios, rhetor, 106–7, 144
Theodoret of Cyrrhus, 203, 208–9, 240–41
  destruction of the Temple of Zeus in Apamea, 8–9, 11–12
Theodosios I, 9–10, 74–75, 76, 182, 183–84, 256–57
Theodosios II, 12–14, 67–68, 86–87
Theophilos of Alexandria, 47–48
Theosophia, 48–49
Third Syrian War, 40
Thucydides, 30–31
Tiberius II (emperor), 110–11
tolerance, 21–22, 72–74, 95, 143–46, 217, 268–69
  Aizanoi, 113
  Aphrodisias, 227–28, 231–32
  Athens, 92–93
  Didyma, 151–52
  Diokaisareia-Olba, 121–22
  Egypt, 134–35, 136–37
  Ephesos, 74–75, 76
  Labraunda, 236
  Lagina, 128
  Palmyra, 120–21
  Priene, 150–51
  Sagalassos, 166–67, 171–72
Trajan (emperor), 69–70, 256–57
Tralles (city), Karia, 35, 36–38
transtextuality, 29–30, 65–66, 106–7, 267–68
Trojan War, 32, 43–44, 138
Troy (Ilion), 12, 43–44
Tübingen Theosophy manuscript, 48–51, 204n.9, 267–68
Typhon (monster), 156–57

unnaming gods, 22–23, 202–8, 254–64. *See also* anonymizing spaces and gods
  Aizanoi, 113, 238–39, 240–41
  Aphrodisias, 224–25
  damnatio memoriae, 22–23, 218–19
  in figural imagery, 204–5
  Labraunda, 232–33
Upper Agora at Sagalassos. *See* Sagalassos
Urartian inscriptions, 4–6, 19
urban *kalos*, 13–14, 145–46
Uylupınar, 221–23
Uzunyuva complex, excavation of, 84–85

Valens (emperor)
  prophecies, 45–46, 51–52, 66–67, 71–72
  spoliating the walls of Chalcedon, 45–46
Valentinian II (emperor), 69–70, 82–83
Vatican, 53–55, 58–62, 212
violence, 8, 152–53, 199–200, 216, 222–23, 249–50
  against inscriptions, 217, 220–21, 236, 247–59, 264, 274
  manufactured, 7–8, 11–12, 120
  against statues, 89–90, 202–3, 208–11, 213–14, 216, 272
  genitals, 212, 214–15, 216, 241n.126
  heads, 79n.36, 215–16
  against temples, 7–10, 11–12, 120, 208
Virius Nichomachus Flavianus, senator, 219
"visual bureaucracy," 88–89

Zacharias Scholastikos, 173–75
Zenobia (Palmyrene queen), 24–25, 121, 160–63
Zeus Casius, dedication to, 43–44
Zeus Keraunios, dedication to, 71–72
Zeus Kersoullos, dedication to, 254–55
Zeus Megistos, 255–56
Zeus of Olympia, by Pheidias, 73
Zorava (Syria), 9
Zosimos (historian), 9–10, 46, 207–8, 263
  Historia Nova, 34